THE BEST OF

The Harvard Gay & Lesbian Review

IN THE SERIES

AMERICAN SUBJECTS

Edited by
Robert Dawidoff

TEMPLE UNIVERSITY PRESS   PHILADELPHIA

THE BEST OF

The Harvard

Gay & Lesbian

Review

FOREWORD BY EDMUND WHITE

ILLUSTRATIONS BY CHARLES HEFLING

EDITED BY

RICHARD SCHNEIDER, JR.

Temple University Press, Philadelphia 19122
Copyright © 1997 by Temple University, except
Essay "A Tragedy of Bees" © Patricia Nell Warren
All rights reserved
Published 1997
Printed in the United States of America

♾ The paper used in this publication meets the
requirements of the American National Standard for Information
Sciences—Permanence of Paper for Printed Library Materials,
ANSI Z39.48-1984

Text design by Kate Nichols

Library of Congress Cataloging-in-Publication Data
The best of the Harvard Gay and Lesbian Review / edited by Richard
Schneider, Jr. ; foreword by Edmund White; illustrations by Charles Hefling.
    p.   cm.—(American subjects)
  ISBN 1-56639-596-8 (cloth : alk. paper)
  1. Gays–United States.   2. Homosexuality–United States.
I. Schneider, Richard, Jr.   II. Harvard gay and lesbian review.
III. Series.
HQ76.3.U5B479   1997
305.9′ 0664—dc21   97-30227

"Lesbian New York" is an excerpt from *Tales of the Lavender Menace*,
to be published by HarperCollins. Copyright © 1995, 1997 by Karla Jay.

CONTENTS

ROBERT DAWIDOFF

O NE OF THE CONUNDRUMS of the quarter century of gay liberation has been the flourishing of lesbian and gay male thinking and
writing with a striking absence of critical exchange. The first
twenty-five years after Stonewall absorbed self-conscious gays and lesbians in
the intense searching out of certainties. Perhaps the energies liberated by a
political and personal consciousness required certainties in order to sustain
what were unprecedented individual and collective transformations. Coming
out is a giant step for people and imperfectly expressed in the restrained gait
of critical intellectual exchange. Gay critical writing formed an important part
of the cultural and political gay movement, as did the resolute and pioneering
work of scholars, theorists, writers, and artists of all sorts.

By 1994, however, the year Richard Schneider began to publish *The Harvard Gay & Lesbian Review,* the need for an independent journal of gay and
lesbian literary, political, and intellectual exchange was real, and the response
of readers and writers to the *HGLR* proved it. Unlike most gay and lesbian
publications, *The Review* risked a nonideological, nonpartisan approach, in
which the good of the lesbian and gay population was advanced through the
candid expression of independent and frequently diverse points of view. *The
Review* refused to be bound by the interests of any single view of the gay movement or by any particular political or ideological position.

The subjects and books covered in the magazine make a powerful display of the heterogeneity of gay people and their lives. The reviewers in general treated the books with care and respect and with an abiding sense of the larger issues each particular subject raised. The past and future have mattered as much to *The Review* as the present. It has courted controversy, not with the object of sensation, but with the purpose of making *The Review* a template of the best and most important lesbian and gay intellectual and literary work. Perhaps most important, the *HGLR* refused the comforts and obscurities that have haunted ideologically driven writing.

Schneider and his colleagues addressed a reader who was educated, independent, and diverse; this reader did not need orthodoxies or bromides but did want informed stimulation. Anybody could read an issue of *The Review* and encounter books she might not have known about, points of view not his own, and challenges to the very certainties on which our identities as gay and lesbian had seemed to depend. Neither the gayspeak of the movement nor the specialist argot of the gay studies movement characterized the writing. Perhaps that is why in its short history, *The Review* has garnered the loyalty of an ever-growing body of readers for the reviews and essays of a remarkable number of the best gay and lesbian writers and intellectuals of our time, as the table of contents shows. Edmund White's welcome and illuminating introduction makes clear how important the *HGLR* has become, and his writing for it emphasizes how successful *The Review* has been in attracting the very writers it needed to establish itself.

There is room and necessity for all manner of journals. What makes the *HGLR* so unusual is that it's the first time that lesbian and gay writers have been able to do serious and independent critical writing in a magazine specifically devoted to such work. Mainstream publications require one to imagine an audience needing introduction and even blandishments where gay issues are concerned. Gay and lesbian publications have tended to be tied to putative orthodoxies and have served populations whose significant common interests were not those of *The Review*. Those publications and the movement that inspired them, it must always be remembered, made the *HGLR* and this anthology possible. *The Review* never aimed to supplant them, but to add a different register to the love that having once dared not speak its name, now happily for us all, has no intention of shutting up. Nor is *The Review* somber or academic in tone. It shares the vivacity and variety that lesbian and gay life encourages, tempered by a certain intellectual standard, but always vital with the vaunted gay sensibility, which may not exist, but which is everywhere!

The pleasures and uses of this anthology are many. It is a rewarding way to learn what gay and lesbian writers have written about and how, what issues and voices have mattered to them. The interviews and extended thematic exchanges, such as those about gay political strategy and the biological origins of sexual orientation, are informed, cogent, stimulating, controversial, and, best of all, good places to start thinking about them and equally good places to revisit. The *HGLR* has kept the long-term intellectual and literary needs of lesbians and gays in mind, which is why this anthology both proceeds from *The Review* and stands on its own. Richard Schneider deserves credit and thanks for founding and editing *The Review,* for assembling a talented staff, and for attracting so many excellent writers and presenting them with such imagination and care. Most important, *The Review* and this anthology have secured a place for serious and independent lesbian and gay literary and intellectual exchange for a broad readership without sacrificing the energy, diversity, and delight that remain its special gifts to our times.

Fresh Beginnings—
The Harvard Gay & Lesbian Review

EDMUND WHITE

T'S A NATURAL HUMAN TENDENCY to imagine that our particular moment in history—the history of a movement, of a country, of a tradition—is late. We're always beset by a feeling of belatedness, as though we're living during a decadent or even fully decayed end of an age. And yet, in reading through *The Best of the Harvard Gay & Lesbian Review*, I kept thinking how *early* this book and these writings will seem someday. Whereas most researchers in the social sciences or most historians or most novelists lament that everything has already been said, every field already exploited, in lesbian and gay culture every investigation strikes me as sometimes tentative but always thrillingly new.

Well, not brand-new, perhaps, since in the earliest gay and lesbian and feminist writings there was more rhetoric than analysis, more passion than skepticism, more polemic than puzzling, whereas what immediately strikes the reader of this volume is that the critical spirit has never been sharper or more discriminating. In the early days of gay liberation everything that was gay was deemed good—or sometimes everything except what was represented by a warring faction. People worked to rewrite gay history (or herstory) to serve as an inspirational example, just as critics constantly exerted a pressure on lesbian and gay novelists to come up with positive role models. The spirit at its worst seemed to combine Stalinism with boy scoutism.

The Harvard Gay & Lesbian Review has from the first represented a virtually unique exception to the old gung-hoism and to more recent glitzy gay journalism, with its fashion spreads and cover stories on celebrated heterosexuals.
In the pages of the *HGLR* a real debate can get off the ground—about the social versus the genetic origins of homosexuality itself, for instance, or about assimilation versus ghettoization (the exchange of letters between Bruce Bawer,
author of *A Place at the Table* and defender of gay conservatism, and David
Bergman, author of *Gaiety Transfigured* and a spokesman for gay identity and
even gay difference, is a model of spunky, significant debate). Reed Woodhouse, elsewhere in the anthology, overturns most hasty preconceptions and
argues that precisely those novels that seem to be the most ghettoized are the
ones that are likely to be the most "universal" (always a loaded word). As he
writes: "I am an Aristotelian in this matter, and believe that universality, if it
is to be found, must come in the form of particulars. I do not think that a literature, or a life, that blurs the outlines of our gay identity represents us fully
to ourselves or to the straight world. While assimilative or queer texts may be
excellent books, therefore, they are only partially 'gay' books. However interesting or beautiful they may be in other respects, they are not the books I
would recommend to someone, gay or straight, who wanted to know what a
gay life was like."

If everything in lesbian and gay culture (even such a concept as "gay culture") seems new, precarious and flourishing, then gay identity itself appears
to have long been perpetually under attack. Lev Raphael, writing as both a religious Jew and a gay man, clarifies the exact threat posed to gay prisoners in
Nazi Germany—a tragic fate but one appreciably different from that handed
out to Jews. Douglass Shand-Tucci, in his study of *Two College Friends*, a previously unknown gay Civil War novel, traces with admirable delicacy the con-
tiguous claims of romantic friendship and homoerotic love—a project inau-
gurated years ago by Simon Karlinsky in his biography, *The Sexual Labyrinth
of Nicolai Gogol*. In this anthology a similar investigation is mounted by
Martha Nell Smith, writing about Emily Dickinson, and Marilee Lindemann,
taking a look at Willa Cather. In none of these essays is the historical subject
stretched or squeezed to fit a Procrustean bed of modern definitions.

Bright moments of recent history (Karla Jay's lesbian New York at the beginning of gay liberation, for instance) are preserved in these pages. The humor in every word of Gabrielle Glancy's all-too-brief "Behind the Door at Red
Dora's," about the seventies in San Francisco, made me wish I were a lesbian
novelist so that I could steal a line from her as an epigraph: "Kris Kovick car-

toonist-writer-producer and self-proclaimed intellectual air guitarist, inventor of the term 'hairball,' which has come to mean the incestuous lesbian tangle in which your lover leaves you for your best friend, read a story about the circumstances surrounding the assassination of San Francisco's gay supervisor Harvey Milk—a story that was so convoluted and brilliantly done, I had to admit I was listening!" Admit it: written out as verse, that sentence could be a John Ashbery poem.

Politics, poetry, gender theories, history, philosophy, postmodernism—all get a chance in this volume to express themselves. There is even room for a personal memoir, Andrew Holleran's "My Harvard," predictably the best-written piece in the collection, given that he is our finest novelist. We learn how to decipher the lesbian content disguised by Gertrude Stein's style ("The name Caesar contains a sound play on 'sees her' and 'seize her,' as well as an allusion to Stein herself, the author with a claim to literary authority and with the haircut of an emperor famous for his homosexual leanings"). We are constantly reminded of Foucault's ever-expanding influence—will our century come to be known as "The Age of Foucault"?—even if Holleran has the wit to poke gentle fun at the excesses and impenetrableness of Foucault's style and that of his followers.

The faithful reader of the *HGLR* is confident that any controversy that besets the community, that any external threat or signal, genetic or historical reinterpretation, or artistic triumph will be recorded in its pages. This anthology represents the best of the publication's first three years, a sampler of the cultural and intellectual life that makes Queer Studies the hot topic on campuses across the country and that deems lesbian and gay fiction and theater and especially poetry to be some of the best American writing being published or staged today. Although AIDS makes its appearance here and there as the ghost at the banquet, this anthology is a potent reminder that gay culture is irrepressible and cannot be reduced to a single issue, no matter how dire and urgent. When AIDS is cured the *HGLR* will be singled out as having served as a major site for the transmission of earlier queer culture to later thinkers and makers, a periodical that resisted the impoverishment and remedicalization of our intellectual life.

THREE YEARS IS NOT LONG to be publishing a journal before putting out a "best of" volume—but that's three years in gay and lesbian time in an era of accelerated cultural change. Since the publication of the first issue of *The Harvard Gay & Lesbian Review* in the fearful Boston winter of '94, scientists have announced the discovery of variant brain structures in gay men and even found evidence for a so-called "gay gene"; the number of out gay characters on prime-time TV shows has gone from virtually none to (at last count) twenty-eight; new drugs such as protease inhibitors have dramatically slowed the death rate from AIDS; the phenomenon of "the Circuit" has emerged featuring huge weekend parties in many U.S. cities year-round; the possibility of legal marriage for gays has made great strides in Hawaii; the Supreme Court has recognized the right of gays *qua* minority to seek legal redress (in the Colorado ruling); and "Don't ask, don't tell" has been implemented in the military (and failed). Meanwhile, gay and lesbian books have been routinely incorporated into venues like *The New York Times Book Review* and *Publisher's Weekly*; and the sheer number of such books has given way to a gay and lesbian "publishing boom" that continues unabated.

The appearance of *The Review* is an aspect of this "boom," to be sure, but also of the more general cultural explosion of the past few years—without which, after all, there would be far less to talk about in a quarterly journal such as *The Review.* In this respect, the sheer density of political and cultural events during this period has made the job of editor easier: These are interesting times, and it's not hard to find people who have interesting things to say about them. One thing *The Review* has tried to do is to capture some of the most important discussions and debates that these times have produced.

To use words like "boom" and "explosion" suggests both rapid and undisciplined change, but in many ways the changes of the 1990s have been in the direction of institutionalizing elements of gay and lesbian culture, which now boasts its own glossy magazines, academic programs, cruise lines, credit cards, "gay days" at theme parks, book clubs and book-of-the-month clubs, and on and on. And it also boasts—if that is remotely the right word—*The Harvard Gay & Lesbian Review,* the arrival of which might be seen as an example of precisely this trend, a publication that exudes legitimacy and matter-of-fact acceptance of "gay and lesbian" as proper subject matter for a serious magazine. (By the way, the use of these terms in the magazine's title was something of a first, as all of the national publications to date—*The Advocate, Christopher Street, Out/Look, The Lambda Book Report, The James White Review, Out, Genre,* even *10 Percent*—had avoided the "g" and "l" words. The name of *The Review* actually derives from the organization from which it originated, The Harvard Gay & Lesbian Caucus and its *Newsletter. The Review* is not a publication of Harvard University.)

But if elements of gay and lesbian culture are being institutionalized or even "commodified," this in itself strikes me as something radical and amazing for a subculture that was still lurking in the shadows of American culture until so recently. Which is more radical, after all, seeing a lesbian couple pictured on a poster at your local travel agency, or not seeing such a poster there? being able to buy this magazine at Barnes and Noble, or not being able to? Furthermore, even if the format of *The Review* is eminently presentable at public libraries, its contents over the first three years will reveal anything but a staid or settled subculture.

To date, *The Review* has featured a number of direct exchanges between people on opposite sides of key issues, two of which are highlighted here. One involved Rep. Barney Frank, who made a point of lambasting gays who support homophobic (Republican) candidates, which elicited a response from Rich Tafel, head of the Log Cabin Republicans, predicting that a "one-party strategy" would fail. The other exchange was kicked off when David Bergman submitted an "Open Letter to Bruce Bawer," strongly criticizing the author of *A Place at the Table* (1993) for promoting an assimilationist agenda, which brought a response from Bawer, who argued that the alternative to assimilation, life in the gay ghetto, can be mindlessly conformist and stultifying. A third chapter, while not a direct exchange, spotlights what has been the central debate among gay and lesbian intellectuals for the past decade, the question of whether homosexuality is an "essential" characteristic of the person, cropping up throughout history, or instead a "social construction" of our own time and place, scarcely comparable to anything that existed, say, in ancient Athens or Renaissance Italy.

The remaining five sections give an idea of the breadth of topics and disciplines in contemporary gay and lesbian studies: history, literary criticism, sociology, and even biology. Two sections offer a range of historical perspectives on gay and lesbian lives and times in the near and distant past. The first section of this book, titled "Being There," presents several first-hand accounts by well-known writers who found themselves embroiled in history in the making. Another section ("Late Sightings") includes studies of several historical settings in which gay people seem to have been present and left traces of themselves, starting with ancient Rome and ending with the "Hollywood watering holes" of the 1930s and 1940s. If the societies described in this section seem quaint and unfamiliar, many readers will recognize themselves in the post-Stonewall venues described in "The Lavender Decades," which includes a description of the lesbian dance scene in the early 1970s and one of the male bathhouse scene that emerged a few years later. Yet another section explores the literary heritage of a number of major gay and lesbian writers, including Emily Dickinson, Willa Cather, Gertrude Stein, and W. H. Auden. Finally, there is a chapter on the "science of homosexuality" that explores the major arguments supporting a biological explanation for homosexuality, along with a couple of sharp critiques of this controversial hypothesis.

That these are the "best" essays featured to date is of course a matter of editorial judgment, in the present case that of *The Review's* associate editors and local contributors, who first nominated their favorites and then voted on the sixty or so nominees. Their votes were tabulated and some forty essays selected for publication in this volume. The following individuals contributed to this process, in addition to myself: Diane Hamer, Charles Hefling, Michael Schwartz, Martha Stone, Ron Suresha, and Alistair Williamson, and I would like to thank them for this and for their many other contributions to this journal. I want to thank Robert Dawidoff, the general editor of this series, for his contributions to the selection process as well as for his vision of a "best of" volume at the outset. I also want to thank Charles Hefling for the brilliant illustrations that he contributes to each issue of the journal, many of which have been reproduced in this volume.

Richard Schneider, Jr.
Boston, June 1997

Being There:
Literary Lives and Times

I F THERE'S ONE GENRE that has played an unusually prominent role in gay and lesbian literature over the past three decades, even a defining role, it is certainly the personal memoir. Indeed the memoir has merged with the novel in many gay works to produce a synthesis that defies pigeonholing as either one—is Edmund White's *A Boy's Own Story* a novel or a memoir?—suggesting a new genre that breaks the traditional wall of separation between fiction and nonfiction. As White himself is fond of pointing out, the central character in some of Genet's novels is named "Jean Genet," itself a violation of literary convention—all the more radical a notion when the life in question is indeed that of Genet, full of thievery and treason along with the dreaded buggery.

Genet's *romans à clef* can be seen as early examples of the "coming out story" that would come to dominate gay writing for some time after Stonewall, serving as the prototype for the gay novel-memoir. The essence of the coming out story is that the writer is disclosing something about himself, something that happens to be radically taboo; and once this barrier is broken there seems to be no further reason not to "tell all" with absolute honesty. This fundamental structure is present, on the one hand, in the "true histories" of sexual escapades reported by Boyd MacDonald in his many pulpy books, but also in the works of serious fiction that started appearing by the end of the 1970s, notably Andrew Holleran's *Dancer from the Dance* and Edmund White's *Nocturnes for the King of Naples*.

What distinguishes these and so many other works of gay literary fiction is not just that they draw from personal experience, nor even that they deal openly with forbidden acts, but that they scarcely bother to cover the tracks of "real life" with the usual conventions of fiction, almost challenging the reader to figure out the exact summer day in 1977 on which Messrs. X, Y, and Z showed up at Tea Dance on Fire Island. In a popular coming out story, *The Best Little Boy in the World* (1973), John Reid captured life at the Boston bar Sporters (its actual name), describing every denizen of the bar with such fidelity that the characters became local celebrities in real life! Bringing it all back home, in a novel published in 1997, *The Boys from the Men*, Bill Mann's Provincetown includes scenes from "The A-House" and the front yard of "Spiritus"—place names that scarcely need quotes around them for anyone familiar with P'town.

As it happens, Holleran and White are two writers who have contributed actual memoirs to *The Review*, republished in this section, and in each case the voice of the novelist is unmistakable: Holleran is wistful and wry when reflecting upon his college days at Harvard, as upon his *"Dancer"* days in New York; White is amazed and amused by the world of up-and-coming gay writers that he mingled with, circa 1980. Both writers are clearly much at home with the personal memoir—not surprisingly, perhaps, but in a way that seems to me characteristic of gay and lesbian writers in a more general sense: They want to tell you what happened accurately and dispassionately, without the shock or guilt that marks the writing of so many straight writers when they delve into the personal memoir, which typically becomes a "confession" of some kind, a tale of wrongdoing followed by redemption.

It is the absence of this "confessional" tone and structure, perhaps, that distinguishes gay and lesbian memoirs, as if the process of coming out as gay or queer frees the writer to examine the details of his or her sexual and emotional life with a knowing detachment, a lack of sentimentality or self-pity (compare the memoirs of the urbane Gore Vidal with those of his guilt-ridden, groveling arch-rival, Norman Mailer). "The worst has already happened," wrote Martin Heidegger, offering this as a reason to confront the reality of one's life, however painful, and tell the truth about it.

These qualities of the gay memoir are present in three additional essays in this section, all of which involve brushes with history that share elements of the classic coming out story. Patricia Nell Warren, in "A Tragedy of Bees," recalls her life as a "poet in exile" in New York's Ukrainian underground, which would become the incubator for the homosexual characters and themes of her later work. Yaroslav Mogutin, a rapidly rising freelance writer in Russia in the early 1990s, came out publicly in a test of the new regime's tolerance, and, after a harrowing flight from Russia, ended up as a journalist in exile in New York. Holly Hughes, one of the so-called "NEA Four," recounts her ordeal in the early 1990s when the National Endowment for the Arts was attacked by Jesse Helms for sponsoring "queer art," and how the NEA responded by shoving its gay recipients back into the closet.

ANDREW HOLLERAN

My Harvard

FIRST, thanks very much for having me to speak. My twenty-fifth reunion, dare I date myself, was last year, but I never even considered coming back, even though I was dying to come back and look around, which I've been able to do last evening and today. The reasons I couldn't imagine coming back are what I think I'm going to talk about tonight. The title I gave this talk is "My Harvard," which only seems megalomaniacal, but is not meant to be—it's from a book published in 1982 by a man named Jeffrey Lant, a collection I contributed to of some twenty or more essays written by people who went here. One of them was Erich Segal. Erich Segal—of *Love Story* fame—wrote another novel about Harvard called *The Class*. So did a classmate of mine named Faye Levine, I learned, reading my 25th Reunion Class Report a few evenings ago. (Faye Levine was a woman who became famous overnight at Harvard after writing an article in *The Crimson* which categorized types of Radcliffe women by comparing them to flavors of ice cream.) Her novel was *Splendor and Misery: A Novel of Harvard*. I don't know if she was alluding to a novel by Balzac, a wonderful novel with a gay character, Vautrin, in it, called *Splendors and Miseries of the Courtesans*, in which a prostitute is sent to a convent to be schooled as the mistress of a jaded Parisian. (Perhaps Faye had a more cynical view of a Harvard education than I did.)

The very first novel I ever wrote was about Harvard, too. I wrote it in a fit of depression after graduation, when I'd lost all my friends and what seemed to me the only place I'd ever been happy. This novel was set not only at Harvard, but in Lowell House, and not only in Lowell House, but on the terrace overlooking the courtyard; it had lots of lilacs, forsythia, roses in it, and the words "balustrade" and "chandelier" occurred a lot; it was, in other words, my sappy attempt at what Evelyn Waugh did so well in *Brideshead Revisited*. What Waugh did in *Brideshead Revisited* was actually make the friends we all have in college, the emotions we feel, the deep nostalgia for that impressionable time of life, objectively matter, seem truly interesting. Because while they

From the Winter 1994 issue

Andrew Holleran

are interesting to the people who lived them, they are often very hard to make important to anyone else. Years later, while working as a nocturnal proofreader for a large Park Avenue law firm, one of my co-workers, a graduate of Penn, asked me to read *his* college novel about a classmate who had made a very deep impression on him. It was hard to say anything about his book, since I wanted to be kind, and the simplest thing to have told him was: "Get over it." I recognized my own first novel in his: the nostalgia, melancholy, hero-worship, or at least desire to worship a hero, or be one oneself. But such emotions are mostly sentimental in print and matter all too often to no one but the author. Which is why I was glad Jeffrey Lant, about ten years ago, asked me to contribute an essay to *Our Harvard*—because an essay seems to me about the right size for a college valentine. I got to not only describe my years at Harvard in this piece, but to discover not how happy I'd been during them, but, in fact, how depressed I was here much of the time; and how a lot of that depression was due to a thwarted attempt to come out—an attempt no one at Harvard seemed to want to contemplate, much less assist, or talk about.

There was another chance I had to write about Harvard, I should add, before Jeffrey Lant asked me for an essay—a chance every Harvard graduate who can't manage a *Brideshead Revisited* or *This Side of Paradise* gets, and that is the *Class Report* that comes out every five years after you leave this place. I'm sure most of you are familiar with them. For the first twenty years they are modest paperbacks, easy to carry, to read on a beach. And from the start, they are fascinating. They have been kept since the 18th century and are used by scholars. They read, however, like novels. They're better than most novels, in fact, because they're not contrived, not literary; they're all true. One can see, if you browse long enough, the whole range of human experience in them— the same amazing variety one finds in the people who go to school here, the different ways in which Fate distributes character, and gifts, and good and bad fortune to people. Of course it's impossible to read them and not compare one's own story with other people's—which is okay, because you do it in private, reading, and you can make what you want of it all, draw your own reflective conclusions. Each essay, each five years, amounts to *A Life Thus Far*; a summing up—and, like all summings up, they seem to be divided into the successful and unsuccessful, the happy and unhappy, in their most extreme form, with all the shades and gradations in between. On the other hand, a lot of people do not write in. Ever. I never did, for instance. Enough people do, however, to make the one that just came out for my class, in its twenty-fifth reunion year, over twelve hundred pages long.

The *25th Reunion Class Report* is hardbound, huge, printed on glossy paper, as heavy as a good dictionary or a small one-volume encyclopedia. The overall impression one gets skimming it is that the whole point of going to Harvard is to become a gynecologist. At least, of all the professions represented, doctors seem to write in most often. Doctors, lawyers, and businessmen. Other than that, it's difficult to generalize. Not all who are successful write in. There is nothing next to the name of a woman in my class, for instance, who's had a very successful career as a pianist who specializes in contemporary music, or another who has gone on to be a famous actress, and whom I took sophomore tutorial with: Stockard Channing. The unfamous also write in. The less successful. People write in, thank goodness, who've changed careers in mid-life, who still don't know what they want to do, who are single and living alone and still write lines like, "I still hope to marry one day and live happily ever after." (*Time is running out, dear*, one wants to write back.) There is always an unreconstructed hippy who is *still* in Burma trying to achieve tantric sex, or a man with a scheme that will guarantee world peace forever, or a harassed suburban housewife trying to sustain her commitment to Marxist humanism, or someone building a harpsichord in his basement in Minneapolis. The overall tone, however, is one of unbelievable conventionality. So it's a shock to come upon someone who announces he or she is gay. There are six or seven in my *Class Report*, I believe, without having read all twlve hundred pages to date. The men seem to make more of a point of it than the women. It may be harder, or more necessary, for them to say; I'm not sure. It certainly was for me, which is largely the reason I never wrote in.

One of my classmates who did, however, came out in the very first report my class published—a man I ran into years later in New York at a book signing when my first novel came out. I'd not known him that well at Harvard; I'd seen him, however, because he used to go around campus in a long black opera cloak, which was eccentric even for Harvard. He had an austerely handsome face and majored in medieval history, and this is what he wrote in the latest class report: "Nothing has turned out as I planned. I planned to be a teacher, probably a college professor. I am an administrator in the bus maintenance side of the New York City Transit Authority. I planned to be a member of a Roman Catholic religious order; I do volunteer work at the Gay Men's Health Crisis of New York. It all started very normally. I wanted to be a medievalist, so I went to Balliol College, Oxford. I was active in the Roman Catholic chaplaincy. I fell in love with a man in my college who denounced me publicly when I hinted at my feelings. I tried suicide, and took a decent honors degree. It was all very commonplace, for Oxford in 1967." And so on. It ends with a description of the grief he feels over the death of friends from AIDS, "a grief," he writes, "that will not go away." This particular classmate, I've thought since the first *Report*, has always been honest. I've always admired his forthrightness, in particular since I could not summon it up myself. And if his entry always seemed to me particularly eloquent, that same courage informs the much briefer opening line of a Radcliffe graduate in this year's report, who writes: "I live in Minnesota with my partner Joan. We lived for many years in the woods."

(*We lived for many years in the woods*—what a novel that might begin.)

At the same time, there are essays in every *Report* that I have always sensed were leaving out an important fact—occasionally, because I happened to know, or know of, the person writing. In my class, for instance, a well-known New York writer has never once divulged the detail that might explain part or much of the sort of life he'd made for himself. Which always seemed to translate into: You can work for *The New Yorker* magazine, and be what the world considers a success, and still not want to have anyone know you're gay, in 1991. The latter surely was one reason I myself never wrote in—what would I say, except the fact that I was gay, and had written novels about gay life? And why did I want to tell them—this mostly straight class—about that?

I was wondering, in fact, as I thought about what I wanted to say here, to this crowd, what it would be like to be at Harvard now, coming to hear this talk. On the one hand, it's impossible to imagine, because this evening would not have occurred when I was here; I couldn't have come to hear me speak; because in 1965 there was no Open Gate, no gay mentor program, no anti-discrimination clause, no newsletter, no Queer Nation going to Brookline High School to distribute condoms and talk about homosexuality, no kiss-ins in house dining halls. Freshman year I was dating a woman I'd gone to high school with who was at Wellesley. Each Saturday night we would return from the French film we'd double-dated at, and stand before her dorm, while the other couples around us puréed each other's lips. Debbie and I talked about Truffaut, then lightly embraced and said good night. Disturbed, I went to Student Health. My question was: Why didn't I want to kiss Debbie? (Debbie's question probably was: What's wrong with my hair and make-up?) At Student Health I had a pre-appointment interview designed to ascertain if there really was a problem; the woman who heard my doubts about my sexuality made a sympathetic clucking noise as she listened—small moans, and sighs; the sound my mother made when watching news of some awful plane crash on TV. I got an appointment the next day with a sun-tanned shrink whose desk held framed photographs of his sailboat and his family on a lawn in Maine. I told him I thought I was homosexual because I didn't want to kiss Debbie. He listened to me wordlessly and then leaned forward and solved the problem by saying: "Next time, kiss her."

Instead, I stopped dating altogether, and freshman year came to an end in utter isolation. After dinner in the Freshman Union—a meal I waited to eat until three minutes before closing, because it seemed easier to sit by myself in that huge room populated by other loners, staring straight ahead as the stuffed moose heads on the wall looked over us at one another—I would go upstairs to an empty room on the top floor to study, and end up instead staring at a young man modeling a swimsuit for Parr of Arizona, Inc., in the back pages of *Esquire*. I remember going to Widener shortly after my visit to Student Health and looking up Plato in the card catalogue; and I remember being very careful no one was behind me who could see over my shoulder just what I was looking up. I think I also found John Addington Symonds, whose title—*A Problem in Modern Ethics*—seemed an understatement at the time. None of this was decisive; to know that great minds had considered homosexuality not only acceptable but noble did not make much of a dent in a twentieth-century middle-class American Catholic upbringing. Another place I went to read was Lamont. I was taking a course in geology at the time: Nat Sci 5. While sitting in the john one day I noticed the partitions between the stalls were sheets of limestone in which the imprints of trilobites could be seen. I also noticed advertisements for nude wrestling scrawled on the doors in Magic Marker. As everyone knows who has gone to school, one can read certain things at a certain age and just not get it: *Moby Dick. King Lear.* Ads for nude wrestling on bathroom walls. Such was the force of my denial, I didn't even associate such things with myself. And when a hand reached under the partition between the toilet stalls one day and stroked my left leg, I stood up, horrified, pulled my pants on, and left. The johns in those days sounded like Niagara Falls when flushed, and the sound, I was sure, let the slimeball who had touched my left calf know just what I thought about *that* sort of activity.

Enter Elizabeth Taylor and Richard Burton. Sophomore year I moved to Lowell House without a roommate. How could I? I still knew no one. The first days there I went to look at places I might live: rooms or suites with people who had no roommates either. One of them was very strange. He chain-smoked while we talked, wore glasses, talked in a low, sepulchral voice and wanted, I learned later, to be a nightclub singer more than anything else in life. Though I ended up in a suite with three sober history majors, I began noticing Richard around Lowell House, with another person—always the same person, a very exotic, aristocratic-looking student who didn't look like the rest of us. He had the sort of expression I'd only seen on the bust of Nefertiti: slanted eyes, wavy blond hair, and a serene but piercing gaze that seemed to regard the world from a mysterious distance I couldn't quite analyze. He often wore a double-breasted blazer, beautiful striped shirts; I decided he must be European, the son of a French count, perhaps. In reality he was the son of a civil servant from the Bronx, and had transferred to Harvard from CCNY. Richard told me about him one day when I found Richard alone at lunch. He said I should get to know Joel, because Joel was in charge of inviting Elizabeth Taylor and Richard Burton to Lowell House for a Ford dinner in the small dining room; part of a series in which undergraduates could invite artists to dinner there. If I got to know him, he might put me on the guest list. The introduction took place. Joel, Richard, and I began eating together, and meeting every night in Joel's room at 11 o'clock. From there we went to Elsie's, ate, came back to Lowell House, and talked till two. They had a remarkable sense of humor—one I liked a lot, but which I knew was not quite right, somehow. When I left Joel's room I thought this was how Macbeth felt after visiting the witches. Harvard, after all, was all about language, the careful and precise use of words. Glib, gabby freshmen like myself soon had ice water thrown on them, so icy my first tutor told me I was "feckless" and I had to rush home to look the word up. Harvard was all about a rational, ironic, critical reserve. Not so with Joel and Dick. I spoke a different language in the room with them. There was a book out at that time about a Princeton student and his relationship with a black prostitute, called *The Hundred Dollar Misunderstanding*, and it had a line of dialogue Joel and Dick used to toss back and forth between themselves that was not very politically correct: "She think hers don't stink, but it do." I couldn't quite fit this in with Henry James, Henry Adams, and Cotton Mather, but after a long day in class learning tropes in Puritan sermons, and the oblivion of Lamont Library, I know I had to go to Joel's at 11 o'clock and hear *some*one say that line.

As it turned out, Elizabeth Taylor never came to Lowell House; she was trapped in her hotel room in downtown Boston—where Burton was appearing in *Hamlet*, shortly after the beginning of their romance. Trapped by fans and paparazzi, if there are paparazzi in Boston, she could not get out to come over to Cambridge. Or so we were told. But by this time, even without Elizabeth Taylor, Joel and Dick and I had become a unit. Or rather I was an appendage; Joel and Dick were the unit, so closely bonded they still seemed to me separate from the rest of the house. They always ate together, for example, at a small table in the corner of the dining hall. Some evenings I would enter that room, see the two of them in one corner, and my roommates at another table, and realize I had to make a terrible choice; a choice Joel watched me make with his penetrating eyes as I walked to the serving line to get my tray—since he knew exactly what I was going through, torn between the conventional and unconventional, respectable and *outré*. Joel seemed to know more about me than I did about myself, in fact. At Joel's I learned a lot of odd things—that perfume is smelled on the wrist, not from the bottle, that Venice is best in September, that I should rinse my face twenty times after cleaning it before bed—but they all seemed mere symptoms of a deeper knowledge he had about what people, including myself, wanted out of life. Really wanted. I of course was too polite to ask, and many nights I simply glanced at Joel and Richard in the corner of the dining room, and sat down instead with my roommates to talk about the closing of the frontier in America.

The frontier may have closed, but finally, in Lowell House, I myself was opening up. I began noticing people besides Joel and Dick; making other friends. One was an assistant professor of English who gave me a part in *An Evening with Oscar Wilde* in the common room, and who led a seminar on Tennessee Williams I took, and whose own book on Emily Dickinson had just come out. Road-signs, it would seem, at this distance. But sexuality is not so easily perceived when young. Once after a lecture on Walt Whitman, we went to lunch in the dining hall, and when we asked if we could sit at his table with him, he looked up, sighed, and said: "If you promise not to ask if Whitman was homosexual." I hadn't been about to, but, like my experience at Student Health, this confirmed my impression that homosexuality was a neurotic bore, a tiresome insecurity of anxious undergraduates and nothing more. Yet I was also aware of this professor's close friendship with another tutor in the house, and the fact that he was thirty-five and unmarried—a fact that must have allowed me to feel closer to him than to other instructors. I was aware, too, of other friendships: another tutor, in particular, and a sophomore, who were both very handsome and went out together in the evening so well dressed they looked like Edwardian fops. And two students, a sleepy-eyed blond and a dark-haired fellow with a faint case of acne, who would walk around our courtyard in spring in black leather pants, actually cracking a big black whip. There was a student playwright whom I saw one morning, just after dawn, walk into the foggy courtyard, while I—having stayed up all night studying for some exam—watched him cross to another entry with his arm wrapped around another man. Cross the courtyard, I sensed (without even making the thought conscious), in a way that was possible only at dawn, in a fog, while everyone else was asleep. There was even a tutor in Slavic studies who looked like the pederast small children are told not to accept candy from—with enormous, liquid eyes, and a pipe at his red lips—a man who contributed drawings to *The New Yorker* and who, rumor had it, flunked his doctoral exams on purpose so he could stay in Lowell House, running both the weight-lifting club and a life drawing class. Both of which seem appealing to me now, but at the time were sub-rosa, off limits, vaguely dangerous. The general atmosphere of the culture, and Lowell House, was macho-competitive. One friend lived with a pack of preppies who would sit in the dining hall Friday nights betting which women coming in as dates were virgins. One of my own roommates was having an affair with a student at Convent of the Sacred Heart, and described his distaste at having to make love in rented hotel rooms with another couple on the adjacent bed. Another roommate was dating a Wellesley student he did more than kiss; he would hang a red tie on his doorknob to mean they were having sex and were not to be disturbed.

Afterwards, I would see them walk into the dining hall with what looked like a radiant glow on their flushed faces. Like the heroine of a Henry James novel I was reading, I suspected everyone was having sex but me. I suppressed the whole issue by spending even longer hours in libraries, searching for the perfect chair, the perfect desk, the perfect lamp that would enable me to imbibe these books I could hardly remember a word of the minute I finished them. By sophomore year you realize, of course, that reading is, in a sense, all you've been sent here to do. And teaching is all about telling a person to read the right book, the one he or she needs.

My friend the English instructor suggested I read one called *The Last Puritan* by George Santayana fall of my junior year. *The Last Puritan* happens to be about a Harvard student, a student who transfers to Williams, actually, and his romantic/idealistic/platonic friendship with an English sailor his father hires to sail his yacht. It's about a love between two men that can never come to sexual expression; it depressed me deeply; I seemed to recognize in the book an emotion that was my fate, a fate that seemed to close off so much of life that should be hopeful and outgoing in a sort of melancholy resignation. I was also given that year a novel by Henry James called *The Ambassadors*. In a famous scene in *The Ambassadors* a middle-aged man from New England, standing in a garden in Paris, suddenly realizes his life has passed him by, and says to the young man he's with: "Live, live all you can, it's a mistake not to!" The words made perfect sense to me. They do to most of us. The question was: How? In the novel, everyone's upset because a young American has lingered in Paris while having an affair with an older woman. This was hard to translate into the opportunities available to a middle-class college student walking with Joel to Elsie's every night for a piece of mocha cake, hearing him say in his sonorous, nasal voice, "Now, *there's* a face." Faces were all we had, though what the significance of their beauty was, I wasn't sure. We did not always agree on the face, but that we both felt them important, and magical, was one of the bases of our friendship, and the glory of this place. Odd. There was no course at Harvard in Faces, the Beauty Of. There was no seminar that dealt with the powerful hold mere physical beauty had on me—at least, no seminars listed as such. Everything was being transmitted obliquely, politely, it seemed—as seeds that would flower, like so much education, later.

Senior year I took a course on the Life Cycle taught by Erik Erikson that made an impression on a lot of people, I realized, reading my last *Class Report*. The Life Cycle consists, in his conception, of six life crises between birth and death. The idea is to pass each one to get on to the next. It always involved a choice. The one that applied to me at the time I took the course seemed to be the Crisis of Intimacy, or Intimacy versus Isolation. The crisis of intimacy involved a member of the opposite sex. Since I now believed I would never pass that one, I concluded my life was permanently stalled—what people used to, and may still, call arrested development; homosexuality as a sort of eternal and terminal adolescence. Well, thought I, since I can't pass the Crisis of Intimacy, I can never move on to Generativity (parenthood), Acceptance, and Death. Or rather, I'd go straight from Crisis Three to Crisis Six without ever experiencing the other two.

There was another concept of Erikson's that I think of now, because it seems to have perhaps more to do with homosexuality in our culture; and that is Negative Identity. Negative Identity is just that—identifying with the reverse of virtues we are supposed to emulate. That homosexuality was a negative identity was a message I'd received all my life; it was, quite clearly, the complete opposite of the pattern urged on us by family, community, custom, church, school, and law: Marriage and Family.

Marriage and Family: the ultimate Goal. The Crisis of Intimacy, successfully passed. When my favorite professor announced his impending marriage my senior year, I was thunderstruck; appalled; felt deserted, abandoned, as if an adored older brother had just told me the news—so deserted, I blurted out without thinking, "Why?" "To enlarge the circumference of my experience," he said, using a phrase from his book on that famous celibate, Emily Dickinson. To enlarge the circumference of his experience? That sounded like an odd reason to get married—like going to Greece. But then the summer I'd gone to Greece, my travelling companion from Adams House kept saying—each time we found ourselves on some matchless promontory above the Aegean—"I'm going to bring my wife here when I marry." Chilling words: I knew I'd be returning solo. When I was talking with one of my other friends, a math major from Oregon who lived across the entry-way from Joel, one night, I remember telling him the difference between us was that he liked Math, and I liked English. In other words, I thought, you're straight, and I'm gay. "Gay" was not the word then, of course. And Harvard, still sexually segregated, all male, let me finesse the whole issue—the dawning sense of isolation, the failure to pass Life Crisis #3—by ignoring everything. No wonder the novel I wrote in a state of depression after graduation was so awful. No wonder it really seemed my life had ended. If homosexuality was a topic the few adults I asked implied was not worth talking about—Kiss Debbie; don't ask if Whitman was—I might as well ignore it, too. In reality I could not. Even ignoring it I was to waste an awful lot of time afterwards, those years when I sometimes wished I'd never gone to Harvard, had moved right to a city like New York, say, right after high school.

Years later the dear friends I couldn't bear to part with in June of 1965 were all leading separate lives. The math major from Oregon got married, took over the family farm, and had two daughters. The friend who wanted to visit Cape Sounion with his bride did. Joel moved to Paris, met someone, he wrote in a letter, "who sees the world the way I do," and began trying to earn a living. Richard moved to Washington, D.C., to avoid the draft, and taught high school. I took the foreign service exam, thinking I would work for the State Department; but each time I scheduled a personal interview, I cancelled—thinking the FBI or whoever interviewed me would know I wasn't straight. (As Gore Vidal said: "I could've been President except for the fag thing!") Instead I went to a writer's workshop—who cared, in the arts, if you were gay?—and after a stint in the Army, moved to New York and became a clone. The few times Joel and I got together on one of his trips back home, our relationship seemed a bit awkward; it was obvious we couldn't reproduce Harvard on the streets of Greenwich Village. He hated New York, for one thing. I loved it. He wasn't "gay." I was. The period of hilarious innocence was over, and Harvard was behind us, and everything had to be, in a sense, re-negotiated.

One summer evening we were walking through Greenwich Village while he was in New York on business, eating ice cream cones, the way we had in Cambridge, and we passed a newsstand. Writers in the news magazines at that time—1975—were fond of saying the love that dared not speak its name now would not shut up. In the ten years since Joel and I had graduated, not only I had come out of the closet, so had thousands of other people. I even knew the man with whom Joel had gone to Europe the summer after I'd met Joel and Dick—a French teacher who now lived three blocks from me in the East Village, where, though he never visited the bars and discos I did, he lived with one lover after another, always Puerto Rican or black, like some man in a story by Joseph Conrad, one Conrad never wrote. Joel of course had been with the same companion for ten years now; without ever once having gone to a bar, baths, or place like Fire Island—the three staples of my existence at that time, places one went ostensibly to find a companion, again and again and again. Which was the reason I felt a little embarrassed taking him down Christopher Street that evening: Part of me was wondering if he hadn't done it in a better way, and didn't consider this pathetic. In fact, by 1975, Christopher Street had turned fairly trashy, the excesses of the seventies already beginning to transform it into something seedy, and as we walked it all seemed suddenly sordid in a way it might not have had I not been trying to sense, as we walked, his reaction. I was already anticipating his disapproval, perhaps, the failure of the scene to match his own standards in life, whether this was Harvard snobbery or Harvard intelligence, when we passed a newspaper stand covered with porn magazines like *Honcho, Mandate,* and *Drummer.* Joel stopped for a moment to look at them, and then said, as we walked on, in a musing voice: "Why do they make so much of it over here?"

Why do we make so much of it over here, indeed? The question struck me then, and still does: I'd made a lot of it, certainly, in my own life. It had become in a sense everything. So I had to ask my own self what he had, what only a visitor, perhaps, could. The easy answer to his question was to say that in Europe, homosexuality was not the basis for a separate category, community, self-interest group that it was here; that people there lived out their sexual preference while remaining in the context of the larger society and culture. And that you could call this either staying in the closet, or refusing to be ghettoized. What was this mob scene I was involved in, anyway, this stampede of promiscuity, this gay life that seemed all too often toward the end of the seventies as predictable and conformist as any in the suburbs? With its rituals, habits, stereotypes, expectations, and burn-out? Perhaps homosexuality was in fact an essentially private and personal fact, something that had to do with the person in one's bed, and nothing more. I could have told Joel that it was a French man, Renaud Camus, who'd written a book that described gay life as well as any I'd read, a book aptly named *Tricks.* But that was not the answer. So I was back to his simple question as we strolled onto the pier: Why did we make so much of it over here?

Nothing is so diminishing as to realize that one was, after all, part of a trend—an era, an historical moment. American life—the sort journalists sum up in decades, or nicknames—is something Harvard people think, I suspect, they are too smart for, too individual, too different, to be a part of. But I was part of something, I guess, that Joel was not. The Age of Clones, 1971 to 1979 A.D. All movements are merely accumulations of many individuals desiring the same thing, of course. When you are coming out, you do not spend much time thinking about what you are doing—you want simply to live, to have a personal life—an approximation at first of the dreams one was brought up with: domestic happiness, fidelity, affection, trust. You want to solve the Crisis of Intimacy. These concepts translate oddly into homosexual life, I learned. There was no education for the sort of life I ended up leading. We are not brought up to be gay. There was a sense of learning new codes, living in New York as a gay man; of going to school all over again in a society which did not recognize the diploma you'd earned. It recognized other things, mostly unrelated to your education—exactly the problem of all education, Henry Adams had pointed out. I who wondered what James meant in *The Ambassadors* was now wondering how to combine brewers' yeast with my morning milkshake because I needed extra protein for the body-building I was doing at the gym. The thing that had not seemed important at Harvard—the body—was now crucial. My roommate would not travel unless he could continue his work-outs wherever he was going, as if he were afraid he would deflate. It often struck me in New York in the seventies that while my friend the math major was writing in letters that Harvard had little to do with farming wheat, I was thinking it had nothing to do with entering the Sandpiper on Fire Island in the right T-shirt and haircut. As the T-shirt said: "So many men, so little time." Life in the seventies was an extraordinary burst of energy and invention. But questions of history and literature were replaced by three: Did you go out last night? Who was there? How was the music? (I did. It was jammed. The music was okay.) In 1977 a Harvard graduate named Toby Marotta came out in his *10th Anniversary Class Report*; he got so many letters, he wrote a book called *Sons of Harvard*—a collection of interviews with gay classmates. One weekend I went down to Washington to visit Richard—Richard who, with classic New England reserve, had never said a word about his private life. Neither Joel nor I had any idea about his sexuality or amorous life. All we knew was that he had been in therapy and was living with 19 cats. One summer evening he and I stood on a terrace of the Capitol, and I asked him what he wanted out of life, and he said: "I want to be successful and have a family." The words stunned me; not only because he seemed far from this goal. When I said goodbye as he dropped me off at Union Station, I did not tell him I felt like the Little Mermaid returning to the sea—the sea of men. I was addicted to cruising. Ten years after graduation from Harvard, where I saw nothing in terms of sex, I now saw everything that way. Re-reading *The Ambassadors* it struck me that the book was really about Chad Newsome's penis—everyone wanted it. And instead of going to Paris to live, live all I could, I headed straight for the Everard Baths the moment the train returned me to New York.

One night the Everard burned down. People died, it was said, because the owners had not hooked sprinklers up. One of the dead was the lover of a man from my neighborhood I used to run into every now and then, infrequently, because he spent six months of the year teaching English in Saudi Arabia and six months back in New York, since, he said, he needed half a year in a strict, puritanical, drugless society to alternate with New York. It was true that, having no limits, thanks to penicillin, there seemed no way the escalation of drugs, muscles, ways to have sex, would stop. The Everard was rebuilt, and now there was also the St. Marks, Man's Country, and the Club. I was reading Henry James now in the waiting room of the Enteric Disease Clinic on 9th Avenue, where I kept running into friends, while waiting for our shit to be analyzed for amoebas. Once I overheard the nurse ask one of the patients the usual question, "Have you been traveling?" and I thought: Yes, in the wrong circles. Yet the moment one was cured, one celebrated by going back into the fray. As a friend said when I asked him what he was going to do with his clean bill of health: "Go to the Mineshaft." In the meantime, a new generation arrived in the City that wanted nothing to do with discos, plaid shirts, or Fire Island theme parties. One day I looked down and saw stencilled on the sidewalk of my block by a group called Fags Against Facial Hair the words CLONES GO HOME. I obeyed. Burnt out by it all, I went home and ended up writing a book about an experience that seemed to have nothing to do with what I'd been educated or prepared for: Gay life. An experience that constitutued an odd, mostly invisible, and very foreign country all by itself.

Oddly, all three of us had ended up living apart—Dick in the inner city of Washington, D.C., Joel in Paris, me in gay America, all equally foreign somehow. What was wonderful was our friendship's surviving everything. The awkward reunions spaced over a decade eventually worked themselves out. Joel even introduced me to a man in New York—a friend of his—who became my closest friend in New York. They were pleased about my getting published. We walked around New York together, the three of us, soon after this. Then AIDS hit in 1983 and took the friend Joel had introduced me to, and the next thing I heard were long distance calls from Paris and Washington asking how I was.

Last night I took a walk around campus. I went down to Elsie's—closed and dark and all changed inside, but still there. Then I went, with some wariness, to Lowell House, wondering if I could even go in. I could, and did, and it was quite spooky. The door to Joel's entry was locked, and two women were in the window beside it facing the courtyard; but I could still feel the spell of those evenings in L-14—how happy and romantic I'd been there—and what a dream world we'd lived in, I now realize. At one point I crossed the grass and stood outside the window of my own first room there, looking out onto the courtyard through the fog. I stood there and peered into the window where I'd sat that night, resting my eyes after a night of studying, separated from that moment by twenty-five years of Time, that densest of all mediums through which many things cannot pass. And all I could think, watching the students talking to each other on the walks, saying good-night before the entry-ways, rehearsing music in the common room, was how fresh they seemed, how utterly hopeful.

Homosexual desire isn't easy. It takes, for all its romanticism, an unending ability to face facts over and over again. Sometimes painful facts. What to tell parents, if anything. What to tell friends, people you work for, where to work, how to integrate sex with the other parts of your life and personality. How to settle the issue of generativity. Of intimacy. How to deal with the temptation to shame. How to find what one wanted to begin with—fidelity, intimacy, affection. Henry James wrote a story called *The Beast in the Jungle* in which a man realized his fate was that nothing whatsoever would happen to him all his life. Well, once you act on homosexual, or heterosexual, desire, a lot of things happen. Many writers have painted a not exactly alluring picture of where all this leads. In *A Streetcar Named Desire*, Blanche gets taken away to the insane asylum for kissing the paperboy. In *Death in Venice*, Gustav ends up sobbing on a beach as mascara runs down his cheeks. (For Thomas Mann, a homosexual life was chaos.) In Proust, the greatest of them all, Charlus is devastated when Morel leaves him for a woman. Homosexuality ends up at some point requiring your best thinking and effort: One's education does in fact have to be used, at crucial times. The past twenty-five years have in a sense illustrated Thomas Jefferson's belief that the best way to find out what is true is to let everything compete with everything else in the free marketplace of ideas. We did make much of it over here. It was an attempt to be happy. Now, surrounded by the litter of a certain amount of human wreckage, we can ask ourselves what should be saved, what should be discarded, in the experiment. A point somewhere between gay cheerleading—the recourse of every minority—and despair should probably be found. One has, after all, to go on, whatever the cards dealt. There is a wonderful story by Colette in which a woman who's spent her life going to lunch with friends on the Riviera decides one day that she is too old to continue this existence. So she tells her friends goodbye, takes off her make-up, and stays home. And stays home. And stays home. Till she can't stand it any longer. So she puts on the make-up, and schedules lunch. Exactly. There's a joke I heard Milton Berle tell on TV this winter which describes the same instinct. A Catskills joke, set in one of the hotels where widows used to go to meet new husbands. A handsome man walks into the lobby one day. A woman goes over to him and says, "I don't think I've seen you here before." He says, "That's because I've never been here." "Oh," she says, "a good-looking man like you?" "I was away at school," he says. "Away at school?" she says. "A man your age?" "I was up the river," he says, "in the slammer. The penitentiary. We call it school. I killed my wife. I hacked her into twenty-seven pieces with an ax." "Oh," she says, "so you're single?"

EDMUND WHITE

Remembrances of a Gay Old Time

WHEN I WAS A KID I was always puzzled by those passages in the Bible that simply presented genealogies of otherwise unknown people, all those series of begats that seemed so mysterious and unnecessary. But after all I've lived through in the last fifteen years, I understand the imperative need to record names, to keep lists of the dead, to inscribe something about them on a quilt or on the page or on a gravestone. I've come to see that those lists of names, which I used to skip over in the Old Testament and in Homer, far from being some annoying caprice on the part of those first authors (themselves un-named, paradoxically), are the essence of literature.

We are all here to do honor to the memory of our friends. A few of them were writers; even fewer published; but most of them, like people everywhere, even the most powerful, are in danger of being swallowed up by oblivion un-less we do something to name them, record their quirks, even their faults, cull a bit of their wisdom, memorialize their pain, do justice to their struggle, cap-ture their moments of bliss.

I suppose since most gay people were not brought up by gay families, and most gay families do not bring up queer children, there is very little of the usual handing down of traditions from mother to child, from grandfather to grand-daughter. Worse, since so much of gay socializing is still based on the mating game, there is less intergenerational contact in our world than there is in theirs. When I was teaching at Brown in 1990 and '91, for instance, most of my lesbian and gay students had never before met and talked with an older gay person; in Paris, where I live now, I'm turned away from most gay bars for being too old.

Of course I realize that there are projects all over the country for preserv-ing the archives of gay men who have died from AIDS; I know that in smaller towns gays and lesbians of all ages socialize with one another, partly out of ne-cessity, perhaps, since there's often only one bar in town, but eventually out of genuine enthusiasm, in most cases. I also know that the lesbian community tends to be a lot less ageist than the gay male community; but nevertheless I

From the Summer 1996 issue. Keynote delivered at the 1996 OutWrite Conference in Boston.

Edmund White

insist that even if normal lines of communication were open between the generations, AIDS has presented us with a major rupture in that transmission, one that we writers are called upon to compensate for.

Because so many men of my generation are dead, I frequently talk to guys in their twenties and thirties who ask me what Brad Gooch has referred to with the title of his new novel, *The Golden Age of Promiscuity*, which is also a book about the much-maligned Robert Mapplethorpe and is an effort to defend him against the trivializing and demonizing that he underwent in the recent Patricia Morrisroe biography. People want to know not only about the sexual spree of the 1970s, say, but also about the lesbian and gay communes of that decade, or the beginning of lesbian and gay publishing, or the representation of queers in the movies. More subtly, they want to untangle the exact relationship that obtained back then between feminism and gay liberation, or black liberation and gay liberation. Or they want to know about the successful fight in the early 1970s to declassify homosexuality as a neurosis in the American Psychological Association. Or they want to find out about the early days of the Gay Academic Union.

Fortunately, we are living through a vigorous period in the production of serious and adventurous lesbian and gay history-writing. The Center for Lesbian and Gay Studies in New York, headed up by one of the great gay historians, Martin Duberman; Joan Nestle's Lesbian Herstory Archives; the creation of a new lesbian and gay study center in San Francisco, the first ever in a public library, which will house the papers of Randy Shilts and Harvey Milk; the important collection of contemporary lesbian and gay manuscripts being assembled at Yale, where the late, much lamented historian John Boswell taught and wrote with such passion and brilliance about gays in the Middle Ages; the continuing achievements of the pioneer gay historian Jonathan Katz, who has never been affiliated with an institution and who has supported himself with odd jobs all these years as he has written his volumes of gay American history and his recent book on "the invention of heterosexuality"—these are just a few of the names that spring to mind. The late Randy Shilts did studies that have already become the history of gays in the military, as did Marianne Humphries and Allan Bérubé. George Chauncey produced a fascinating history of "Gay New York" as it was at the beginning of the century. Richard Plant has written about gays in the concentration camps.

And then there are all the biographies of lesbian and gay artists, thinkers, doers, books which not only depict the homosexual life of earlier periods but also give us heroes and heroines or even villains—in any event populate the past with familiar faces where before there had been nothing but blank picture frames. There have been recent biographies of Djuna Barnes, for instance, and Willa Cather and Marguerite Yourcenar and Mary Renault. In the last two years there have been four new biographies of Thomas Mann. I just read Tony Heilbut's excellent biography of Mann, in which he talks openly about Mann's largely unconsummated homosexuality and the real-life background for *Death in Venice* (apparently the model for Tadzio was Count Wladyslaw Moes who, in the 1960s, fifty years later, recalled that an "old man" had watched him attentively in Venice when he was ten).

If I mention my own biography of Jean Genet, I do so only because it is the one I know the best. To me there was nothing more fascinating than tracing out the evolution of Genet's attitude towards homosexuality, for instance, from his youthful shame and defiance in the 1930s and his total lack of solidarity with other gay men, to the point that he encouraged fellow thieves to rob and beat up gay men—to the very different attitude he assumed in the 1970s, when he concluded that homosexuality could predispose someone towards revolutionary politics. He was sufficiently irritated by the Black Panthers' repeated references to their white male enemies (especially Nixon) as "faggots" or "punks" that he made strong objections, which caused his ally, Panther leader Huey Newton, to issue his ground-breaking essay, "The Women's Liberation and Gay Liberation Movements, August 15, 1970." Newton said that "through reading and through my life experience and observations" he knew "that homosexuals are not given freedom and liberty by anyone in the society. They might be the most oppressed people in our society." Newton called for the freedom for each person "to use his body in whatever way he wants." He said that although some homosexuals were not revolutionary, others were: "maybe a homosexual could be the most revolutionary. When we have revolutionary conferences, rallies and demonstrations, there should be full participation of the gay liberation movement and the women's liberation movement." I can remember when Newton issued that statement, but until I did research for my biography I had no idea that Genet had influenced Newton's thinking.

What I'm trying to suggest is that since there is little direct, intergenerational oral transmission of gay culture, we writers—whether we are poets or novelists or historians or biographers or sociologists—have a crucial mission to keep our culture alive, especially since AIDS has wiped out most of the male members of a key generation, the very Stonewall generation that legitimized the idea of such a culture in the first place. And, of course, I'm also acknowledging that, since Stonewall, an immense part of the past has been recovered and brought to light, a past that had never been known at all to earlier generations because few people were researching queer history and no one was publishing it. I'm thinking of Foucault's *History of Sexuality*, for instance, or Dover's *Greek Homosexuality*.

More narrowly, I want to talk about our need to remember and celebrate the earlier writers who have influenced us. Acknowledging our debt to them does credit to them, but also to us, since tracing out our spiritual heritage gives us a weight, a tradition, a resonance that all alone we do not possess. I think it must help a visionary, experimental lesbian novelist like Carole Maso to know that she is part of a tradition of like-minded women such as Willa Cather, Virginia Woolf, Djuna Barnes, and the poet Elizabeth Bishop, especially in a period as vulgarly commercial and unadventurous as our own. I know that Alan Hollinghurst is quick to honor his descent from such writers as Ronald Firbank (Hollinghurst edited *The Unknown Firbank*) and E. M. Forster (although *Maurice* was not published until 1970, and the stories in *The Life to Come* till later still). Before Hollinghurst published *The Swimming Pool Library*, serious gay male fiction of great artistry had almost died out in England; luckily Hollinghurst could look back to the 1910s and 1920s and take up where Firbank's *Concerning the Eccentricities of Cardinal Pirelli* and Forster's gay stories and *Maurice* left off. Certainly the pleasure for me of editing *The Faber Book of Gay Short Fiction* was to bring to readers works such as Denton Welch's story "When I Was Thirteen" and Henry James's "The Pupil" or the love scene from James Baldwin's *Just Above My Head*—fiction that either had never been read in a gay context or that had mysteriously remained unknown.

But for me the most important gay writer of the past has always been Christopher Isherwood, whom I had the chance to meet in the late 1970s and who became my friend in the early 1980s. I was lovers in 1978 with Christopher Cox, another member of my writers' group, the Violet Quill, and he was working for the famous composer and music critic, Virgil Thomson, who was already up in his eighties at that point. Anyway, Virgil had lived in France for fifty years and was a great cook and had written two operas with Gertrude Stein and seemed to know everyone. When Isherwood came to New York with his lover, the much younger American artist Don Bachardy, Virgil naturally invited them to dinner—and somehow Chris and I were also invited.

Isherwood was as inspiring as a man as he was as a writer. So many writers I've met I've liked—in fact I agree with Proust that writers are the best company—but most of them don't resemble their writing very closely. But Isherwood had the same graceful sense of humor linked to the same unvarnished truth-telling that I'd always admired in his writing. His response to flattery, for instance, was a great roar of laughter; there was not a pretentious bone in his body. When I had been a teenager and in my early twenties, there were very few gay books that crossed my path. I now know of course that there were quite a few important gay books in print, including Gore Vidal's *The City and the Pillar* and the novels of John Horne Burns, but the only ones I came across were the journals of André Gide and his memoir, *If It Die*, James Baldwin's *Giovanni's Room*, John Rechy's *City of Night*, which I read in installments in little magazines as it was coming out, and Isherwood's groundbreaking novel, *A Single Man*. What was remarkable about Isherwood's book was that, unlike

Rechy's or Jean Genet's fiction, it wasn't about marginal people—hustlers, pimps, thieves—but rather about an Englishman, a professor living in Los Angeles whose lover has recently died and who seeks solace with another expatriate, an Englishwoman, who lives nearby. There is no effort to apologize for homosexuality or place it in a medical context, no plea for compassion from the heterosexual reader, no suggestion that a gay man's life is more or less rewarding than that of his heterosexual colleagues and neighbors. The protagonist has his problems, including a nagging feeling that when he drives his car or teaches his classes he's a robot, but these problems are not linked to his condition as a homosexual.

If I mention this novel of the early 1960s now, thirty years later, I do so because I wish to remember Isherwood's contribution. Not only did he write gay fiction and memoirs of an extreme lucidity and eloquence, but he also shed before anyone else the excess baggage of shame, psychoanalysis, and religion. I suppose the authoritative English biography that is being written now about Isherwood will determine how he managed to be so many steps ahead of everyone else, but I would hazard that he must have been affected by two factors: his contact with the first gay liberation movement in Berlin in the 1920s, the movement of Magnus Hirschfeld that was wiped out by the Nazis; and his later contact with the homophile culture that sprang up in California after the war, the period of *One* magazine, the burgeoning gay world that had been born during the war and that was nurtured by beach hedonism. To be sure, Isherwood did not admit in print that he himself was gay until his 1970 memoir about his parents, *Kathleen and Frank*, but he had already written superb gay fiction in such books as *Down There on a Visit, The World in the Evening*, and *A Meeting by the River*, as well as his masterpiece, *A Single Man*.

Before I met Isherwood I had been writing very differently. I can see my own work as a gradual and uneven movement away from a totally imagined kind of writing with an emphasis on a strict formal organization and an invented content and an ironic tone, towards an autobiographical fiction that generates its sparks, if it does, through its tone of veracity and sincerity and its conformity to the natural trajectory of a life, my life.

Nabokov had been my first great influence, and my first two novels, *Forgetting Elena* and *Nocturnes for the King of Naples*, were written under his spell. *Elena* is a very coded novel, but already in *Nocturnes* there was some homosexual content, partially autobiographical but largely generated by wish-fulfillment.

Then I met Isherwood and I wrote a nonfiction book, *States of Desire: Travels in Gay America*. In it I began to experiment with a technique that Isherwood had pioneered—a gradual self-disclosure, a flirtatious unveiling of the self, but in my case I was coy not because I was afraid of complete candor but because I was searching for a device that would make the reader want to continue reading what was necessarily an episodic, fragmented travelogue. What Isherwood responded to in this book, however, was its political content, which he emphasized in his very generous blurb. The year was 1980 and we'd just lived through the Anita Bryant days; Isherwood was supremely aware of the full extent of religious bigotry and homophobia in the United States and he knew just how lethal these sentiments could be.

I suppose all my work could be seen as existing in a dialectical relationship between Nabokov and Isherwood, and the relationship has never been a simple one. Nabokov cannot be pegged as an irresponsible aesthete; his brother was gay and died in the Nazi camps, and his wife was Jewish, which caused the Nabokovs to flee Germany for France and eventually the States. His hatred of fascism is evident in *Bend Sinister, Invitation to a Beheading,* in many short stories, and in the scornful details about bullies and despots in all his postwar work. Nor can Isherwood be read as merely a political activist; he was at least as influenced by a quietist Vedanta philosophy as by progressive politics, and his work was sober and reserved in the English tradition of E. M. Forster. Moreover, at a certain moment I felt Isherwood's understatement and control were linked to an internalized homophobia, a desire to appear masculine in the stiff-upper-lip English fashion. Fifteen years ago, when I was still making pronouncements about the gay sensibility, I declared that the true gay style is elaborate, even overwrought and highly metaphorical. My theory was that a chaste style like Hemingway's (or in our day Raymond Carver's) that spells nothing out and leaves everything up to the reader's interpretation is a style appropriate only to the dominant culture; the reader can only draw the conclusions he or she has already learned, and those conclusions are necessarily conservative or at least familiar. An elaborate style that spells everything out like Proust's or that re-imagines everything through extended metaphors like Genet's is appropriate to queers, since they want the reader to think new thoughts and feel her or his way into entirely new moral and psychological sympathies.

But a lot has happened in the last fifteen years. Gay and lesbian life has been mainstreamed and even our values have become less separatist; I suppose the fact that gay marriage and adoption by lesbians and gay men have become the current hot issues shows the full extent of our real or attempted integration. Moreover, the very growth of gay culture—an expansion that can be sampled by looking at the growth of the gay bibliography in any bookstore or by the success of OutWrite, for instance—this growth means that our literature can explain less, can lower its voice, can speak casually.

At least it can speak casually to the converted, to an audience that is already gay or sympathetic. Genre fiction, humorous fiction, small-press fiction, and nonfiction can address themselves to sophisticated lesbian and gay readers without seducing or explaining. Most of the year I live in France, and if a recent visit to the States has taught me anything it's that homophobia is still raging in the U.S. I was appalled to discover how homosexual marriage and the possibility that Hawaii might legalize it have become a political football for the Christian Right. On C-Span at the time of the Iowa Caucus I watched one Republican candidate after another enter a church during an anti-gay rally and publicly sign a pledge to protect heterosexual marriage and family values against the satanic spectre of homosexual marriage. One speaker even dug up a 1972 radical gay text that had called for multiple gay marriages! Horrors! Every time the word "lifestyle" was uttered in ominous tones, I knew exactly who was being evoked.

When I think of launching a mainstream lesbian or gay novel before such a nation, I remind myself that every effect must be calculated or at least conscious. I at least certainly intend to make my work as honest and in-their-face as it's been since I first published *The Joy of Gay Sex* in 1976. I do not subscribe to the conservative, assimilationist, low-profile principles of books such as *A Place at the Table* or *Virtually Normal*. I do not want to melt into the crowd, because I know the crowd wants to lynch us. I do not want to disassociate the gay movement from drag queens and leather boys, partly because I don't want to be one of those dull normals normaling about—I identify too closely with drags and once used to be a leather boy—but mainly because I know that bigoted straights hate a middle-class gay man or woman much more than they hate a drag queen. Straight people made *La Cage aux Folles* a huge hit; straight people are worked up to a frenzy about homosexual marriage. Because middle-class gay life is more objectionable to straights than is marginal lesbian and gay life, a book such as Isherwood's *A Single Man* will always be more disturbing to straight readers than *Our Lady of the Flowers*. I am calling for defiance, for self-assertion, but I want every lesbian and gay author to be aware of the consequences and to know that we're playing a dangerous game with high stakes.

My excitement has carried me far from my subject, which is memory. I suppose I was led into this political excursus inevitably by the memory of Isherwood, who even now, ten years after his death, is my model, my interlocutor, my sparring partner. But if I think about my artistic and personal debts, I must not forget my contemporaries either, especially the members of the Violet Quill. The group itself met only less than a dozen times in the late 1970s and early 1980s, but our informal, friendly contacts preceded the club by many years (Robert Ferro and Andrew Holleran were college friends in the 1960s; George Whitmore and I met at a reading in the mid 1970s and were briefly lovers; Ferro and Michael Grumley were lovers, as were Chris Cox and I), and even today I remain in close contact with Felice Picano and Holleran, the only other members who are still alive.

This group has been resented and attacked by other gay writers partly because of its very success. What's important to remember is that before 1978 the modern gay literary movement scarcely existed. A few nonfiction books such as those by Dennis Altman or C. A. Tripp's *The Homosexual Matrix*, or Donn Teal's *The Gay Militants*, had been published, as well as that landmark feminist work, Kate Millett's *Sexual Politics*, but gay male fiction became a recognizable movement only in 1978 with the publication of Larry Kramer's *Faggots*, Holleran's *Dancer from the Dance*, and my own *Nocturnes for the King of Naples*, the least noticed of the three and the most modest seller. (On the West Coast the first volume of Armistead Maupin's *Tales of the City* and Paul Monette's *Taking Care of Mrs. Carroll* were published in the same year.) Suddenly American critics and readers were being asked to take notice of gay male fiction that wasn't apologetic, that showed (at least in Kramer's, Maupin's, and Holleran's books) not just a gay man or a gay couple but a whole gay population with its bars, its dialect, its folkways, and its watering places. Kramer was even confident enough to criticize the gay community for its promiscuity rather than apologize, as earlier books had done, for our very existence. Soon Ferro, in *The Family of Max Desir* and *Second Son*, was able to take up the theme of the gay son's fight to be accepted on his own terms, with his male lover by his side, by his conservative Italian-American family. Grumley, in a posthumous novel, *Life Drawing*, broached the delicate subject of black and white men together. Chris Cox, who became an editor at Ballantine, published many gay writers, including the haunting fairy tales written by Patrick Merla, for many years the editor of the *New York Native*. Our friend Vito Russo read to us at one of our meetings excerpts from the book he was writing, *The Celluloid Closet*, about the depiction of lesbians and gays in the movies. Our friend, the editor Michael Denneny, brought out an oral history of a contemporary gay love affair called *Lovers*. George Whitmore was one of the first journalists to give real-life accounts of the first PWAs before he himself died of

AIDS. Now Picano has given us a sweeping epic about the 1970s and 1980s before and after the onset of AIDS in his novel *Like People in History*. I've just read Holleran's new novel, due to be published next summer, which is a dark, powerful account of the loneliness and isolation of a survivor, someone who has left New York, outlived his friends and parents, and now must make do with radically diminished expectations.

I hope this brief overview of the work of the Violet Quill members will dispel the notion that all we could think about was Fire Island and tricking; if that is the image we projected, the stigma is due to Holleran's *Dancer from the Dance*, which is clearly the most beautiful gay novel of our times and the one most likely to be read a hundred years from now. Our enemies suggest that we constituted an arrogant New York hegemony, but we just happened to live in New York; that we crowded our rivals out of the field, but the field didn't exist before we came along; that we used our cunning and power-mongering and money to get where we got, but I was a humble ghost-writer writing college textbooks, Whitmore was a secretary, Ferro and Grumley were very poor, Picano tells me he is still just hanging on by a thread, and most of us were in our late thirties before we had even a first small taste of success.

I'm certainly not complaining, since I'm grateful that I've been able to live by my pen, even if I have to flesh out my income with journalism assignments and teaching; I know how privileged I am. I'm sure all of us in the Violet Quill are grateful that we were able to make our mark; so many writers of our generation were struck down by AIDS before they could get a book published or find their voice. If you think of the great writers in history, we would remember almost none of them if they'd died before age forty, yet that has been the fate of so many gay writers of our times, of my generation and younger.

Which returns me to my theme of memory. The other day I was at a party for Salman Rushdie and there I was introduced to the parents of a student of mine at Brown who died two years ago from AIDS while he was still in his twenties. His name was John Russell and he left behind a marvelous play, *Stupid Kids*, that will finally be put on next year in New York. As everyone else at the party was gawking at Rushdie or calculating the risk they were running by being in the same room with him, the Russells and I were oblivious to our surroundings. We were weeping and hanging on to each other and smiling because we knew that John's work would have its moment in the sun, even if it was just the brief neon sun of a New York theatrical season.

PATRICIA NELL WARREN

A Tragedy of Bees: My Years as a Poet in Exile, 1957–1973

> Like a tragedy of bees,
> Like a questing of beetles,
> The sun circles the bush of the sky . . .

THESE WERE the first lines of the first poem—tentative, eager—that I wrote in the Ukrainian language. My struggle to escape from a tragedy of my own making would produce a couple hundred more poems, as well as a tentative first novel, before I finally came out in 1973 and wrote the novel that most people know me by, *The Front Runner*.

Like any new Greek temple, *The Front Runner* stood on an older foundation of an older temple hidden deep beneath it. Every writer's work is a layered archeological site of personal anguish and growth. Mine was no different. Without that Ukrainian-language poetry, there would have been no *Front Runner*, nor the other novels I wrote. During the long years that I was a closeted writer, my poetry fed my hurting spirit in secret, and found its own secret code.

If anybody had told me when I was a tomboy ranch-girl in Montana in the early 1950s that I would some day write in Ukrainian and find an international readership through that tongue, I would have laughed. Yet I had already felt the first mysterious heart-throb for this great Slavic country, Ukraine, then a captive of Russia and Communism, and second-largest republic in the Soviet Union. In Powell County High School, my history book described Ukraine as "the breadbasket of the U.S.S.R." A photograph showed the land north of the Black Sea—an immense flat steppe that was once grasslands, now one of the richest farm belts in the world, striped with wheatfields and fallow. I knew something about wheatfields: our ranch was striped with them.

Languages came naturally to me. Our ranch household wasn't exactly polyglot, but we spoke smatterings of this and that. My Prussian great-grand-

From the Fall 1995 issue

Patricia Nell Warren

parents spoke German at home. My rancher dad knew a little Latin, German, French, and Cree. My mother taught herself Latin and Greek so she could read the inscriptions on ancient coins. In high school, I had no trouble with Latin and Spanish. In college came French and Italian, which I honed during the summer of 1955, studying art in France and Italy.

In 1956, as a converted Catholic about to leave the church, twenty years old and a senior at Manhattanville College in New York, I met a real live Ukrainian student named Olha Dyhdalevych. She and her mother had survived the hell of World War II refugee camps. Now Mrs. D, as we called her (because we couldn't wrap our Yankee tongues around her name), was head nurse at the college infirmary. We students loved her warmth and motherliness. Here were two people from those steppes on the other side of the world. I was intrigued. Mrs. D and Olha introduced me to the Ukrainian ghetto in downtown Manhattan.

At Surma Book and Music Store, I leafed through art books and Soviet magazines, and fell in love with more photographic vistas of that great land so like Montana—the Karpaty Mountains with their Hutsul mountaineers on little horses, and the eastern steppe, flat and luminous, like the Great Plains, and the Dnipro River with its willow islands, so like the Missouri. Lonely Scythian grave mounds against the skyline stirred a feeling of déjà vu. I had never been so intimate with a foreign place. I wanted to go there, of course.

Now Olha introduced me to a friend, namely a twenty-two-year-old electrical engineer and poet, Yuriy Orest Tarnawsky. Yuriy had Mongol intensity and looks that probably went back to the Horde. I was a dyke in denial, looking for a man. Yuriy was possessive, intense—and swept me off my feet.

Yuriy's mother had died as the Nazis invaded the Ukrainian S.S.R., and his father vanished in the fighting. In 1945, at age eleven, he and his two siblings and aunt were liberated from a Bavarian slave-labor camp along with other surviving Slavic *untermenschen* ("subhumans"). After the war, their father found them through Allied refugee networks. The reunited family came here as DPs (displaced persons). Yuriy was living the nihilism of European youth who had cut their teeth on World War II.

My parents didn't like Yuriy. I did feel uneasy about his traditional (the word "macho" wasn't in common usage yet) European possessiveness. But in 1957, after graduation, I married him anyway.

At first I learned Ukrainian in self-defense, as most of my new friends and in-laws didn't speak English. Yuriy's family and friends accepted me. Who could resist an *Amerikanka* who was learning *nasha mova* (our language) so well? My spouse and I settled in Westchester County, where he worked on machine translation for IBM Research. I went to work as a *Reader's Digest* editor. Most of the time, however, we commuted in and out of the Ukrainian ghettos in New York City, Newark, Philadelphia, Chicago, and Canadian cities.

Three million Ukrainian emigrés now lived in North America. Most of them were from Galicia, or western Ukraine, because the turmoil of the Nazi invasion enabled them to escape to the free West. In the central Canadian provinces, many Ukrainians were farmers and striped the prairie with wheat. In the United States, "Ukes" (as they wryly called themselves) were mostly city people and members of the intelligentsia. They got very weary of being called "Russians" by Americans who were ignorant of their part of the globe. Many were the fiery letters I wrote to *The New York Times*, taking the editors to task for their unsophisticated attitude. No letter was ever printed.

Around 1958, Yuriy and I helped form a publishing group with several other young emigré poets who drifted together in the Greenwich Village coffeehouses of the mid-fifties. There was Emma Andievska, Bohdan Rubchak, Boydan Boychuk, Jhenya Vasilkivka, Marko Tsarynnyk. Our favorite hangouts were Cafe Rienzi and the Orchidia Restaurant on Second Ave. The Lower East Side didn't feature junkies then—it was still heavily Slavic and Jewish middle-class neighborhoods. We weren't even into marijuana, but we drank like Cossacks. At the Ukrainian Arts Institute, in a decaying Manhattan mansion on East 79th Street, the receptions and balls of Uke intelligentsia saw us all soused and standing in a circle, arms linked, to howl Ukrainian folk songs.

We poets were also active in the International P.E.N. Club, one of the few U.S. organizations that was sensitive to Soviet cultural complexities. Our group was always reading the latest poems to one another. Naturally, I couldn't resist taking my own shot in this melodic and noble language.

From 1957 to 1973 my life would revolve around this group of poets, and the heterosexual marriage tagged to it. Most of my poetry was written during this time. Roughly half my output was in English. Of these, only a few were ever published in the United States, because my style and themes were at odds with U.S. literary trends of the 1950s and 1960s. For a time, I faithfully mailed my works around to the little magazines, who always rejected them. Finally I said to myself, "Screw you all," and went into exile myself—writing seriously in a foreign tongue.

My first book of Ukrainian poetry, *Trahediya djmeliv* (A *Tragedy of Bees*), came out in 1959. It expressed my search for stripped-down truth. But if there was no sexual truth in my life, what good was any other truth?

> I want to live without reds and without blacks,
> night without shadows, motion without wind.
> I want to see horses who don't run by means of silk,
> who don't run on lightning and gleams.
> In dreams I see an unheard peal of thunder,
> a thunder shaped like an urn.
> I want to be without reds and without blacks,
> night without shadows, motion without wind.

My colleagues and friends were the *enfants terribles* of Ukrainian literature in exile. Their childhoods had focused on running for their lives, staring into mass graves, and learning new languages to survive. Most of my friends knew five or six languages well. At our parties, it was the thing to tell Polish jokes— in Polish. I had an inkling about mass graves, as I'd grown up near an old one on the ranch, where a lot of Indians and mixed-bloods were buried after a massacre in the 1860s. Dragging all my half-native rage about that kind of repression and atrocity, I fit right in.

We were the *Novi Poety*, the New Poets, the Uke answer to the Beat Generation—polyglot, pornographic, pessimistic, pugnacious. Our work was gruesome, and wildly lyrical. We put out a poetry annual called *Novi Poezii*, and published our individual books under the *Novi Poezii* imprint. With time, we added art into the annual edition—with artists like Jakiv Hnizdovsky, whose striking woodcuts were becoming known to American art collectors. A local printer ran our books off. Distribution was simple: We schlepped our books over to Surma Books and Music. With time, we sent out review copies to literary magazines and universities, where interest in Slavic studies was starting to stir.

Other than Beatniks and rock bands, our most-admired artists were foreign iconoclasts—including Albert Camus, Jean-Paul Sartre, Simone de Beauvoir, Marcel Proust, Federico García Lorca, Gabriela Mistral, Arthur Rimbaud, Pablo Neruda, Georg Trakl, Yukio Mishima. Yuriy, by the way, was very homophobic; how odd that many of his writer idols were gay.

Older emigrés who'd lived through the war expressed the horrors in more traditional fashion, and viewed our little circle with mingled shock and fascination. Ukrainian celebrities like the modern sculptor Archipenko were cordial to us, but from a safe distance. We did have our elder champions, like critic Yuriy Lawrynenko.

Those thirteen years were a blizzard of wonderful and terrible experiences, from poetry readings at Canadian universities, travels in France and sojourns in Spain, to quarrels with Yuriy and two suicide attempts on my part. It is strange, perhaps, that a young woman leading such an "interesting" life would be desperate enough to think seriously about dying. But, as one poem put it:

> Now I'm looking for tragedy
> Because one good tragedy
> is worth a thousand chimeras

My college conversion to Catholicism had collapsed into a black hole of disillusion. Now, still searching, I read Hindu, Buddhist, Taoist, and Islamic philosophy. Most of all, I yearned not only for a new spiritual path, but also for the courage to write openly about homosexual themes that secretly gripped me. But since Yuriy was given to spiteful comments about the gay men and lesbians we glimpsed on the Village streets, I felt I had no choice but to retreat into opaque personal allegory. Traditionally, Ukrainian women had enjoyed a certain measure of independence; now and then in our social circles we met the halfway-out lesbian. A couple of these Slavic Sapphos psyched me out, and made passes at me. Naturally I was cordial, but from a safe distance.

> What should I do today?
> Watch the sea make sand?
> What should I do today?
> Watch the sea make sadness?
> What should I do today?
> Die?
> Or watch the sea make sand?

During those sixteen years, I also wrote an English poetic drama, *The Horsemen*. Here, I edged away from deep symbolism, and hazarded the creation of my first gay character—an androgynous figure named Kah-Lee, who commits suicide by jumping a horse off a cliff because he/she can't choose between men and women. When the *Novi Poety* did a reading of *The Horsemen*, thinking to produce it, my spouse questioned me sharply about Kah-Lee.

"What dark place in your mind did that monster come from?" Yuriy wanted to know.

Generally, my writings were terse, like the folk songs I loved, and wrapped thickly in metaphor. Being so deep in denial, I felt cut off from life, though my spirit kept struggling towards life and beauty. The poetry was obsessed with death, violence, the gloomy lessons of history. Lovers embraced, and as they slid to earth, moss covered them—their caresses turned to the slow foldings of the earth's crust. People lived out their lives trapped in museum corridors, in glass display cases. A man went about with a hole in the front of his rib-cage; inside him lived a white bird.

In one poem, a girl comes home carrying a cow's skull in her apron. The family is sitting at the table. She tells them that the skull is the only thing she could find. The mother puts the skull on the table and arranges parsley around it. The last we see the girl, she is running away through the woods, disappearing among the trees.

> The grandmother's chair was empty.
> *Stürm*, said the barometer
> on the wall of the old room.
> "Did grandmother go away?" asked the little girl.
> "Yes," said her mother.
> "When will she come back?"
> "I don't know," said her mother.
> Through the window, you could see
> how the lilacs were blooming
> by the fresh grave of a pet dog.

There was a nagging déjà vu, a feeling that I'd lived on Earth many times. The déjà vu gave me a perspective, a voice, that spoke across a wideness of time, instead of through the narrow doorway of a single life. Through my poems ran a leitmotif of archaeology—of striving to dig ancient women's graves and alabaster goddesses out of blowing sand-dunes that were lost somewhere on the edge of some empty desert. Another motif ran to visions, dreams, legends, and prophecies. One literary critic—Lawrynenko, as I remember—called me a latter-day Cassandra.

Unlike my friends and my spouse, I hadn't survived a physical world war. But I felt like a war was going on inside.

Said one poem:

> Spring came
> and I forgot to turn green.
> Usually I wait for spring,
> I pray to puddles,
> go silly over pussy willows.
> But this time . . .
> spring came
> and I forgot to turn green.

Eventually our review copies got into the right hands. By the mid-sixties, our works were becoming known in Europe and Brazil through translations into French, Portuguese, German.

At one point, during the decade that Yuriy and I were in and out of Spain, we were in touch with Spanish novelist Camilo José Cela. He wanted to publish translations of some of our work in Spain, including my Ukrainian poem "Lament for Antonio Rizo Pastor." Spain was another country that stirred up all those déjà vu shivers for me. But General Franco was still in power, and evidently the government censors did not care for my poem.

INEVITABLY, as the communist system started to falter, our work filtered into the Eastern Bloc countries. In the U.S.S.R., when Khrushchev became premier, he allowed "the thaw"—precursor to 1990s *Glasnost*. It was Khrushchev who publicly admitted to the Soviet people that Stalin was a bad guy. Controls on nationalist culture creakily relaxed a bit. Right away, a whole wheatfield of Soviet Ukrainian dissident writers sprang up greenly—to be debated, criticized, sometimes harassed and jailed. Literate Ukrainians were tired of censored writing and proletarian platitudes. They wanted something fresh and ornery.

The sex-beauty-death-rock-and-roll of the New Poets stood the hair of puritanical communist censors on end. So our fans behind the Iron Curtain had to tread carefully. Official policy still viewed emigrés as traitors to the Motherland. But finally some of my poems came out in Poland, then in Czechoslovakia. They'd been translated by a wonderful Czech woman, Laryssa Molnar, writer and critic, whom I knew only through her letters.

With time, copies of our poetry books found their way, through the underground, into Soviet Ukraine. There, dissidents risked arrest and prison by merely retyping our poems for mimeographing, then hand-circulating these smudged copies secretly through the capital, Kiev, and other Ukrainian cultural centers. The most dangerous of their own works got out this way, through *samizdat* (self-publishing). In the U.S.S.R., anything self-published was automatically illegal. Technically, these Soviet citizens' copying and distribution of our work constituted copyright infringement. But we didn't dream of protesting.

In the late 1960s, as Soviet communism continued to thaw, three dissident poets were finally allowed to visit the United States and fraternize with emigré "traitors." This was a highly emotional moment in history for us.

Our visitors, Ivan Drach and Dmytro Pavlychko, were allowed six months in New York City as cultural attachés to the Ukrainian UN delegation. We attended UN sessions and watched the two putting in their time, with translation headphones on their ears. Drach was from Kiev, slender, blond, somber, already emerging as the young literary leader. I had a hard time understanding Drach, because he spoke the eastern Ukrainian dialect. But I had no trouble communicating with Pavlychko. He was stocky, ebullient—a mountain Hutsul with a puckish sense of humor.

One night we shepherded the two to a gala P.E.N. Club affair in their honor. I gave an introductory lecture on them. Then they read their work to a packed house.

Through succeeding nights, the two were wined and dined till they swore they couldn't handle another party. Ukrainian society hostesses fought to have them as guests. They visited our own homes, and while the KGB "tail" waited in his car on the street ouside, the two cultural attachés got roaring drunk with us New Poets, and howled folk songs in perfect pitch with us, like the wolves of the steppe. They listened to me howl in my Galician dialect, and shook their heads with disbelief that an *Amerikanka* could do this—one who was born in that land of cowboys and Indians that they'd heard of.

"When we first saw your poetry at home," they told me, "we thought you were born of Ukrainian emigré parents."

About a year later, journalist Vitaliy Korotych, a dark intense six-footer, another native of western Ukraine, came for a long stay. We yearned for a visit by Lina Kostenko, the reigning diva of Soviet Ukrainian poetry, and questioned the visitors about her. She wrote fiercely expressive poetry of a kind that was unthinkable before the thaw. But Kostenko had serious troubles with the police and censors, so she was not allowed to come.

Our friendships—the knowledge that we were under constant KGB surveillance—were careful, yet intense. Only on the last day did tears flow freely, and good-bye hugs and kisses go wild. We knew we might not see the three men again.

Back home in Soviet Ukraine, the dissidents finally managed to publish several of my poems in the country's biggest literary magazine, the *Literaturna Hazeta* in Kiev. I was the opening wedge, because I was the *Amerikanka*, not a "traitor." Hence I was "safe." It was an outstanding surprise to get a battered copy of the *Hazeta* via international airmail. This coup went a long way to salve the wound of rejection in my own country.

I tried hard to publish the dissidents' work in the United States, seeking insider publishing contacts through the *Digest*. Among other things, I translated Korotych's book O *Canada*, as well as a whole passel of poetry. It broke my heart as I translated works by Lina Kostenko, wondering if she was in prison. Dissident colleagues of hers, notably Siniavsky and Daniel, had been dragged to a highly publicized trial. But in the United States, editors yawned at my translations. American media and American trade publishers had yet to discover that many non-Russian cultures were smouldering, ready to explode, in the U.S.S.R.

Finally, Drach and his circle dared to invite me and Yuriy to visit Soviet Ukraine. Again, I was to be the door-opener—the "safe" *Amerikanka*. Drach wrote that it would be possible to read our poetry in major cities there.

We were tempted. It was now possible to get U.S. visas to go there. A trickling of American tourists had visited Ukraine. I had debriefed with one American-born college student who told me how he had actually hitchhiked around the Ukrainian boonies, right into the high mountain country where Pavlychko was from. Doubtless the student had been allowed to do this, so that word would get out that Ukraine was "safe" now. But was it safe? The KGB had continued to keep an eye on us. At large Ukrainian social affairs, the KGB was casual about letting one of their guys be visible, with a drink in his hand. Now and then foreign travelers to the U.S.S.R. still found themselves in trouble with the authorities—they wound up in prison, or even disappeared.

We decided that our trip would be safe only if the Soviet Ukrainian government would issue an official invitation.

Regrettably, in the late 1960s, an official invitation was still not possible. My dream of seeing the steppe now faded.

As 1970 ARRIVED, I was shifting creative gears, from poetry into prose. Dial Press bought my first novel, *The Last Centennial*. Other gears were shifting too—spiritual ones, sexual ones. I was moving towards the moment of dreadful decision about writing honestly and coming out. In Spain I had actually begun writing a novel whose characters wrestled with homosexuality; this book was kept in the bottom drawer, so my spouse didn't see it.

During this time, two more literary events happened. A pair of battered manuscripts arrived from Soviet Ukraine, via the underground. One was a bundle of mimeographed reports on the trials and imprisonments of Soviet Ukrainian intelligentsia, complete with all kinds of details, even names of KGB officers. These became known as the *Chornovil Papers*. I showed them to colleagues at the *Reader's Digest*, and finally turned them over to staff Soviet expert Eugene Lyons. Were they authentic? Were they disinformation? Lyons pronounced them genuine—the most vivid evidence of communist repression of free speech that he'd seen. Subsequently the *Chornovil Papers* provided research material for several major books and magazine articles by Soviet commentators.

I stood back—this kind of writing was not my chosen path.

The second bundle, for Ukrainians, was even more startling and exciting. It was a primitive Xerox copy of a thick book—the long-lost *Volume III* of Hrushevsky's sixteenth-century Cossack epic poetry. It still had the KGB file number on it.

To Ukrainians, this was the equivalent of finding the sequel to *Gone with the Wind* after Margaret Mitchell's tragic death. A distinguished folklorist, Hrushevsky started his research during the 1920s, when Premier Lenin was more lenient towards Soviet republics expressing their native cultures. Hrushevsky haunted Ukrainian villages, looking for the old bards who still knew how to sing these colorful epics, called *dumas*. Accompanied by playing on the zither-like *bandura*, and sung in a strongly Turkic style, the *dumas* are every bit as poetic, earthy, and gory as *Beowulf*.

Duma plot-lines tell of Ukrainian Cossacks who lived on islands in the Dnipro River. The steppe was still unplowed prairie, with grass so tall that horsemen disappeared in it. Poles, Tatars and Turks were trying to seize control of the steppe. The Kozaky were like samurai, fierce in silks and swords, fighting the Tatars, outwitting the Poles. When things went well, the Kozaky captured much booty, and went home to their islands, where they had great feasts and governed themselves as a free nation, with a democratic council called the Hromada. When things went badly, the Cossacks languished in Turkish prisons and slaved on Turkish galleys. Or they died brave and lonely deaths on the steppe, in the shadow of Scythian grave mounds, leaving their bones for the wolves of the steppe to chew.

Mostly the *dumas* celebrated the deeds of men. A few of them celebrated intrepid Cossack women.

I loved those *dumas*. They had the same wild spirit as the native-American stories I was raised on. Yuriy and I had started doing the first English translations of *dumas*. And lo! We had finally gotten the attention of a major American institution, namely Harvard University. The school had just established the first chair of Ukrainian studies in U.S. history.

But . . . we only had *Volumes I* and *II* of the *dumas*. By the early 1930s, Professor Hrushevsky had published these two volumes. But Lenin was now dead, and the new premier, Stalin, was clamping down on nationalism throughout the different Soviet republics. Stalin saw festering nationalistic spirit and ethnic freedom as a danger to Soviet unity, and was determined to stifle it everywhere. The professor had just taken *Volume III* to the printer, when Stalin launched his great purge. Angry at the great folklorist's stubborn devotion to

Ukrainian culture, Stalin had Hrushevsky arrested. The secret police raided the printer, and confiscated *Volume III*. Like one of his Cossack heroes, Hrushevsky died a brave and lonely death in a Siberian prison camp.

Now here was *Volume III*. Some people in high places in Soviet Ukraine evidently wanted to make amends for the past—maybe a KGB agent who was a closet dissident.

The translation project became a joint venture of Harvard and the University of Toronto, which also had Slavic studies. Several years after I divorced Yuriy in 1973, Toronto finally published the *dumas*. Ironically, our two names appeared as a joint by-line.

YEARS LATER, in 1991—long after I left the Ukrainian emigré scene and came out and published *The Front Runner*—the Soviet Union was finally falling apart.

Festering nationalism had been the cause, just as Stalin had always feared, as well as people's long-denied yearning for greater personal liberty. I read in the press that my old friend Ivan Drach was now heading the Ukrainian Rukh (independence movement). With Drach at the helm, the second largest republic in the U.S.S.R. slowly changed course, like a great tanker, and headed into her own destiny for the first time in three centuries. With her went every resource that had made her valuable to the Soviet Union—not only her fabled wheatfields, but her iron mines, oil fields, and Black Sea ports, as well as her troops and nuclear warheads.

Vitaliy Korotych's name cropped up too. He now edited a major Soviet pro-democracy magazine, and was deeply embroiled in those catastrophic events. The *San Francisco Chronicle* described Vitaliy standing on a van in Red Square with a bullhorn, speaking to the crowds. It was quite a shock to see their names in print, after all those years. I couldn't hold back the tears.

Fittingly, perhaps, a steady attrition destroyed most of my unpublished writings from these years. Some poetry and story manuscripts blew away on the winds of divorce. Subsequent losses were due to moves, fires, and my own penchant for destroying writings I wasn't satisfied with. I don't lament these losses too much. The writings of these years were too heartbroken to put on record. It was time to move on, and work on leaving a more positive legacy. As a poem put it in *Legends and Dreams*:

> Oh lichen, lichen
> you journey on your stone

you wander slow but sure
I want to travel with you

In 1993, in Los Angeles where I now live, the Northridge earthquake collapsed a section of the Santa Monica Freeway on top of my storage company. Under the ruthless blades of CalTrans bulldozers, the last of my Ukrainian memorabilia disappeared. They included a copy of the *Chornovil Papers*, as well as my Ukrainian books of poetry, and the last unpublished English poems.

Today, all that remains of those thirteen years is three volumes of Ukrainian poetry. There is A *Tragedy of Bees, Legends and Dreams*, and *Rose-Colored Cities*—slender European-style paperback volumes, long out of print. The original printings were one or two thousand copies, at most. Poems from a fourth book, *Horse with the Green Vinyl Mane*, were published in *Novi Poezii* around 1971. These portrayed a coldly beautiful universe in which the poet roamed space like a comet, devoid of all feeling. I'd run out of things to say about tragedy. Today, copies might be found in private book collections in the Ukrainian community, or in the Slavic libraries at Harvard, Rutgers, or the Universities of Toronto and Ottawa. Copies of *Ukrainian Dumy* are probably still on library shelves somewhere.

On these works, and on my first English novel, I used the pen name Patricia Kilina. I had desired to have a literary identity independent of my spouse. Ultimately my surge toward "identity" provoked his heterosexual frown, when I finally told him I am gay. Kilina is an ancient pagan female name. It comes from the word *kalyna*, meaning "holly tree." In those Ukrainian folk songs that I howled at the moon, this evergreen tree with its blood-red berries is the symbol of woman.

The tragedy was over. Tragedies always end in defeat and death. I'd decided I was more interested in victory. Kah-Lee wanted to live.

YAROSLAV MOGUTIN

"Invitation to a Beheading"

Bastard Mogutin! For a long time I had a suspicion that you were nasty shit and a greasy Jew. But I was absolutely shocked by your last writing. Who gave you, reptile, the right to write this kind of things? All kinds of pederasts like you have a great desire to destroy our Orthodox country, to corrupt our children. It will never happen! Our power is still strong! And tell this to your owners (or sexual partners?) in Washington and Tel-Aviv! You have signed your own death warrant. Take care! If you are so courageous and principled, why do you hide under an idiot's pseudonym and why don't you disclose your real (Jewish) name? I can answer: you are afraid of the revenge of the Russian Nation which was offended and humbled by you! But remember: we are sick of your rotten provocations! Enough! Death! Death! Death!

I RECEIVED THIS LETTER shortly before I was forced to leave Russia this past March [1995] due to the last in a series of criminal prosecutions brought against me for my position as a gay rights advocate and the only openly gay journalist in Russia. Messages of this kind were not unusual for me, as I had received them regularly through the mail and over the telephone, but this one arrived via fax machine, in a country where faxes are rare. These anonymous threats were not the most frightful compared with the threats by the state authorities and militia of physical violence and extortion, political harassment, criminal prosecution and long-term imprisonment for what I wrote or said.

IN 1990 I BEGAN WORKING as a freelance journalist. I was widely published in new, independent papers like *Yeschyo (More)* and *Novyi Vzglyad (New Outlook)*, as well as influential larger circulation publications like *Nezavisimaya Gazeta (Independent Gazette)*, *Stolitsa (Capital)* and *The Moscow News*. Most of my articles were on cultural and literary criticism and homosexual issues. I

From the Fall 1995 issue

also published several interviews with a number of famous cultural and pop personalities, most of whom were gay and for the first time spoke openly about their homosexuality.

I worked at Glagol Publishing, the first and only publisher in Russia publishing international and Russian homosexual literature. I was editor and author of the forewords of ten books, including: *Giovanni's Room*, by James Baldwin; Burroughs' *Naked Lunch*; and *Suicide of Tchaikovsky: The Myth and Reality*, by Alexander Poznansky.

When I first came out and began to publish my articles on homosexual issues, I was in an extremely dangerous and risky position. Homosexuality was absolutely taboo in the Russian press, culture, and public sphere. Perestroika and Glasnost had scarcely changed this situation. Although in 1993 Yeltsin repealed Stalin's law punishing homosexuality with up to five years in prison, gay men and lesbians in Russia still feared harassment and imprisonment from the militia. Homophobic agitation is a tacit state policy, with homosexuality considered criminal and morally abhorrent by most Russians. As recent polls have shown, almost half feel that homosexuals should be killed or isolated from society. Only a couple of years ago, a few first gay bars and discos were opened in Moscow and St. Petersburg.

There is no gay community per se in Russia. There is no gay civil rights movement, nor any influential political, social, or cultural gay groups. Needless to say, there are very few openly gay people in Russia. Most gays and lesbians, especially in the provinces, are deeply closeted, married, and have children. The foreign journalists who interviewed me in Moscow told me that it was difficult for them to find any Russian gays or lesbians who would agree to show their faces or give their real names even for a Western audience. My open gayness was shocking for closeted gay journalists and editors in the Russian press, who supported me in the beginning of my career, but then decided that it was too dangerous for them to have any contact with me. "Don't press homosexual issues," one editor told me. "I don't want to lose my job for publishing your homosexual articles, and my wife will think I'm a queer."

From Recognition to Surveillance

In 1993 my writing began to receive a large response and significant public recognition. In 1994 I was called the best critic of contemporary culture by *Nezavisimaya Gazeta*. Although increasingly popular, most of my articles and interviews were partly censored by editors for their homosexual references and content. For example, "Homosexuality in the Soviet Camps and Prisons" (*Novoye Vryemya*, No. 35–36, 1993) was censored before publication by the editor, Leonid Mlyechin. What he excluded concerned homophobia among anti-Soviet dissidents. "Even if it's true that these dissidents were homophobic, it's still not a good reason to kick them!" said Mlyechin. "Who cares about homosexuals, their rights and their problems? Only Mogutin does," Sergei Chuprinin, editor-in-chief of the literary magazine *Znamya (Banner)*, wrote in his article in *Moscow News*. These kinds of homophobic declarations are common for the so-called democratic and liberal press. After I published an interview with Simon Karlinsky, professor of Russian literature at Berkeley University and a specialist on Russian homosexual tradition, critic Nina Agisheva wrote in her article in *Moscow News*: "Mogutin and Karlinsky try to present all Russian classics as homosexuals! Even Gogol!" According to Soviet propaganda, which is still very real, there weren't any homosexuals in Russian and Soviet history: homosexuality is a "foreign disease," and, as famous writer-patriot Valentin Rasputin put it, "it was imported into Russia from abroad."

In July 1993, I published in *Yeschyo* an interview with Boris Moiseyev, an openly gay and hugely popular singer and performer. In it, Moiseyev stated that at the outset of his career he was the victim of "sexual terror" by the Komsomol and Communist Party leaders, who were "the fans of the beautiful bodies of young boys." He described graphically how he was forced to perform strip dancing and oral sex on "the dirty peckers of those old bastard Komsomol leaders . . . all of whom are still in power." The interview with Moiseyev created a minor scandal. When that issue of *Yeschyo* sold out, Xeroxed copies of my interview were disseminated in *samizdat*, like anti-Soviet literature in the USSR before Perestroika.

A highly edited version of the interview with Moiseyev was published without my permission by *Moskovskyi Komsomolets (MK)*, one of the most popular and official Russian dailies. In *Novyi Vzglyad* I published an article of protest against the illegal publication of my interview ("Dirty Peckers," NV, No. 34, 1993). In that article I reconstructed all the pieces from the original interview censored by *MK*. On September 10, instead of charges against *MK* for the unauthorized and illegal use of my interview, the Presnenskyi Interregional Prosecutor's Office of Moscow used my publication in *Novyi Vzglyad* as pretense for bringing criminal charges against me under Article 206.2 of the Criminal Code, for using "bawdy language and obscene expressions," "touching upon the subject of perverse sex, illustrated with the sketch of homosexual subject matter, and bearing a photographic picture of naked men." Article 206.2 ("malicious hooliganism with exceptional cynicism and extreme insolence"), providing for up to five years' imprisonment, was typically used against dissidents by the Soviet authorities. Following the Soviet prosecution system, the same charge of "hooliganism" is used against gays in China and Cuba. I found out about the Prosecutor's Office decision through accounts I read in the press, as there is no due process in the Russian judicial system.

After the attempted coup in October of 1993 the Yeltsin government shut down those newspapers it deemed "oppositional." Unexpectedly, the independent erotic newspaper *Yeschyo*, where I was published, was on that black list. On October 6, the militia, with a detective named Matveev, came to the apartment of Aleksei Kostin, the paper's publisher. Without official warrant they searched the apartment and arrested Kostin. "We should have destroyed the sexually anxious a long time ago!" exclaimed an officer who didn't give his name. For three days Kostin was held in custody without any formal charges.

Yeschyo was singled out from all other erotic publications, because it was the only paper in Russia to regularly publish positive and serious material on homosexual issues. In fact, *Yeschyo* was shut down after publishing my interview with Boris Moiseyev and the opening of the criminal case against me. The procurator's and militia's repressive actions against *Yeschyo, Novyi Vzglyad*, and me were part of a new homophobic campaign and a broader campaign against freedom of speech, independent journalists, and press. This campaign was supported with great enthusiasm by the former Soviet press and the official papers such as *Rossyiskaya Gazeta, Rossyiskiye Vesty (Russian News), Solidarnost (Solidarity)*, and *Vechernyaya Moskva (Night Moscow)*. A dozen homophobic articles against me and other journalists from *Yeschyo* and *Novyi Vzglyad* appeared during the next few weeks. One author proclaimed all of us "agents of the Israeli secret service MASSAD, who have received instructions to corrupt Russia."

On October 28, 1993, three militiamen came to the office of Glagol Publishing and shouted through the door to Alexander Shatalov, editor-in-chief of Glagol, inquiring as to my whereabouts. He answered that I was not in. They then said that they would break the door in and check it themselves. They obviously were informed that I was at the office at the moment. When the door was opened, they came in and showed me their documents. Their chief lieutenant Andryei Kuptsov put me under arrest. They drove me in handcuffs to the Regional Militia station. On the way there all of them used far more "bawdy language" and obscene expressions than the ones I had allegedly used.

At the station I was interrogated by Kuptsov three times during five hours without break or the presence of a lawyer: as a witness to the crime (i.e., writing and publishing of my own article!); as the prime suspect in the crime; and finally as the one charged with committing the crime. He asked if I understood that "Dirty Peckers" was illegal and that in writing it I had broken the law. I answered that this whole case seemed absolutely absurd. At the end of interrogation I was forced to sign a document prohibiting me from leaving Moscow. (I did not have the right of travel and was for all intents and purposes under house arrest until the end of 1994. I was also banned from receiving my foreign-travel passport.) "You're lucky we don't put you in jail like Kostin!" Kuptsov said to me.

Later, I found out that on the same day Kostin was also arrested. He was charged under Article 228 of the Criminal Code: "production, distribution and propaganda of pornography," subject to up to three years in prison. During the Soviet period this article was regularly used against dissidents. Three months later Kostin was arrested again and placed in a general holding cell in the most notorious prison in Moscow, Butyrki. Despite the considerable press attention given to the cases of *Yeschyo* and Kostin, along with numerous letters of protest from Russian and international human rights organizations, Kostin was held in the prison for thirteen months without trial.

The day after my arrest, Genrikh Padva, Russia's most famous human rights lawyer, took on my case pro bono. His great authority is based on the role he played in several high-profile political trials during the Soviet era. Padva was a founder of the first professional lawyers' union in the USSR. He was also the first lawyer to petition the Ministry of Justice to end the anti-homosexual Article 121.1 of the Criminal Code.

Out Comes Zhirinovsky

At around this time, at an exhibition in Moscow, I was introduced to Vladimir Zhirinovsky, leader of the Liberal Democratic Party of Russia who ran for president in 1991 in Russia's first free elections and became one of the most popular politicians with his nationalistic slogans. His extravagant image, speeches, actions, and manners made him an idol for many teenagers. He is often invited for the opening of rock clubs, galleries, punk, and heavy metal concerts.

Zhirinovsky was with his bodyguard, formerly the bodyguard of Babrak Karmal, the head of the Soviet regime in Afghanistan. Zhirinovsky was surprisingly interested in me. He told me that he had read my articles. "Why didn't you come to me before?" he asked. "You could have come to me and said: I wanna work for you and for your party! Why didn't you do it, like many other young Russian guys have?"

It was hard to know if he was serious or not. Zhirinovsky invited me to join him at the restaurant of the Central House of Architects. There we suddenly met two young boys, twelve or thirteen years old. Zhirinovsky was very interested in them and asked me to invite them to our table. "They can be good party members in military uniforms," he said. His manners, toasts, and speech were really bizarre to me. He felt comfortable in my company, as he knew I was gay. He proposed vodka to the boys, but they declined. He openly flirted with them, but ended up frightening them off. Disappointed, Zhirinovsky shot down another glass of vodka and went off to the dance floor into a clutch of young female admirers.

Zhirinovsky's obsession with young boys is not a secret to his inner circle, but it can not be a subject for discussions among them. The issue of his sexuality is seemingly taboo for the Russian press as well. Although a number of major papers published Reuters's photo of Zhirinovsky kissing a Serbian soldier on the mouth, both naked in the sauna, during his visit to Yugoslavia, none made any comment on it. He always has seventeen- or eighteen-year-old men around him—the youngest members of his party, the so-called *sokoly Zhirinovskogo* (Zhirinovsky's falcons). He lives separately from his wife and spends almost every weekend at his private dacha outside Moscow. One young reporter, who was there trying to do an interview with Zhirinovsky, told me that he was propositioned by Zhirinovsky to pose naked for the camera in the shower.

. I received another proposal from Zhirinovsky—he wanted me to be his press secretary. My reputation as an openly gay journalist obviously didn't embarrass him. I suppose he had more sexual than political interest in me. On the other hand, I was already a well-known writer, and he may have wanted to use my name to get more votes from my readers as well as from gay people. I realized that collaboration with Zhirinovsky could put an end to my persecution and protect me from other possible troubles with the authorities. I was an easy target for them, as I had no political backing or protection. One telephone call from Zhirinovsky to the Prosecutor's Office and the criminal case against me would be closed. But I declined his proposal as I had no interest in politics and I have tried to remain independent from any political parties, groups, or organizations. Now I would say that it's almost impossible to be politically independent in today's Russia.

Two months later, in December 1993, after an incredibly successful political campaign in the nation's parliamentary elections, Zhirinovsky became the leader of the largest party in the new Parliament. With promises of cheap vodka for every man, a boyfriend and flowers for every woman, and legalized drugs for all, he was the only politician in Russian history to use slogans in support of private life for all citizens, including homosexuals. Many of his 12.3 million voters were in fact homosexuals. "We are against any interference in the private life of our citizens," Zhirinovsky said in one interview. "Somebody is fascinated by eastern religions, somebody spends all day standing on his head in the pose of yoga, somebody has particular sexual preferences. Why do we have to interfere in their private life? We don't want to! The American president had the same slogan. And I was the first Russian politician who did the same, wasn't I? That's good! And note my, let's say, progressive ideology." When he was asked about me, what he thought of my reputation, he answered diplomatically: "We have a lot of work now, and we need people. It's why I proposed to work with him. . . . You can find some discriminative characteristic on everyone: one—dirty, another—poor, the third one—stupid, the fourth one has a different religion, the fifth one has a different ideology. . . . And what will happen?"

The Marriage

On March 22, 1994, the Presidential Legal Commission on Informational Disputes held a hearing regarding a number of my articles on homosexual issues published in *Novyi Vzglyad*. The Commission is a censorship organization founded by a special Yeltsin decree for control of mass media and information. Its chairman, Anatolyi Vengerov, is an ex-communist bureaucrat in his late sixties. The Commission consists of ten political appointees, all of whom are former Soviet *apparatchiks*. The legal status of the Commission is not clear, as its position is outside the Constitution, but its decisions, in effect, have the same power as presidential decrees. The work and the existence of the Commission have been criticized in the Russian independent press and Parliament, although most of the press tries to placate the Commission, which tacitly controls all legal issues affecting the mass media.

Ironically, I was not even invited to my own hearing, and found out about the Commission's decision in the press. I was proclaimed "a corrupter of public morals, a propagandist of psychic pathology, sexual perversions and brutal violence . . . including the use of profane language," etc. My writing "produces especial danger for children and teenagers." This decision was issued to all of the licensed press in Russia with a strong warning to editors not to publish my writing. From that time only the most liberal papers continued to publish me—*Nezavisimaya Gazeta* and *Novyi Vzglyad.*

On April 12, 1994, I attempted with my partner, American artist Robert Filippini, to register officially as the first same-sex marriage in Russia. We had lived together since January of 1994. The marriage action was announced in the press, and we had concerns that authorities would prohibit it. In the press release we wrote that the act was a "protest against the policy of homophobia and sexism, puritan public opinion and hypocritical morality," and "the primary objective for us was to draw public attention to the problems of gay and lesbian people in Russia."

On the eve of the marriage action we went to the United States Embassy to register Robert's intention to marry me, as per the rules regarding marriage of foreigners and Russian nationals. Surprisingly, even telling the consul to take note of the genders involved, we received the certificate with the signature and stamp of the Embassy consul Paul Davis-Jones.

On April 12, at three P.M. we arrived at Wedding Palace No. 4, the office for registering international marriages in Moscow. More than one hundred reporters and friends were waiting for us there. Karmen Bruyeva, the head of the Palace for over twenty-five years, was informed about our visit through friends. Surprisingly for us, she was polite and sympathetic. Bruyeva said that personally she understood our desire to get married, but "marriage is a voluntary union between a man and woman," according to a Soviet law that has remained unchanged since 1969. "I'm really sorry, but I cannot register your union. If I accepted an application from two men I would be reprimanded and the marriage would be declared invalid," Bruyeva said. "Why don't you apply to Parliament and ask to amend the law? By the way, raise your hands, those of you, journalists, who favor amending the law?" And all of them raised their hands.

The action drew a huge public response. The event was widely covered in the Russian and Western press, including CNN, Reuters, AP, *The Philadelphia Inquirer, The LA Times*, and *The San Francisco Chronicle*, among others. Most of the Russian press was very sympathetic and positive, except for an article in the Communist *Pravda*, where we were proclaimed "agents of Western drug trafficking and porno business," and a couple of other homophobic articles in government papers.

The Trial

The trial concerning the criminal case against me under Article 206.2 was set for April 14. Starting on April 13, Robert and I became the targets of militia harassment. That evening, two uniformed militia came to our apartment on Arbat and explained the reason for their visit: They had received letters of complaint from our neighbors claiming that we "corrupted our neighborhood." After looking around the apartment they left.

A few hours later two plainclothes detectives came to our apartment. The lead man, stout and with a prominent scar on his face, demanded to see our documents. When we asked to see their identification, "Scarface" responded, "Fuck off!" He and his partner, "Pretty Brute," wearing long black leather jackets, walked us into our kitchen and began an hour and a half interrogation on every aspect of our lives. Again, they told us that they received a neighbor's letter accusing us of holding "orgies with young boys"; they rambled on about their loathing of homosexuals and what they perceived to be the farce of our marriage attempt. "We can do anything with you two, put you in a psychiatric clinic, see you to jail, deport you from Russia! And neither PEN Center nor the American Embassy will be able to help you!" boasted Scarface.

They indicated that they were members of Zhirinovsky's party. Their belligerence was unrestrained until I told them that I knew Zhirinovsky personally and I would call him immediately to ask him to order them to stop their actions against us. "Don't give us this shit!" Scarface yelled. "How can you, queer, know Zhirinovsky personally?" I showed them his business card and his private number in my telephone book. After they drank nearly a liter of our vodka, they extorted $250 from us, promising that it would be the end of our "troubles with the neighbors," and left the apartment laughing. The visit was utterly animalistic. We were absolutely demoralized and in shock, to the point that we were afraid to tell even our friends of the incident.

On April 14, 1994, the Presnenskyi Interregional Court held a hearing concerning the criminal charges brought against me under Article 206.2. Against code, I received no official notification for the date of the trial. I was not even familiar with the documents of the case against me, as well as with the indictment as it was written. When I protested this to the presiding judge, Elena Filippova, she was completely indifferent. My lawyer argued that I was targeted for prosecution because of my homosexuality. He said that this was the only case in the history of Soviet or Russian jurisprudence when a journalist had been charged with hooliganism for his use of language. Use of so-called profane language has a long tradition in Russian letters and classical literature, and it has become increasingly common in the media, including large newspapers and on the government TV channel. Padva mentioned a number of examples when profane language was used by President Gorbachev, Vice President Rutskoi, President Yeltsin, and other Russian officials. Padva said that the case should be closed because of a variety of violations of the Criminal Code on the part of the Prosecutor's Office. He pointed that this is not just "a minor point, but . . . a crass violation of human rights."

After the lawyer's speech Judge Filippova took a break for "consultation," which was odd, as she was alone in her chambers. Evidently, she "consulted" with the Prosecutor's Office or other initiators of the case against me. Though, as written in the new Russian constitution, the judicial system is to be independent of the Prosecutor's Office, in Soviet and present-day Russia judges still represent the Prosecutor's Office. After about forty minutes the judge returned and read her resolution. She proclaimed me guilty of all charges, but sent the case back to the Prosecutor's Office on technical grounds for a new investigation.

On the night of April 16, the two detectives returned. For the next two hours a vodka-drinking Scarface, whose profanity-filled speech was a bizarre mix of foul Russian, English, and German, told graphic sexual stories, spoke of politics, religion, the philosophy of Hegel, Zhirinovsky's glory, the Motherland, his poor old mother, the dangers of militia work, the Orthodox Power, family life, and the general moral disorder of the world, emphasizing their hatred of homosexuals and the corrupting influence of the West. Thus did I discover the sophisticated spiritual and intellectual world of a militiaman. Midway through this monologue a large cellophane bag of hashish was laid on our table. The detectives laughed and proceeded to tell us of the prison terms one faced if found in possession of drugs. They then proposed to find young girls to bring up to our apartment for group sex. Pretty Brute asked if we preferred eleven- or twelve-year-old-girls. Repeatedly during their visit both of them demanded money. Again, they left the apartment drunk to the point where they could hardly walk.

A couple of nights later Scarface returned alone. He showed us a handwritten letter full of homophobic scribblings, describing graphically orgies with young boys that took place in our apartment. He asked if we wanted for him to kill our "motherfucking" neighbor, the purported writer of this letter. He raised his full glass of vodka, swilled it and said that he would now do us a favor, at which point he burned the letter in front of us, filling the room with smoke, yipping when he singed his fingers.

After our attempted marriage, due to the extensive press coverage it received, we were frequently recognized and regularly stopped on the street by the militia. This was especially true in our neighborhood, where we could not walk past the roving militia without being harassed. Though the anti-homosexual law was abolished in Russia, the militia continue to keep and collect files on known homosexuals. "I control all of them in my district," the Moscow local militia chief said in a TV interview. "I have to do it, because homosexuals are physically and psychically abnormal people. Every one of them any time can take the ax and kill somebody. Easily! They have to be isolated. They are sick!"

Flight from Russia

On September 20, 1994, under pressure from the liberal press, Russian and international human rights organizations, and legal efforts, the criminal case against me was closed by the Prosecutor's Office because "of the changed circumstances, the personality of Mogutin has ceased to pose danger to society." I was familiarized with that decision only on October 10, when I was invited to the Prosecutor's Office and had a three-hour conversation with Igor Konyushkin, First Deputy Prosecutor of the office. He was surprisingly young, intelligent, and gentle for his job. He spoke with me very frankly and seemed outwardly friendly. I realized that he was being provocative. Konyushkin introduced himself as a "big fan of my writing." "According to the duty of my job I have to read all your articles," he said. "We have a big file on you. You're a very good writer but the content of most of your articles is criminal. We could open a criminal case against you concerning anything from these articles as easily as we did with the 'Dirty Peckers' case. I just want to let you know that we dropped this case, but we can always open another one. We're giving you a chance to rehabilitate your mind: you must stop your writing or change your subject! You know what I mean? That's my advice as your big fan!"

My conversation with Konyushkin reminded me of Nabokov's *Invitation to a Beheading*. There was something sado-masochistic about it. He was completely obsessed with me, my criminal prosecution being an extension of this obsession. Konyushkin told me that he was most wounded by my article where I wrote that homophobic people in the Prosecutor's Office were just repressed queers. After my conversation with him, I was all the more convinced that what I had written was true. I walked out of there feeling ambivalent towards him.

A few weeks later the General (State) Prosecutor's Office issued a statement proclaiming their disagreement with the Regional Office's decision to close my case, and they brought it into their jurisdiction for future prosecution.

In February, the Presidential Legal Commission on Informational Disputes held two hearings concerning an article I had written on the war in Chechnya, "Chechen Knot." The article was highly critical of Yeltsin's government, the Parliament, the military complex, as well as Chechens and the Russian press and intelligentsia. "Chechen Knot" was not the only article of this kind in the Russian press. I was again being singled out because of my open homosexuality. Like my earlier case, this one had a strong political motivation.

Both hearings of the Commission were closed, and only reporters from the government press were invited. The trial was in typical Soviet character. When I tried to say something in my defense, the microphone was turned off. The Commission's members and reporters laughed. The chairman Anatolyi Vengerov was screaming: "It's scandalous! Stop this ugliness immediately or we shall call the militia! Where is security? Somebody, call security right now!"

The members of the Commission accused me of violating the Constitution by "inflaming national, social, and religious division" and recommended to the Prosecutor's Office that he bring criminal charges against me, and to the Committee on Press and Information that it close *Novyi Vzglyad* and rescind its license to publish. The official government TV channel Ostankino announced on its nightly news program, *Vremya (Time)*, the Commission's decision, which was also noted in *Rossyiskaya Gazeta* and other government papers.

I was almost unanimously vilified in press coverage of the new trial, in over a dozen aggressively homophobic articles. One of the authors called me a "hysterical mama's boy" and appealed to the authorities to put me in a psychiatric clinic. Another writer, the first secretary of the Moscow Union of Journalists, suggested that it was too bad that the earring-wearing Mogutin hadn't been killed instead of Dmitry Kholodov (the journalist of *Moskovskyi Komsomolyets*, who was killed by a letter bomb in the editorial office in October of 1994 while working on a report on corruption in the Russian army).

I was afraid to stay home or even be on the street, waiting to be rearrested by the militia. On the advice of my lawyer I chose to leave the country due to the likelihood of imprisonment and further harassment. Robert and I arrived in New York in March. Expecting the situation to settle down in my absence, we fled Moscow in the hope of returning in a few months. But shortly thereafter I found out that the case against me had in fact been opened under Article 74 of the Criminal Code. With that, my way home was closed. I decided to ask for political asylum in the United States. The history of asylum on the grounds of sexual orientation is a short one, but my lawyers here feel that I have an exceptionally strong and well-documented case. I have also received support from many international human rights organizations, including Amnesty International.

I left behind in Russia not only my political troubles but also my culture, my readers, my fame. When people ask me how I find my present life, I tell them that anonymity in New York is much better than a "prominent position" as a famous homosexual writer in a Russian prison. I hope one day to return to Russia to continue my work as a writer and gay advocate without risk of prosecution for what I write or say.

HOLLY HUGHES

Reverberations of "The NEA Four" Affair

FOR SIX YEARS I have been plagued by a single question concerning my "membership" in the so-called NEA Four, the four artists singled out by conservatives in Congress as examples of government funding of depravity: "Wasn't it the best thing that ever happened to you?" The question has been following me around to the performances I give and those I attend, to demonstrations and dates, to panel discussions and parties.

What is the source of this question? It is coming from a mainstream culture that believes there's no such thing as bad publicity and a queer movement with a one-word agenda: visibility. Behind the query is the sense that it doesn't matter that I'm better known for being rejected by a government agency than for having achieved something worthwhile; what matters is that I'm "known." Didn't I see that any kind of fame was a valuable tool? So I had been handed this implement and now it was up to me to figure out what to do with it, how to make it work for me.

If my experience over the past several years had not proven otherwise, I would have assumed that most artists would find that being attacked by Jesse Helms made, not for great publicity, but for some great material! In fact, I approached the debate as if it were a gig that just fell into my lap at the last moment, a chance to perform for a larger audience than I had ever dreamed possible. For an artist who spun political parable from personal experience it seemed I had gotten my big break at last.

I wanted to shape my story into something that would carry us—me and my audience—toward other stories, such as the attacks on rap music, on the multicultural curriculum, on reproductive rights, and on affirmative action. Being a performance artist I would then connect these dots through song, dance, and monologue. Perhaps I could even build a theatrical time machine that would put my story in the context of those of Joe McCarthy, Anthony Comstock, and the other great American party animals of yesteryear.

But this new show would be different from my other work. First, it wasn't

From the Summer 1996 issue

going to be a solo performance. Moments after learning of the de-funding I was on the phone with one of my collaborators, a prominent leader of the anti-censorship movement, who began by saying she hoped I wasn't going to turn this into a gay issue. She insisted that John Frohnmayer's decision to cut funding from me and two other gay artists, John Fleck and Tim Miller (along with non-gay artist Karen Finley) had nothing to do with homophobia. No one cared enough about lesbians to bother discriminating against them! In the ensuing months I would struggle with many of those who had mobilized to fight the attack on arts funding. No one seemed willing to build a case for the work that was under attack, art that was provocative, "in your face," and featuring a queer body as both its subject and its object. Instead, the focus was on the NEA, the organization under attack, which was presented as a fine, All-American, red-blooded, suburban institution that funded Up With People–style revues. At their worst, anti-censorship activists loudly distanced themselves from the art and artists under fire, noting how little controversial work the NEA had funded over the years.

I began to realize that the show in which I was starring was following someone else's script—several someone else's. I found myself cast in central roles in several versions of "What's Wrong With America?" ranging from that of the Christian Coalition's to that of Robert Hughes in his *Culture of Complaint*. What was most disturbing was how difficult it was for me to interrupt the other narratives projected onto me. After Jesse Helms called me a "garbage artist" on the Senate floor, after David Gergen wrote in *U.S. News and World Report* that I performed "skits that threatened our national security," audiences came to my shows, not to see my work, but to witness the freak show the Right had promised them. For the first time, critics took me to task for not being shocking enough!

Six years later, a composite of Hughes's representation of the NEA Four as spoiled brats whining about their allowance, and the religious Right's image of us as depraved monsters, lingers on, resisting efforts to reframe who we are and what all the fuss was (is) about. When asked what got us into so much trouble, I describe how the man who de-funded the NEA Four never saw our work and how he arrived at his decision after a brief consideration, not of our artistic merit, but of our sexual identities. But even queer and queer-friendly journalists often act as if homophobia weren't enough of an explanation, even after I tell them that all John Frohnmayer ever had to say about me was, "Holly Hughes is a lesbian and her work is very heavily of that genre." (I had never thought of it as a genre before.) Recently a lesbian interviewer not only dismissed my account, but accused me of evading the question of what had I done wrong. Didn't I do something outrageous on stage? Defecate? Masturbate? I'm sure this woman was aware of the *Bowers v. Hardwick* decision, the gays-in-the-military flap, and the recent Defense of Marriage Act, but somehow she couldn't make the connection between the NEA debate and other acts of federally sanctioned homophobia. Jesse Helms had gotten to her, too.

My chance to respond in the media usually came in the form of sound bites. How best to use my fifteen seconds? Should I try to counter the perception that this was just a big publicity stunt on my part by detailing all the death threats received by the artists, not to mention the loss of funding, the consequences to the venues that presented us? But wouldn't that just feed the idea that we were just a bunch of whiners? Should I try to put the debate in a larger political context? But which one? Should the context be explicitly queer; but what about the controversies about rap music and multicultural curriculum? Should the frame of reference be the First Amendment; but then, how to avoid coming across like a civics teacher? Perhaps I should focus on the NEA itself and suggest that it needed to be expanded and take more risks, or about the problematic place of art in American culture? And how could I represent my work as something other than the freak show the Right had led people to expect—without sounding apologetic? And what stand to take toward the general public?

According to polls, most Americans supported the idea of an unrestricted NEA, although it was hardly the issue for which they'd go to the barricades. Perhaps I could appeal to queer intellectuals. But after Richard Elovitch and I co-authored a *New York Times* op-ed piece that focused on homophobia, I found myself under fire from lesbian scholars like Lynda Hart, who dismissed the piece as just more identity politics, and Richard and I as merely "gay," not "queer." The only real "queer" in the NEA Four, according to Hart, was the lone heterosexual among us, Karen Finley. Other scholars opined that the best way to democratize art was for artists to reject all funding, public or corporate (but I noted that they did not make the same demand of institutions of higher learning).

A final question must be raised: Does all this matter, in the end? I think it does. Whatever its effects on me personally, the NEA de-funding has proved disastrous for others. The attacks on art, particularly queer art, not only proved to be a big fund-raising tool for the religious Right, but helped move organizations like the Christian Coalition from the political margins to center stage. When a young feminist writer wistfully remarked that she wished it had happened to her, all I could say was, It has.

CHAPTER 2

Origins: The Science of Homosexuality

THE SCIENTIFIC INVESTIGATION of homosexuality is essentially as old as the word itself, for the term "homosexual" was invented as part of a new scientific quest to explore sexuality in the late nineteenth century. The (in)famous coinage of the word "homosexual"—along with countless other sexual abnormalities and personality types—was part of a general mania to label and classify things in that taxonomic age; but, soon enough, scientists and psychologists began to inquire into the origins of this newly discovered phenomenon, the homosexual, and (faster still) they began to propose various biological explanations for its occurrence, as did people like Krafft-Ebing and Havelock Ellis and even Freud.

The invention of "the homosexual" as a distinct social type, an object for scientific study, has come to be viewed as a kind of founding act in the latter-day construction of the phenomenon so named, and has played a pivotal role in the contemporary debate over the origins and meanings of homosexuality. A legacy of Michel Foucault's analysis, the general position known as "social constructionism" (or "postmodernism" or "queer theory") takes this as a starting point and implicates science as the progenitor of the entire modern definition of homosexuality. For if the object of investigation is just an invention of science, then anything that science finds out about it will be merely self-confirming and self-referential.

Despite the skepticism, science has marched on over the past decade or so and produced a subfield of biological research that explores the origins of variant sexual orientation with reference to genetic or physiological variables. A number of methods have been used to test this general hypothesis, such as twin and sibling studies, brain structure analysis, and DNA research. Each of these three methods has in fact yielded findings that suggest a biological cause of homosexuality. Perhaps the most famous study, as well as the most controversial one, was that of Simon LeVay, who found a significant difference in the size of the hypothalamus (or a portion thereof) in gay and straight men. Sibling studies conducted by Richard Pillard, among others, have shown that (male) homosexuality may in fact run in families irrespective of environmental factors. And Dean Hamer reported finding an actual genetic marker (Xq28) differentiating gay and straight men.

The articles in this chapter are intended to provide a general overview of the arguments and evidence for a biological explanation of homosexuality, along with a couple of rebuttals to this hypothesis. Richard Pillard offers a solid general introduction to "The Genetic Theory of Sexual Orientation" with evidence from hereditary research, while William Byne and Edward Stein ("Varieties of Biological Explanation") attempt to lay out a clear paradigm for what a biological or genetic explanation would have to look like to be plausible. Chandler Burr focuses on Hamer's discovery of a "gay gene" and the confused frenzy to which this discovery gave rise in the mass media (which asked, "Does this mean it's not a choice?"). While the evidence for a biological link with homosexuality seems to be mounting where males are concerned, the research on females suggests a weaker biological link, a finding that's explored by Carla Golden, who raises the question, "Do women choose their sexual identity?" Finally, Vernon Rosario argues that we should be skeptical of genetic explanations if only because we seem to have a vested interest in believing in them, a formula for self-deception and bad science.

RICHARD PILLARD

The Genetic Theory of Sexual Orientation

MY MEDICAL SCHOOL textbook of psychiatry, now more than thirty years old, discussed homosexuality in a section sandwiched between "inadequate and infantile behavior" and "sexual intercourse with domestic animals." Within one professional lifetime, the scientific study of sexual orientation has left the ghetto of psychopathology and moved to the gentrified neighborhood of mainstream culture. Perhaps the celebrity status of gay and lesbian studies is not so surprising when we reflect that what steers some people toward being straight is as little understood as what leads others to be gay. Everyone is curious about the origin of his or her desires, why we are attracted to men or to women, to a hairy partner or a smooth one, to someone blond, brunette, or (as some of us hope) bald. The precise delineation of human lusts remains, strange to say, relatively unknown territory.

Members of my profession have, to be sure, described the more obscure sexual desires. My favorite case vignettes come from psychiatrist and jurist Richard von Krafft-Ebing (1840–1902). In his famous *Psychopathia Sexualis*, Krafft-Ebing described several hundred individuals referred for forensic evaluation. There is, for example, the young man who, in the dark of night, dug open the graves of the freshly dead and with his bare hands clawed open their coffins "in nowise sensible in his excitement to the injuries he thus inflicted on himself." I will spare the reader further details, which the author has discreetly rendered in Latin.

On a more mundane line, Krafft-Ebing wrote of a man attracted to women who limp, and remarked that, as a youth, this man had a nurse with a lame leg. He speculated that "in the life of every fetishist, some partial sexual impression occurs with the first awakening of the *vita sexualis*." Here, I think Krafft-Ebing was on to something. First attractions probably have unusual power to fixate the libido, particularly if combined with some degree of anxiety. The more modern ideas of imprinting and instrumental conditioning come to mind. Pair an unconditionally pleasant stimulus such as genital fondling with

From the Winter 1997 issue

a neutral stimulus like the feel and smell of undershorts in the process of re-moval and you can make a reasonable case for the popularity of Calvin Klein.

I have to admit, however, that when it comes to being gay or straight, en-vironmental explanations—learning, conditioning, imprinting, and so on—fail to strike me as deeply convincing. It may indeed be that as infants all of us were pleasured and intimidated in ways that shaped our adult sexual orienta-tion. Parental influences account for a lot, but my vote is that sexual orienta-tion comes from a different place. Wherever that place is, it must originate in the earliest years of life if not prenatally, because most lesbians and gay men are marked as such early in childhood by virtue of their play behavior, which tends so often to be gender-atypical. The sissy boy and the tomboy girl may be stereotypes, but they are also powerful predictors of adult sexual orientation.

A more serious rebuttal to simple learning explanations comes from the work of anthropologist Gilbert Herdt. Herdt studied the Sambia tribe in New Guinea and their mythology of masculine development. A Sambia boy must imbibe quantities of semen in order to become virile and able to ejaculate se-men himself. Thus, the pre-adolescent boys fellate older adolescent and young adult men to fill their bodies with the masculinizing fluid. Later, they will be fellated in their turn by the younger initiates. It works for the Sambia. Since Sambian youth are having homosexual orgasms year after year, taking first one part and eventually the other and having a perfectly enjoyable time, why don't they become "conditioned" to same-sex arousal and continue to seek it after their time comes to leave the men's hut, to court and marry? They just don't. The occasional older man does want to keep doing it with guys (it's a small tribe) but he is the rare exception. (Cf., Gilbert Herdt, *The Sambia: Ritual and Gender in New Guinea,* 1987.)

I want to advance a different theory, simple and rather general: Sexual ori-entation resides in the deep structure of human personality. It is wired into our brains. For the vast majority of humans, an orientation develops au-tonomously, largely independent of environmental circumstances, and is al-most impervious to change. Even people with quite atypical brains, schizo-phrenics and the mentally retarded, almost always have a sense of being either gay or straight.

If sexual orientation is indeed wired in, is it so wired genetically, or is it due to some accidental influence in the early environment, inside or outside the womb? An example of a prenatal influence is the increase of schizophrenia in the offspring of Dutch mothers pregnant during the great famine winter at the end of World War II. Presumably, the lack of a particular amino acid in the mother's diet affected the developing brain of the offspring. In the same vein, German endocrinologist Günter Dörner suggested that more gay men are born to mothers who experience prenatal stress. Dörner's argument is hard to prove or disprove. One woman's stress is another's exciting challenge; however, on balance, the maternal stress theory lacks convincing data.

THAT SEXUAL ORIENTATION is genetically endowed is hardly a new idea. The great sexologists of the past, including Freud, Magnus Hirschfeld, Havelock Ellis, and others, have all accepted it as probable. One way to test whether genes influence sexual orientation is to see if it is familial. Should being lesbian or gay turn out to be familial, the genetic theory gets a boost—though of course traits run in families for other than genetic reasons. On the other hand, if orientation is not familial, the genetic hypothesis dies. Some years ago, I thought it would be worthwhile to make a careful study of this issue. I was aware of families that had lots of gay kin, and as I reviewed the literature, there seemed to be certain families that were gay-loaded, the French Bourbon monarchy for one.

Our team at Boston University recruited as random a sample as we could find of men and women willing to provide a sexual history. We then located as many of their siblings as we could coax to join the study. Of the heterosexual men, about four percent had brothers exclusively or predominately gay. This was reassuring because four percent is close to the national average for men with a lifelong history of same-sex attraction, suggesting that our sampling and interviewing techniques were working properly. The picture was very different for the gay male subjects. They had five times as many gay brothers as the straight men, over twenty percent altogether. Any reader of this article can do a low-tech replication. Ask a random sample of the gay men you know how many brothers they have and then how many of those brothers are gay. Average the results from as few as twenty respondents and you will become a believer. The lesbians we interviewed also had more lesbian sisters than the heterosexual women, although the difference wasn't as large. Some families had both gay brothers and lesbian sisters and some had interesting patterns of gayness in their more distant relatives.

Shortly thereafter, we participated in a study begun by psychologist Michael Bailey at Northwestern University. Bailey gathered a group of gay twins, some identical and some fraternal, and then ascertained the orientation of the co-twin. A genetic hypothesis predicts that the identical twins will be concordant (both gay) in the fifty to seventy percent range, while the fraternal twins will both be gay only as often as the gay brother pairs in the family study, about twenty percent. Adding a sample of adopted siblings of gay probands is an important control; the adoptees should be gay no more often than the general population, about two percent for women, four percent for men. This was indeed the approximate result obtained from several large samples.

Twins and siblings can be alike for other than genetic reasons. It is commonly supposed that sexual orientation is shaped to some extent by family influences that are naturally more alike for identical twins. To our surprise, the heritability calculations revealed that the most powerful environmental influences were not those that the twins shared but those they did not share. In other words, insofar as life circumstances contribute to sexual orientation, it isn't having the same mother and father, living in the same house, getting beaten up by the same bully that matters, but instead the different experiences twins might have (e.g., one takes piano lessons, the other becomes a Boy Scout)—although what those different experiences might be, this research design could not identify. The problem is that nobody knows what's relevant to the development of sexual orientation. It may be true, for example, that gay boys have distant fathers and protective mothers, but what is the cause-effect relationship here?

One powerful way to get an idea of the relative contribution of nature and nurture is to look at identical twins, one of whom is gay, who have been separated shortly after birth and raised in separate environments. They are rare persons, of course, and only a few have been reported in the medical literature. Among the four known women pairs, none were concordant for being lesbian, but among the men, several pairs were both gay. Moreover, the concordant twins, beside being gay, tended to share other aspects of their personality, including their particular sexual tastes. Taken as a whole, the family and twin data strongly suggest a genetic influence on sexuality, though perhaps a stronger one in men than in women. It might seem that heredity can be only part of the story because, if genes were everything, the identical twin pairs, however they were raised, should *always* be concordant—assuming they have an identical genetic endowment. However, recent genome research shows that identical twins in fact acquire some interesting differences. This happens because after the fertilized egg separates into two individuals, there is a period of genomic instability during which subtle changes occur in the DNA sequencing of the two, now separate, fetuses. Whether these changes have anything to do with personality, much less with sexual orientation, is not known, but this opens the possibility that heredity may play an even more important role in determining how we behave than the classical twin studies have led us to assume.

The ultimate test of a genetic basis for a behavioral trait is of course to find the gene or genes and discover what they do. This will not be easy, judging from what we know about genes. The search for the gene for Huntington's Disease serves as a caution against optimism. Huntington's is a stereotyped neurologic disorder, easy to diagnose, and transmitted as an autosomal dominant with complete penetrance. The Huntington's gene ought to be easy to find, but it took ten years and tens of millions of dollars to locate and sequence it. We now know that Huntington's Disease is caused by one gene of large effect, but we assume that the genes influencing behavior act in a chorus, each contributing only a small part. Moreover, the expression of some genes depends on the presence of specific genes elsewhere in the genome, or on an environmental trigger that amplifies or damps a gene's potential. One imagines, therefore, that the genetic analysis of complex behavior traits will be extremely difficult. The path from gene product (a protein structure or enzyme) to the eventual behavior remains a black box. Still, molecular biology is perhaps the most rapidly advancing science within medicine, so it is likely that the genetic analysis of "normal" behaviors is going to move ahead very quickly.

A PROBLEM FOR THOSE of us who favor a genetic basis for sexual orientation is why, from an evolutionary point of view, gay attractions should exist at all. My suggestion is that both orientations are genetically programmed, that both appeared during the evolutionary history of our species and therefore may exist at least in rudimentary form in our close primate relatives. This is one reason that I read with interest descriptions of other primates' sexual behavior. The study of same-sex behavior in animals is emerging from a void. Almost every class of animals has individuals who copulate with members of their own sex. But what does it mean? Does the mounting of one male monkey by another male monkey express dominance, pair bonding, reassurance, sexual attraction, or all of the above? Primatologist George Vasey makes an interesting observation that homosexual mounting occurs rarely in New World (platyrrhine) monkeys but is more frequent and more clearly expressed among Old World (catarrhine) primates, who are more recently evolved and more closely related to us. Catarrhine males will sometimes show a preference for a male partner and will compete with other males for such a partner.

Sheep are another species in which males occasionally show what looks like preferential homosexual mate choice. Biologists Anne Perkins and James

Fitzgerald, working at the U.S. Sheep Experiment Station in Idaho, are trying an interesting experiment. They identified rams who show an interest in mounting other rams, electro-ejaculated them to collect sperm, and used the sperm to impregnate ewes. The offspring rams, as they are interbred, will be tested to see if they show a homosexual mounting choice more frequently, which they should if there are "gay genes" concentrated and passed on from parent and grandparent ancestors.

The discussion so far still leaves bare the question why an orientation that appears so inimical to reproduction might nevertheless persist in human or animal populations. Homosexuality needs to demonstrate a survival benefit sufficient to offset the reproductive cost that the orientation would be expected to exact. Most reproductively disadvantageous traits occur because of occasional and random mutations which are gradually selected out of the kindred. Huntington's Disease, for example, occurs in only about four people per million. The gay/lesbian phenotype is far too common to be entirely the result of deleterious mutations. If genetic, it must have undergone some degree of favorable selection. One concept to understand about "reproductive success" is that it can be realized by different strategies. The oak produces thousands of acorns and is lucky if one or two grow to make acorns of their own. The larger land mammals, on the other hand, have relatively few offspring and are metabolically expensive to bear. A successful strategy for big creatures like ourselves is to invest heavily in guarding and protecting the relatively few offspring that we are able to have.

This line of thinking, elaborated by biologists Robert Trivers and James Weinrich, among others, is that gay people may have evolved character traits of an altruistic nature that prompt them to work harder for the protection and advancement of closely related family members rather than invest in having children of their own. This idea, called "kin altruism," results from the simple calculus that two nephews or nieces are genetically equivalent to one son or daughter. Reproductive sacrifice explainable by a theory of kin altruism has been demonstrated in some animal species but remains speculative for humans, most of whom, sad to say, seem rather short in the department of altruism. (Cf., Jim Weinrich, *Sexual Landscapes: Why We Are What We Are, Why We Love Whom We Love*, 1987.)

Ray Blanchard and his colleagues at the Clarke Institute in Toronto recently analyzed thousands of families and found that gay men have a later birth order than straight. Specifically, the gay men had more older brothers but not more older sisters once the older brothers were taken into account. A psycho-developmental explanation springs to mind: A young boy might develop homosexual at-

tractions more readily if an older brother is in the picture. But a biological explanation is also on the horizon. The placenta supporting every human pregnancy
has small protein fingers that engage the mother's bloodstream by digging into
the wall of her uterus. When the placenta is shed, some of the placental cells remain in the uterine wall and can be demonstrated to be alive and well years later.
These cells came from the fetus and contain its genome. Is it possible that some
cells of an early pregnancy remain behind and, by an unexplained mechanism, try
to capture the resources of subsequent pregnancies, a sort of biological primo-
geniture? I like this odd (and admittedly remote) possibility because it shows how
much is still unexpected in the biology of human sexuality.

Behavior genetics applied to sexual orientation encounters a variety of
criticisms. In this debate, I feel like a detective who's presenting his case to the
district attorney. I have scraps and clues, hypotheses that sometimes hang together but that also have gaps. But the DA must be a skeptic. He has to put
my case before a jury whom he must convince beyond a reasonable doubt. The
standard of proof rises as the investigation proceeds. (Thanks to Jim Weinrich
for the analogy.) The most I can say is that no one has yet put forward evidence
that is devastating to my case.

There is one criticism I want at least to touch on, namely that genetic theories pander to homophobia. If "gay genes" are discovered, how much easier
will it be to eradicate them? Opinion surveys are unanimous that people who
endorse a genetic hypothesis are more sympathetic to lesbians and gays than
people who hold to a purely environmental theory. Still, technology has a way
of biting back. No scientific knowledge is risk-free, and this must surely include genetic investigations of sexual orientation. One might take a sort of reverse comfort in knowing that homophobia, like racism (and all the xenopho-
bias), exists regardless of whatever might be considered "the facts" of the
moment. Research on human sexuality will, by its nature, evoke resistance and
fear, to some extent legitimately. Here is where I think social science research
has a valuable role. There ought to be funded research programs not only to
unravel the genome but to unravel the ethical and psychological dilemmas
that accompany the new insights that behavior genetics will generate.

Scientific research is permeated by values. Mine are that it is better to
know something than not to know it. I believe that same-sex desire will remain
a topic of interest and study for a long time. I'm confident that biological
knowledge will prove it to be a valuable trait, selected by evolution precisely
because it contributes some quality that was useful, perhaps even essential, to
the sudden ascendancy of human beings among all the primates.

WILLIAM BYNE AND EDWARD STEIN

Varieties of Biological Explanation

AT THE RECENT opening of a psychotherapy center for lesbians and gays in New York City, a speaker, himself a gay psychoanalyst, stated: "At last gays and lesbians have a place to come for psychotherapy where the orientation is that homosexuality is immutable, familial, and probably innate." Notably absent from his address was reassurance that the center will provide an atmosphere where it is okay to be gay, regardless of the etiology of sexual orientation. The tacit assumption that the acceptance of homosexuality—particularly one's own—hinges upon the innateness or immutability of sexual orientation may ultimately prove to be detrimental to the self-esteem of gay men and lesbians as individuals, and to their collective struggle for social acceptance and legal protections.

We will begin by considering the ways in which biology might contribute to sexual orientation and conclude by arguing that gay men and lesbians should not appeal to etiological arguments as they make their case for fundamental human rights and social tolerance.

Because we are biological beings, all of our thoughts, actions and emotions must have a biological substrate at some fundamental level. Thus, we should not ask if sexual orientation is biological. Indeed, we should not even ask if it is *primarily* biological. How could biological and psychosocial factors be teased apart, and what are the units of measurement that would allow them to be assessed and weighed against one another to determine which is more important? From a scientific perspective it would be more productive to ask about the alternative pathways through which biological and experiential factors might interact to influence sexual orientation.

The alternatives through which biology may influence sexual orientation can be illustrated by three models.

1. In the *formative experience* model, biology plays a permissive role
   by providing the neural machinery through which sexual orienta-

From the Winter 1997 issue

tion is inscribed by childhood experience. Formative experience is the subjective internalization of the environment and should not be equated with the environment itself. Internalization involves the biological processes of perception and the neural activity involved in interpreting and integrating ongoing experience in the context of the moment and within the broader context of one's life history. The same events in the external environment would be expected to generate unique formative experiences for different individuals. Thus, attempts to find the origins of sexual orientation in parental relationships and objective environmental factors alone are unlikely to be successful. The subjective internal representation of the environment must be considered. In this model, biology could also delimit the period during which the relevant formative experience(s) must occur. For example, some songbirds must learn their species' song by hearing it during a restricted period of early development. While the song is clearly acquired through experience, biology determines the period during which that experience must occur. Once a particular song has been learned, it will be that bird's song for life; and the bird will not be able to learn another. Thus even phenomena acquired through experience may be immutable. By giving this example, by no means do we wish to imply that sexual orientation is acquired through simple mimicry. Instead, the example suggests only that a particular experience or set of experiences might have a greater or lesser impact on sexual orientation depending on the developmental stage in which it occurs, and that sexual orientation could be impervious to change even if inscribed by formative experience.

2. In the *direct model*, biological factors would exert their influence by directly organizing brain circuits that mediate sexual orientation. This model is called "direct" because the arrow of causation goes directly from biological factors such as genes or hormones to sexual orientation. This model also allows for the possibility that direct biological effects could be subsequently modified by experience. For example, the sexologist John Money has speculated that the majority of women who were exposed as fetuses to masculinizing hormones become heterosexual because "social factors override their biological predisposition toward lesbianism."

3. In the *indirect model*, the arrow of biological causation does not go

directly to sexual orientation. Instead, biological factors would influence sexual orientation only indirectly via some intermediate
characteristic such as personality or temperament. Such a characteristic would then influence how one interacts with and modifies
the environment in shaping the relationships and experiences that
influence the emergence of sexual orientation. This model is similar to the formative experience model, but goes beyond it by addressing the possibility that the relevant formative experiences may
themselves be strongly affected by hormonally or genetically influenced personality variables.

Importantly, the existing biological data relevant to sexual orientation are
equally compatible with both the direct and indirect models. The distinction
between these models can be readily appreciated by showing how they lead to
different interpretations of three of the more robust findings in the sexual orientation literature. The first of these findings is that the propensity to engage
in rough-and-tumble play appears to be influenced by prenatal exposure to an-
drogens, the so-called male sex hormones. This finding holds up across species
and laboratories and may even apply to humans. The second finding is that,
compared to heterosexual men, more, but not all, homosexual men recall a
childhood aversion to competitive rough-and-tumble play. The third robust
finding is that, compared to heterosexual men, more, but again not all, homosexual men remember their fathers as having been distant or rejecting.

In a direct model interpretation, the aversion to rough-and-tumble play is
merely the childhood expression of a brain that's been pre-wired for homosexuality. This is the position of the analyst Richard Isay, who suggests that biological factors wire the brain for sexual orientation and reverse the polarity of
the Oedipus complex. In addition to shunning rough-and-tumble play, pre-ho-
mosexual boys would be sexually interested in their fathers during the Oedi-
pal period. The father might recoil from his son's sexual interest and gender
nonconformity, but even if the father didn't distance himself, Isay suggests
that gay men might distance themselves from their father in their memory in
order to avoid recognition of their early erotic attachment to him. Thus gay
men would be more likely to remember their fathers as distant or rejecting
even if that had not been the case.

Alternatively, the indirect model suggests that the biologically influenced
aversion to rough-and-tumble play does not imply pre-wiring for homosexuality at all. Instead, this aversion would become a potent factor predisposing

someone to homosexual development only in particular environments—perhaps, where it is stigmatized as "sissy" behavior and causes the boy to see himself as different from his father and male peers. In this scenario, the father's withdrawal from his son would contribute to rather than result from his homosexual development. Importantly, the son's aversion to rough-and-tumble play would arguably have different consequences in environments where it was accepted, perhaps making no contribution to sexual orientation at all.

By offering the above example we do not wish to imply that either an aversion to sports or a rejecting father is a feature of all or even most pathways to male homosexuality. Based on the indirect model, one can conjecture how a number of temperamental variants could influence sexual orientation. A particular temperamental variant might predispose one to homosexuality in some environments and to heterosexuality in others, while making no contribution to sexual orientation in still other environments. To the extent that the indirect model approximates reality, the search for predisposing biological factors will result in incomplete and misleading findings until their interactions with environmental factors are taken into account and controlled for in adequate longitudinal studies.

ACCORDING TO MANY popular accounts, biological research into sexual orientation is something new. These accounts are wrong. The role of biology in sexual orientation has been a topic of recurring debate for the past century-and-a-half. Because appeals have often been made for this debate to inform social policy, it has been mired in politics from its inception. While the study of the biological underpinnings of any and all behavioral phenomena is in principle a valid endeavor, before we can even hope to approach objectivity in studying sexual orientation we must extricate the valid scientific questions from the purely political ones.

Historically, many advocates of lesbian and gay rights have tried to support their claims by saying that people do not choose their sexual orientations. That is, they argue that people should not be punished or discriminated against because of things beyond their control. This *lack-of-choice* argument can be persuasive. A 1993 *New York Times*/CBS News poll found that, compared to people who believe homosexuals could change if they really wanted to, people who believe that homosexuality "cannot be changed" are more likely to believe that social and criminal sanctions against homosexuality should be eliminated. Unfortunately, the phrase "cannot be changed" is often interpreted to mean "biologically determined." Consequently, the results of this poll are mischaracterized as showing that those who believe homosexuality to be chosen or change-able are less tolerant than those who believe it to be biologically determined. As a result of this misinterpretation, research findings suggesting a major bio-logical influence on sexual orientation have been popularly interpreted as "good news for gays," while even constructive criticism of the biological evi-dence is often misconstrued as motivated by an anti-gay agenda.

It is important to recognize that the chain of reasoning from biology and sexual orientation to tolerance and social policy is misinformed. For starters, "not chosen" does not mean biologically determined. The fact that we do not choose our native language does not suggest that it is innate. As we have shown above, animal research has demonstrated that behaviors which are so-cially acquired can, nonetheless, be immutable. By analogy, sexual orientation could be equally impervious to change whether it were directly determined by biological factors or shaped by formative experiences.

Biological evidence is not needed to bolster the lack-of-choice argument. That sexual orientation is neither chosen nor freely mutable is shown clearly in the psychological literature reporting the ineffectiveness of therapies de-signed to change it. Very few if any of even the most highly motivated have been able to change their sexual orientation despite subjecting themselves to dehumanizing aversion therapies, or investing tremendous emotional and fi-nancial resources in years of psychotherapy.

But why should lesbians and gay men have to appeal to the lack-of-choice argument at all? The issues of choice and immutability seem to be selectively applied to homosexuals and not to other minorities. Members of religious mi-norities are not asked to demonstrate that either their religious affiliation or their religious practices are innate or immutable. At best, the lack-of-choice argument can lead only to an impoverished form of gay rights. Arguments for the rights of gay men and lesbians, like rights for religious minorities, should be cast in terms of justice, privacy, equality, and liberty, not in terms of lack-of-choice or genetic determinism.

Another problem with the lack-of-choice argument is that while sexual ori-entation is not consciously chosen, choice *is* involved in decisions to partici-pate in sexual behavior and to publicly acknowledge one's homosexuality. Even if we agree that individuals should not be penalized for matters over which they have no control, proof that sexual orientation is genetically deter-mined would not preclude legislating against all conscious expressions of ho-mosexuality. The "Don't ask, don't tell" policy of the U.S. military penalizes the choice to disclose one's homosexuality, not homosexuality itself.

Some advocates of lesbian and gay rights seem implicitly to make a *pragmatic* argument to the effect that genetic and other biologically deterministic arguments should be embraced merely because they are persuasive and seem to have a desirable political effect. However, it is a risky strategy to link anyone's rights to the ups and downs of research that is, at best, in its early stages. Biological research into sexual orientation has an extremely poor track record when it comes to reliability. Noting the unreliability of brain findings in this area, Heino Meyer-Bahlburg of Columbia University suggests that no such findings should be accepted as reliable until they've been replicated by three independent laboratories—provided that there are no intervening failures of replication. To date, no neuroanatomical or genetic linkage study meets that criterion. What some may believe to be valid results today could turn out to be mistaken. Making fundamental human rights contingent on a particular scientific finding is, therefore, precarious. That people are persuaded by biological arguments may suggest a public relations strategy that can succeed in the short term, but it does not suggest a strategy for solidly grounding lesbian and gay rights.

One form that the pragmatic argument sometimes takes is to urge critics of the biological evidence to keep silent. This is because of the popular misconception that sexual orientation must be freely chosen if it is not biologically determined. Even constructive criticism of the biological evidence may then be misconstrued as suggesting that homosexuality is simply a chosen lifestyle. And yet, are we to suppress valid scientific discourse in order to advance a humanitarian political agenda? The answer to that question has to be "No." Such a strategy is potentially self-defeating. If it becomes known that political aims are the primary justification for favoring one scientific theory over another, the persuasiveness of the biological argument will be undermined and the distinction between science and propaganda lost.

Finally, the lack-of-choice argument does not necessarily lead to social tolerance. The genetic basis and immutability of skin color, for example, do not seem to have a mitigating influence on racism. In the absence of social tolerance, any theory for the origins of sexual orientation may be turned against lesbians and gay men.

It is worth noting that Magnus Hirschfeld's efforts to link gay rights with a biological etiology in pre-Nazi Germany ultimately backfired. Although he argued in favor of rights for homosexuals on the grounds that they constituted a biologically defined third sex, prior to his death he conceded that not only had he failed to prove his biological thesis, but that he had unwittingly contributed to the Nazis' persecution of homosexuals by stigmatizing them as biologically defective. Thus, homosexuals were imprisoned, castrated and sent to camps to remove them from the breeding stock. At the same time, however, the Nazis also embraced social theories of homosexuality. Thus, homosexuals were imprisoned and sent to camps to prevent contamination of the German youth by exposure to adult homosexuals. These historical observations suggest that homophobia, like other forms of bigotry, does not need a reason. What it needs is a rationalization, and that may be premised on any etiological theory that happens to be convenient at the moment.

The fate of homosexuals under the Nazis certainly does not support the notion that embracing biologically deterministic theories will necessarily lead to social tolerance. In fact, the very terminology of these theories may contribute to the social stigmatization of homosexuality. Within the neuropsychiatric literature, these theories are almost invariably stated in pejorative terms such as hormonal abnormality, deficiency, aberration and "gene-controlled disarrangement of psychosexual maturation patterns." The danger here lies in the fact that states perceived as undesirable *and* of biological origin are often assumed to be amenable to medical remedy or prevention. Even while lobbying for homosexual rights in pre-Nazi Germany, Hirschfeld nevertheless referred at least a few homosexual men to a physician for a surgical "cure."

Within the past thirty years, physicians have used a variety of biological approaches in attempts to "cure" homosexuality. These have included various hormonal therapies, castration, and brain surgery. The rationale for the brain surgery was to destroy the hypothetical "female mating center" in homosexual sex offenders. As recently as 1974, the *Journal of the American Medical Association* reviewed the results of this surgical approach and glibly concluded, without moral commentary, that the brain surgery was more effective than chemical castration. Today, the concept of a female mating center is considered naïve, demonstrating that biological interventions do not need to be valid in order to be carried out. More recently, there has been discussion of amniocentesis to detect genes for homosexuality or aberrant hormonal levels that might predispose one to homosexuality. Thus, recent evidence for links between biological factors and sexual orientation is not necessarily the good news that some gay advocacy groups had hoped for.

Thus the anticipated political consequences, beneficial or otherwise, of a theory do not constitute a valid scientific argument either for or against it. Instead, socially responsible research into the biology of sexual orientation must

begin with the realization that biological evidence is not a cure for homophobia, and that the self-esteem and civil rights of lesbians and gays should not
hinge upon assumptions about the etiology of sexual orientation. As Frank Ka-
meny stated in an address to the New York Mattachine Society in 1964, "We
are interested in obtaining rights for our respective minorities as Negroes, as
Jews, and as Homosexuals. Why we are Negroes, Jews or Homosexuals is totally irrelevant, and whether we can be changed to Whites, Christians or Heterosexuals is equally irrelevant."

CHANDLER BURR

The "Gay Gene" Hits the Big Time

ONE OF THE WEIRDEST things about the search for the biological origins
of sexual orientation, if you were one of the scientists involved in it, would
have to have been the total misinterpretation, or over-interpretation, that the
news media universally applied to what you were doing. Science is about genes
and neurons and hormones; the media were interested in politics, which was
to say the ubiquitous question in the political debate, "Is it a choice, a
'lifestyle'?" The fact is, homosexuality being a "choice" is a laughable non-
issue in science, and has been for years; the media didn't realize that the very
search for a gay gene revealed this fact.

It was on July 16, 1993, when geneticist Dean Hamer published his study
of Xq28 in *Science* magazine, that the press's fundamental misunderstanding
of the gay gene caused politics to collide with science full force. Television, in
all its self-serious hype, found Hamer immediately. He, in turn, found television quite trying.

Most of the questions made sense. On *CBS This Morning* at seven A.M.,
Paula Zahn asked Hamer about the outmoded theories of environmental causation. "It's really important," Hamer responded diplomatically, "to realize that
there was never any hard evidence, never any experiments done to test that. And,
in fact, when some researchers looked at more than a thousand gay and heterosexual men a few years ago, they found very little difference in environment or
parenting style." On ABC's *Good Morning America*, Charles Gibson asked how
sure he was of the results. "Well," said Hamer over his satellite feed, "one good
way to test it is to take a coin, flip it forty times, and get thirty-three heads. You'd
get that less than one percent of the time. That's our confidence level."

It wasn't the science per se that they got wrong (which meant Hamer didn't
see their fundamental mistake immediately). Sure, there were a few minor errors.
Gibson announced: "Researchers at the National Cancer Institute have identified a similar genetic pattern in thirty-three pairs of gay brothers, a finding which
suggests the tendency to homosexuality may be inherited." Hamer joined Gib-

From the Winter 1997 issue

Chandler Burr

son via satellite and explained he hadn't found a "similar genetic pattern" in the brothers but a high percentage of markers inherited from the same chromosome. (*The MacNeil/Lehrer News Hour* made a similar mistake.)

But these were quibbles, and the reporting of the study's facts was generally excellent. What increasingly struck Hamer was a larger problem, the media's misunderstanding of the study's larger implications.

First, they suggested that "the gay gene" meant that homosexuality was good. On *NBC Nightly News* Tom Brokaw opened with the Hamer story, going to science correspondent Robert Bazell, who reported: "This latest research . . . shows that homosexuality is a natural genetic variation, like left-handedness or blue eyes." ABC's George Strait reported, "Gay activists intend to use today's discovery to support their argument that homosexuality is not deviant behavior."

The use of expressions like "natural" or "not deviant" implied that a genetic origin made a trait acceptable. However, this reporting by the media was fatally imprecise. For one thing, "natural" does not mean "benign." By that logic, the discovery of a gene for colon cancer would render colon cancer a "natural" variation of human biological development "like left-handedness or blue eyes." In fact, cancer is, in a strictly biological sense, natural. But in that same sense so is having Hodgkin's disease or fingernails. The crucial distinction, one that neither NBC nor ABC elaborated, is that Hodgkin's is pathological, destructive to the organism, and certainly does deviate from the healthy norm; while having fingernails is not and does not. A trait can be "genetic" or "natural"—and absolutely lethal. Genes may also play a role in alcoholism, violence, gambling, pedophilia, and other states of mind expressed behaviorally, but that does not make them any more "natural" or "good."

But it was another of the media's assumption, one diametrically opposed to the scientific reality, that so perplexed Hamer that it took him several days to fathom what was being asked. Announced the *Today* show: "There is new evidence that homosexuality may be inherited in some cases and not a matter of choice." Stated ABC *World News* Peter Jennings: "There is a new medical study which may have a significant impact on the debate about the nature of homosexuality: is it choice or is it biology?" Tom Brokaw opened with, "There's new medical evidence that homosexuality is genetic, not acquired, behavior." On *Good Morning America*, Hamer was asked, "So, if you say that genes are part of the reason, you're really saying it's not a choice." Hamer paused, and then responded with an observation about phenotypic variation that bypassed the question. The media could not understand why Hamer would not address the question of choice; Hamer could not understand why they were asking him about it.

Nightline began at 11:35 as usual. Theme music: trumpets and strings. From the ABC studio in Washington, Ted Koppel raises his head, places his hands before him, and fixes on the audience. Hamer is sitting in a cramped, remote studio, staring wide-eyed at a camera's eye and trying to pretend, as the producer advised, that it is a person. He has an audio plug stuck in one ear. Through the plug he hears Koppel begin: "Tonight: the genetic link to male homosexuality." And then he hears Koppel give the popular—and fundamentally incorrect—view: "More authoritatively than ever before, a scientific study is suggesting that a man's homosexual tendencies may not be a matter of choice."

Koppel looks grave, leans ever so slightly into the lens:

Think about it for just a moment, think only about the legal implications. While it is constitutional for example to prohibit certain behavior, it is not constitutional to make status such as race illegal. If the findings of this study are confirmed, it will not quite raise homosexuality to the same legal level as race, but it moves it a lot closer.

Cut to science correspondent Dave Marash, who begins his report with a clip from the play *The Twilight of Golds*, about a woman who aborts her baby because a genetic test determines that it will probably be gay. He then listens to sociologist Charles Moskos suggest, bizarrely, that homosexuals constitute a "third sex"; and then goes to Robert Knight of the conservative Family Research Council, who asserts that homosexuality is a "lifestyle." Marash concludes that if there is a gene—ergo, if homosexuality is not a choice—gays will find more acceptance in society.

Back to Koppel, welcoming Hamer, who appears as a giant face staring wide-eyed out of a screen. The geneticist is clearly nervous and out of his element, his slate blue eyes wary under the TV lights. Koppel asks the political question, "If the findings of the study, Dr. Hamer, are confirmed, will it then be accurate to say that homosexuality is not optional behavior?" It is the very first question, and, to a biologist, it makes no sense.

"Well," Hamer begins, carefully but gamely enough, "that portion of homosexuality or heterosexuality that is genetically influenced is, of course, not optional because people don't have an option over what genes they're going to inherit."

Hamer has given a scientific answer, which has not addressed the political question. Koppel tries again: "In a sense that's begging the question." Quickly: "Or maybe I don't understand the refinement that you have just made."

Hamer is confused. He has been quite clear that the genetic region that he has isolated—or maybe any number of genes that influence sexual orientation—are not the sole factors involved in the creation of the trait, sexual orientation (since, in genetics, there are frequently non-genetic biological factors contributing to the trait). So he tries another answer. "What we've found is that one specific region of the X chromosomes is linked to homosexuality, at least in some men. And what that demonstrates is that part of being gay, or part of being straight, is determined in the genes. The reason I say that it doesn't mean it's not an option," explains Hamer, using Koppel's word, "is that homosexuality is not simply determined by a single gene, as your eye color is determined by a single gene."

But Koppel is interested not in genetics but in whether it's a choice, while

Hamer is under the impression they are talking about genetics. Koppel: "Will it be possible, at least, to say that it is not a purely—behavioral thing?" Hamer, trying to be helpful, jumps in. "There are definitely inherited characteristics which are very important," he says supportively. "That's correct."

This is not the answer Koppel wants. "And—," he tries, "how important—I'm—just trying to get you to put it in as commonplace language as you can so that we all understand it."

"Sure," says Hamer, clearing his throat. (Afterwards, he will describe how he was furiously wondering why Koppel would not accept his scientific answers. He *is* trying to make it simple.) He tries again. He talks about related research; he describes his own study, gives a heritability estimate, and reaffirms that there is evidence of a substantial inherited component of homosexuality. "We can measure it, we can assess it in the laboratory. The important finding is really the proof that there is such a component." He means proof that there is a biological component influencing this trait, not proof about "choice," which cannot be assessed by looking at genes.

After *Nightline* comes back from its commercial break, Koppel introduces the Reverend Peter Gomes, Professor of Christian Morals at Harvard, and Arthur Caplan, the Director of the Center for Medical Ethics at the University of Minnesota. The mood seems slightly more tense. There have clearly been some hurried negotiations during the break because Koppel then adds, "And joining us again—and I should point out that Dr. Hamer wants only to refer and to comment on the scientific aspects of the story—is Dean Hamer."

Koppel immediately tries Gomes for an answer to the political question. "Professor Gomes, my sense is that those who want to be accepting of homosexuality are going to be able to use this information to help their case and, as Professor Caplan was just suggesting, those who do not want to use it will be just as able to use it for theirs. Your thoughts?"

Finally Koppel has his answer. Gomes—whose business, after all, is made of this stuff—correctly identifies the question and answers in political terms, stating in his round tones his belief that, yes, in the end, the research will be more helpful politically than harmful. "I think part of the whole conversation about homosexuality has been to confuse it with some deliberate choice of lifestyle, confuse it with 'a lifestyle,' and suggest that it is somehow an option that other people who are normal, as it were, do not have," he says. "In the sense that homosexuality is now to be seen as part of the equipment with which some people are born into the world, in some respects I think normalizes the debate, and I think that's helpful."

Having finally received an answer to his question about choice, Koppel visibly relaxes. He talks to Caplan for a minute, then circles back one more time: "Let me come back to the science of this, Dr. Hamer. To what degree is that kind of reassurance for gays warranted? In other words, is it appropriate, based on the findings that you have reached, that gays can say, Look, it's not a matter of choice, it's predetermined?" asks Koppel. "In a sense, genetically," he adds.

Hamer pauses, very briefly: he's finally gotten it. He takes a reluctant breath and, almost angrily leaving the questions of science for the alien realm of politics, gives the answer Koppel has been searching for. "I think," says Hamer, tightly and conservatively, "all scientists that have studied sexual orientation already agree that there's very little element of choice in being gay or heterosexual." And with that, he turns and heads back into science, pointing out tersely, and correctly: "The question is whether there's a defined genetic component to homosexuality and if we can ultimately understand how that works."

Nightline is almost over. They've survived. As a wrap-up Koppel, now slyly playing devil's advocate, allows himself a final question by returning to the odd interpretation of Hamer's genetics made by sociologist Moskos. "Are we here—and this may seem like a ludicrous question to each of you—but are we talking about a third gender, a third sex?"

Hamer looks as if he is going to raise an eyebrow, but doesn't. It is, indeed, a ludicrous question. Hamer gives the precise, scientifically correct answer: "There are, of course, some people who have been called a 'third sex,' essentially hermaphrodites. The locus we've discovered is not related to that in any way, shape, or form, and as far as we can tell from our research results, the locus we've identified is just a normal variant similar to the sort of variants that cause differences in eye color or handedness or perhaps in other behavioral traits." And he is done.

WHAT DOES the gay gene mean to the scientific question of how sexual orientation is created biologically? Everything. The way hormones and genes interact, mold neurons, create traits—these processes are the essence of biology. What does the gay gene mean to the political question of "choice"? Nothing at all.

An analogy can help here. The human trait most closely analogous to human sexual orientation is human handedness. Both traits have a majority orientation and a minority orientation. Now we all know that people don't choose to be left-handed. Do we know this because we've found the gene for left-handedness? No, we have no idea what genes and hormones create left-handedness. We know it because we ask them, and they invariably say, "I didn't choose to be left-handed. It's part of me."

After all the fuss raised over it, the fact is that this is also how we know that gay people don't choose to be gay. It's a bit anticlimactic, and so obvious to Hamer and other scientists that when ABC anchors don't understand it, they find it difficult to respond. We no more need a gene for left-handedness to know whether left-handedness is chosen than we need a gay gene to know whether being gay is chosen.

Weeks later, in his office, Hamer recalls the whole experience with good-humored amazement. The fact is that among researchers and clinicians, the idea that homosexuality is chosen has been dead for decades. It is empirically absurd. But, sighs Hamer, among people who hate homosexuality, there is simply an emotional, irrational, ascientific refusal to give up the idea that people choose to be gay. Hamer realizes reluctantly that in this purely political, emotional debate, the gene is not a gene; it is a symbol—a symbol of certainty, of a reality that's too politically distasteful, too morally unpalatable, too theologically terrifying to be accepted alone. Those willing to accept the clinical evidence understand that "choice" is a non-starter.

"The fact that homosexuality is not chosen was one of the mandatory biological preconditions to our concluding there was a gene for this trait," Hamer observes. He pauses, incredulous. "Can you imagine any sane, reputable biologist spending years of their life and their resources looking through chromosomes for a gene for something that's a chosen lifestyle? I suppose you could do it, but you'd have to be a complete idiot, because it would be the genetic equivalent of staking your entire scientific career and reputation on finding the gene for"—he searches for an example—"being a Presbyterian." He sits in his office shaking his head, smiling.

CAMILLE PAGLIA

Where Gay Boys Come From

WHAT IS THE MEANING of male and female, homosexuality and heterosexuality? At the end of the century and the millennium, there is not a single important question about sexuality that we can fully answer. I am simply one of a number of contributors to this worldwide debate.

My work is energized by my own combat with my conflicted drives. I was born in 1947; I grew up in the very repressive 1950s and certainly had what would have to be called a massive gender dysfunction. I didn't know whether I was male or female. I've often said in public I'm glad I hadn't heard of Christine Jorgensen: If I had thought that a surgical sex change was possible, I would have become obsessed with that and been convinced that that was the answer to my problem. I now think that I was a kind of pioneer: What I wanted to be as a woman was not possible in the conformist fifties, given the kinds of Doris Day–Debbie Reynolds sex roles that women were expected to play—the docility, the deference towards men! I was simply not capable of this. I think there was something in me right from the start, something that is probably unmeasurable by any known mechanisms today. I've described myself as a sexual mutant, born between the sexes in some way.

That was the first of my problems, the gender dysfunction. Then, was I gay or straight? I began falling in love with women from the age of three or four. Most of these stories now, after gay liberation, have a reasonably happy ending. Once you know that you're gay, you join other gay people and you feel that you have a place. My experience after Stonewall was that, far from being accepted by lesbians, or being able to date lesbians, I have been totally blocked out by them. This is why I'm such a strange and heterodox personality.

Now the one class of person that I have always gotten along with is gay men. I've identified totally with gay men, and my most intimate human con-

From the Spring 1994 issue. This reading is an excerpted transcript of a talk delivered by Dr. Paglia as part of a day-long symposium, "The Biological Nature of Homosexuality and the Psychological Development of Gay Men and Lesbians," at the Harvard Medical School in March 1993.

Camille Paglia

tacts have been with gay men. The way investigations are going now, the new and still very sketchy kinds of data supporting a biological cause of homosexuality suggest a direction that makes sense to me. Because I have lived so intimately with gay men for so many years, I have to say there is something strange and wonderful about the gay male mind. It is my belief that science will eventually demonstrate that there is a measurable brain difference between gay men and straight men. Right now we simply have hypotheses and a few studies suggesting a biological difference; we need to exercise great caution in any generalization we make.

On the Origins of Homosexuality in Men

I have been teaching in art schools for twenty-two years and have a lot of close contact with male dancers and artists who are gay. And I have put together an account that I think makes sense about the origins of homosexuality in men at this stage in Western culture. We have to be careful about the parochialism of our terms. These paradigms simply do not apply to far Eastern cultures; Freud, for example, does not transfer over to Japanese culture.

Here is my working hypothesis about gay men: It is not homosexuality that is inborn; homosexuality is an adaptation after the fact, an adaptation to a certain kind of personality which may in fact be inborn. Researchers were suggesting as long as twenty-five years ago that artists—all artists, gay or straight, but visual artists particularly—possess from earliest childhood a kind of perceptual openness, a kind of hyper-responsiveness to color and form. This trait could even have some relationship to autism, in which there's a tremendous influx of sensory phenomena that the person has difficulty organizing. I think that this hyper-responsiveness may be what begins the pattern that ends up in male homosexuality.

Let me take the case of a gay male dancer, a type of man that I frequently encounter in my classes. Now in our society, unlike in Russia or Europe, there is no prestige accorded to a male dancer—except maybe in downtown New York. He is treated as a sissy and abused right from the start. The young man has to just cleave to that vision of wanting to be a dancer. Again and again in my classes I encounter a male dancer born into a family in New Jersey with five jock brothers. This boy is different from the outset. He is "sensitive"; he is dreamy. The mother knows he's different and he knows it, too.

It is not that he wants to *become* his mother, but he is attracted to what is in his mother's boudoir: the fabrics, the objects that make up her world. He is drawn to the beauty, the tactile pleasure of the fabrics in her closet: the silks, the nubby wools, and so on. Men in our society are denied any kind of expression of aesthetic impulse. In the eighteenth century men were able to wear beautiful silken clothes. For all the talk about how women are fashion victims, it is men who suffer from aesthetic deprivation in our culture. The boy is also attracted to her makeup, not because he wants to put it on, but because the lipsticks are essentially paint. He admires the beauty of the perfume containers, these beautiful objects on his mother's dressing table. This boy's mother likes him because he is more like her: He is quiet; he is integrated much better into her world. Right from the start, the father dislikes him as a soft thing and rejects him, as do his straight brothers and the neighborhood boys, who may treat him horribly.

My hypothesis is that the homosexuality is an adaptation to this type of personality. The boy soon realizes that there is something beautiful that is masculine, but it is something other than himself, something out there, and he falls in love with it. Now feminism is obsessed at present with the idea that masculinity is a social construction that is false and oppressive, the source of all evil. Marilyn French has declared that masculinity is an illness, a disease. My view is that masculinity is something real and simple and primary. All of the world's cultures have recognized it, all the way from Hawaii to Siberia to India, even those in which men have a much more languid, feminine body language, as seems to have been the case in ancient Egypt among the aristocracy, which valued the beauty of gesture and whose men wore eye makeup. Still, there is a sense of the masculine. I believe the masculine is something that simply exists, however differently societies may present it. The gay boy feels early on that he is in between in some way, and he has this longing for something that is not him. When he falls in love with another man, he is falling in love with something that he does not possess. It is not that he wants to become what he falls in love with, but rather that he longs for something, is drawn magnetically to something, which he himself lacks.

This is my working hypothesis about gay men. So many gay men that I know were born into a middle-class family in Indiana or Iowa, the most ordinary family without any kind of aesthetic interest. Right from the start he knows that he wants to be a fashion designer. Halston is a good example of this. He feels alienated in that very macho realm, and he eventually escapes it by traveling to New York or to another city where he can find other gay men to hang around with. There is a clumping phenomenon in all the big cities of the world, as gay men form their urban ghettos.

This responsiveness to color and beauty is what ties me to gay men, and also what separates me from gay women. I don't know why I am the way I am, but my response to art happened all at once in the middle of upstate New York, under the steely grey snow-belt sky. Every time I saw an art object, I fell in love with it. I have never met a gay woman who had this obsession with the way things look. There is a kind of elitism here, an elitism based upon beauty that is very foreign to the more egalitarian ethic of lesbian-feminism, which prefers a kind of consoling pat on the back to heal people's wounds and soothe them—or put them to sleep. Lesbian-feminism is now worried about "look-ism," saying that we never should comment upon how someone looks, insisting that everyone is equal. Gay men know that this is not true. They say that someone is "to die for"; they talk about "buns of death." When straight men make such comments about women, feminists complain, "That's objectifying. It's the male gaze that's making us passive objects." But that is not true at all: This is a form of admiration. The beautiful person is something to be admired and put on a pedestal. A beautiful young man in a gay bar is like a superior being. In *The Picture of Dorian Gray* Oscar Wilde created a young man of electrifying beauty. The Greeks knew this being, too: that's what the *kouros* sculptures are all about.

Nature Retaliates

There are a number of things that I think are missing in the current discussion of sexuality. First: the way in which AIDS is constantly discussed without any reference to nature, as if AIDS were somehow the invention of a series of Republican administrations. AIDS is something that happened in nature.

It is my generation that first experienced AIDS, the generation of the Sexual Revolution. We thought, coming out of the repressive church teachings of the 1950s, that we would make sex totally free. It would be a utopia, a whole new age. And we hit the wall, the wall of nature. We must begin to recognize that nature does not care about us as individuals—the way it has destroyed a whole generation of gay men! *Newsweek* was quite right to put "A Lost Generation" on its Nureyev cover—a lost generation of artists, of fashion designers, and so on. The blow that the art world has taken from the loss of so many of these talented men is staggering.

We have a situation in gay activism where you cannot raise certain types of questions. You cannot ask, for example, is this possibly a behavior that nature is disapproving of? My attitude is not, Obey nature. Everywhere in my work I have said, Defy nature, like Captain Ahab shaking his fist in the face of nature. But stop complaining if then you suffer, and nature takes her revenge on you. If you refuse to discuss these issues, you are forcing them underground and you are helping the far Right. Because if only the far Right will say these things out loud, you are causing the rise of fanatics such as David Duke and Pat Buchanan. You have got to allow free debate of these issues: critique from within the gay world.

For example, how can we talk about sexuality in human beings and other species without referring to procreation? It seems pretty obvious that sexuality in the animal kingdom is destined for that purpose. What about sodomy, then? When you have examples among mice of males allowing themselves to be mounted by other males, is sodomy actually occurring? Now, as far as I'm concerned, any area of pleasure in the human body should be exploited. Nevertheless, as we women have been long aware and have been warned by gynecologists, one must be very careful about going directly from anal sex to vaginal sex. Right now in gay activism you'll find an absolute equivalence made between the vagina and the anus, and it's only "homophobes" who say there's any difference. There are all kinds of things that are being said on the far Right that have some truth in them, but no one will listen to them. If one simply tries to silence them, you end up with an increasing stridency and an increasing homophobia in the way these issues are phrased.

Wherever I see that there's a taboo upon utterance I feel that it's my obligation as an intellectual to go there and open it up and force people to think about it. I approve of sodomy; I want all laws that forbid it to be repealed. I am a libertarian; I don't believe the state has any right to dictate to one in the private realm about anything, whether it's suicide, drug taking, gambling, or the like. Nevertheless, it may be that sodomy is dangerous. We have this idea of "unsafe sex," but people don't want to think about that.

On the Origins of Homophobia

I am doubtful that we will ever reach a situation in any culture where gay men are fully tolerated by straight men. Every boy has to make a passage out of the shadow of his mother toward manhood. Many cultures have ceremonies in which the men of the village come and kidnap the boy from the women's quarters and throw him into a pit or mark his body, or force him into other kinds of hazing rituals to make him a man. A girl simply has her period, something that happens to her internally and passively. She knows she's a woman, and she's calm in her womanhood. But there is no marker for a boy to become a man in the way that there is for a girl to become a woman.

I believe that boys, in making this passage from boyhood to manhood, may go through a necessary period of homophobia, and that's why it is so dangerous for gay men in the streets. That's why we have groups of young men spontaneously acting out this hostility toward gay men. Maybe that is not bigotry per se, something that one is taught, but instead part of this terribly dangerous passage that boys make into manhood. If so, we're facing a more serious problem than one of mere toleration. Perhaps not everything can be solved in the sexual realm through passing rules and regulations. Maybe there are ambiguities and ambivalences that are very profound and that we will simply have to accept. Gay activism has to start developing the discourse with which to deal with these ambiguities.

The one thing that we must want is something that is as close to the truth as possible. We must put ourselves into a receptive frame of mind to search for the truth. Gay scholars and scientists must think of themselves as larger than their gay identity. Once people put their gay identity before their scholarship, before science, then it is propaganda, and that's a recipe for disaster for gay rights from the rise of the far Right.

Footnote on Gay Activism

When my book *Sexual Personae* came out three years ago, it was in a period when social constructionism was absolutely the dominant code, especially in Ivy League literature departments. I'm happy to say that in the last three years French theory has started to break apart. You can just hear the ice cracking and the ships going down and the cries of the drowning! Unfortunately, the one place where French theory is still going strong is in "queer studies." Foucault is as strong as ever. Now if you need Foucault to explain your sexuality to yourself, if you need the work of a guy who was so alienated from his own body that he never mentioned a woman in all of his work—! This is a leader? This is the queer Big Daddy that "queer studies" has elevated? This is disastrous! We don't need Foucault. False theorizing, dead, abstract theorizing, removed from science, removed from the direct study of history, that is a cul-de-sac that the gay world has gotten itself into.

At the same time, I think that gay activism has gotten off track in its insistence on a gay-versus-straight polarity. That kind of a tension, which is now everywhere in the culture, ensures the survival of homophobia. I would prefer to educate people toward the idea of sexuality as a continuum, something like what Kinsey first talked about. I got this idea first from studying literature and art: In Shakespeare's comedies gender and sexual orientation are presented as something that is fluid. I don't like the gay-versus-straight dichotomy because it's terrible for gay men. They are the ones who will pay the price for this, not lesbians; gay men will be beaten up and die in the streets from the kind of rhetoric that's in the air. Anything in gay activism should be phrased in a larger context of libertarian principles. We should ask for protection for all nonconforming behavior, of which gay behavior is only a subset. There has to be a more general philosophical perspective.

CARLA GOLDEN

Do Women Choose Their Sexual Orientation?

RARELY IS THE ROLE of conscious choice taken seriously in scholarly discussions of sexual orientation, an oversight resulting from the failure to include women in much of the research. Listening to the ways in which women talk about their sexuality reveals that, in contrast to men, a significant minority of women experience themselves as having made a choice about the gender of their sexual partners.

Over the last decade, I have conducted in-depth interviews with more than one hundred women actively engaged in the process of sexual self-definition. From an initial study of lesbian college students, I expanded the scope of my research to include non-student lesbians in their twenties, thirties, and forties, as well as heterosexual and bisexual women of varying ages. The women were primarily white and from a range of social class backgrounds; interviews were open-ended and involved asking women to tell the story of how they came to know and identify themselves as lesbian, bisexual, or heterosexual. This research led me to believe that the contemporary feminist movement has had a significant influence on how some women make choices about—and reflect upon—their sexuality, highlighting the importance of considering cultural and historical context in discussions of sexual orientation and its causation.

From the interviews, I was able to identify women who experienced their sexuality as a conscious choice, as well as those who felt it was not a matter of choice at all, but something innate and beyond their control. While some women described their sexuality as fixed and unchanging, others experienced it as more changeable, or fluid, over the course of their lives (Cf., Golden, 1987, 1994, 1996).

An overview of the growing literature on women's sexual identities confirms that, for some women, choice has been a determining factor in their sexual orientations and/or identifications, and that their sexuality is best described as fluid (Brown, 1995; Esterberg, 1994; Golden, 1996; Rust, 1992; Whisman, 1993, 1996). While many lesbians mention choice only in the con-

From the Winter 1997 issue

text of accepting and embracing a sexuality they believe to be inborn, others describe choosing to be lesbians because they prefer women and because the feminist movement has legitimated that choice. Some women who identify as bisexual speak about how the idea of bisexuality appealed to them, and recount that they found it easy to move in that direction after deciding to do so. Some heterosexual feminists also use a language of possibility and preference. Although many have not actively questioned their sexuality, some have considered their options and chosen to pursue the most socially acceptable path. Others leave open the possibility of change in the future, when the situation is right or the appropriate woman comes along. Women's choices around their sexuality are evident not only in the acceptance and adoption of a lesbian or bisexual identity, but also in the conscious rejection of such an identity because it would make life too difficult.

My research reveals that one cannot predict simply on the basis of sexual attractions and involvements whether a woman will consider herself to be lesbian, bisexual, or heterosexual. Among the interviewees, all permutations of attraction, experience, and identity were evident. There were women who had only heterosexual experience, yet reported that they were lesbian, or bisexual; women with bisexual experience who considered themselves to be lesbian, or heterosexual; and women in sexual relationships with women at the time of the interview, who nonetheless reported that they were "really" heterosexual or bisexual. Nor does sexual attraction neatly predict sexual involvement. Some women have experienced same-gender attractions but have never acted on them, while others have made a conscious decision to experience and pursue such attractions. And to complicate the picture further, any part of this system (i.e., attraction, experience, identity) can change over the course of a lifetime.

Are such cases rare exceptions or do they represent common experiences among women exploring their sexuality? The women I interviewed were not randomly sampled from the population, and no claim is made that they represent most or even a majority of lesbians or bisexual women. From a phenomenological perspective, however, numbers are less important than what the interviews reveal about women's subjective experience of their sexuality, and about the variability and diversity among women as they explore their sexuality.

A brief consideration of the ways in which psychologists think about sexual orientation and sexual identity will serve to highlight what is "different," and hence most important, about the interview data. Psychologists define sexual orientation in terms of whether a person's "primary affectional and/or erotic attractions" are to people of the same gender, the other gender, or to both (Gonsiorek and Weinrich, 1991; Greene, 1994). In research on sexual orientation, people are characterized as if they clearly belong to one of four discrete categories: lesbian, gay, bisexual, or heterosexual, even though many psychologists, following Kinsey, Pomeroy, and Martin (1948), acknowledge that human sexuality exists along a continuum and that dichotomous categories represent a distortion of the multiple forms that human sexuality may take.

Sexual orientation is generally considered a stable characteristic that is established by adolescence, often before sexual activity has occurred. People are believed to know their orientation through a subjective awareness of their attractions (Bell, Weinberg, and Hammersmith, 1981; Gonsiorek and Weinrich, 1991). It is assumed that a person's sexual orientation will be consistent with his sexual behavior and sexual identification. Much of this research is based on men and, as with most areas of psychological research and theorizing, may not be generalizable to women's experience. My research suggests that a woman's sexual orientation, when defined by attraction and arousal, is not always consistent with her sexual behavior or the sexual identity she adopts. Similarly, the claim that sexual orientation is clearly established by adolescence and stable across the life-course is not consistent with the research conducted with women.

For women, there may be more to sexual orientation than "affectional/erotic attraction." Money (1988) argued that the definitive criterion for sexual orientation is falling in love; a homosexual person is one who falls in love with someone of the same sex. Money also identified other criteria, such as "being sexually attracted to" and "aroused by," assuming that these always occurred in concert. My interviews suggest that they do not. Some bisexual women reported sexual attraction to other females without being in love with them; some heterosexual women described themselves as being in love with their girlfriends without experiencing sexual arousal; and some lesbians reported loving but asexual relationships.

Improving on Kinsey's assessment of sexual orientation according to the two factors of attraction, fantasy and sexual experience, another early model of sexual orientation identified three critical components: the sex of the people one fantasizes about, the sex of the people one has been sexually involved with, and the sex of the people one affectionally prefers (Shively and DeCecco, 1977). While this conceptual scheme allows for multiple defining features of sexual orientation, it fails to take into account that these factors may not always be consistent. For example, the majority of North American women describe affectional or emotional preferences for women but experience sexual relationships exclusively with men, a pattern that Nancy Chodorow (1978) characterized as heterosexual asymmetry.

My own discussions with women have identified a range of components as contributing to sexual orientation, including: (1) sexual fantasies; (2) sexual attractions, and how easily they are interpreted as such; (3) falling in love; (4) emotional and affectional preferences; (5) sexual experience and the quality of that sexual experience; and (6) self-identification in the context of social and political affiliations. The interviews revealed striking variability in the criteria women used to define their sexuality. What is apparent is that there is no simple relation between sexual desire, experience, orientation, and identity, and that for some women, choice is seen as influencing their sexual decisions.

Some might argue that the problem here is a failure to distinguish between *sexual orientation* as a biologically-based substrate of desire over which people have no control, and *sexual identification* as a process of labeling by which people choose to identify themselves with one or another social group. The argument here would be that women may choose to call themselves lesbians or bisexuals because they prefer women emotionally or because of political considerations, but that does not mean that they actually choose the objects of their desire. In other words, they may choose their identity, but not their orientation. And yet, women spoke *as if* they chose more than just their self-label; they described themselves as deciding to become sexually attracted to and involved with other women. Without any previous same-gender sexual experience, women talked about becoming "open" to their attractions to women and overcoming years of heterosexual socialization. When I asked when and how the possibility had first occurred to them, they mentioned a range of different experiences that kindled their interest: women's studies classes, exposure to lesbians within feminist groups, or more discrete events such as viewing a film or TV program, hearing a lecture, reading an article, or having a discussion with a lesbian friend. These had often prompted ongoing reflection on their part, which sometimes involved their reinterpreting close female friendships and/or attachments to teachers and camp counselors as evidence of the possibility that they had been sexually attracted to women all along but had never recognized it until now. This kind of reinterpretation is consistent with the dominant view of sexuality as fixed and unchanging; such reinterpretation of one's history would be unnecessary if sexuality were recognized as fluid.

The argument could still be made that the women described above were "really" bisexual, and that their openness to sexual relationships with women, after a history of sexual attractions and relationships exclusively with men, merely reflects a predetermined (bi)sexuality. This is the view of John Money (1988), who asserts that it is incorrect to use the term "sexual preference," because people cannot choose their sexuality. He argues that sexual orientation "is something that happens . . . like being tall or short, left-handed or right-handed, color-blind or color-seeing." According to him, no one prefers to be homosexual rather than heterosexual, or bisexual rather than monosexual. One wonders whether he has ever listened to women's accounts of their sexual choices.

The growing body of research on women makes clear that some women undeniably experience their sexuality as fluid. Whether this is a result of an underlying bisexual orientation that was always present or a conscious choice cannot be definitively determined. But the case of heterosexual women is illustrative. In my interviews with heterosexually identified women, some indicated that they had sexually "experimented" with other women and found the experiences less than satisfying, concluding that they were "really" heterosexual. In some cases, however, they acknowledged that there were other factors that contributed to the less than fully positive experience, including fear, inexperience, and internalized homophobia. Based on multiple discussions and interviews, I conclude that there are many more women who have considered the lesbian choice and rejected it than have elected to adopt it.

Given the particular tensions around intimacy in heterosexual relationships, with women wanting more emotional openness and intimacy from their male partners (Rubin, 1983; Chodorow, 1978; Eichenbaum and Orbach, 1984; Stiver, 1984), one might expect lesbianism to be an obvious choice for women. A relevant question is why so many women avoid it. One answer is that sexual orientation is locked in early and neither changeable nor subject to choice. Another is that women find it very difficult to overcome the social mandate of compulsory heterosexuality (Rich, 1980). The latter seems more likely to me, and the current increase in visibility of bisexuality among women on college campuses would support this view.

Taking into account the role of choice allows for a more comprehensive understanding of sexual behavior and self-identification in women. Identities and behaviors that appear puzzling and difficult to explain become clearer within a framework that acknowledges women's fluid sexuality. For example, it helps in understanding those women who have always considered themselves heterosexual but then become aware in adulthood that they are attracted to women as well as men. Some of these women act on their sexual attractions, despite no previous experience, and develop strong identities as lesbians. Other women may consider themselves bisexual, whether or not they ever act on their attractions. If sexuality is fluid, then it is understandable why some women consider themselves "bisexual lesbians," having chosen to be sexually involved with women and to identify as lesbians while acknowledging that they sometimes experience sexual attractions to men. It makes clearer the experience of so-called "transient lesbians," women who for a period of time identify as lesbians and are involved with women, but who subsequently become involved with men. It explains so-called "political lesbians," who decide based on feminist beliefs that it is preferable to be sexually involved with women, and for whom this becomes a distinctly erotic as well as a political choice. And it may explain the increasing visibility and expression of bisexual choices among women who previously assumed but never questioned their heterosexuality. Bisexuality may be the one area of sexual "deviation" in which women not only express more interest than men, but have more experience as well.

From this perspective, bisexuality can be conceptualized as a distinct form of sexual expression, and bisexuals as women who recognize and act according to their sexual fluidity. Some lesbians consider bisexuals to be lesbians who are unwilling to forego heterosexual privilege; some heterosexuals believe that bisexuals are simply confused and have not made up their minds. But if sexuality is not essential (fixed and unchanging) or dichotomous (focused exclusively on women or on men), then bisexuals are neither confused, nor passing through a stage in the process of coming out, nor unwilling to give up heterosexual privilege.

Conceptualizing sexuality as fluid and as subject to personal choice also helps make sense of the fear of—and preoccupation with—lesbians and gays in mainstream American culture. Consider the virulent anti-homosexual sentiment that characterized recent efforts in Oregon, Colorado, and Georgia to deny civil rights to lesbian and gay people. If sexuality is not fixed and it is possible to choose one's sexual attractions, then exclusive heterosexuality is indeed in danger. As the visibility of lesbian and gay people increases, and as individuals who are "out" and very comfortable with their sexuality are perceived as acceptable, it is more likely that people of all ages could decide that a lesbian, gay, or bisexual lifestyle is as viable a choice as any other. If deviations from the prescribed path of heterosexuality were not a real possibility, people so vigorously committed to the superiority of exclusive heterosexuality would have less to fear from the open integration and inclusion of lesbians, gays, and bisexuals into public life.

For all the current scientific and media emphasis on the biological bases of homosexuality, women's stories suggest that homosexuality may not be as biologically predetermined for women as for men. There is no similar interview research with gay or heterosexual men that explores this issue, but from reading gay male literature, speaking with a small sample of gay men, and exchanging views with therapists who work with them, my impression is that gay men do not experience their sexuality in the fluid manner that some lesbian, bisexual, and heterosexual women do. I suspect that very few gay men could be characterized as having chosen their homosexuality. As for why the experience of sexuality might be so different for women and men, psychoanalytic theories of mothering offer some insights. Feminist analyses of British object relations theory provide a framework for understanding how the conditions of early infancy might lead women to have greater bisexual potential than men. To the extent that infants and young children are primarily nurtured by women (and depending on the importance one attaches to this experience as contributing to later sexuality), one might expect boys to be more predisposed toward heterosexuality and girls to be more directed toward lesbianism (Chodorow, 1978, 1994; Dinnerstein, 1976). Adding in the cultural imperative toward heterosexuality, one might expect a greater incidence of bisexuality among women, or at least greater expression of interest in that possibility.

When one incorporates the experiences and words of women into theories of sexual orientation and its development, it is no longer possible to ignore or reject notions of sexual choice and preference. This is not to suggest that sexuality is experienced as a choice by all women, or even by most. That choice is a salient feature of sexuality for a significant minority of women means we must begin to explore its implications.

REFERENCES

Bell, A. P., Weinberg, M. S., and Hammersmith, S. K. *Sexual preference: Its development in men and women.* Indiana University Press, 1981.

Brown, L. "Lesbian identities: Concepts and issues," in A. D'Augelli and C. Patterson, eds., *Lesbian, gay and bisexual identities through the lifespan: Psychological perspectives.* Oxford University Press, 1995.

Chodorow, N. *The reproduction of mothering: Psychoanalysis and the sociology of gender.* University of California Press (Berkeley), 1978.

Chodorow, N. *Femininities, masculinities, sexualities: Freud and beyond.* University of Kentucky, 1994.

Dinnerstein, D. *The mermaid and the minotaur: Sexual arrangements and the human malaise.* Harper and Row, 1976.

Eichenbaum, L., and Orbach, S. *What do women want? Exploring the myth of dependency.* Berkeley Books, 1984.

Esterberg, K. "Being a lesbian and being in love: Constructing identities through relationships," in *Journal of Gay and Lesbian Social Services,* 1(2), 1994.

Golden, C. "Diversity and variability in women's sexual identities," in *Lesbian psychologies: Explorations and challenges.* University of Illinois Press, 1987.

Golden, C. "Our politics and choices: The feminist movement and sexual orientation," in B. Greene and G. Herek, eds., *Lesbian and gay psychology: Theory, research, and clinical applications.* Sage, 1994.

Golden, C. "What's in a name? Sexual self-identification among women," in R. Savin-Williams and K. Cohen, eds., *The lives of lesbians, gays, and bisexuals: Children to adults.* Harcourt Brace and Co., 1996.

Gonsiorek, J., and Weinrich, J. "The definition and scope of sexual orientation," in J. Gonsiorek and J. Weinrich, eds., *Homosexuality: Research implications for public policy.* Sage, 1991.

Greene, B. "Lesbian and gay sexual orientations: Implications for clinical training, practice, and research," in B. Greene and G. Herek, eds., *Lesbian and gay psychology.* Sage, 1994.

Kinsey, A., Pomeroy, W., and Martin, C. *Sexual behavior in the human male.* Saunders, 1948

Money, J. *Gay, straight, and in between: the sexology of erotic orientation.* Oxford University Press, 1988.

Rust, P. "Who are we and where do we go from here? Conceptualizing bisexuality," in E. Weise, ed., *Closer to home: Bisexuality and feminism.* The Seal Press, 1992.

Rich, A. "Compulsory heterosexuality and lesbian existence," in *Signs: Journal of Women in Culture and Society,* 5, 1980.

Rubin, L. *Intimate strangers: Men and women together.* Harper and Row, 1983.

Shively, M., and DeCecco, J. "Components of sexual identity," in *Journal of Homosexuality,* 3, 1977.

Stiver, I. "The meaning of dependency in female-male relationships," in J. Jordan, A. Kaplan, J. B. Miller, I. Stiver, and J. Surrey, eds., *Women's growth in connection: Writings from the Stone Center.* Guilford, 1984.

Whisman, V. "Identity crises: Who is a lesbian, anyway?" in A. Stein, ed., *Sisters, sexperts, queers: Beyond the lesbian nation.* Penguin, 1993.

Whisman, V. *Queer by choice: Lesbians, gay men, and the politics of identity.* Routledge, 1996.

VERNON ROSARIO

Genes in the Service of Gay Pride

IS HOMOSEXUALITY HEREDITARY? And why does it matter? These questions have been debated since the mid-nineteenth century, when psychiatric forensic doctors and homosexual rights advocates both claimed that there was a congenital form of "sexual inversion." This immutable and "true" homosexuality, they argued, was a "natural" variant of sexuality that could be distinguished from willful, "unnatural" sodomy or pederasty. As such, congenital homosexuality should not be considered immoral or, at least, should be decriminalized, since "true" homosexuals were no more responsible for their passions than lunatics were for their deranged actions

After falling into desuetude for a number of years, the genetic hypothesis has recaptured media attention in the past five years. The "gay twin" studies of J. Michael Bailey and Richard Pillard and, most recently, the molecular biological research of Dean Hamer and his team at the National Institutes of Health have been widely touted as proof that homosexuality is genetic. Gay and lesbian legal defenders and political lobbyists have propped up their arguments for homosexual civil rights on this scientific evidence.

Many legal scholars and biomedical scientists, however, realize that biological claims are an unstable and superfluous foundation for human rights. Religion, for example, does not have to be congenital for it to be constitutionally protected. Nevertheless, the "argument from immutability" is tremendously appealing to courts and to the general public. A *New York Times*/CBS News poll of March 5, 1993, showed that Americans who believe that homosexuality is immutable are generally more sympathetic to gay rights. Vera Whisman's sociological study, *Queer by Choice*, despite its title, argues that the majority of American lesbians and gays sense their sexual orientation to be innate and biologically determined (while being "out" is their choice).

Although scientific support for this belief is tantalizing, more research and replication of existing studies are necessary to make it credible. It is with only scant evidence that many gays and lesbians have jumped on the genetic band-

From the Winter 1997 issue

wagon. Some queer critics of science argue that internalized homophobia is responsible for these quick converts'—and the gay sexologists'—medicalization of homosexuality. But this accusation of false consciousness is not very satisfying. What *positive* symbolic functions might the elusive "gay gene" satisfy? Let me start with the man who literally wrote the book on gay genes, Dean Hamer.

In *The Science of Desire*, Hamer opens with an epigraph by Darwin: "We do not even in the least know the final cause of sexuality. The whole subject is hidden in darkness." Darwin's second appearance in the volume is even more portentous. Hamer claims that while reading Darwin's *Descent of Man* and *Selection in Relation to Sex* he suddenly realized that homosexuality "most likely has a significant genetic component." Thereafter, his life took a sharp turn from boring oncological research to the pursuit of the gay gene—ultimately resulting in evidence of genetic markers for male homosexuality on the X chromosome. His literary recourse to the "father of modern biology" marks Hamer's research as a teleological quest—a search for final causes. By invoking the Darwinian legacy, Hamer alludes to the notions of natural selection, evolutionary progress, and genetic fitness.

More than any other scientific figure, Darwin is associated in the popular imagination with the idea that the great diversity of animal forms and behaviors is the product of "natural" forces (except where breeders intervene), and that all these variations contribute to the fitness and survival of individuals and species. A deeply religious man, Darwin refused to portray the "moral qualities" as evolutionary products. But E. O. Wilson, the leading proponent of sociobiology, argues that even morality is an *evolved instinct*, and that genes for homosexuality may have persisted because our altruistic works favored kinship survival. No matter how little contemporary homosexuals might *actually* contribute to the child-rearing of their kin—or, indeed, how homophobes might panic at the thought of armies of gay child-care workers—a genetic theory of homosexuality evokes a prehistoric, imaginary narrative and invokes a Darwinian evolutionist teleology to prove that gays are natural and good.

Furthermore, the geneticization of homosexuality founds imaginary vertical and horizontal lines of queer kinship. Extending vertically into the past, the "gay gene" figuratively establishes our consanguinity with other famous homosexuals in history: Plato, Leonardo da Vinci, Shakespeare, Michelangelo, Bessie Smith, Virginia Woolf, and Oscar Wilde. We would all share the genetic seed of queer genius. The "gay gene" also establishes a paternal link to collateral gay offspring who otherwise would have been brought into the family only by gay acculturation (or, as homophobes would claim, homosexual recruitment). This imaginary horizontal kinship provides the objective, biological confirmation of "gaydar," which assures one that the cute guy (clinging to his girlfriend's arm in Greenwich Village or in a gay disco) really is "family," but just hasn't figured it out (his genes) yet. Beyond national boundaries, a genetic, essentialist model also assures us that every cultural manifestation of same-sex affection is really the expression of a singular gay sexuality. The "gay gene" thus legitimizes the cultural imperialism epitomized by the bible of gay tourism, the *Spartacus International Gay Guide*, which cheerfully identifies where to find exotic "gay" sexual partners from Abu Dhabi to Zimbabwe even if "they don't believe that there is anything homosexual about their actions."

A gay gene would also be a particularly crafty and subversive one. It must have endured since prehistoric times despite shirking the Darwinian heterosexual imperative: The best breeders triumph in the evolutionary struggle. Instead of E. O. Wilson's altruistic gay gene, both Hamer and Simon LeVay evoke the image of *selfish* genes operating through time and individuals for the genes' own good. Nostalgically alluding to 1970s gay male hedonism, LeVay claims in *The Sexual Brain* that "genes do not care about these long-term prospects [of the species] any more than they care about the general welfare of the planet. Genes demand instant gratification." This saga of our genetic Id, managing to survive the evolutionary wars by whatever means necessary, uncannily mirrors (while historically trivializing) those fearless and ingenious gays and lesbians who struggled to gain social visibility and political clout for homosexuals in the twentieth century. As a bio-historical operon, the "gay gene" secretly reassures us that, no matter what social and cultural oppression gays may suffer today, or whatever political activism or inaction we personally espouse, gayness will inevitably survive.

Perhaps, then, support for the genetic model of homosexuality is based not on internalized homophobia, but on homo-chauvinism. Biological and genetic "reality" can be a queer source of orthodox cultural approbation and a mythical history of gay paternity, endurance, wiliness, and social utility. Scientists may or may not confirm the genetic hypothesis of homosexuality. And it's anyone's guess whether "gay genes" will be closely linked to altruism, selfishness, artistic ability, hairdressing skills, or other associated gay traits. But it is unlikely that the subtle, mysterious actions of genes alone will improve the social condition of gays and lesbians. It will still take the craftiness and courage of politically astute gay people to make the United States a better place for the efflorescence of queer traits.

Recent Sightings of an Old Desire

DO GAY PEOPLE have a history? The question seems a frivolous one in light of the explosion of books and articles on gays in history and the history of gays. But this has occurred against a backdrop of skepticism, especially among academicians, as to whether it makes any sense to apply our concept of "gay person" to people of the past, such as Michelangelo or even Sappho, or to assume any resemblance between our concept of homosexuality and that of historical societies like Renaissance Italy or ancient Greece. They would deny that gay people have a history in the conventional sense.

This skepticism has not, however, stopped historians from continuing to search for evidence of same-sex desire or behavior in pre-Stonewall societies, only that they've become more cautious about inferring any resemblance between these exotic examples and contemporary gay American culture. Nor can these essays be dismissed for having made crude assumptions about the universality of concepts like "gay" or "homosexual." Someone like Bernadette Brooten, who finds evidence for female same-sex relations in late antiquity, is very much aware of these "essentializing assumptions," avoids the term "lesbian" when describing these relations, and does not assume that same-sex relations of the past have anything in common with contemporary lesbianism. What is known is that the Catholic Church became alarmed enough to respond and formulate a position on such relations—a homophobic and misogynist one, as it turns out (no surprise there). Very much later, but still long be-fore today's "gay man" was a gleam in anybody's eye, soon after the American Civil War, a novel was written that describes the love and intimate relations between two men before and during the war. Douglass Shand-Tucci, who brought this novel to light in *The Review*, far from treating this as a 1990s-style gay partnership, shows how very different this relationship *had* to be from any-thing we know today.

Moving into the early twentieth century, the scenes describing gay people become more familiar but still a distant mirror of ourselves. In *Gay New York* (reviewed by Robert Dawidoff), for example, George Chauncey found a sub-culture of men who clearly identified themselves as "homosexual"—but how different they seem from today's citizens of Chelsea or the Castro! The same can almost be said of the denizens of the "Hollywood Watering Holes" of the 1930s and 1940s, where the men didn't touch each other and communication was all in code. Meanwhile, in Europe, a far more sophisticated gay world was thriving at this time, notably in Isherwood's Berlin. Germany's burgeoning gay culture would come to an abrupt end with the rise of the Nazis in the 1930s, producing a "gay holocaust" in which thousands were put to death, an inci-dent that Lev Raphael explores in this section. Precisely because these mur-dered souls have been romanticized by latter-day Gay Lib (e.g., through the symbolism of the pink triangle), Raphael is careful to avoid finding parallels between their social situation and our own.

BERNADETTE BROOTEN

Early Christian Responses to Female Same-Sex Relationships

EARLY CHRISTIANITY EMERGED in a world in which people from various walks of life acknowledged that women could have sexual contact with women. Close textual analysis of several early Christian writers demonstrates that they knew more about sexual relations between women than previous scholars have assumed, which accords with a heightened awareness of female homoeroticism within the cultural environment of early Christianity. Whereas pre-Roman-period Greek and Latin literature contains very few references to female homoeroticism, the awareness of sexual relations between women increases dramatically in the Roman period, as a detailed study of astrological texts, Greek love spells, Greek medical writings, ancient dream interpretation, and other sources reveals.

Because a strict distinction between active and passive sexual roles governed the prevailing cultural conceptualizations of sexual relations in the Roman world, it shaped the way that people viewed female homoeroticism.[1] The distinction between active and passive shaped Roman-period definitions of natural and unnatural: free, adult male citizens ought never be passive, and women should never be active. Should they transgress these boundaries, society deemed their behavior "contrary to nature" (*para physin*). This concept of "unnatural" and its dependence on the active/passive distinction aids us in understanding early Christian condemnations of male homoeroticism and usage of the phrase *para physin*. If early Christians had not condemned sexual relations between women within a gendered framework of active and passive, natural and unnatural, then they would have been unique in the Roman world in so doing.

Roman-period writers presented as normative those sexual relations that present a human social hierarchy. They saw every sexual pairing as including one active and one passive partner, regardless of gender, although culturally they correlated gender with these categories: masculine as active and feminine

From the Fall 1996 issue. Adapted from the Introduction to *Love Between Women: Early Christian Responses to Female Homoeroticism* (University of Chicago Press, 1996).

Bernadette Brooten

as passive. The most fundamental category for expressing this hierarchy was active/passive—a category even more fundamental than gender for these writers. They often defined "passive," that is, penetrated, males as effeminate. Males could be either active or passive (such as when they were boys or slaves), whereas females were always supposed to be passive. The division between active and passive was, therefore, not biological.

Drawing upon a broad range of sources from the Roman world, I illustrate in my book that early Christian views of female homoeroticism closely resembled those of their non-Christian contemporaries. Some prior researchers have tended to take an apologetic pro-Christian stance and to see early Christian sexual values as of a higher moral level than those of their environment. Other researchers have viewed early Christians as proto-Puritanical and repressive in contrast to the more sex-positive pagans around them. My research is more in line with those researchers who see a continuity between non-Christian and Christian understandings of the body.[2] A focus on female homoeroticism makes this continuity clearer than would a focus on male homoeroticism, since nearly all extant sources on sexual relations between women condemn such relations, whereas some Roman-period, non-Christian sources express tolerance toward male-male sexual relations, which masks the similarity between Christian and non-Christian understandings of masculinity. Because the reasons for condemning female homoeroticism run deeper than the reasons for promoting marriage or celibacy (on which there was much debate in the Roman world), there is a cultural continuity of views of female homoeroticism.

Although ancient Christian writers resembled their non-Christian contemporaries in their views on erotic love between women, both groups differed from our own culture in their overall understanding of erotic orientation. Whereas we often dualistically define sexual orientation as either homosexual or heterosexual, they saw a plethora of orientations. (When we in the late twentieth century think about it, we also recognize bisexuals and transsexuals, leading us to speak of a spectrum, rather than a bifurcation.) Their matrix of erotic orientations included whether a person took an active or a passive sexual role, as well as the gender, age, nationality, and the economic, legal (slave or free), and social status of the partner. For example, for the second-century astrologer Ptolemy, the configuration of the stars at one's birth determines a person's lifelong erotic orientation. A man born under one configuration is oriented toward females alone; under a second configuration, he desires to play a passive role toward males (i.e., to be penetrated); under a third, he desires to penetrate children; and under a fourth, he will desire males of any age. But the list does not end there. Other configurations give rise to men who desire low-status women, slave-women, or foreigners. In this schema, female homoeroticism constitutes one erotic orientation out of many, rather than a subcategory of two orientations (heterosexual and homosexual). Ptolemy and other authors reveal a gender bias in that they present far more differentiated pictures of the male erotic life than of the female one, even attributing more orientations to men than to women. By keeping in mind the larger picture of ancient classification systems for erotic orientation, the reader will better understand the specific discussions of female homoeroticism that I analyze in my book.

My research in this area contributes to women's history by documenting the existence of woman-woman marriage, of the brutal surgical procedure of selective clitoridectomy for women who displayed "masculine desires," and of women seeking out magical practitioners to help them attract other women. It contributes to the history of sexuality by analyzing the differences between the cultural conceptualizations of female and male homoeroticism in antiquity, by documenting the concept of a long-term or lifelong erotic orientation in ancient astrology and ancient medicine, by demonstrating that nineteenth-century medical writers were not the first to classify homo-erotic behavior as diseased, by analyzing the interplay between ancient religious views and understandings of sexual behavior, and by delineating the gendered character of Roman-period understandings of the erotic. It contributes to theology and New Testament studies by explicating the meaning of "unnatural" in Paul of Tarsus and in Clement of Alexandria, by showing Paul's use of natural law theory and of the Jewish law to undergird his teachings about sexual relations and about gender, by clarifying how homoeroticism was an issue of gender in the early church, and by providing a historical-exegetical basis for contemporary church discussions concerning same-sex love. Finally, this project contributes to ancient history generally through the sheer number of sources presented in it. Prior to this study, these sources have never been collected in one place, and some have never been translated.

NOTES

1. In some cultures today, the categories active and passive still shape the way people view male same-sex love. See, e.g., Ana Maria Alonso and Maria Teresa Korek, "Silences: 'Hispanics,' AIDS, and Sexual Practices," *Differences: A Journal of Feminist Cultural Studies*, 1:1 (1989): 101–24; reprinted in *The Lesbian and Gay Studies Reader*, eds. Henry Abelove, Michèle Aina Barale, and David M. Halperin (New York: Routledge, 1993) 110–26, esp. 115–20; and Tomás Almaguer, "Chicano Men: A Cartography of Homosexual Identity and Behavior," *Differences: A Journal of Feminist Cultural Studies*, 3:2 (1991): 75–100; reprinted in *The Lesbian and Gay Studies Reader*, 255–73.

   In the earlier part of the twentieth century, the categories active and passive played a greater role in defining gay male identity in the United States than they do today. See George Chauncey, *Gay New York: Gender, Urban Culture, and the Making of the Gay Male World, 1890–1940* (New York: Basic Books, 1994); and George Chauncey, "Christian Brotherhood or Sexual Perversion? Homosexual Identities and the Construction of Sexual Boundaries in the World War I Era," Journal of Social History, 19 (1985): 189–212; reprinted in *Hidden from History: Reclaiming the Gay and Lesbian Past*, eds. Martin Bauml Duberman, Martha Vicinus, and George Chauncey (New York: New American Library, 1989) 294–317.

2. E.g., Aline Rousselle, *Porneia: On Desire and the Body in Antiquity*, trans. Felicia Pheasant (French original, Paris: Presses Universitaires de France, 1983; London: Basil Blackwell, 1993).

DOUGLASS SHAND-TUCCI

A Gay Civil War Novel Surfaces

A GAY U.S. ARMY NOVEL, published 124 years ago, focusing on two Harvard students who enlist together to fight for the Union cause in the Civil War, has recently come to light.

Although homosexual themes have been identified in several nineteenth-century classics, the outrage that greeted the 1860 edition of Walt Whitman's *Leaves of Grass* points up how controversial such a theme was then and for years to come: E. M. Forster's *Maurice*, written before the First World War, was not published until 1971.

Brought out exactly one hundred years earlier, Fred W. Loring's *Two College Friends* is the record of a stormy but steadfast relationship between Ned and Tom and their unnamed older mentor, and is immediately unusual in the frankly homoerotic quality of the author's descriptions of the two younger men, and in the way they meet. Tom is described as having "soft, curly brown hair, deep blue eyes and dazzling complexion"; with Ned "the complexion is of olive, the eyes brown, the lips strangely cut [and he has] a curious grace and fascination of manner." They meet in their mentor's professorial study in Harvard Yard in a scene that is surely the closest thing to a classic gay pick-up that 1871 could handle.

A Battlefield Love Affair

Tom has sought out the professor's counsel, in the course of which both are rather taken aback by the unexpected arrival of Ned, who, having invited himself, forthwith belies rather a dull reputation by exhibiting a newfound wit and charm. Its stimulant, clearly, is Tom, who is soon "radiant with enjoyment." As for the professor, it is not long before he is uncorking his best Madeira.

It is only at the conclusion of this jolly session that the older man, detaining Ned at the head of the stairs as Tom exits below, asks earnestly: "Why

From the Spring 1996 issue

have you never shown me what you really are?" This rather coded query is understood at once by Ned:

> "It wasn't for you, sir," said Ned, with a certain frankness that was not discourteous. "It was for Tom, sir; though I like you and hope we shall be friends. But the moment I saw him come up here I felt that here was a chance to get acquainted."

No persiflage there. This is very much a young man's book. Its author wrote it at age twenty-one.

Though frank, Loring was not foolhardy. He disarmingly deflects any objection that Ned was "morbid on the subject of Tom" by making the former an orphan. Equally adroitly, and in more treacherous waters, the author has it, so to speak, both ways with the professor, a bachelor with whom Ned and Tom remain close throughout the book. On the one hand, the professor is affirmed as a man of "tender sympathy, . . . exquisite delicacy of thought and life and [of] wit and scholarship." On the other hand, one of the young men allows that for all his affection for the older man, the professor's "liking for us boys is very queer to me."

"What you really are"; "morbid" young men; "very queer"—this is not a tough code to break. But modern readers should be wary of being lulled into reading our own values and attitudes into those of a century ago. Both Tom and Ned, for instance, plan to marry women and have children and take their place in the conventional society of their day. (We are inclined to forget there was a *Mrs.* Oscar Wilde.)

Though both Tom and Ned show a due appreciation of the possibilities offered by the opposite sex, any such interest by either invariably provokes the other man to a furious jealousy, suggesting that much more is at issue. Ned, for instance, fancies one young lady sufficiently to produce some verses for her and send them to Harvard's magazine. But when they meet up and she inquires about the initials on a locket of Ned's, asking coyly, "Is she pretty?" Ned's reply is devastating to her *amour propre*: "'She!' he answered; 'it isn't any girl; it's my chum Tom, you know.'"

Nor do advancing maturity and the rigors of the battlefield—after both men, who are depicted as ardent patriots, leave Harvard to enlist—alter this attitude. *Two College Friends* depicts no schoolboy crush! At one point during their time together in the Army, Ned writes in his battlefield journal: "When this war is over, I suppose Tom will marry and forget me. I never will go near his wife—I shall hate her. Now, that is a very silly thing for a lieutenant-colonel to write, I don't care; it is true."

One possible reason is that, just as the attitude toward heterosexual marriage of the author and his protagonists is distinctly at odds with that of most gays today, so too is what seems (at first glance, at least) their somewhat Mediterranean attitude toward same-sex relationships. Certainly Tom is depicted as noticeably more like a woman than Ned. Shown a photograph of Tom in drag for a student theatrical production while still at Harvard, the professor opines: "'What a mistake nature made about your sex, Tom.'" Later, in the army, a grisly old soldier says to Ned of Tom—all but abandoning the code of the closet—"'You care for him as you would for a gal, don't you?'"; understandably describing Tom as "'pootier than any gal I ever see anywhar.'"

While it is Ned who courts Tom, making the first approach, and Ned who enlists first, expecting Tom to follow, the fact is that throughout the book both are always fighting for dominance, Tom declaring at one point that he "will not accept dictation" from his friend despite liking him more than anyone else. In fact, their relationship in this respect hardly accords with the Mediterranean same-sex model in which one man invariably plays the aggressive and penetrating role, which is not seen as homosexual, while the other man, who is seen as such, plays the receptive and passive role.

The extent of their belligerence is clear in this account from Ned's journal:

Quarreled with Tom! How we have fought, to be sure! I don't know what this quarrel was about, but I know how it ended. We didn't speak for two days, and then came another attack from that restless creature, Stonewall Jackson. . . . I didn't see Tom, but I knew he was near,—we always kept close together at such times;—still, if I had seen him, I wouldn't have spoken to him. My horse had been shot from under me, and I had cut open the head of the man who did it; it seems strange, now that it is all over, that I could do such a thing. Suddenly I saw the barrel of a rifle pointed at me. The face of the man who was pointing it peered from behind a tree with a malicious grin. I felt that death was near, and the feeling was not pleasant. However, the situation had an element of absurdity in it, and that made me laugh a little. The man who was going to kill me laughed too. I heard a little click, a report, and his gun went up, and he went down. Tom had shot him.

"Tom," said I, with some feeling, "you have saved my life."

"There!" said he, triumphantly, "you spoke first."

I saw that I had, and I was dreadfully provoked. However, he admitted that he was wrong; and so, under the circumstances, I decided that a reconciliation was advisable.

Such stubborn masculinity on each side surely implies a rough equality and, upon closer consideration, it would seem that the comparisons of Tom to a woman are meant, not to imply Tom is *less masculine* than Ned, but rather that he is *more beautiful*. Certainly Ned is pronounced "not as handsome" as Tom, and much is made throughout the book of "Tom's beauty." But nowhere is it suggested that either is effeminate.

Cracking the Code of the Time

Two College Friends is rooted firmly in what is often called muscular Christianity, to see the homosexual aspect of which one must recall that many if not most men then of whatever sexuality (clearly including Fred Loring) took the view—certainly the prevailing one today—that unmanly-behaving men were problematic, and that it was gender-inappropriate behavior, not homosexuality as such, that affronted masculine values, heterosexual and homosexual. In today's terms one can hardly avoid noticing that neither Tom nor Ned—despite a relationship open enough that the grisly old soldier recognizes it at once as comparable to one between a man and a woman—seem to have at all troubled unit cohesion! One is reminded instead of the battalions of lovers in the Theban army of ancient Greece.

Nor should any of this in the American Civil War come as a surprise, for Ned's journal is a striking literary corroboration of the historical findings of Yale Professor Peter Gay, whose study of the real-life nineteenth-century diary of a Yale student disclosed,

> a capacious gift for erotic investment [in] men and women indiscriminately without undue self-laceration, without visible guilt or degrading shame, . . . inclinations [that] seemed innocent to [him] and apparently to others, because his bearing and behaviour, including his emotional attachments to others of his own sex, did not affront current codes of conduct. He preserved the appearances; it never occurred to him, in fact, to do anything else.

We have entered here, of course, what has been called by Brian Pronger in his book of that title, "the arena of masculinity": *Two College Friends* deals finally and most importantly with men at war, and in this connection gays always, I believe, do well to consider the brilliant observation of A. L. Rowse, the legendary Oxford historian, that both the Japanese samurai warrior tradition and the Greek homosexual warrior tradition "do not see manliness as instinctive, but, rather, as something to be gained by moral effort." The mustering of that effort, on several levels, is really Fred Loring's fundamental theme in this book.

Confronted, and at a disadvantage (as a prisoner of war), by Stonewall Jackson's assertion—"I love war for itself, I glory in it"—Ned stalwartly answers back, "I hate war"; here he is making—and exemplifying—a moral effort not all men would be capable of. He will only fight, Ned insists, "when there is a cause at stake."

Similarly, when he finds himself at odds with a much larger man, a civilian troublemaker whose antics are distracting his men during drill, Ned finally concludes:

> remonstrance would be in vain; so I knocked him down, seeing my opportunity to do so effectively. My men laughed. The giant raised himself in astonishment.
>
> "You can't do that again," said he. Another laugh from the chorus.
>
> "I know it," said I. Still another laugh.
>
> "I could just walk through you in two minutes," he growled with an oath.
>
> "I believe you," said I; "and I shall give you a chance to, if you don't keep quiet."

After this sterling exchange it is hardly surprising that Ned shows yet more pluck by quickly seeing the man's underlying ability and convincing him to enlist; whereupon Ned makes him his first lieutenant!

Although *Two College Friends* in these and other ways opens a welcome and timely window into the homosexual feelings of two American youths one hundred years ago, the climax of Loring's book will perhaps seem curious to the modern reader. Not that it is not passionate enough. Ned, Loring recounts, visiting his wounded friend in a field hospital, directs his orderly to "let no one enter [the room] under any pretext whatever," and then "threw himself down [on the bed] beside Tom—kissed his hot face" and, all the time lying in bed next to his chum, who is described as "sleeping restlessly under the influence of some opiate," delivers himself of rather a scorcher for 1871. For all its cloying tone it is still oddly moving:

> O my darling, my darling, my darling! please hear me. The only one I have ever loved at all, the only one who has ever loved me. . . . O Tom, my darling! don't forget it. If you know how I love you, how I have loved you in all my jealous, morbid moods. . . . Don't you remember when we were examined for college together? . . . I saw you there; and I wanted to go over and help you. And your picture, Tom . . . it was the night when I determined to go to war that you gave me that picture; it was just before we enlisted. . . . You won't forget Ned, darling; he was something to you. . . .

There is an age-old and honorable romantic heterosexual tradition of finding passionate love and even erotic fulfillment in relationships which, because of religious prejudice, age asymmetry, social custom, or whatever, are nongenital in nature. Of an affair of Henry Adams, for instance, a biographer writes: "some *lovers* [my emphasis] found it nobler—and perhaps even erotic—not to act on their physical impulses." But though homosexual love, with its ancient heritage of Platonic self-mastery, evinces historically an even greater affinity for such relationships (as in *Maurice*, for instance, where Forster writes, "it had been understood between [Clive and Maurice] that their love, though including the body, should not gratify it"), for the modern reader the idea founders on the fact that even if gay men are no longer seen as lust-crazed sexual outlaws, all men are seen today as sexual predators if only because genital sex now seems for us a necessary validator of passionate romantic love.

Just as it has been argued of Bayard Taylor's 1870 *Joseph and His Friend*, that it is not a gay novel even though the deepest and most fulfilling relationship is between the male protagonists—one of the protagonists finally marries a woman—thus will it probably be argued of *Two College Friends*, where, of course, the same thing happens. But how could it not? It has ever been the classic solution whenever a permanent union is not possible between two lovers (whether for reasons religious, racial, social, or whatever): one has to die and the survivor, happily wed, can almost be depended upon to name the first child after the lost love; in this case Ned is shot for violating his parole to save the life of Tom, who is depicted at book's end as looking tearfully into his son Ned's eyes.

But does this mean *Two College Friends* is not a gay novel? As if homosexual relationships that fail (for whatever reasons) are any the less homosexual; or as if gay people never marry the opposite sex, or cease to be gay when they do! How many homosexual "acts" makes a homosexual anyway?—if that's what makes one. One? Two? Three dozen? Three thousand? Will just the desire suffice? How about masturbation? Better yet, consider Robert K. Martin's sage remark of what a tip-off it is when someone is prepared to "assume that anyone is heterosexual until there is proof, not of homosexual feelings, but of homosexual [i.e., genital] acts." Who was it who said, "you don't have to be it to do it, you don't have to do it to be it"?

Is *Maurice* a gay novel? If so, then so is *Joseph and His Friend,* as well as *Two College Friends,* the author of which also died, in real life, as if to foreclose further inquiry, in an Indian attack on a stagecoach out West, in the very year he wrote the book, at age twenty-one, in 1871. Who was it who said most gay history lies buried in bachelor graves?

What Became of Loring and Friend

If Loring's early death defeats much additional investigation, something further still can be ventured. His Harvard class notes do hint, for example, at a certain discomfort about *Two College Friends*—the not inconsiderable achievement of a first book at age twenty-one is dismissed in a phrase without even noting the novel's title—and what little survives of Loring's remaining published work suggests he quickly turned to more conventional heterosexual subjects. The most noticeable of these to us, many years later, is a slim book of verses which takes its title from the "Boston Dip," a popular dance of the period—"One way to dance it thoroughly/ Is much champagne to sip;/ Or,—rub your boots with orange peel/ Till they are sure to slip."

Also of interest is that one of Loring's poems in this work is entitled "Tom to Ned" and announces the former's forthcoming wedding in a tone of somewhat defensive false heartiness. ("I really think that bachelors/ Are the most miserable devils"). Taken in conjunction with Loring's departure after graduation for the western frontier, a dangerous enough place in the 1870s, this just possibly hints at the sort of real-life situation that in the gay literature of the late nineteenth century is what Forster's *Maurice,* for instance, turns on: the break-up of a same-sex relationship under the weight of society's pressure on a man to marry, in aid not only of his social but also his professional or business success.

That there is at least some element of autobiography about *Two College Friends* is suggested by Loring's dedication of the book to a classmate, William Chamberlain. Moreover, the tone of Loring's dedication seems to echo more than a little of Tom and Ned's quarrelsome relationship when he writes, in the book's "Preface and Dedication,"

> Indignation at my dedicating this book to you will be useless, since I am at present three thousand miles out of your reach. Moreover, this dedication is not intended as a public monument to our friendship;— I know too much for that. If that were the case we should manage to quarrel even at this distance. . . . But I can dedicate it to you alone of all my college friends, because you and I were brought so especially into the atmosphere of the man [the professor] who inspired me to undertake it.

Loring's reason for the dedication, however, rings as false—why not just dedicate it to the professor, hardly an unexampled proceeding among teachers and students—as his address to his absent friend about his quarrelsomeness rings true. Indeed, its testy tone is that of all of us when we feel betrayed by someone we are still drawn to, and is reminiscent of Maurice's tone with Clive in Forster's novel when Maurice comes out (as we would say today) and Clive does not, electing instead to marry.

This is, of course, all very speculative, but the Harvard class notes of Chamberlain also are supportive of such possibilities. Loring and Chamberlain went very different ways upon graduation—Loring on a bachelor adventure out west, Chamberlain within a year back to his Massachusetts hometown to marriage and a son; but the son was not named after Loring (who had been dead over a year). Yet hints surface in later class reports by Chamberlain, who outlived Loring by forty years, of a much less conventional history. Chamberlain is noted as having "lived abroad a considerable portion of [his life]"—always suggestive in the coded discourse of the day—and seems also to have quickly abandoned the family business for journalism and the theatre. In fact, he formed at one point a very successful partnership with a leading figure of Boston's Bohemian gay circles of the 1880s and 1890s, the playwright Thomas Russell Sullivan, with whom Chamberlain wrote a comedy that in 1880 enjoyed wide popularity in Boston.

The comedy was titled *A Midsummer Madness*, which sounds a very different type of tale than *Two College Friends*, but in the game of mask-and-signal and reveal-and-conceal that gays were forced to play then (and well enough to still amuse today: witness *The Importance of Being Earnest*), one can hardly be sure.

About one thing, however, there seems to have been no dissembling. Just as Tom and Ned were described as ardent patriots for the Union cause, so are both portrayed as, above all else, Harvard men. In his last letter before he is shot, Ned evokes the mood of his generation well enough:

> I can see the Yard, with Holworthy and Stoughton and Hollis beam-
> ing away from their windows at each other . . . I hear the voices . . . I
> can see fellows sitting around the tables in their rooms, studying and
> not studying; . . . the bell for morning prayers, which I still hate, be-
> gins to clang upon my memory . . . if you ever want to think of me, and
> to feel I am near, walk through the Yard . . . I wonder how many visions
> of its elm-trees have swayed before dying eyes here in Virginia battle-
> fields.

ROBERT DAWIDOFF

On Being Out in the '90s—The 1890s

A Review of Gay New York: Gender, Urban Culture, and the Making of the Gay Male World, 1890–1940
by George Chauncey
(Basic Books, 1994)

YOU THOUGHT PERHAPS you knew the rough outlines of gay male history in the twentieth century—the grim years of the closet startled by the Stonewall outbursts into the modern era we inhabit. It turns out that the conventional view, the post-Stonewall Whiggish view, of gay history is at best limited. In this very important and superb new history, George Chauncey shows that there was a thriving gay life in New York. In place of the stereotype of a century of shadows and closets, Chauncey presents a panorama of gay male public and private life, performed and lived by a variety of men and witnessed not only by the police and moral vigilantes of a society threatened by sexual freedom but by a fascinated New York public.

On one level, *Gay New York* is a series of scholarly ripostes to the accepted narrative of gay male history; on another, it is an excursion into a lost past, the days before the day before yesterday, when the men who were to become homosexual or gay had developed an urban culture comparable to those of other urban groups, and a response to the virulent if inconsistent prejudice against them. Chauncey, a historian who teaches at the University of Chicago, has written a book that no reader interested in the gay past, present, or future will want to miss.

In brief, the argument of *Gay New York* is that in the fifty years between 1890 and the Second World War,

a highly visible, remarkably composed and continually changing gay male world took shape in New York City. That world included several gay neighborhood enclaves, widely publicized dances and other social

From the Summer 1994 issue

events, and a host of commercial establishments where gay men gathered, ranging from saloons, speakeasies and bars to cheap cafeterias and elegant restaurants. The men who participated in that world forged a distinctive culture with its own language and customs, its own traditions and folk histories, its own heroes and heroines.

Chauncey's story begins in a New York stoked and stressed by the economic and social changes of the late nineteenth century. Cities like New York were home to extraordinarily large and transient populations of men. Immigrants, working men, and new industrial and labor conditions challenged an American society already worried about its cohesion in the face of social change.

Chauncey shows how a gay male culture developed in the midst of and on the fringes of this urban male culture. Against this backdrop of urban growth and the fear of social dissolution, Chauncey shows how a gay life began to take shape as a class of effeminate men known to themselves and others as "fairies" held a place in the working-class culture of the time. Each chapter reveals more of a history rich with evidence of life lived resourcefully in the teeth of vicissitude. Successive waves of gay men claimed different parts of the city and different identities, but the growth in their number was inexorable: Events and the inhospitableness of non-urban America proved a constant source of new men. Against the background of New York's urban history and the social history of the United States, Chauncey shows how the gay men discovered themselves and one another, learned how to communicate their desires, and to make the best of the opportunities for individual satisfaction, love, community, and culture. And the kind of men who were fairies, queers, and then gays—their class, ethnic, racial, social distinctions—emerged with fascinating variety and clarity.

Chauncey identifies three myths that disguise the truth about gay history before 1940. "The myth of isolation" has gay men before the rise of the gay liberation movement condemned by pervasive cultural prejudice to solitary lives. "The myth of invisibility" insists that even if a gay subculture in fact existed, it existed in secret, and was invisible to the society and thus was generally inaccessible to gay men. "The myth of internalization" presumes that gay men "uncritically internalized the dominant culture's view of them as sick, perverted, and immoral, and that their self-hatred led them to accept the policing of their lives rather than resist it." Readers will surely recognize these myths as part of our intellectual furniture, and Chauncey is surely right in seeing them as critical to the current understanding of the gay past.

Gay New York marshals the evidence that explodes these myths. Chauncey shows how gays were like other marginalized peoples, targeted by repressive laws but "able to construct spheres of relative cultural autonomy in the interstices of a city governed by hostile powers." The book glows with the complicated, changing, overlapping networks of gay life on the streets, in apartments, bars, cafeterias, and bathhouses, and the regular communal events, like drag balls that attracted thousands of participants and spectators by the 1920s. The stories of these people and places give the book a warmth and an emotional power that is rare in a work of such unsparing evidentiary care. Similarly, Chauncey explodes the notion that gay life was "invisible." *Gay New York* details the visibility of gay New Yorkers in terms of their own efforts to be visible: the red ties, bleached hair, gatherings on certain corners and certain haunts. He shows that gays were tourist sights by the 1920s and fairies a public craze in the early 1930s.

Chauncey does not deny the repressive forces that constantly threatened and intermittently suppressed and punished gay men individually and collectively. What he does do is show that gay men were victimized in part because they were visible and that they fought with honor and courage to stay visible to one another and, in many instances, to the world at large. The third myth is in many ways the most powerful because so much of gay life remains invested in battling the internalization of culture-wide prejudice. Chauncey shows that a significant number of gay men "celebrated their difference from the norm, and some of them organized to resist anti-gay policing." He brings to light the small but steady stream of pro-gay writing and protest that gays produced in their own cause. Even more subtly, he disputes the claim that the absence of widespread protest necessarily equals internalization. The forces arrayed against gays were so totalizing that resistance was carried out in "the strategies of everyday resistance that men devised in order to claim space for themselves in the midst of a hostile society." The history of that resistance, the claiming of the YMCA as a gay space, the appropriation of Greenwich Village Bohemia or Harlem, certain apartment buildings, the doings at the Astor Bar, certain benches on Central Park West, is what makes *Gay New York* thrilling reading, because Chauncey is scrupulous in detailing the threat, the repression, that gays lived under.

Critical to Chauncey's accomplishment is his extraordinary research. He has delved into every kind of public record, private recollection, archival and cultural source. He is a careful, judicious, and balanced reader of it all. He has been careful to respect the work of the gay scholars and writers who have flourished outside the Academy. Indeed, it is hard to think of an example of scholarship that blends the professional and the subjective interest more successfully. Chauncey shows a clear awareness of the "theoretical" debates that enliven contemporary gay studies. I would call him a social constructionist historian of an essentialist phenomenon. Perhaps most important, he shows how gender identification in the 1890s was crucial to the thriving of a gay culture enmeshed in a working-class male culture, and that the reconstruction of gay identity in terms that suited bourgeois individualism and the interest of social order had tremendous implications for how gay men were seen and understood and how they saw and understood themselves. I am not doing his compelling and subtle argument justice, however; his "theory" is especially interesting because of its deep connection with the evidence he presents. Most stirring of all is his sensitivity to the varieties of class, ethnic, and especially racial history.

With this remarkable study of gay men in New York from 1890 to 1940, George Chauncey has transformed our understanding of gay history and given back to us a history most of us never knew existed.

LESTER STRONG AND DAVID HANNA

Hollywood Watering Holes, 1930s Style

MOCAMBO, Ciro's, the Trocadero—Hollywood during its Golden Age would not have been Hollywood without its famous clubs and night spots. Part of the mystique of the world's movie capital, their names were nearly as prestigious as those of their celebrity patrons.

Much less renowned but equally important to Hollywood's social life were its gay bars. These bistros—called queer bars by their customers in the 1930s—also served many big-name celebrities over the years, as well as a host of lesser-known and unknown individuals who worked in the movie industry. They differed in size and décor; they ran the gamut from hole-in-the-wall dives to elegant nightclubs. But all were disguised in some way to hide their identity as gay bars.

The origin of these establishments can be pinpointed to the end of Prohibition in 1933. Like gay bars all over the United States, their survival was marked by the kind of uneasy relations with local officials, police, and organized crime associated with speakeasies during the 1920s, not with the mainstream bars and nightclubs that sprang up after Repeal. Additionally, in Hollywood, gay bars operated within the shadow of the world's most powerful movie studios and within the political structure of greater Los Angeles, both of which impacted greatly on their development.

The Montmartre

A typical early Hollywood gay bar was the Montmartre, located on Hollywood Boulevard plunk in the center of its shopping district. The Montmartre had been a posh spot in its day, catering to prominent movie people. But by the mid-1930s it had fallen on harder times. It had been allowed to decay since its earlier days of splendor, and no attempt was made to beautify the place for its incarnation as a gay bar.

From the Summer 1996 issue

A speakeasy is a good analogy for the Montmartre. It did not advertise its existence, its patrons were subject to arrest, and it was run by a gangster. All this stemmed from one basic problem: by the mid-1930s, drinking alcohol was again legal in the U.S., but homosexuality was not. Gay people wanted the kind of social space for themselves that the non-gay population could take for granted. But such a place was not easy to come by, in Hollywood or anywhere else. Gay bars were chancy propositions, possibly even illegal, since they offered roofs under which so-called morals offenders might assemble. They were subject to raids, and were under constant surveillance by the Vice (the term used for undercover police officers planted to entrap gay people in places where they were known to congregate). To function at all, such clubs needed someone to run interference with local police and officials, and the mob was perfectly positioned to do this.

The Montmartre was run by Les Bruneman, a small-time hood whose influence, aside from the bar, extended no further than a few betting and bingo parlors. Seedy though it was, the Montmartre was welcomed with outstretched arms by its patrons. Like all gay bars, it provided a public place where gay men could gather and socialize, meet new friends, exchange personal confidences, and for fleeting periods be themselves. Most of its patrons were young newcomers to LA from other parts of the country, lured by dreams of the good life and by the excitement of Hollywood's movie industry. Only a few found success. They lived in the many Hollywood rooming houses, paying three or four dollars a week in rent, and scrounged for jobs. On any given night at the Montmartre, perhaps half the patrons were regularly employed. The rest scraped by on whatever part-time work they could find. This meant the faces changed constantly, as those unable to support themselves moved elsewhere and were replaced by newer aspirants to Hollywood's good life.

Yet for the run of its existence the Montmartre was a happy watering hole. A visit was no ordinary night out for its patrons. They dressed to the nines— suit, white shirt, and tie. On Saturday nights especially the bar was filled to capacity. Young people got to know each other, romance flourished, and everyone put up a bright façade, going to great lengths to conceal his poverty.

But the semi-legal status of the Montmartre had an effect upon its patrons. As in all gay bars of the period, same-sex dancing was not allowed, and fear of the Vice was never far away. Everyone had to be careful. Vice cops were to be found all over LA—in the public lavatories of bus and train stations and department stores, at the YMCA, along Sunset and Hollywood Boulevards in their squad cars, and even along the lovers' lanes of the Hollywood Hills. Out of uniform they would sometimes patrol the bars undercover, and were not easy to identify. They too were young, dressed in suits, white shirts, and ties. They sounded gay, and many of them probably were. But as slight a suggestion as "How about coming to my place?" was enough for an arrest.

Fear of the Vice meant the Montmartre was not a place for those with jobs or social positions to protect. There were few older customers, and no major movie stars. Occasionally someone with a face recognizable from the movies sauntered by, glancing in at the bar with an interest suggesting that he wanted to enter. But few ever did—the consequences might have been disastrous.

Finding the Formula for Success

For all its popularity, the Montmartre was short-lived. This had something to do with the poverty of its patrons, which meant any profit the club made must have been small. Its closing was also related to its location within the LA city limits. The constant harassment of its patrons indicates Les Bruneman had little clout with the LAPD. He couldn't stop the entrapment and was unable to stop the local newspapers from printing the names of those arrested. Still another problem can be summarized in one word: glamor—or the lack thereof. To attract a big-money crowd that would ensure financial success, a bar or nightclub had to offer an exciting ambiance well beyond that found at the Montmartre.

To stop police harassment and attract wealthier patrons, Hollywood's gay bars adopted several strategies. One was to change location. Bars were opened outside the city limits of LA, in pockets of land administered by Los Angeles County, whose sheriff's department took a more casual view of such establishments than did the LAPD. Another solution was to assume a protective cloak—to cater to a mixed crowd of men and women, gays and sympathetic straights. This eliminated the threat of entrapment even inside the city limits of LA. It also helped solve the problem of attracting a big-money crowd since it widened the potential base of customers who could spend big bucks. No one needed to worry about being seen at such an establishment.

One of the first areas to attract bar entrepreneurs was a slice of Sunset Boulevard (later dubbed the Sunset Strip) leading from the geographic boundary of Hollywood to the incorporated city of Beverly Hills. And one of the first gay bars to open there was popularly called Bruz Fletcher's after its owner. Bruz was a gay entertainer who sang "naughty songs." He hoped his bar would attract a mixed crowd of gays and straights, and for a while it did. But the sort of success he expected did not materialize. There were no obvious reasons for this. Perhaps customers did not like the entertainment. There might have been pressure from organized crime. In any case, the club did not prosper.

In Hollywood proper, there were other attempts to open upscale nightclubs that would appeal to both gays and straights. One of these was located on Cahuenga Boulevard. The bar was short-lived—a few weeks at most—but was interesting for the effort put into making it a success. It started off with Dora Maugham as the headliner. Maugham was a one-time vaudeville star who had taken to the nightclub circuit with a program of naughty monologues and songs. Her show at the bar was a modest success, and she was followed by America's best-known female impersonator at the time, Julian Eltinge. But here there was a hitch. . . .

Eltinge, whose billing read "The Most Beautiful Woman in the World is a Man," was a quintessential drag star who had enjoyed long runs in New York and on the road. Despite his retirement a few years earlier, he was still very much a star name. Even in retirement Eltinge would dig into his wardrobe once a year to perform a one-man show at the private, all-male enclave called the Friars Club. Eltinge nights at the Friars Club were hot tickets, so it came as a surprise to both the management of the Cahuenga nightclub and Eltinge himself to learn at the last minute that the LAPD distinguished between wearing drag at a private club like the Friars and at a public bar. To put on his show, he would have to go to the police to be mugged and photographed before being issued a permit. Instead, on opening night Eltinge went on stage dressed in a tuxedo. Pulling gowns off a rack, he told the history of each, recounting performances attended by the King of England, Woodrow Wilson, and other famous individuals. A few songs rounded off the performance. But after a couple of evenings of this, Eltinge disappeared and went back into retirement.

The club next turned to a performer who had become a gay institution in LA and San Francisco: Ray Bourbon, a tall, well-muscled man whose speech retained the accent of his native Texas. Bourbon could be described in a simple way as "deliciously sissy." His routines were strewn liberally with the use of sissified phrases and words like "Get you, Marge," "nelly," "swish," and "dearie." He used chatter and patter songs such as "I'm a Link in a Daisy Chain," "Sailor Boy," and "When I Said 'No' to Joe." For some reason, the LAPD had it in for Bourbon. Away from Los Angeles he worked in drag. But in Los Angeles—even on the Strip—he didn't dare. Even so, time and again he was hauled off to jail by the police and charged with giving a "lewd, inde-cent performance." Bourbon turned out to be the Cahuenga club's undoing, for it did not take long for the police to stage a raid. Bourbon was taken to jail and the place closed down, never to reopen.

Many gay bars were even more fly-by-night than the Cahuenga Boulevard establishments. Doubtless some of these were run along the lines adopted by one individual who called himself Mother Goddam, after a character who ran a brothel in the 1926 Broadway play *The Shanghai Gesture*. Mother Goddam's assets amounted to a mailing list of gay men he'd built up over the years who trusted him with their names and addresses. His method was fairly simple: ap-proach a bar whose business was faltering and suggest the bar provide the lo-cation and he provide the customers. Unfortunately Mother Goddam had no police or political connections. The arrangement worked well enough for a short time, but the bars were always closed down.

Hollywood also had lesbian bars. Run by women, they were usually smaller and somewhat quieter than the gay male bars. Their owners had no apparent connections to organized crime, but they did obviously know their business. There were no raids or closings by the police, despite a gay ambiance that flowed as freely as the liquor; and there were even male-impersonator shows on occasion.

One of these spots was Jane Jones'. Like Bruz Fletcher's, it was located on the Sunset Strip, but it flourished for a considerably longer time—not only during the late 1930s but through World War II and beyond. It was presided over by Jane Jones herself, a hugely fat woman with a deep bass voice. Jane also appeared in movies. She was not a big name, but sang in *Alexander's Ragtime Band*, the 1938 musical starring Tyrone Power and Alice Faye, where her role was large enough to be listed in the credits. At her bar she surrounded herself with a small group of male impersonators.

Another lesbian bar was run by a woman named Tess. A warm, friendly per-son, she cut a striking if somewhat matronly figure. She wore a great deal of makeup and always dressed fashionably in basic black and pearls. She usually stood near the door of her place to greet her "girls," most of whom she knew by name. Tess's was really a series of bars. Always located within the lines of Los Angeles County, not on the Strip but nearby, each had the same name: The International.

There were rumors that Marlene Dietrich dropped by Jane Jones's and The International. She probably did—Dietrich was likely to pop up anywhere. But she was the only woman of any prominence in Hollywood who dared. A gay star like Agnes Moorehead might show up with a woman companion at a lesbian bar in Paris or even New York, where no one paid much attention. But in Los Angeles, never. For gay female stars as for gay male stars, to be spotted at a gay bar there was tantamount to career suicide.

Café Gala

The march of world events in the late 1930s and the outbreak of World War II produced a new economy in Southern California, and a new prosperity that made itself felt in every area of the region's life, including the gay scene. With the buildup of the defense industry and the introduction of the draft, the poor young men and women of the Depression days suddenly found themselves eminently employable. Those not drafted, including lesbians and gay men, rushed into well-paying jobs from one end of LA to the other. People who a few years before had barely been able to pay the quarter-dollar price of drinks at places like the Montmartre found they could afford more.

It was this new economy that made possible the success of the Café Gala, which appeared on the Hollywood scene early during World War II. The handiwork of Baroness Catherine Derlanger and her longtime companion John Walsh, always referred to as Johnny, this spot from its start attracted a large gay following. Not that it advertised itself as a gay bar or even had an exclusively gay patronage. But a gay bar it essentially was, and it appealed to everyone, celebrities and non-celebrities alike. Johnny was aware of its popularity among gays. He wanted their patronage, although on occasion he was heard to mutter, "Everybody thinks I'm running a gropeteria."

The Baroness Derlanger was a titled Englishwoman and heir to a substantial fortune. She belonged to the fabled list of American and British expatriates who collected in Paris during the 1920s, and was among those who had stayed on through the 1930s until forced out by the war. Once resettled in LA the Baroness bought a small estate on a hill just north of the Sunset Strip. Down the road was another house, occupied by Johnny. At the foot of the hill, less than a hundred yards north of the Strip, stood still another house. It was this building they converted into their nightclub, an exquisitely decorated establishment with a warm, intimate atmosphere.

Johnny was at once manager, doorman, and a performer at the Café. He was also gay, and this contributed very much to the success of the club. Night after night Hollywood's gay population turned out to enjoy the atmosphere of a nightclub in which they felt at home even while being superbly entertained. The Baroness and Johnny had reproduced the formula for success pioneered by such earlier gay bars as Bruz Fletcher's. The club was located within the jurisdiction of Los Angeles County, and appealed to everyone, gay and non-gay alike. It was chic, fun, and very profitable. Under Johnny's management it remained a popular place to visit for over a decade.

For gay people, it felt safe. As doorman, Johnny saw to it that no undesirables entered. And while the Café was not overly expensive, it was considered classy. Patrons had to meet a dress code, and Johnny enforced standards of behavior inside. At the bar, which was often crowded with people—mostly men—two or three deep, Johnny would tell someone to sit facing forward. The inference was obvious: no groping on the premises, which in effect meant, "Don't provoke the Vice." Johnny clearly knew how to handle things. Because there were no raids or arrests, patrons enjoyed a real feeling of freedom that gave the place a very gay atmosphere.

The Gala was a special gift for gay men and women in the film industry. It meant for the first time in their careers that they could openly spend an evening with other gay men or lesbians at a Hollywood night spot without fear of exposure. This was especially true for stars. In the huge mix of patrons that were always showing up, no one could tell gay from non-gay, and no one even cared. The gossip columnists treated it no differently than they did other clubs, and artists who performed there were reviewed just as they were when they appeared elsewhere. All this gave the place a measure of respectability that was rare for night spots where gay people congregated with any regularity. At one time or another during its decade or so of popularity, everyone in Hollywood who did the nightclub scene sampled Café Gala's pleasures. It brought gay people together in surroundings that were attractive and accepting of their ways, and helped open their eyes to the fact that their lifestyle was nothing to be ashamed of.

Eventually, though, Johnny grew weary of the long nights and constant work that went into making it such a success. He allowed others to take over the management, and patronage began to fall off. Some time after he and the Baroness sold the club, it closed. Later in the 1950s he opened a place on La Cienega Boulevard named Johnny Walsh's. Johnny's second nightclub venture tried to recreate the atmosphere of the old Gala, but it was not a success, and Johnny retired from the nightclub business altogether. Its failure to attract a following was symptomatic of larger changes in Hollywood after World War II. Chi-chi gay was out, while a whole new atmosphere that could be called gay-assertive was starting to make itself felt.

Partly this had to do with changes in the film industry. By the 1950s, American tastes in movies started to change and audiences began demanding greater realism. Not coincidentally, the Motion Picture Production (Hays) Code censorship was beginning to lose its grip over Hollywood, as new amendments widened the definition of what was acceptable subject matter. The Code was abandoned altogether in 1968. Extremely tentatively at first, but then with growing assertiveness, homosexuality itself became a subject to be explored in films.

Movies began to be shot more on location, so that studio back lots were less important. The studio system itself started to collapse, helped along by the U.S. government's antitrust actions in the late 1940s, which separated American movie theaters from studio control. The Golden Age of Hollywood was over, in the sense of Hollywood's absolute centrality to the American movie industry. The upshot was a lessening in the stranglehold the studios held over the lives of those who worked for them. Gay stars had to remain vigilant about their reputations, as gay stars still do. But the smaller gay star found the heat somewhat less intense. This led to profound changes in the mores of Hollywood's gay and lesbian population.

The gay men and women who entered Hollywood after World War II were a different breed from their predecessors. Unlike the Depression generation, they were relatively prosperous. Economic times were better, and gay men and lesbians were learning how to demand what they wanted, not just accept what the powers that be would allow. But the most important factor was World War II itself. The war produced a heavy concentration of gay people in the big cities and in the military. For many, it was a new experience to see how many others like themselves there were, not just in the U.S. but in foreign lands and capitals. Gay men and women started to see themselves in a new way—as part of a community. This had repercussions after the war, which could be sensed even in the Hollywood bars.

A visit to the popular 1950s gay male bar the Cherokee House would have revealed a bolder crowd. The old uniform of white shirt and tie was gone, as patrons felt less of a need to appear "respectable." The young men acted tougher and less amenable to being pushed around. Police still staked out the bus and train terminals and patrolled the Hollywood Hills to make busts, but inside the bar there was less talk of the Vice.

There was also less fear of the Vice. One undercover policeman, young, blond, and handsome but notorious for his brutal entrapment methods, finally stepped over the line and the unthinkable occurred: One night he was set upon by a number of young gay male bar patrons and severely beaten. This was an isolated incident, a mere straw in the winds of change in the 1950s, a small salvo in the cataclysmic changes that were yet to come.

SOURCES

All information on gay bars themselves is based on reminiscences by David Hanna. The following sources were consulted: Kevin Starr, *Material Dreams* (New York: Oxford University Press, 1990); Otto Friedrich, *City of Nets* (New York: Harper & Row, 1986); Lillian Faderman, *Odd Girls and Twilight Lovers* (New York: Penguin, 1992); Vito Russo, *The Celluloid Closet* (New York: Harper & Row, 1981); John D'Emilio, *Sexual Politics, Sexual Communities* (Chicago: University of Chicago Press, 1983); Allan Bérubé, *Coming Out Under Fire* (New York: Free Press, 1990).

LEV RAPHAEL

Deciphering the "Gay Holocaust"

THERE IS an historical irony to the adoption of the pink triangle as one of the symbols of the gay and lesbian rights movement. We have actually known very little about what happened to gays and lesbians under the Nazis in the years 1933 to 1945. Our memory is in fact "empty memory," in the words of Klaus Müller, a gay consulting historian to Washington's Holocaust Memorial Museum. Müller uses that term because we are not "haunted by concrete memories of those who were forced to wear [pink triangles] in the camps."

In his introduction to the new edition of *The Men With the Pink Triangle* (1994), Müller notes that gays and lesbians have been among the "forgotten victims" of the Holocaust, rarely spoken of or studied. Likewise, homophobia has not been sufficiently examined "as an important part of Nazi propaganda, racism, and population politics."

Until this past year, Richard Plant's meticulously researched *The Pink Triangle* (1986) had been the major work in English helping to fill the historical void (Frank Rector's 1981 *The Nazi Extermination of Homosexuals* is full of blatant inaccuracies). Plant's short study is valuable on many levels, not least for the clarity and strength of his writing.

Plant fled Nazi Germany for Switzerland in 1933, and ultimately fled to New York. His book opens with a moving prologue in which he describes both his fear at the time, as the son of a Jewish socialist, and the ways in which he and so many other Germans that Hitler had declared enemies were unable to take Hitler seriously. One of Plant's friends was gay and was smuggled into Switzerland after brutal treatment in jail, but others were not so lucky. The book is thus in part fueled by a personal wish to bear witness to the suffering of his friends, though it never becomes polemical. Plant also clearly demonstrates the widespread taboo among noted historians and biographers on reporting gay experiences in the Holocaust.

Plant takes us from debates about the nature of homosexuality in nineteenth-century Germany through the Nazi persecution before the war and

From the Summer 1995 issue

into the concentration camps. He starts the book with a crisp overview of German thinking about homosexuality and the ways this dialectic played itself out socially and politically. One of Plant's most distressing observations is that charges of homosexuality emerged in Germany as potent political weapons used by many different parties, not just the Nazis. Plant describes the gay movement's repeated attempts to repeal Germany's anti-gay law, focusing on the major protagonist, Magnus Hirschfeld. Hirschfeld was a walking composite of Nazi scapegoats: a liberal, Jewish, gay sexologist. His internationally-renowned Institute for Sexual Research was one of the Nazis' early targets, and its ransacking, followed by a bonfire of its books and files, came a year before the well-known Ernest Roehm Affair, or the "Night of the Long Knives."

It's easy to misread the Affair as mainly a brutal expression of Nazi anti-gay sentiment, but Plant disabuses us of that notion. In the summer of 1934, Hitler ordered the purge of the Brown Shirts, the Nazi party's long-time private army. While its leader, Ernest Roehm, Hitler's friend and second-in-command, was openly gay, Plant says that his gayness was "a sideshow . . . never really the cause of his downfall." Homosexuality was used as a propaganda excuse to explain the purge—along with the far more serious (but bogus) charge of plotting against Hitler. The Nazis would likewise later use false charges of homosexuality in an attempt to weaken the Catholic Church, to eliminate youth groups that rivaled the Hitler Youth, and to police the armed forces.

The Roehm purge served Hitler politically in a number of ways. Roehm wanted his SA to absorb the German army, a goal that made its generals his bitter enemies. Hitler wanted the army to swear allegiance to him personally, rather than to the German state. A deal was struck and Hitler got his loyalty oaths. Murdering Roehm and eliminating the SA also eased party conflicts between paramilitary and political factions. And the purge burnished Hitler's "image as a tough leader capable of imposing discipline and high moral standards on his own party." Far more insidiously, it established "the legalization of crime in the name of the state," setting a precedent for the murder of any German group conceived of as a state enemy, whether Jews, gays, Jehovah's Witnesses, or anyone else.

Plant devotes a bizarrely fascinating chapter to explicating SS leader Heinrich Himmler's background and the development of his "curious blend of cold political rationalism, German romanticism, and racial fanaticism." Plant admits that despite all the details, as with other Nazi officials, the biographical facts explain only so much; one is still left puzzled by the cold ferocity of hatred translated into murderous policies. Himmler was in charge of the Final Solution, and his youth seems to have been filled with constant humiliation over his physical weaknesses and his family's low status and financial decline. Lots of adolescents harbor wild dreams of revenge against their perceived tormentors or as recompense for unbearable shame, but few get the power to enact them as Himmler did. His inner world eventually became a slumgullion of anti-Semitism, superstition, homophobia, and paranoia about a Germany facing defeat by a low birth rate, and lunatic fantasies for turning the SS into Europe's new nobility, with blond and blue-eyed Germans spreading across Europe.

Among the groups Himmler loathed, homosexuals were stereotyped as effeminate, pacifist criminals, bearers of a dangerously contagious disease found only in the degenerate bourgeois and upper classes. This profile was not exactly *sui generis:* it was composed of various views popularly held by a wide range of Germans. Some of them sound a very contemporary note, calling to mind anti-gay rhetoric in the U.S.

Plant shows those policies being enacted into laws even crueler in practical effect than on paper, as judges in Germany were increasingly given the latitude to punish any act at all "if the inborn healthy instincts of the German people demand it." In other words, they could completely overturn a basic principle of Western law, that only acts explicitly listed as criminal can be punished. Plant's chronology at the end of the book usefully lists Nazi legislation and activity against gays, Jews, and other targets, year by year. More powerfully than the narrative from which it is drawn, this schedule shows growing Nazi lawlessness masked as law.

Life in the Camps

Though gays could elude the Gestapo far more easily than Jews, once they wound up in concentration camps, they fared very badly, and were almost always among the numerically smallest of the various groups of prisoners. All prisoners were supposed to be brutalized, terrorized, and constantly reminded they were enemies of the State. But gays suffered in different ways. Homophobia existed in the camps just as much as elsewhere, here taking many forms like suspicion. Attempting to join an anti-fascist underground, you might be suspected of only being after sex, or of spying because you might trade sex and information to guards. Being classed as a State enemy didn't automatically make other "enemies" feel any kind of bond, and gays were "blamed" for sado-masochistic acts of guards and *kapos* (the prisoners appointed by camp officials to keep order).

Plant estimates that as many as fifteen thousand gays were murdered by the Nazis. Because they came from such widely divergent backgrounds, gays never united with any sense of group solidarity as did other groups. Few gays became *kapos* (who were mostly criminals or anti-fascists) and thus they couldn't intervene with camp officials or guards to help other gays. Gay prisoners also rarely received mail or packages from families or friends, who were ashamed of their incarceration, or afraid of being caught in the net of Nazi terror themselves. Finally, homophobic officials assigned gays to work details with the highest mortality rates, like quarries and cement factories. Some gays were also the victims of bizarre medical experiments attempting to alter their sexuality.

Plant relays these horrors dispassionately, which is no easy achievement. But he warns that the persecution of homosexuals has a long history in Europe, and that the Nazi "hurricane of hatred" can be heard whistling in the rhetoric of Fundamentalists calling for a "holy war" against their society's "most vulnerable and vilified minorities."

The Pink Triangle is probably less well-known than the play, *Bent*, Martin Sherman's 1979 opus about gays in the Holocaust. That's unfortunate. While *Bent* is at times powerful art based on gay suffering in the Holocaust, it's skewed in some not-so-obvious ways, creating a distorted image of the Holocaust in general and the role of gays in particular.

Bent is the story of Max, a shallow, coke-dealing, S and M–loving Berlin homosexual who winds up in Dachau after a 1934 round-up of homosexuals. In the course of two acts, he helps murder his roommate by finishing the beating an SS guard began, commits necrophilia to prove to the SS that he's straight and thus deserves a yellow star rather than a pink triangle, has "verbal sex with a fellow prisoner he comes to love," sees that man killed, and kills himself—after donning the pink triangle.

Max is a frivolous charmer, impossible to care about, a man whose deepest insight into himself is that he's "a rotten person." If the play is an attempt to show that even men like him can learn to respect themselves and to love, it seems extremely cruel. Does it take Dachau to make someone deepen as a human being? If so much suffering is necessary, he must be hopelessly unfeeling—which Max doesn't seem to be—so the play fails as the portrayal of a man's development into a *Mensch*.

Before *Bent* opened on Broadway in 1979, New York papers were filled with articles about the play's success in London and interviews with the author. The common theme was the controversy the play had caused by asserting that Jews had it better off in concentration camps than homosexuals. Sherman was reported again and again to have done "years" of research in the British Museum, and so the play was supposedly based on accurate information. One negative review said the only research you needed to write *Bent* was screenings of *Cabaret* and *The Night Porter.* I'd add: being tuned into urban gay life of the late 1970s, American style.

I saw the original Broadway production and have read the play several times since. I still think it's less the story of survival of human dignity under the most atrocious circumstances, or even of gay pride, than it is a sexual fantasy. The heavy sexual atmosphere is created in the opening scene with references to leather, chains, and cocaine, making the play feel at that point like a transposition of the late-1970s Village to 1930s Berlin. The atmosphere is heightened when Max's big blond pick-up of the night before struts out of the bedroom nude.

In Dachau, Max's new friend Horst is openly gay and pressures Max to admit the truth about himself. Remember—he's not suggesting that Max come out to his parents at a family dinner—he's telling Max to wear his pink triangle proudly in a concentration camp! It's grotesque. So is the fact that despite lifting and carrying rocks twelve hours a day, they manage to chat and flirt like they're at a bar:

HORST: Your body's beautiful.
MAX: I take care of it. I exercise.
HORST: What?
MAX: At night I do push-ups and deep knee-bends in the barracks.

Horst doesn't believe it, but Max says he does it to stay strong, to survive. This ludicrous exchange is heightened on-stage by the actors' undeniably healthy and attractive shirtless bodies that nothing can disguise. Even when it was Richard Gere, his beauty could not blind me to the fact that his line was ridiculous. The play titillates the audience here by offering beefcake and saying, "Okay, pretend you're in a concentration camp and there's this really hot guy—!"

Max says that everyone in the camp talks about sex and misses it: "They go crazy missing it." This is nonsense. Richard Plant points out, as many other writers about the camps have done, that in a brutal and unpredictable atmosphere of terror, torture, starvation, filth, with no medical care, most men's sexual desires faded away. Prisoners were obsessed with food, not sex. While sex may have occurred, food was far more important, and in memoir after memoir about the camps, you encounter tales of dreaming about food, fantasizing post-liberation feasts, or memories of pre-war meals.

Given the play's sexual emphasis, it's not surprising that its real highlight is an act of fantasy sex achieved through talking. This act ostensibly proves that Max and Horst are still alive, still human. If anything proved that during the war, judging by Holocaust victims' stories, it was kindnesses like sharing food or helping the weak stand during a role call. Such acts challenged the barbarity of the camps and "salvaged the highest values" of Western civilization, in the words of Anna Pawelczynska, the Polish sociologist who was in Auschwitz and wrote *Values and Violence in Auschwitz* thirty years later. Max does perform such an act when he gets medicine for Horst's cold, but once again sex is central in Sherman's vision. To get the medicine, Max has to blow an SS captain.

Bent's greatest strength is shining a light on an unexplored region of the Holocaust Kingdom, but it is often one-dimensional, poorly written, dramatically unconvincing, and even absurd. It's believable and historically accurate when a guard throws a prisoner's hat onto an electrified fence so that, when forced to retrieve it, he'll electrocute himself. But that's undercut when a guard is unbelievably explicit and almost solicitous in his instructions to Max and Horst; he'd be more likely to shout some orders and beat the two men. The SS actually knock on Max's door when they come to murder the man he picked up. The Nazis in this play can seem like figures out of a melodrama, but then the cardboard nature of the characters is well-suited to a sexual fantasy. *Bent* reveals the poverty of Sherman's imagination: he could not conceive of gays in a concentration camp without sex being central. Ironically, he confirms straight stereotypes about gay men, that even in that hellish environment, sex is still more important than anything else.

How Vast a Horror?

Just as distorting as *Bent's* foregrounding of sex is the play's claim that Jews were more fortunate in the camps than homosexuals. This claim forces you into making obscene comparisons of suffering. Do we give points? How many for a man who has to beat his dying lover, as compared, say, to a woman watching a guard smash her baby against a wall? At various times Jews, Gypsies, and homosexuals were all subjected to insane medical experiments. Should we find some way to rank them? Wouldn't it have been enough to add the anguish of German homosexuals to the world's picture of the Holocaust—why must that suffering be greater? By letting a polemical aim distort his dramaturgy, Sherman in his own small way ends up aligned with those who for different reasons ignore or blur the incontrovertible truth: Jews were always the Nazis' prime target of destruction.

Nor is this statement meant to set up a hierarchy of suffering. Gays were indeed Holocaust victims and died in higher proportions than other small groups of prisoners like Jehovah's Witnesses. It doesn't, however, serve the cause of gay rights to make exaggerated claims about their fate. Isn't it damning enough that homophobia was part of the Nazi world view, and that gays and lesbians were one of their many targets?

Writing in the 1980s, Richard Plant found assessing both the numbers of gay deaths and their circumstances difficult, given that some records had been destroyed and many were locked behind the Iron Curtain. The situation has changed dramatically since the re-unification of Germany, and we now have an invaluable book that can be read as a documentary companion to *The Pink Triangle*, namely the collection *Hidden Holocaust?* edited and introduced by German historians Gunter Grau and Claudia Schoppman. This book is essential for understanding the Nazi reign of terror against homosexuals, as well as the radically inhuman mindset that can justify any means to achieve "moral renewal" or the "moral stability of the state."

Grau and Schoppman have brought together and translated over one hundred important and representative items: Gestapo directives, speeches, legal discussions, letters, excerpts from books and articles, minutes of meetings, medical reports, newspaper articles. Amplifying upon Plant's work, their two introductions create a clear framework for this mass of carefully annotated documents, all of them deeply compelling.

The collection takes us through pre-Nazi-era homophobia in Germany through the increasingly punitive and bizarre stages of the Nazi campaign against homosexuality. Weimar Germany saw a burgeoning gay culture and an active movement to reform laws against gay men, as well as growing social and political homophobia. The early and mid-1930s brought bar closings, surveillance, beatings, censorship, and tougher anti-gay legislation. From the mid-1930s on, the campaign escalated, with stricter sentences, registration of homosexuals, "preventive detention" in concentration camps for some, and the institution of the death penalty for homosexual activity in the SS and the police.

While thousands of homosexuals were ultimately tortured, worked to death, castrated, and experimented on in concentration camps, Grau and Schoppman conclude that there was no "holocaust" of gays—hence the question mark in the book's title. This assessment is based on the wide range of contemporary documents, including court records maintained with "Prussian meticulousness." Grau discounts the current wild estimates of the number of gays killed by the Nazis, suggesting a figure closer to five thousand.

Grau finds that fifty thousand gays were sentenced during the period of 1933–1945, and five thousand of those were deported to concentration camps. While serving a prison term could mean detention in a camp afterwards, it wasn't automatic. The Nazis wanted to stifle homosexuality, but they had no interest in exterminating every homosexual. They wanted every man who could contribute to building the population to do so; they were obsessed with fighting anything they thought would result in "a general weakening of [the] nation's strength [and] military capacity."

How, then, are we to read the widely-quoted incendiary statements by Nazis like SS leader Himmler, who consistently called for the "eradication" of homosexuals? After all, Himmler commended what he claimed was the ancient German way of dealing with homosexuals, drowning them in marshes: "This was not a punishment but simply the snuffing out of an abnormal life. It had to be removed, much as we pull up nettles, put them in a heap and set fire to them." Much of this rhetoric, Grau says, was propaganda meant for public consumption.

Grau holds that in this case we have unfortunately failed "to differentiate what was said in Nazi programmes from what was actually carried out." "Extermination" is an inappropriate term to describe the panoply of Nazi "decrees, directives, orders, and prohibitions" dealing with homosexuality. In the framework of a bizarre eugenics theory, what the Nazis really wanted was to dissuade homosexuals from practicing sex through intimidation and terror. If successful, these "punishments and deterrents" would supposedly keep the birth rate high, avoid contaminating public morality, prevent the formation of anti-social cliques and the possible corruption of minors. The initial goal was "reeducation through deterrence. And anyone who could not be deterred was sent to a concentration camp: reeducation through labor. Psychology was also brought into service: reeducation through psychotherapy." Gays were "watched, arrested, registered, prosecuted, and segregated . . . re-educated, castrated and—if this was unsuccessful—exterminated."

Despite these efforts, gays were never the subject of pogroms, and never faced the danger that Jews did in Germany and occupied Europe, because all Jews were eventually targeted for extermination. Jews were doomed by their very identity—whether they practiced their religion or not. Gays could hide far more easily, and could avoid prosecution even if questioned by the Gestapo. Once arrested, if you maintained you weren't an active homosexual, you were freed unless there was proof to the contrary.

Grau makes clear that the Nazis did not have to create anti-gay policy and feeling in 1930s Germany. When they came to power, there was already "a police and judicial apparatus" in place, along with anti-gay laws. Fervent anti-gay rhetoric also marked public debate. Though there were many calls for liberalization and tolerance before 1933, and there was an active gay rights movement, all this was balanced by the clamor for harsher laws, compulsory medical treatment, preventive detention, castration, and sterilization. Under the Nazi regime, these demands were enacted into law, so that ultimately all homosexuals were victims, "whether they were interned in concentration camps, imprisoned by a court or spared actual persecution . . . the racist Nazi system curtailed the life-opportunities of each and every homosexual."

If the fate of gay men in the Holocaust has been unclear, that of lesbians is even murkier, as Claudia Schoppman writes in her separate introduction to *Hidden Holocaust?* Lesbians in the Nazi era were never uniformly seen as "a social and political danger capable of threatening the male-dominated 'national community.'" Women could, after all, bear children no matter what their proclivities, and so lesbians were not threats according to "a majority of Nazi figures specializing in population policy." Debate continued for years about enlarging the chief anti-gay law, Section 175 of the penal code, to include lesbians, but it never happened, and thus lesbians were never prosecuted with any intensity. Some may have been interned as "anti-socials," but there's little evidence of internment in concentration camps as lesbians.

What is certain is that the Nazis wiped out a "collective lesbian life-style and identity" that had developed over several decades. Lesbians suffered "destruction of clubs and other organizations of the homosexual subculture, the banning of its papers and magazines, the closure or surveillance of the bars at which they met. This led to the dispersal of lesbian women and their withdrawal into private circles of friends. Many broke off all contacts for fear of discovery and even changed their place of residence."

All this took place in a climate of intense propaganda for motherhood, incentives for marriage, and the banning of abortion. From 1936 The Reich Office for the Combating of Homosexuality and Abortion recorded all homosexual activity it came across, registered transvestites and abortionists, and monitored the production and sale of contraceptives and abortion-inducing drugs.

Hidden Holocaust? may be a collection of documents, but it is by no means dry. Time and again, voices leap out at us. Two of the most shocking pieces are in the earliest section. One is a published report of the Vatican's praise for Nazi efforts to ban obscenity. The other is a heart-wrenching anonymous appeal from soldiers to a Bishop to intervene in the mistreatment and torture of gays held in prisons without being criminally charged. The desperate soldiers appealed not only to the love of Jesus but the Fuhrer's mercy—surely he would save them if he knew how they suffered. It's bitterly ironic to contrast this hope with an article from the SS newspaper declaring that homosexuals are promoting a state controlled by other homosexuals, "just as a gangster wishes for a state run by gangsters." This, in a police state founded on terror.

How Like the Present Day?

Echoes of contemporary American intolerance make the book even more disturbing. There's an especially bizarre item that makes the current U.S. military policy on gays in the military seem almost enlightened. It's a long series of instructions on suppressing homosexuality, written by the head medical officer of the German Air Force that's so detailed it begins to read like soft-core pornography. Medical officers are warned to see that men don't sunbathe or tell dirty jokes or wrestle or listen to sexy music, because these activities (and many others) will lead to an "overheated sexual atmosphere" and gay sex among "healthy, sexually needy young men" living "in close physical and psychological companionship."

It's important to have a solid understanding of the reality faced by gays in the Holocaust before one turns to the new edition of Heinz Heger's *The Men With the Pink Triangle*. The account in Heger's book is apparently the story of an anonymous Viennese gay man as told to Heger. This man hoped his book would help change the law in Austria, which it seems to have done.

This crucial memoir offers rare insight into the period, but is hampered by everything Heger's informant could not have known about the larger context of his suffering. He mistakenly believed that gays were slated for exactly the same fate as Jews at the time, that they died by the hundreds of thousands, and that gay sex was rife in every camp. The memoir is one of the few written by gay Holocaust victims, because after the war homosexuality was still a crime in Germany. As many gay men were convicted in the 1950s and 1960s as during the Nazi era. Unlike other victims, their stories were not welcome, and the trauma of reliving what they'd suffered was allied with their continuing, very real fear of exposure.

It's a harrowing story of sudden arrest, imprisonment and subsequent beatings, humiliation, slave labor, and torture. Especially powerful is the demonstration of how prisoners were turned into "dumb and indifferent slaves of the SS." But although he was degraded and terrorized, Heger's source was ultimately lucky. He survived six years of imprisonment because he was protected by *kapos* in return for sex, and because he eventually became a kapo himself and was spared a great deal of misery. He was in no danger of starving, and could also get out of situations that might otherwise have led to his death.

Heger's book was originally subtitled "The True, Life-and-Death Story of Homosexual Prisoners in the Nazi Concentration Camps," but the publisher (Alyson) has unaccountably changed that to "The Life and Death Story of Gays in the Nazi Death Camps." It's a completely inaccurate and hyperbolic label. Heger's source was a *prisoner* in *concentration* camps (Sachsenhausen and Flossenburg), not an internee with no hope of release in an *extermination* camp like Auschwitz or Treblinka.

We're not talking about a mere semantic confusion. Both types of camp "existed outside any legal restrictions," as Plant puts it. But however horrific the conditions he witnessed and endured, Heger's Viennese gay man was not in an infernal factory whose purpose was the destruction of human beings. The introduction to the first edition of *The Men With the Pink Triangle* (1980) made this important distinction clear. It also noted that "at no time were homosexuals as such sent directly *en masse* to Auschwitz" and that during the war there was a slackening of anti-gay persecution while the frenzied assault on Jews kept mounting. For a sense of what the death camps were like, readers should consult a memoir like Primo Levi's *Survival in Auschwitz*, or Terrence Des Pres's study *The Survivor*. The death camps were infinitely more brutal and inhuman than the camps described in Heger's book.

Robert C. Reinhart's novel *Walk the Night* is an earnest attempt to create fiction out of some of the material in *The Men With the Pink Triangle*, which he acknowledges as a source. Reinhart starts the book in 1970s New York, where a dying German refugee pianist, Leda Kohl, reveals the truth of her past to her son Peter. His father was actually a gay man swept up in the 1930s by the Nazis. She lost contact with him when she fled to America, and now wants to make sure he's all right. Peter sets off for Germany to find his father, who turns out to be a rich and successful designer. Though Peter decides not to reveal his identity, he does fall in love with Sybella, his translator-guide, and they get married.

The novel has a lovely scene in which Peter finds a record store in Germany whose window is full of his mother's recordings, and there's a chilling confrontation with anti-gay neo-Nazis in a small New England college at the novel's end. Otherwise, Reinhart's ambitious book never really comes to life. The characters and the settings are flat, and the novel shows its inspiration too clearly. There are long undigested quotes from books about the Nazis and gays, and the novel reads as if the idea—fiction based on *The Men With the Pink Triangle*—was never developed beyond early drafts. If you've read Heger's memoir, you don't gain much from reading *Walk the Night*.

I hope that *Hidden Holocaust?* is just the beginning of a new wave of eye-opening scholarship about the life and death of lesbians and gay men in our century's darkest years. I also hope it is read widely in the gay and lesbian community, where there is often deep ignorance of the Holocaust. On *Gaynet* and in many gay publications, I've encountered consistent misuse of Holocaust metaphors to describe any and all incidents of discrimination. The U.S. is often compared to Nazi Germany, and any public expression of anti-gay sentiment is dubbed "Nazi." Infringement of rights are routinely dubbed a first step on the road to a fascist state—"Look what happened in Germany," the argument inevitably seems to run. Republicans get called "*Ubermenschen*," and so on. If we lambaste Rush Limbaugh for his use of the insult "feminazis," how can we speak the same debased language ourselves? It's offensive and pointless to use the Holocaust—a unique act of destruction—as a handy club with which to beat your opponent. As Elie Wiesel has said, the Holocaust is not a metaphor of anything. To use it as such is to misunderstand its reality.

The Lavender Decades

THE TITLE OF THIS SECTION is a nod to Tom Wolfe's *The Purple Decades*, a collection of his own essays that capture curious or glorious moments in New York's hip culture of the 1960s and 1970s. Lavender was of course the color of choice for the Gay Lib culture that emerged during these same decades; and that color's proximity to purple, which Wolfe associated with psychedelia, urban night life, decadence, "radical chic," and political correctness, seems quite appropriate in light of the prevailing gay culture of the day.

It was somewhere in the 1980s that the colors of Gaydom shifted from lavender to "the rainbow," a shift that can serve as a marker for two fairly distinct periods in gay and lesbian culture and politics. In the "lavender" period (ca. 1969 to the mid-1980s), gay life remained largely underground, still an "outlaw" subculture that inhabited the night and the most dangerous parts of the city, wildly vibrant in remote places like Fire Island yet all but invisible to straight society. The shift to the rainbow as a symbol coincides with a second "coming out" that started in the 1980s and is still underway, in which a national gay and lesbian subculture has emerged and gained widespread recognition as a legitimate part of American society. One feature of this change is that gays have increasingly come to be viewed as a minority group comparable to African Americans or women, albeit one whose struggle for equal protection is only partially realized. Further evidence for this mainstreaming trend is the appearance of gay and lesbian characters in movies and TV shows, increasingly in a matter-of-fact way that suggests routine acceptance of these characters. But perhaps the best evidence for this second "outing" is that gay people have become a market niche, a demographic segment that companies and advertisers recognize and pitch products to.

The commercialization of gay culture, however inevitable in the larger context of American culture, has been much lamented by many gay and lesbian writers over the past few years—and by people as politically diverse as Michelangelo Signorile, Sarah Schulman, Andrew Sullivan, Urvashi Vaid, and Daniel Harris. One senses here a certain nostalgia for the good old days, or one's own version thereof, and it seems to me that this too attests to the closing of a period in the history of the modern gay and lesbian movement: the lavender decades.

The essays in this section provide glimpses into some of the venues being frequented and times being had during this earlier period, whether at the bars, the baths, or the literary salon. The first two essays focus on the period immediately before, during, and after the Stonewall riots of June 1969. Michael Denneny, in an effort to understand what prompted the riots, takes us back to the bar scene of the Stonewall Inn and its rough-and-ready social dynamic. Karla Jay picks up shortly after the riots, again in New York, again in a story that begins in a sleazy bar scene, only this time the women decided to revolt by staging their own lesbian dance! No treatment of the lavender decades would be complete without a piece on the gay baths: Ira Tattelman provides an architectural tour of the bathhouse as a design for sex that arose in the big gay cities by the mid-1970s. Two additional pieces concern literary salons of quite different sorts. Gabrielle Glancy delves into a 1970s-style salon that was also a saloon, a San Francisco club called Red Dora's, where women read poetry and presented performance pieces in a bohemian atmosphere. Felice Picano offers a firsthand account of the first out gay literary group, the Violet Quill Club (sometimes "Lavender"), whose members, including Andrew Holleran, Robert Ferro, and Edmund White, met in each other's apartments to read their works, followed by dessert. Finally, in a long, far-ranging interview, Larry Kramer charts the history of the lavender decades' most important and devastating event: the onset of AIDS, and documents the gay world's fledgling but often heroic response to its biggest challenge.

MICHAEL DENNENY

The Stonewall Riot as Event and Idea

AS WE CELEBRATE the twenty-fifth anniversary of the Stonewall riots, much is being written about that now mythical event which is generally taken as the birth of the contemporary gay and lesbian rights movement. Much of what I have read strikes me as wrongheaded, especially the revisionist attempts by the currently politically correct to downplay the role of white males in that event. "Middle-class white men" is the term generally used, but considering the reputation of the Stonewall, or just glancing at the few photos left from that time and place, one wonders about the term "middle class"; one wonders, in fact, about the word "men." "Randy white boys" might be more accurate. Recently I read a manuscript proposal (generated by a PBS television series on gay rights) that asserted that "middle-class white men" had "stolen" (their word) Stonewall as an event, appropriating to themselves an action generated by lesbians, transvestites, and people of color. The authors offered no evidence for this statement, just blandly asserting this revision of history with the same smug and self-righteous certainty that Stalin's encyclopedists must have felt as they dutifully revised their history decade after decade.

Personally, I doubt that the Stonewall, while clearly a racially mixed bar, was ever a popular dyke hangout, or that its clientele was anything like equally divided between men and women. And while anyone who knew Marsha or Sylvia knew what a force Street Transvestite Action Revolutionaries (their term) could be in a confrontation with the cops, the contribution of either to the ongoing organizing of the gay movement is a different question.

But, in retrospect, all these squabbles to claim credit are not only petty but beside the point, except when they interfere with the attempt to ascertain historically what actually happened. They are beside the point because they misunderstand how an event like Stonewall actually comes to interact with his-

From the Summer 1994 issue

tory, becomes a part of history, or not. Stonewall was not the first time gay people had confronted the police, nor the first time we stood up for ourselves. John Preston once told me about a remarkably similar event that took place at a gay bar in Chicago a year or so earlier. The police were harassing the owners and made the patrons walk a long gauntlet of cops while being photographed entering and leaving the place. For the people involved this confrontation was as harrowing and as heroic as Stonewall, but it had no echo across the country and is now almost forgotten. There had also been a similar confrontation in L.A.

So what made Stonewall different?

Kant wrote of the French Revolution that it was not so much the event itself that was going to change the world as the quality of attention paid to it by its spectators, by those observers across Europe who watched the unfolding events in Paris and knew that something momentous had happened. It was what the spectators made of the events of the French Revolution that would change history, not what the rioters in Paris had done. In other words, it is when an event is raised to the level of an idea that it has the power to alter history through changing the consciousness of people.

I would argue that something similar is the case with Stonewall. It was definitely not the first sign of the emerging gay revolt. A year-and-a-half before Stonewall a couple of guys had started *The Advocate* in Los Angeles, at about the same time that Troy Perry established the first of the Metropolitan Community Churches, today the largest gay organization in the world. Clearly, something was afoot with gay people even before the events at Stonewall. What was missing was any sense of possibility, any alternative, to the oppression gay people faced daily everywhere they looked.

To get a sense of the mental oppression our people labored under, this lack of possibility which was so spiritually suffocating, one might look at Mart Crowley's play, *The Boys in the Band*, a much maligned work that precisely delineates the pre-revolutionary emotional situation that would lead to Stonewall. The play is about eight gay men and one straight; in essence, the gay guys, who are very unhappy and bitchy, start the evening beating up on each other and progress till their anger is directed at the straight man. What is amazing in this play is that none of the gay characters has any sense of possibility, of any way out of the trap of gay life as it was then led. Although they are clearly angry to the point of fury, the idea of gay liberation is the furthest thing from their minds. As someone who remembers the years before Stonewall, I can testify that the very concept of gay liberation would have then struck most of us, even those of us who were intensely politically active, as absurd. Being homosexual was a psychological situation, maybe a medical situation, but certainly not a political matter.

Luckily for everyone, the women's movement came along and got us to consider the notion that the personal was political: a major step forward. Then what was needed was a crystallizing moment, and the four continuous nights of rioting that the raid on Stonewall provoked offered that moment. What was decisive was not the event itself, but how people responded, the immediate, spontaneous and utterly decentralized flurry of organizing, leafletting, and pamphleteering that resulted (and which was so well documented in Donn Teal's 1971 book *The Gay Militants*). It was this response, and perhaps above all the late Craig Rodwell's determination to commemorate the event the next June with the world's first Gay Pride March, that made Stonewall the shot heard 'round the gay world.

The event had become an idea, the idea that gay people would fight back, would stand up for their rights. And ideas can change the world.

KARLA JAY

Lesbian New York

OF ALL THE MISCONCEPTIONS about the early days of lesbian-feminism, the one that rankles me the most is that we didn't have sex or fun. Maybe it's the same psychology as thinking that your parents or grandparents never had sex except for procreation. Sure, we sat in a lot of meetings, picketed and zapped a lot of establishments, but we sure did have fun. By 1980, I had slept with well over one hundred women (but who was counting?). We went to parties, and some people held orgies in their homes. And we loved to dance.

Far harder than finding someone to sleep with was finding a public space in which you could dance with another woman, strut your stuff, and show the world you had found someone special—or several someones special. Although there were many bars in New York City for men, usually only one bar for lesbians existed at any moment. In the late 1960s, Kooky's replaced the Sea Colony, and it was Kooky's that I most often frequented. Kooky's had been open for a few years on West Fourteenth Street near Seventh Avenue, and Kooky presided over the bar like a spider hovering over a web. Once you had paid your three dollars to Kooky or one of the large bouncers (all of whom smoked cigars and were named Harry), you were admitted to her premises— if you were white. Women of color were repeatedly asked for identification or "carded." While I was once stopped for being a runaway teenager when I was twenty-three, I had no trouble sauntering into Kooky's domain. Well, not "hers" really because all New York City bars were rumored to be owned by organized crime families (we called them "the Syndicate" in our leaflets). They stayed in business by regularly paying off the police.

Kooky was certainly their gatekeeper, and a formidable woman she was. She had a shellacked beehive of blond hair and favored pink crinoline dresses. A friend of mine was convinced that Kooky was really a drag queen, and in a moment of insanity brought on by alcohol, she tried to grope under Kooky's stiff slips. My companion was tossed out the door and never allowed back in. Kooky forever had a cigarette in her hand, which she would put menacingly

From the Winter 1995 issue

under your chin if you were causing any trouble or simply not drinking fast enough. "If you goils want to talk, go to choich and talk in a pew," she would intone in a thick Brooklyn accent. Then she would order you another drink, for which you would pay as fast as you could detach the three dollars from your sticky, sweating palm.

I know the bars have been the subject of some hagiography lately. Joan Nestle and others seem to have fond memories of these places. Probably they had better luck than I did. From 1964 to '68, I was a student at Barnard. By 1970, my hair was so long that it cascaded about halfway down my back in wavy disarray. I had given up ironing it to make me look like Joan Baez. For my twenty-first birthday, I got my ears pierced. (My mother saw ear piercing as akin to losing my virginity and had forbidden it—it was easier to get a drink illegally than have your ears pieced.) For years I wore long, dangling earrings. I looked more like a hippie than a femme; okay, I *was* a hippie, but I'll tell you about why I never got to Woodstock another time. Bar denizens weren't interested in Woodstock! "Are you butch or femme?" they would inquire even before asking my name. "I'm butch Monday, Wednesday, and Friday and femme Tuesday, Thursday, and Saturday. On Sunday I'm ki-ki. What day is this?" I'd answer in my most innocent manner. Potential suitors would flee, which was the point, because one time I did let a bar butch pick me up and the event turned into a nightmare.

She seemed attractive enough, her hair slicked back into a Bryl-Creemed D.A., a T-shirt under her long-sleeved Oxford shirt, and tight dungarees. She drove me to her apartment in Queens, and after we had undressed, I discovered she was completely tattooed from her collarbone to her ankles with the names of women. There was still one vacant spot over her heart, and I saw my name (probably misspelled) flashing there with a trashy valentine surrounding it. I had just read Ray Bradbury's "The Illustrated Man," and we all had learned in Psych 101 that only sailors and psychopaths wore tattoos, so I hopped back into my mu-mu and tried to figure out where the hell I was. Now I was a rather parochial Brooklynite whose family talked of Manhattan (which we called "the city") as if it were a foreign country. I realized that I had probably never been to Queens before, except passing through in my father's car. Where the hell was I? It was a scary trip home for an eighteen-year-old baby dyke at three A.M. in the subway. After that, I certainly wasn't going to allow any more bar butches to romance me into their beds, though occasionally they tried. Later on, my bar buddy Michela would get really tight sometimes and tell the meanest-looking butch in the bar I had the hots for her, just to cause me endless trouble. And though those butches would grab me and waltz me about the dance floor, crushing me against the unfiltered Camels rolled up in their sleeves and their un-camel-like breasts flattened by binders, I never let them get me as far as Queens again.

As I said, others must have had better luck! My trips to the bar usually left me broke—entry and two drinks and a tip came to ten dollars versus the fifty cents it took to get into a double feature with my student ID. I preferred vodka drinks, sugary screwdrivers, or creamy white Russians. Mixed drinks cost about the same as a beer, but the harder stuff was watered down, and the glasses were filthy. It was rumored that you could get hepatitis from those glasses as there wasn't enough alcohol in the drinks to kill even the most feeble germs. I didn't like beer much, which nevertheless I sometimes ordered. Not only did it come in a clean bottle, but it took me the whole night to get a bottle of the offensive substance down.

The one thing worse than the quality of the drinks was the endless line for the toilet. There were only two individual bathrooms at Kooky's for maybe two hundred women, so you had to plan ahead to get in line before you really had to go. As you neared the entrance to the bathroom door, a woman would hand you exactly three squares of toilet paper. I don't know why we got three rather than two or four, but it was totally humiliating for someone else (never mind that Kooky could say she was employing members of the community) to decide this intimate matter for you. Joan Nestle has written an extensive account of the ubiquitous bathroom lines. Though she views them as an attempt to keep deviants from going into the bathroom together for illicit purposes, I suspect that an equally strong motive for Kooky was to pressure you into getting back to the bar so you could order another drink. Not that she should have worried: the bathrooms were hardly a place to linger—this wasn't exactly the Ladies Powder Room at Roseland Dance City.

In short, for many of us, conditions in the bars were so oppressive and dancing was so relatively expensive that my friends and I were delighted when the Gay Liberation Front decided in late 1969 to put on dances at the Alternate University (a short block from Kooky's on Fourteenth Street and Sixth Avenue). I never did figure out what you could actually learn at the Alternate U. It was one flight up in a loft-like space. There was a large unfurnished room in front and a few smaller rooms in the back with tattered sofas, battered armchairs, and splintering foldup chairs.

IN PRINCIPLE, the dances seemed like a perfect antidote to the bars. In our post-Stonewall political fervor and naïveté, we believed that if gay men and women came to the dances, they would join the movement and show up the following Sundays at our meetings, which in the beginning met in a Village church or the Alternate U. before moving uptown to another church in Chelsea (the movement got me into far more religious institutions than my family ever could have). We were more than slightly quixotic in that out of maybe four or five hundred revelers, maybe three or four would show up at a meeting, less than a one percent return. We did best if someone got a crush on a GLF member—that might ensure meeting attendance so long as the dalliance lasted.

The dances worked better as a fundraising technique. We would collect a few dollars at the door, and because it was illegal to sell liquor without a license, we sold soda and beer for a stated "donation."

The lights would be dimmed, and fast dancing records would be played by a volunteer DJ. The room was often thick with the smell of pot and poppers, and many of my friends also took "uppers" to keep going until the dance ended at about two or three in the morning. Only about ten percent of the crowd were women. The lesbians couldn't even see each other as we were engulfed in a dimly lit, densely packed, swirling sea of men who were generally taller than we were. It also annoyed some of the lesbians that the men could take off their shirts while we could not—it was often intensely hot. Between the smell of amyl nitrate and the river of men's sweat, many of the women felt as if we had stumbled into the men's locker room at the YMCA.

Though the women never equalled fifty percent of the GLF membership, many of us were active. Lois Hart (who died many years ago) and I were among the first chairs of the organization. Many of the women, including myself, worked at the dances—collecting money at the door, selling drinks, chipping ice, running out to replace exhausted supplies of drinks and cups, and sweeping up mountains of trash after the dance ended, a chore that usually took us until about four A.M. to complete. After that, a few of us would then go to an after-hours transvestite bar around Washington Square or on lower Broadway, dance some more, and finally stagger home around seven or eight A.M., squinting all the way in the cruel morning light.

Still, most of the women were dissatisfied with the arrangement. We had long discussions at GLF meetings—almost any topic would engender debates, heated arguments, and shouting matches. When I was the chair, I went to the meetings with my softball bat, because I couldn't shout down some of the men. No, I didn't hit them: I hit a pole, but it did shut them up. At first, we were given a separate room at the Alternate U.— the one with the lovely furniture—for the women to socialize in. We would take turns guarding the door to keep men out. The couches quickly became socializing and necking meccas. The latter became a source of tension for some. Who wanted to walk in there and see your two ex-lovers getting it on with each other? Or worse yet, your current lover and your ex-lover *in flagrante delicto*? Even if you weren't involved, you didn't want to sit on anyone by mistake—it was pretty dimly lit.

I did have better luck in the back room as I met the first woman I would live with there. It wasn't exactly love at first sight, though. She had just returned from living in Amsterdam, and I had heard about her the winter before from another lover of mine, May. May often mentioned Alice nostalgically because she had been quite smitten with Alice, who had refused to "bring her out," as we called it. I clearly had no such compunctions. I had also heard about Alice from a guy I worked with at Collier's Encyclopedia. Henry was straight, but I didn't care. Underneath his teddy bear exterior topped by a mountain of curly hair, there lurked a radical pacifist with a wicked sense of humor. He did fabulous things, like trying to index Lyndon Johnson under "American Cattle Rancher" and Richard Nixon under "Dictator, American." He also mentioned a woman he was in love with. She had gone to Amsterdam and left him heartbroken. "That's cool," I said, "everyone's in Amsterdam." I didn't have a clue that they were both talking about the same woman! So when they both appeared with Alice at a dance at the Alternate U., I said, "Oops!" and ran to hide myself in the forest of tall men. Being short is an advantage at times.

But Alice pursued me, and we spent five years together. That's yet another story, but the dances were good vehicles for women to meet one another. Unlike life in the bars, only Pat Maxwell, who was also called "Peter Pan," was greatly concerned about butch and femme. She would come over to my apartment, and with the seriousness of a therapist trying to unwind some knotty problem, she would attempt to help me figure out which I was by running through a list of who had been to a meeting or dance. "Do you think Emily is hot? How about Cecile?" But much to her horror, I was omnivorous, finding everyone attractive. Occasionally, a new-age lesbian would ask me my sign at a dance—and then scurry away when I revealed I was a Pisces. Astrology was no advance over butch/femme when trying to get lucky. At several dances, one woman asked me my sign. She was extremely cute, but hers was no bear-trap memory. I hoped she was trying to find out more about me, but when I revealed my sign, she would frown, "Yuk, my husband was a Pisces!" and run away. The third time I lied and said I was a Taurus, her sign. "You're lying," she said, pointing her finger at me accusingly. And she ran away.

Yes, there were times in those days that I was definitely nostalgic for the bars. Even those sexy bar butches, now classified as politically incorrect, held you when you danced. In the hip seventies we rarely touched on the dance floor. Free drugs were easier to find than a slow song. The only time we went into the old bars was to "liberate them." On Sundays, after our meetings, some of the men and women would walk over to a bar—or pile into cars and vans if it were cold. We'd regroup in a bar we had all agreed upon, a men's bar one week and a woman's the next. On Sunday afternoon or evenings there was often no cover charge, so we would whisk past the bouncer Harry and dance in a huge circle or in three's or four's, men and women together, much to the horror of the *habitués*. Gay women almost never went into men's bars—the few times I had to go into one to wheel out a disabled friend, someone would inevitably ask in a hostile tone, "Are you lost, girl?" If I couldn't pass as a butch or femme, I certainly wasn't going to be mistaken for a fag hag! Harry kept most men out of the lesbian bars because these "dyke daddies" would stand around the edge of the dance floor and masturbate while they watched the women gyrate. It was truly gross, so Harry did have one good function anyway. It seemed crazy for gay men and lesbians to want to be in the same bar: that was for small towns where you had no choice. We danced and danced—which was also a good way to avoid having to buy a drink—and then, after an hour or so, we left. In retrospect, though we made some points about alliances between brothers and sisters, we surely did disrupt one of the few places most gay people could go to in those days.

ONE OF THESE SOLUTIONS seemed very satisfactory, so in the end the women demanded money from the GLF for a separate lesbian dance. Endless arguments later, we got the money and the reluctant acquiescence of the majority of the men, though some gay brothers were strongly supportive of our needs. We picked a date in April 1970 and booked the Alternate U. And then we panicked. What if we had a party and no one came? What if we couldn't attract more than the fifty or so regulars? Fearing failure, we turned to our heterosexual sisters in the women's movement. We asked them to come to the dance as an act of support. Many of the women I knew from Redstockings and *Rat* magazine agreed to come. I mistakenly asked one woman twice, though, and she accused me of trying to make her become a lesbian. I wasn't at all attracted to her, so I was surprised by her allegation. A year later she came out. But at this point, they didn't come out—but they came.

We also wanted to let the women in the bars know that there was now an alternative. But how? Aside from *Rat* magazine, an underground paper that had been seized by feminists and which was unlikely to be read by the denizens of the bar, and *The Village Voice*, there were few venues in which to advertise. So a few women stood outside Kooky's and Gianni's (another lesbian bar that opened in early 1970, I think) and passed out leaflets. One night, a few of us made forays into Kooky's, but she spotted us after only a few minutes and had Harry toss us out into the snow. Kooky clearly wasn't big on First Amendment rights. She read the leaflet and threatened, "If you goils keep dis up, there ain't gonna be no gay lib!"

The night of the dance was wonderful. Though it was still cold, the weather was clear. The place was packed. We were thrilled. My straight Redstockings sisters sat nervously on the make-out couches and hoped no one would ask them to dance. No one did, and they were insulted. The rest of the women seemed to be having a fabulous time as they danced to their favorite songs. We were ready to congratulate ourselves on our success. One detail made us nervous, however: we sent a spy over to Kooky's and Gianni's, and she reported that they were both fairly empty—on a Saturday night, too! We tried not to worry and kept ourselves busy chipping ice, selling drinks, and dancing.

When the dance came to a close, we began the massive cleanup. But we had made little progress when we saw several extremely large men in trench coats with guns in their belts, filling up the door of the Alternate U. They announced that they were the police. There was general panic as some women stashed pot under the couches in the back room—only the most foolhardy and least fastidious would reach under those cushions!—and other women, who were less economically minded, flushed pot, acid, and all sorts of goodies down the overworked toilets. The men said that we were selling liquor without a license. We knew that they were too large to fit into a police uniform and that police don't wear their guns in their belts. When asked for identification, they flashed something shiny and started to shove and punch some of the butcher women.

Before the dance had started, I had been given the number of Flo Kennedy, a radical African American lesbian lawyer. She said to call her in case of trouble at the dance. I had her number inked on the back of my hand—the 1970s version of the Filofax. Someone had to escape and contact her. There were no phones in the place, and even if there were, calling for help would have gotten me reprocessed into Swiss cheese. Another woman and I headed for the back stairs—it was always good to know more than one way out. One of the guys saw us make a dash towards the fire exit, and he charged after us—actually, he lumbered. I ran down the stairs and heard what I hoped was the metal door slam behind me. I had never heard a gun fired, and I wasn't about to inquire now. When we got into the cold night air, we decided that the closest pay phone was in front of Kooky's bar, less than a block away. We ran over there and called Flo, who she told us she'd get the police—it wouldn't hurt to call more cops if the others were real—and the press.

As we finished our business in the phone booth, two men emerged from Kooky's. They were not employees but drunks who had accidently walked into a lesbian bar and were tossed out. They were enraged and looking for the first lesbians in sight in order to kill them. And there we were in the phone booth. (In those days there were still self-contained phone booths, which doubled as urinals.) This was obviously not our lucky night. They asked us if we had been in the bar, and we truthfully told them no. They didn't believe us and show-ered us with a stream of abuse calling us "pussy suckers" and other names. They threatened to kill us. I again denied having been in the bar. They asked us what we were doing in a phone booth at that hour of the night? "Fixing it, we're from the phone company," I replied nervously. I was so upset that I lit-erally pulled the receiver out of the phone. "See, it's broken." They had to agree and tottered down the street.

When we got back to the loft, the fray was over. The media had come, the men had fled, and the police had also arrived. The police denied that anyone from the vice squad or alcohol commission had been sent over. They left, but never found the culprits. The media left, after receiving our thanks. Several women had been bullied and hit, but no one was seriously injured.

Despite our close escape and the message that we were supposed to get from those thugs, we were not deterred. We started to have women's dances on a regular basis. Each dance drew more women. When the bars saw that they would not go out of business from an occasional dance, they stopped harass-ing us and even let us leaflet outside (some let us inside).

What does this story mean for us almost a quarter-century later? It means that some of the things we take for granted today, such as the right to dance outside the confines of the bar, did not always exist, and in many states same-sex couples couldn't dance publicly, even in a bar. This story is an example of how we must fight for what we want and never give in in the face of resistance, even at the risk of our lives. And when we do choose to fight, eventually we will win—although certainly not all battles are won as quickly as this one was.

The message is also not to be complacent. We could have been while we were singing and dancing in circles and in pairs at our dance, but we weren't. We could have immediately considered our efforts a success, but we always kept a wary eye on the door. So must we, whatever victory we win or however joyfully we celebrate Stonewall or some legislative gain, be wary, for the tiger is always outside the gate, ready to pounce. It is foolish to think that those who have power and oppress and those who profit from power and oppression will just give up their privilege without a struggle. What appears to be a gift may be fraught with danger. Few gifts are bestowed without a purpose or without something that must be given in return.

We must also not be complacent in another way. We must not celebrate those gains we have obtained without keeping one eye open so that our oppressors do not take those small "gifts" back from us. The few victories we have won are not inalienable rights. Ask any gay man or lesbian who has been attacked in the streets. Ask anyone who has lost a job or an apartment or a child. Yes, celebrate, but do so with caution.

IRA TATTELMAN

The Rise and Fall of the Gay Bathhouse

BATHHOUSES have long been places where shared activities of various sorts occur. In Greek, Roman, Islamic, Japanese, Finnish, and Turkish cultures (among others), they have acted as spaces for gathering, repose, communal ritual, and physical stimulation.

New York, as a city of immigrant groups, has a unique history with bathhouses because of this built-in constituency. Public bathhouses gained popularity at the beginning of this century, but only for a brief period of time. A change in health standards and economics motivated landlords and builders to bring bathing functions into private homes. By mid-century, the public baths had closed or were renovated for other uses.

Private baths opened as commercial ventures. Some developed as an urban counterpart to the country club, a private space for gentlemen to gather. The Everard Baths, for instance, located on Twenty-eighth Street, was easily accessible from major hotels and travel routes. Other bathhouses developed into places where the surrounding ethnic communities gathered, places for bathing, relaxing, and recreating. Through the years, many of the baths began to attract and/or cater to homosexuals. In time, some began to exclusively serve homosexuals.

The shifting nature of bathhouse type is important to my study. As built structures, the baths have been amazingly adaptable to the changing communities that have used them. I am interested in the layering of use onto this building type that produced a texture unforeseen by the original designers. Unfortunately, few photographs or documents have been collected regarding their history and development. Many have been torn down or rebuilt for other uses, and the few that remain are in danger of being closed or gutted. My own research will need to excavate individual buildings to understand how the present lives of these baths relate to the past physical and architectural experiences that took place within them.

From the Spring 1995 issue

The Public Bath

The public bath movement developed out of a desire to upgrade the standards of public health and morality in the city. Reformers believed that a reciprocal relationship existed between character and a clean environment. Like the museums, libraries, and parks that were also developed at the turn of the century, the baths were built to embody and promote "Victorian" propriety among the working class and immigrants. Proponents wanted to Americanize these people by teaching the mainstream values that would enhance the lives of the poor. They also hoped to create a community center with the bathhouse as a replacement for the bar.

While most middle- and upper-class apartments had bathtubs, few tenements were equipped with one. The first successful indoor public bathhouse opened in New York City on the Lower East Side in 1891. An inscription above the doorway arch proclaimed "Cleanliness is Next to Godliness." By 1902, there was one municipal bath open year-round, fifteen floating baths open during the summer, and several smaller ones under the sponsorship of private organizations. By 1912, no fewer than twelve municipal baths were in operation year-round. The inclusion of bathtubs in all new tenements, however, slowed the public bath movement. By 1934, only eleven percent of the apartments in New York City were without baths or showers and most public baths had closed their doors.

The bathhouse building was generally designed to contrast with neighboring tenements. But compared to other public buildings, the exterior was deliberately modest as a "welcoming" gesture to the poor. Architects designed the interiors of the small buildings for speed and sanitation. The shower and dressing chambers were divided by partitions and screens. Men were kept separate from women not only in the baths but also in the waiting rooms and lobbies.

The baths were scattered throughout the city to cater to individual neighborhoods. This not only brought baths directly to the people, but insured that different ethnic, racial, and class groups would not mix. Homosexuals, however, are not physically identifiable, nor did they congregate in one neighborhood. Their "difference" could be masked and then unveiled to certain people at certain times. Bathhouses and public showers were plentiful in major urban centers during a period when many people could not afford private washing facilities. Although they were not, by and large, the gay sexual institutions of the pre-AIDS 1970s and 1980s, a few baths in New York City were notorious as meeting places for sex. After meeting in these public spaces, men generally made appointments to see each other in more private locations.

The Russian and Turkish baths used the principle that supplying heat to the surface of the body was good for hygienic, remedial, and curative purposes. Food, conversation, games, and sometimes sexual pleasure became part of the experience. Because the user spent long hours at the baths, the owners needed to promote a sense of ease for their patrons. The sites were easily located and accessible, and the layout and program offered efficiency, comfort, and cleanliness.

The bathhouse also relied on its physical setting; the artistry of the space had commercial value. Decorations and fittings, while rarely extravagant, were desirable and necessary features. From glazed tiles, painted murals and mosaic floors to stained glass domes, ornamental wooden partitions, and brass water spouts, the owners paid attention to spatial design and social arrangement by creating the illusion of foreign luxury. An 1893 marketing brochure for the Everard Baths reads: "This most complete and beautiful bathing establishment in the world was opened to the public on May 3, 1888 . . . at a cost of over $160,000." Nothing was left undone to render it the most complete and elegant institution of its kind. The bathhouse offered a sense of historical continuity with many of the people who used them. It also established a sense of solidarity and pride within the communities who inhabited them.

The Gay Bathhouse

> More amenable to the interests of gay men were the private Russian and Turkish baths that dotted Manhattan. . . . Gay patronage and sexual activity were concentrated at two kinds of baths: baths visited by straight as well as gay men but whose management tolerated limited homosexual activity, and those that catered to gay men by excluding non-homosexual patrons and creating an environment in which homosexual activity was encouraged and safeguarded.
>
> —George Chauncey (*Gay New York: Gender, Urban Culture,
> and the Making of the Gay Male World, 1890–1940* [1994]).

The St. Marks Baths on the Lower East Side in Manhattan provides a good example of the gradual change in patrons. Built in 1913 as the St. Marks Russian and Turkish Baths, it catered to businessmen in the area. As businesses began to move, the baths became popular with neighborhood residents. In the 1950s, the establishment served older Jewish men during the day and gay men at night. In the 1960s, it became exclusively gay, although St. Marks was considered unclean and uninviting. Bought and refurbished by Bruce Mailman in 1979, the baths were redesigned for gay sexual expression in all its variety. In 1985, the bathhouse was closed by the city due to the AIDS crisis. The building has been boarded up ever since and is currently for sale.

> Bruce Mailman did not invent the gay bathhouse, he merely perfected it. . . . The Penn Post baths, near Madison Square Garden, had been popular at rush hour in the fifties. The Continental Baths in the Ansonia Hotel had a cabaret that spawned Bette Midler and Barry Manilow in the early seventies. The Everhard [*sic*] catered to the Greenwich Village set. And then there was the St. Mark's Baths, a local fixture since 1907 [*sic*]. At its peak, the St. Marks Baths was the hotbed of a revolution in public sex that crystallized for many homosexual men of his generation the very essence of what it meant to be gay in America in the late seventies and early eighties.
>
> —Brooks Peters ("The Sexual Revolution Mailman Delivered,"
> *Out* magazine, July/August 1994)

The proliferation of gay bathhouses is part of a particular period in the gay movement, the years between the Stonewall Riots and the outbreak of AIDS. The bathhouse offered gay men the safety and freedom within which to explore a multiplicity of interactions, social as well as sexual ones. Sensual pleasure was the predominant motive, one that sought not just the achievement of orgasm but also the exploration of the erotic possibilities of the whole body, and the promise that almost any fantasy could be fulfilled. As such, the bathhouse became a place of difference for closeted, bisexual, and openly gay men. Assumptions and beliefs were questioned by the disparate mix one could find and the possibilities of unrestricted sexual activity. The place, however, was not without the biases of the surrounding environment. Racist, competitive, and phobic social relations from outside were brought into the baths.

Even so, gay bathhouses were extremely popular. In 1973, there were close to a half-million members nationwide in the Club Baths chain, making the Club Baths the largest national gay organization. In 1982, before the discovery of HIV, there were at least 169 gay baths located in most major cities. In 1994, a similar listing in *Steam* magazine had a total of 61.

THE GAY BATHS tried to remain inconspicuous. Visibility represented risk; the institution could only operate and survive if it did not attract public attention. Appearing timeless and separated from the world, the bathhouse represented an attempt to break the barriers that separate people. It tried to equalize the patrons through a uniform dress code, namely the distribution of a white towel, and through the dimness of the lighting, which favored the other senses over sight. As the individual retreated behind the door, one's "street" identity disappeared.

Entering the bathhouse involved some screening as well as a number of locked doors; no one entered the system unannounced. Inside this closed environment, communication among patrons often occurred through codes rather than words. The codes of the bathhouse included body placement, eye contact, hand gestures, and the arrangement of the towel. The places were often wordless but not silent. A patron heard endless music, urgent moans, the jangling of keys, and the latching and unlatching of doors.

The boundaries of the bathhouse were clearly marked and developed in relation to the body. They formed an exact but incomplete enclosure; the wood panel dividers between cubicles never reached the ceiling. Even when a room was closed to view, it was never closed to sound. One's erotic utterances were linked to all the others that were happening at the same time. The spectator and spectacle had merged. At the St. Marks, a particularly fragile boundary occurred in the café where clothed men awaiting entry sat on one side of the counter while men in towels or nude sat on the other. The interaction of these two groups defined the bathhouse as much as the sexual contact that took place upstairs. Entering the building, one accepted a position in the performance and rituals of the space.

The baths, through the infrastructure of security, the placement of a support staff, and the spatial juxtapositions of activities, suggested certain paths and practices. The choreography of the spaces, the marks and boundaries that indicated what was seen/scene and not seen/scene, became particularly relevant in this culture of looking and touching—but also, looking and not touching, or even touching without looking.

In studying the St. Marks, I have discovered some of these spatial relations in the building construction. The east wall compared the tight individual spaces of the upper floors to the large collective spaces of the lower floors through the placement of plumbing and interior "walls"; one can contrast and relate the water of the sink and toilet to the water in the pool or Jacuzzi, or the space of a 4′ × 6.5′ cubicle to the space of a 16′ × 26′ orgy room. The west wall describes the circulation spaces, a circuit for cruising. The bathhouse invited a continuous flow of traffic repeatedly passing each room, sometimes finding a door open and inviting, sometimes closed. The red toned corridors that separated the long array of numbered rooms were as cramped and constricted as the cubicles.

The safety these spaces offered cannot be overemphasized; the bathhouses were places where mainstream society came under question. The variety of sexual contacts and the number of sexual partners a man could have were considerable. This strategy of exploration and exchange opened up new relations between and among men. The authority of desire was celebrated, and with it the promise of repetition and diversity. The baths became a magnetic force for many gay men, who perceived the bathhouse to be without limits or prohibition.

The boundaries of "traditional" values were constantly being tested and threatened. The actions of the men who visited the bathhouses celebrated their difference from the mainstream even if, outside the bathhouse, they helped make up the mainstream. As an example, some married men used the bathhouse as an anonymous outlet for homosexual experimentation.

> He goes there purely for the sex and has no interest in having any social contact with any of the people in the baths other than the most casual of conversations. He does not reveal his identity in any way. He signs the enrollment book with a false name and address.

One of the attractions of the baths, of course, is the almost complete anonymity that they offer:

> Such a setup is perfect for a respectable married man, such as Jack, who wishes to have some homosexual satisfaction without becoming involved in the social and interpersonal aspects of the homosexual community. . . . He goes in and has sex. This may happen once or twice. When he feels sexually gratified, he will leave the baths and go home.
>
> —Martin Hoffman (*The Gay World: Male Homosexuality and the Social Creation of Evil*, [1968])

Bathhouse buildings, which had begun with one purpose in mind, often shifted to another. The changing communities who appropriated these buildings had different needs and wants; they and the owners made modifications to the architectural space to effectively serve these new purposes. By placing one use on top of another, by altering and innovating old structures rather than building new ones, diverse environments were produced.

The communities and owners intensified material surfaces and boundaries; arranged and rearranged the hierarchy of spaces; heightened issues of scale, sensuality, and surveillance; eroticized encounters through intimacy and surprise; and established relations between things, relations that were implied by the proximity of bodies and the juxtaposition of different kinds of activities.

The sites of the bathhouse are again being transformed. During the 1970s and early 1980s, a total of sixteen gay bathhouses operated in New York City. Today, six have been torn down. Five have been converted for other uses including: restaurant, wholesale market, dance club, and personnel office. Two, although closed, retain the remnants of the bathhouse. Only three remain open for business, and they operate very differently now as a result of AIDS.

In an attempt to rediscover the bathhouse, I hope to uncover the possibilities in these social spaces, the potential of these "inaccessible" sites. As we approach the millennium, many architects are attempting to re-inscribe architecture with new possibilities. I believe the role of the architect is to expose the displacements to which we have become immune and to carve out forgotten spaces to allow occupation to take place. Taking on such charged spaces as the bathhouse is a step in the right direction.

FELICE PICANO

The Real Violet Quill Club

IF YOU HAPPENED to be in or around New York City in early March of 1980 looking for something interesting and fashionable to do, and if you happened to turn to the "in" newspaper of the time, *The Soho Weekly News*, you would have come across an article by Australian scholar Dennis Altman titled "A Moveable Brunch: The Fag-Lit Mafia."

Altman used this quite sizable essay to announce and at the same time to gently tweak a group of seven openly gay Manhattan authors who had not only come out in their work, but who willy-nilly had formed a writing group, sometimes called the Lavender Quill and at other times the Violet Quill. Altman had been observing and critiquing the American gay scene and he—and the editors of the paper—evidently found the group both unique and, after all, not that unusual. Since Stonewall, gays seemed to be grouping together to do *something* or other all the time. What neither Altman nor the editors nor indeed the members of the Violet Quill realized at the time was that in a few years his joking title for them, "Fag" or "Gay Lit Mafia"—would be taken up in a more sinister fashion, used by others—usually outside New York, sometimes on the fringes of American life altogether—who had *not* interviewed the seven writers, *not* read their work, *not* followed their careers as Altman had; others who'd never met any of the seven, or had done so only in passing, say, at a reading in their city.

These out-of-town writers were often disillusioned by their failed attempts to break into publishing, their work having been rejected by the same book and magazine publishers who so regularly, and to them so egregiously, featured the work of the New York seven. No wonder they came to believe that this group controlled gay publishing in the country, though even a cursory study of the industry would reveal otherwise. No wonder they came to blame the writers for their own lack of success, and, later on, when other, younger writers were published, saw them as cohorts, all of it a conspiracy to establish a stranglehold over American gay literature.

From the Spring 1995 issue

Felice Picano

The few glimpses of these disaffected writers' handiwork that I managed to see—letters to the editor, reviews, essays—showed them to be deeply paranoiac and aggrieved. Several of us in the New York writing group, especially those who'd received the most public attention, Andrew Holleran, Edmund White, and myself, came under attack: vicious, slanderous, indeed, our lawyers assured us, libelous attack. These attacks might have gone on indefinitely if some of us hadn't countered with threats of legal action. From then on, the snipers operated from a distance, resorting to bizarre schemes: false telegrams and reports of our activities to various news organs, even letters to one of us purporting to come from another—all to sow dissent.

Naturally, we were astounded by all the publicity and even more astounded by the vituperation, and mostly that anyone cared what we did in private. Because that's what the Violet Quill Club was, after all, a private and really kind of desultory meeting of seven gay men who knew each other socially and happened to be writers, who decided to get together less than a dozen times over the course of a year-and-a-half to read and discuss works in progress. So why did we attract both articles and arrows?

Perhaps because of who we were. The members of the Violet Quill Club were Edmund White and his lover of the time, Christopher Cox, Andrew Holleran, George Whitmore, Robert Ferro and his lover of many years, Michael Grumley, and myself. Our one guest was Vito Russo, who read from his book in progress, *The Celluloid Closet*.

Edmund read selections from what would become A *Boy's Own Story*, Holleran from what would become *Nights in Aruba*, Ferro from *The Family of Max Desir*, Whitmore short stories published in *Christopher Street*. Grumley read novel excerpts: one from a never completed novel titled "A World of Men," published as "Public Monuments" when it appeared in my 1981 anthology, A *True Likeness*. Other sections appeared in Grumley's posthumously published novel, *Life Drawing*. Chris Cox read short stories and a piece from his nonfiction book A *Key West Companion;* and I read pieces published in various magazines and eventually in the books *Slashed to Ribbons in Defense of Love* and *Ambidextrous*.

That list of books might justify Altman and *The Soho Weekly News'* interest in the group—it might even justify the "outsiders'" outrage. You may have read several, possibly all, of those books. After a decade-and-a-half, most are still in print, and as a group they've come to represent a kind of early high-water mark in gay writing.

But more crucially, that list explains why a reading and discussing forum was needed in the first place. At the time, the seven of us found ourselves in the position of being just about the only serious openly gay authors we knew of with whom we *could* discuss how to present the gay material we were struggling with. Even a writer as sociable and well-connected as Edmund found little camaraderie or comfort in this area from the older, better known, mostly closeted gay authors he dined and partied with.

Let me stress that. We were alone and we were first. How alone? How much first? Take this example. In the late summer of 1978, when I completed a final draft of my novel, *The Lure*, and was just meeting most of the members of what would become the Violet Quill Club, my agent and my editor at Delacorte, both far-seeing yet practical women, took me to dinner. They told me they loved my novel and would push it as hard as they could. But I must be realistic. If the book failed, or even if it succeeded, I might never again be published—at least not by a mainstream press, not under my own name. No one had ever gotten away with what I was trying to do: that is, to write and publish a provocative tell-it-like-it-is openly gay novel. My promising writing career might be ended. A month after our dinner, *Dancer from the Dance* was published and was a wild success: but Holleran was an unknown author and had written under a pseudonym. So I went into the year 1979 believing it very well might be my last as Felice Picano the author.

As recently as 1989, I was in the Brill Building, where many of Hollywood's New York-based film directors and producers had offices, meeting Frank Perry for lunch, when Paul Schrader and Brian de Palma came out of an elevator. Several years earlier, I'd met de Palma to discuss a project that had never taken off, so we shook hands. As Perry and I stepped into the elevator, we overheard de Palma say to Schrader, who'd evidently just asked who I was, "he wrote that cult best seller . . . that gay thriller." So, my agent and editor had been partly right. Even though since then I had published two well-received non-gay books, in their eyes, I was type-cast: a gay writer.

But when we seven writers gathered for that first session of the Violet Quill Club in George Whitmore's not-quite-legally-sublet Washington Square North apartment, we were not—as others later said—planning a takeover of world gay literature.

Instead we felt it was us against an incredulous, uncaring world. Yes, it was a sort of mutual admiration society. We each liked what the other was writing. And we did share the view that there was so much of gay life around us to write about, and that few had written about it before with any authenticity, from inside as it were, nor in much detail. At the time, gay culture seemed to us to be on an unstoppable upward spiral: by the late 1970s, fashion, design, and the pop music worlds were almost completely dominated by gays and gay values. Places like Greenwich Village, San Francisco's Castro, and West Hollywood were dynamic gay areas; and there were even newer gay communities in Boston, D.C., Chicago, Houston, Dallas, Atlanta, and Denver, with Fire Island, Laguna Beach, and Key West bursting into existence as gay resorts. Just writing about the people and places, the new modes of behavior and relationships, could take years, there seemed to be so much that was fresh and different.

How were we to present this brave gay new world in literature? Did we take old forms and remodel them to fit the material? Or was it necessary to break new formal ground? How much sex should be included in our writing? Some of us thought: as much as possible to push it in the straights' faces. Others thought we ought to be more blasé and write as though everyone in America felched twice a day, discussed varieties of smegma, and personally knew a Golden Shower Queen. At times we got hung up in grammar itself. For example, if a first-person narrator referred to another male character by the female pronoun "she" only and always, would the reader ever guess that "she" was a male? Everywhere we turned, there seemed to be a new problem!

That we lasted as a group as long as we did was amazing given how quickly gay literature grew at the time. By the middle of 1980, we were all on crazy schedules, often a continent apart, and it would take weeks for us to mesh schedules to meet for a single evening. By then, too, philosophical differences had arisen. One example: Robert Ferro insisted that it was crucial that gays and lesbians reconcile with their—mostly homophobic—families, and that this reconciliation be a major theme in gay literature. Whereas I felt that while separation from family—no matter how it had occurred—made lesbians and gays uniquely able to critique the disaster of American heterosexuality, our literature ought to ignore their dysfunctions and concentrate on how to make a new world.

Another problem was that in the space of a year we were no longer equal: some had become more famous than others. Of course, some had always been more ambitious than others—not necessarily the most successful. Divahood came to full bloom at our meetings. And adding to the difficulty, several of us were involved in relationships which now ended—with the usual messiness. George Whitmore and I had stopped sleeping with each other early on in the club's life, but Edmund and Chris broke up after we'd met several times. Then, too, unsuspected rivalries arose. One reader would take umbrage at another "poaching" on what he'd come to see as some locale of his "literary territory," and would retaliate by taking longer to read than he was supposed to— far, far, longer—and then become irate when we forced him to shorten or altogether forgo his discussion time.

From the beginning, we'd always had dessert. At first it was a simple coffee-and-sweets break between two sets of readers. But as the readings became longer and our meetings further and further apart and more difficult to arrange, the desserts became more elaborate, larger and more expensive: I particularly recall an enormous, glittering castle of Black Forest cake. Finally, Andrew Holleran admitted, "I'll come to the next meeting. But only for the dessert."

He managed to draw criticism from the others, especially house-proud Robert Ferro, because although we were supposed to meet in each apartment on a round-robin basis, after five meetings we'd still not been invited to Holleran's flat. I was sent to look at the offending East Village apartment, and one look was enough for me to agree that the "Tomb of Ligea," as Holleran had named the place, was indeed deadly accurate. I declared it unfit for human occupancy, offering my apartment for him to serve as host.

Even with all these problems, it required but one utterly stupid argument for the group to end. It happened in my apartment. George Whitmore was reading and stopped suddenly and asked where Holleran was. After a search, Holleran was discovered behind my big sofa on the floor. I couldn't tell whether he was laughing himself into hysterics or simply holding his ears because he didn't want to hear what was being read. George walked out of that meeting, and a series of telephone and in-person negotiations followed to try to keep the group together.

Innocent me, I thought the source of the problem was merely Whitmore being annoyed by Holleran, which anyway would have been turnabout-is-fair-play. Earlier in the year, Holleran had complained that Whitmore's story, "Last Dance," was a rip-off of his own work, and even I'd had cause to complain to George about his turning my anecdotes about friends into "The Black Widow," a story he'd published in *Christopher Street*. That had gotten me into Serious Dutch with the real-life characters, including one dangerously bad-tempered body-builder.

But no, this turned out to be a great deal more complicated: the story Whitmore had read, "Getting Rid of Robert," was a more-or-less satirical look at the effects of a gay couple's breakup on their social set, and some details were evidently—but unbeknownst to me—a bit too close to Ed and Chris's own recent split. They were naturally mortified. Worse, Robert Ferro and Michael Grumley, whose long-term marriage was open enough to include "boyfriends," had just themselves gone through a rocky patch, and I suppose one of them had mentioned it to George and now they were both offended, certain the story was about them.

George defended his right to write about anything and anyone he wanted, and my own diplomatic skills were too poor to get past these resentments and put the Violet Quill back together again. Six of us, with new boyfriends and lovers, continued to socialize after George left. We never met again as a group but we did continue to read each other's work pre-publication, making comments and suggestions, until illness and death pulled us apart forever. The three of us left—Holleran, White, and I—still do send each other work or read it aloud, although it's always one-on-one, and far friendlier.

And, while we weren't looking, the Violet Quill has become "legendary" as the first gay writing group. At least one book-length biographical study on us and our work has been signed up by a publisher, and last year's *Violet Quill Reader* came in for the expected share of kudos and barbs, genuflections and— as always and without any surprise—vicious attacks. Professors used to come to my apartment and scour my extensive journals for relevant data. Now a distinguished library has collected our papers—even George Whitmore's—and they go there.

It's an odd sort of notoriety, and not nearly as useful as you might suppose. At a recent literary do, I was flirting with a young man who began telling me that his favorite writers were members of the Violet Quill. "Oh, really," I said, meanwhile checking my wallet to make sure I was carrying protection for the stupendous bout of lovemaking that would doubtless ensue, "I was one of them." He didn't believe me! Even when I pulled out my driver's license. In his mind, if I really was a member of the Violet Quill, I should not be middle-aged and hitting on him, but instead ancient or, better yet, dead.

We seven never took ourselves all that seriously. In the early 1980s, we used to visit the Ferro family beach house on the Jersey shore, a rambling Victorian with decks and sunrooms looking out to a tidal estuary and colorful Catamarans atilt on the sand. We all referred to it as Gaywyck, and we'd retitled the guest rooms, "The Princesse Louise sur Mer Suite," "Garbo's Garage," and other such sillinesses. One weekend Robert and Michael drove to the Sea Girt train station to pick up Edmund, Cox, Holleran, and myself. As we headed toward the shore, Robert stopped short, swerving the midnight blue Firebird wildly on a bridge to avoid hitting another car.

"Careful!" Edmund chided, "If we all died in this car, think how long it would take for gay literature to recover!"

A moment of silent thought was followed by one of us saying, "Ten minutes! At the most!"

"Five," someone else piped in.

"Three and a half!"

And finally, "It wouldn't even notice!"

GABRIELLE GLANCY

Behind the Door at Red Dora's

FOR THE FIRST three years I lived in San Francisco, I was married to a performance artist and I never went out of the house. The literary scene seemed to me dormant. Of course, the fact that I wasn't open to it makes it hard for me to tell if it was out there at all. There was this place we had heard of, Red Dora's—a cabaret-café-performance space owned and run by the lesbian duo Lynn Flipper and Harriet Poon—but it seemed boring or dangerous or something. Stuff was going on there, we sensed that, but who knew what it was? It had this aura of the speakeasy for me, a place you had heard about but were never sure was real.

In fact, until I actually went to Red Dora's, six months before Martha and I broke up, I thought the place was called The Red Door. And I pictured it as just that—a threshold with nothing behind it. A kind of queer literary underground where performance art simply went in and came out, I imagined that the place literally was underground. Boring, dangerous, exotic, Red Dora's had that air of mystery so familiar to me: it seemed to occupy the same space that lesbians did before I came out.

So one day Martha says, "Let's go." Some of her new journalist friends were performing, and she wanted to check it out. Curious, I grudgingly agreed. (In all honesty, my main goal in those days was to intercept any passes that might be thrown her way.) We sat on "the shelf," which is what I have come to term this long six-inch-wide bench that goes the length of the place, itself as narrow as a bowling lane. That night the theme was "the hairball," taken from a Penny Perkins story, and the title of the show was "What is a Lesbian Date?" Everyone was wearing cat fur scotch-taped to their clothes like some new armband or coded souvenir. This handsome yellow lab romped like the rest of us between girls' laps and chair legs, and I was mesmerized. I had entered, really for the first time in my life, the free-wheeling heady world of girls watching girls make art.

Kris Kovick, cartoonist-writer-producer and self-proclaimed intellectual

From the Spring 1995 issue

air guitarist, inventor of the term "hairball," which has come to mean the incestuous lesbian tangle in which your lover leaves you for your best friend, read a story about the circumstances surrounding the assassination of San Francisco's gay supervisor Harvey Milk—a story that was so convoluted and brilliantly done, I had to admit I was listening! "She's a genius," I whispered to Martha, whom I had almost forgotten was still there next to me. There was this singer-songwriter, I seem to remember, and then a report-back about some insane "women's farm" by Robin Stevens, former editor of *Out/Look*, and her journalist friend, this small, dark, brainy girl with Trotsky glasses. Six months later, Martha and I would break up; our house burned down two days before we moved out of it and I ruptured a disk and had emergency back surgery. In the months that I was recuperating, having moved into a new neighborhood, it turned out Kris Kovick lived around the block. I met her in the park one day walking her dog Sam. Suddenly, I had a private invitation to Red Dora's, first to hear a torch song cabaret, then to one of Kris's shows. How Red Dora's has figured in my personal life is a story in itself. Suffice it to say that little dark-haired girl, who was herself a well-known journalist, became Girlfriend #2, which seems an appropriate name for her, as both her story and Martha's appeared in a Red Dora's anthology (edited by Robin Stevens) entitled *Girlfriend Number One*.

At Red Dora's I have heard the work of brilliant unknowns and mediocre knowns from all over the country in shows with titles as diverse as "Lesbian Literary Binge and Purge Night" and "Ain't I a Woman?" starring Kate Bornstein. "Cross-Pollination" is how Kovick would describe what she's aiming for in the mix of queer talent she attracts and showcases here. The shows, often riffing off of or contorting themes Kovick facetiously concocts, are, according to the emcee herself, "often political and sometimes dreadful." The fun is not only in the shows themselves but in the people who come to them: the performers come right out of the audience. At Red Dora's in a single night it would not be unusual to see Jewelle Gomez read from a new novel, Alison Bechdel (*Dykes to Watch Out For*) narrating a slide-show retrospective tracing the origin of her present comic characters, a hilarious homeless street musicologist singing country and western queer, and Joan Jett Blakk in high drag lambasting the news. At Red Dora's I have seen, to name a few, Justin Bond, Miss Betty Pearl, Juliana Leuking (a New York performance artist), Alison Wright, Louise Rafkin, Jacqueline Woodson (*Autobiography of a Family Photo*), and even the twisted ukelele-plucking Pineapple Twins.

When I was finally healed, I read there myself (at Kris's request) from a book I had recently finished called *Fire*. It was that moment the seeds for this article were planted. When I looked out over the audience, girls packed in "tits to clits"—that night was free to butch girls in femme drag—the aroma of intimacy, talent, and sex was palpable and pervasive. I was struck with what I could only call "nostalgia for the present." That is, I had the sense I would remember this night, this place, this moment. "Red Dora's is a moment in history," I said to myself, and then a moment later to the audience who, I sensed, knew exactly what I meant.

AN INTERVIEW WITH LARRY KRAMER

by BETSY BILLARD

"Life Is about Climbing Mountains"

I CONDUCTED the following interview with Larry Kramer for the *HGLR* the spring of 1995. Larry Kramer, founder of ACT-UP and co-founder of the Gay Men's Health Crisis (GMHC), is known both as an activist and a writer. His writings include the groundbreaking 1978 novel *Faggots* and his widely produced play, *The Normal Heart*, about the AIDS epidemic in its early years.

BETSY BILLARD: In your book, *Reports from the Holocaust*, you say that you bristle when you are referred to as an activist. Why does that word bother you?

LARRY KRAMER: Because I don't think I'm doing what anyone else shouldn't be doing and I consider activism part of my daily schedule. It's the makeup of my life. It implies that if I didn't do it I'd be a pacifist, I guess.

BB: But, you were a pacifist before AIDS.

LK: Well, you shouldn't have to get AIDS to do what you do. I don't do it particularly because I want to. I do it because I have to. I would just as soon not have to do it. All of this stuff just makes me so angry that it makes me do it, because nobody else seems to be out there doing it, or very few are. I've discovered that I'm good at it. The word activist doesn't bother me. I think what you're referring to was at an earlier time. I think in those days the word had connotations of the great unwashed or being a scruffy troublemaker, which I proceeded to become.

BB: You are very judgmental in your writings. You attack people who don't do as you do. At your age and with your knowledge, isn't it unrealistic to expect all gay men and lesbians to have your concerns?

LK: I think most accomplishments in life are achieved because you do attempt to reach the impossible. Life is about climbing mountains. Expectations should be high. There's nothing wrong with that. It doesn't mean it's going to happen, but it doesn't mean you can't want it.

From the Summer 1995 issue

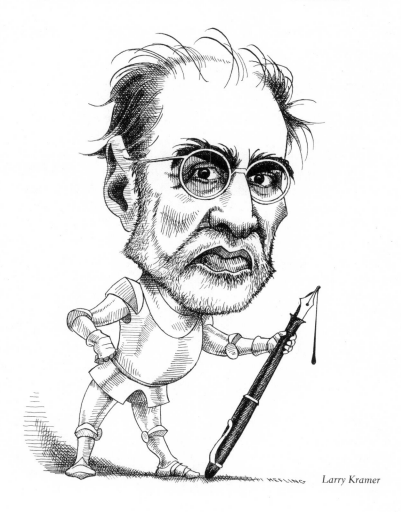

Larry Kramer

BB: What was the general reaction to most of your writing and speeches? Did most people say, "Larry. Enough. Don't tell me how I should live my life"?

LK: I've had every reaction possible. No matter what you do, there will be certain people who will approve and certain people who will disapprove, so you might as well do what you want to do. Some people don't like what I do and others give me a lot of support. I get a lot of mail. But that's irrelevant. You don't do things because of what people think. You do them because you have the need to do them. If you can be dissuaded because of public opinion, then you aren't the person who should be doing them.

175

BB: When you think back on your life before AIDS, is it hard to think about where you were then and where you are now?

LK: My mind doesn't work that way, but as a writer I'm certainly conscious that there have been different periods. But everyone has that. Friends you have now, you may not have in ten years because you outgrow them or you get bored with them. Or the things that seem so meaningful to you when you're twenty-two—they may not seem terribly important to you now.

BB: I came to speak with you about the gay and lesbian movement because you are a person who doesn't speak a lot about that topic. You are better known for your writings and lectures regarding the AIDS movement.

LK: I consider myself more of an AIDS activist than a gay activist and I'm not as interested in the politics of the gay movement as I am in getting a cure for AIDS and in getting the research done. I've been involved peripherally almost. I guess people find that hard to accept and believe almost because the two are so inextricably bound. I've not been a part of organizations that have been primarily political, like NGLTF [National Gay and Lesbian Task Force] or HRCF [Human Rights Campaign Fund], even though Urvashi Vaid is a very close friend. It's not because it doesn't interest me, but I think I'm a one-issue person. As I get older, there is only time to do certain things. I'm not even an AIDS activist across the board. I'm a research activist, a treatment activist. I'm not going to become involved in problems of education or condom release, or needles or all the many issues. It's not that I'm not interested in those issues, but the only thing that's going to make AIDS go away is a cure, and I only have so much energy, and so I'm going to focus it on that issue. I think that's what ACT-UP was supposed to be about and it became very watered down because it dealt with so many other issues. Many of those issues, I confess to having welcomed into the fold.

BB: Where did it become watered down?

LK: Oh, I think it was just a long history of growth and like any living organism it grows the way it wants to grow and there's very little you can do about it. The same with GMHC [Gay Men's Health Crisis]. They turn into adults. There comes a point in every organization's life, if it's got any organic blood in it at all, where you can't do very much to change it. It was too bad for me, because both of them became things that I didn't want them to become. For different reasons they became out of my control, although I should say that I didn't set out to control them. With ACT-UP particularly, people were nervous that I was going to become a dictator. I made a point of trying to be an advisor from the sidelines and not really to get involved unless I saw something going radically wrong. There comes a point where the organization gets too big, or people get too tired, or too many people die. I think ACT-UP had a longer life of success than many grassroots organizations and of course it's still going, sort of. But there was a point where it really was not useful.

BB: Do you think it became watered down because it's difficult to sustain the kind of anger required to fuel that organization?

LK: I think people have a wrong idea of what ACT-UP was. It wasn't sustained by anger. It was actually sustained by love. For the first years it was a remarkable, exciting place to be. It was that way in the beginning of GMHC, too. People really worked well together. Men and women got along in ways I'd never seen before. There was this feeling of Mickey Rooney and Judy Garland putting on a show. There was a lot of love and support. That's hard to sustain, too. A lot of people died and a lot of people came in with a great deal of hope that they would save their lives, or that the drugs that we were fighting for would save our lives, and I think because that was the intention of the organization, perhaps there were more people who wanted to join it. It sustained an enormous amount of death and that's awfully hard emotionally when people are working together and someone gets sick.

It also became kind of a home for every crazy after awhile. In the beginning there were more people with balance and judgment. It was good because we all have crazy parts and we all have rational parts. It sort of made for a good mix. Slowly, the more rational ones couldn't take the crazies anymore. They either peeled off and started their own organizations or stopped being activists. What became a residue was everyone who had an agenda, talking about problems in El Salvador. There were so many representatives of different groups who felt alienated. In the beginning we had an amazing ability to accept each other's differences. The women actually were most responsible for helping us get through that. Gay men are used to being with mostly their own kind and quite unknowingly were sexist or rude. The women in a rather loving way helped us to understand, and that was a very moving experience. That was replaced by other groups coming in and ramming their alienation down everyone else's throats. Everything had to be translated into eighteen different languages and while that has a certain rationale to it, that's not what we were about.

BB: Do you think that is part of the problems with the gay rights movement, that it is so disenfranchised and that there are so many different pockets?

LK: I know that's what people say, but having helped to start two organizations, I know what is possible when it comes to bringing people together in the beginning. GMHC was a very moving and viable experience for three or four years and ACT-UP was that for six years. Both organizations really achieved great things. ACT-UP really made historical changes in the way drugs are delivered and in the way people are included in clinical trials. When we started, all government protocols for treatment were done on straight, white, middle-class men. We expanded it to people of color, to women. We got women included in the definition of AIDS. There are eight zillion drugs that wouldn't be out there if we hadn't fought for them. We lessened the approval time for most drugs from literally ten years to sometimes less than one year. And that goes for all illnesses. So, the world has a great deal to thank ACT-UP for. I know what we're capable of.

BB: So, why can't we translate this same kind of action into groups like NGLTF and HRCF

LK: I think a lot of it's got to do with our truly remarkable inability to respond to leadership: to anoint, appoint, elect, or accept a leader. Somehow we have to have more structure to our goals. We need to learn how to locate, find, and accept money. No movement, in the end, can go anywhere without being financed. ACT-UP's really good years were when we had a lot of money. We were enormously successful in fundraising. There was one year where we made over a million dollars and that was literally from having art auctions and selling T-shirts. However, the money was pissed away and in some instances stolen by democracy. Anyone on the floor who had a plan could say they wanted to buy an icebox for a poor person in the East Village and before you knew it that person would have an icebox. It would have nothing to do with getting drugs or having AIDS. The stuff that quite often got voted on was ludicrous and the stuff that quite often got voted down was very valuable.

I say this in the "Report from the Holocaust" essay: that there is no real payoff for anyone in this movement and I think that after a few years of taking shit, anyone who could be a leader says, "Fuck it, I can't be elected senator, I can't get a great job out of this, it's not going to look wonderful on my resumé. I'm not getting paid anything, I'm working my ass off, and I'm getting shit from everybody." Doctors, writers—everybody deals with a great deal of shit and vitriol. But for straight people there's a payoff somehow. You do a good job and you get a reward. You don't in the gay community. So, we've lost wonderful leaders like Ginny Apuzzo and Urvashi Vaid, who finally say, "I've got to go out and make a living. No one is supporting my organization." Or else you have to be a superb fundraiser, which we also haven't had. That was Ginny's big problem. She came at a time when people weren't giving and it was hard to get financial support.

BB: You talk about these organizations that have a lot of money like the Human Rights Campaign Fund and then accuse them of not doing anything with it. What prevents them from accomplishing more?

LK: That comes back to the leadership thing and this is where I always get accused of elitism. All of the boards of these organizations are such hodge-podges of people who are thrown on not because they're good or because they can raise money. They're thrown on because they represent something, gender equality or color equality. We need to have so many people of color, we need to have so many lesbians. In a well-run corporation, a board member has to be responsible for doing something. He or she has to either come in with some money or some contacts, or a skill. The GMHC board is a joke and the NGLTF board is an even bigger joke. When it comes to electing leaders, it's the most mediocre person who's chosen for that job. Yes, that person is making fifty, sixty, a hundred thousand dollars, but he or she is very middle-of-the-road, somebody who is not going to make any waves, and you wind up having a very mediocre organization. That's why they wind up not doing anything.

BB: Would you also agree that the message they put out to most gays and lesbians is unclear?

LK: I think that's absolutely true: it's too unfocused, too diffused. All these organizations are trying to take care of the world. There is no straight organization that attempts to do half of the things that every gay organization attempts to do. They're enormously protective of their territory, so that NGLTF can only go four blocks on this side of the street and HRCF can only go four blocks on the other side. In essence they should really be the same organization. It should be funded with a lot of money from David Geffen, who isn't doing it. I don't think things are going to change very much until we have a substantial amount of money as well as a substantial number of people with good skills who are willing to contribute them and open their mouths.

BB: Do you think HRCF tried to do that when they hired Elizabeth Birch from Apple Computer?

LK: Well, she's been there a year and I don't know what she's done. That is not to say that she hasn't done anything, but my vision of a leader is someone I can see. I don't know what the woman looks like and I don't know what she says. It sounds like she's got an impressive résumé, but I don't see our place in Washington any stronger because of HRCF's presence there. When I started getting involved in all of this in the early eighties, there were three lobbyists in Washington. It's 1995 and we now have four lobbyists in Washington. We have not made any progress. When you think of the Israel lobby, the auto lobby, and the pharmaceutical lobby, which all have thousands for each issue, you begin to realize why we don't have any rights.

I put forward an idea many years ago to NGLTF and to HRCF which seems so sensible and easy and no one ever takes it up. It only costs between seventy-five and a hundred thousand dollars a year to finance a lobbyist. Every gay community in this country could be responsible for raising that amount of money per year. We'd have four hundred lobbyists in Washington next week. One big fundraising campaign in Cleveland, Chicago, Columbus, Des Moines could raise a hundred thousand dollars in a weekend. It's like pledging to support that person and they should all be affiliated with one organization in Washington.

BB: So, if we took up the idea of HRCF and NGLTF merging into one, what should the mission be?

LK: I don't know. This has not been my issue. Urvashi and I have talked about it. I see something along the lines of a national organization of gay and lesbian organizations. All in one building in Washington. Like United Jewish Appeal or National Organization for Women: an umbrella organization. I think we need a big physical presence there. A big building that people see and from which people fan out all day long. I don't think it's impossible. There's an awful lot of money in this community. If I were younger and healthier, I would certainly be interested in starting that organization. In 1986 I had a meeting with five or six of the really wealthy guys out there— Sheldon Andleson, who is now dead, Barry Krost, Gil Garfield, to name some of them. I said that we have to have this kind of organization in Washington and we need to have it for AIDS and everything else. But everyone was already involved with other organizations.

We are very bad at having a sense of the big picture. Not whether we're going to welcome in the transvestites or whatever. The big picture is power and having a place at the table and getting everything we deserve. That requires major bucks and major commitments. David Geffen gives a million bucks to APLA [AIDS Project Los Angeles] and you want to cry that he does it so blithely and so blindly. The movement and all activism have historically been achieved and perpetuated by people who are disenfranchised and who don't have money and who are very suspicious of giving power up to those who do. While one understands all of that, it has also served to defeat us a great deal of the time. The energy has kept the movement going, but it has also been the wall that has kept the movement from going anywhere. This is the first time I think I've voiced that or seen it that clearly.

BB: Do you think the Clinton administration's inaction has a lot to do with why people are stepping back and are more laid back about the movement than they should be?

LK: It's more cumulative and goes back further than that. I think we're dealing with the eight hundredth president in a row who doesn't give a shit about us and, yes, he had said a lot of stuff and he got us all full of hope and hasn't delivered on any of it. So, I think that's sort of the nail in the coffin. I think we feel extraordinarily powerless right now and it comes after the twelve years of Reagan-Bush. It's actually worse under Clinton. We were better off under Bush. In terms of AIDS we certainly were.

BB: How can you say that?

LK: Because there was a chain of command and because there were people who had a modicum of power in charge of the AIDS research establishment. Most important, though—and people won't accept this—the minute Hillary Clinton opened her mouth about drug companies, accusing them of making too much profit, every single drug company practically shut down research and development and switched their resources. They claimed their profits were being used for research and development. Eli Lilly overnight shut down their AIDS research. I hate to be in a position of supporting the drug companies because I support what Hillary wanted to do, but in this instance we've got a plague and we can deal with the profit motive later. I'd just as soon they would do the research. In some instances, a few companies are, like Merck and Abbot, but a lot who were, aren't now. George Bush was very much for the drug companies, so in some cases we were better off under Bush. It applies to a lot of illnesses: breast cancer, Alzheimer's, not just AIDS.

BB: Do you feel that Clinton at least started a dialogue going about gays and lesbians? Many people feel that he brought us to the table at least. Okay, so he left us there and didn't feed us, but he gave us a chair.

LK: I know there are more appointments than there were under Bush, but it's such extraordinary tokenism that you'll forgive me if I find it offensive. It's one thing to bring Bob Hattoy to Washington and let him make speeches at the Democratic National Convention and then, once that's over, to put him in an office that's so far away from power that he's useless. Even though he's a gay man appointed by Clinton, I don't consider that anything.

BB: What about the Manhattan Project? Do you think it will ever get off the ground?

LK: Well, it's had many names, but the answer is no. Over the years it's been re-jiggered to reflect where we were at the moment in research and I don't know if the one we conceived of five years ago is quite as applicable today. Too many second-rate people are running the show and the NIH [National Institutes of Health] is such a cesspool of mediocrity that most of the important stuff seems to be coming out of private labs, maybe having some government funding, but being controlled privately. Like the Aaron Diamond Research Foundation in New York, like the Salk Institute, like the Howard Hughes Medical Foundation fellowships. In some instances out of universities, but less and less out of the NIH.

BB: If there were a Manhattan Project, who would you like to see running it?

LK: The man we've always wanted is David Baltimore, who is now at MIT, and surprisingly enough most scientists want him, too. He's enormously respected, but he's been dumped on so many times that, quite rightly or sadly, he says, "Leave me alone."

BB: Do you have any regrets at all about referring to AIDS Project Los Angeles and Gay Men's Health Crisis as Dachau and Auschwitz?

LK: No. Each day I'm more and more convinced of it. I know the rhetoric is probably so far out that it's not a useful way to make my point. I think these organizations are sad and shameful and become more so as they become more bureaucratic. I didn't start GMHC to behave that way and to become so bureaucratic. This organization probably spends a quarter of a million dollars a year funding the AIDS Action Council in Washington, which is another useless organization, also founded by me and Paul Popham to lobby in Washington. It has become nothing but a bunch of ladies who lunch. I don't understand how things can turn into such bureaucracies. These organizations were started in order to hold the system accountable and they have become the system. It never fails to amaze me what happens to people. So when I say they are Auschwitz, I mean that they are literally helping people to die and are not fighting to keep people alive.

BB: How many of the founders of GMHC are still alive?

LK: Three of us are still living but no one is actually involved with the organization. Edmund White lives in Paris and was never really involved even in the beginning. He was just along because we wanted his name. Larry Mass was a doctor and a great hero in the early days. He was literally treated so shabbily by GMHC that he quietly and nobly just withdrew. Unlike me, who keeps ramming it in their face.

BB: And the other three guys?

LK: Are dead.

BB: When you think about them, what do you suppose they'd be thinking about all of this bureaucracy?

LK: I had most of my early fights with Paul Popham, which I dramatized in the play *The Normal Heart*. By the time he died, we had long since made up our differences, and he was enormously supportive of my anger. It was very moving that he had made that journey. If the organization reflects anyone's philosophy, it's Paul's. Paul was a closeted gay man and exceedingly conservative and the organization is pretty much the same now because of that early training, so to speak. But I know he came to be very angry with GMHC, particularly with the last executive director he had to deal with, a guy named Richard Dunne, who was—well, one should not speak ill of the dead.

BB: Do you think you're a hard person to be around for a long period of time?

LK: It depends where you're around with me. My lover and I seem to have a lot of fun together and we laugh. I was, if I may say so myself, a wonderful film producer and knew how to get good work out of people and how to inspire them to do their best.

BB: I mean, are you hard to be around because it seems that you're always challenging people to think about things that they might not want to think about?

LK: Well, I think most of my friends are probably like me. People who are interested in issues and who have achieved and who are interested in bettering themselves, and climbing mountains, and learning. I think I'm actually a great deal of fun and I think the people with whom I spend most of my time would agree. Especially as I get older and my health more problematic, I spend a great deal of my time with my friend David and I'm not as social as I used to be. I do not suffer fools or incompetence easily and the friends that I have don't either. So, if you were a fool or a laggard it would probably be very difficult for me to spend time with you.

BB: Do you mind speaking about the state of your health?

LK: No, I've been honest about everything else. I'm fairly stable. I'm on AZT, ironically. I'm still in the normal T-cell range. I do have a very problematic liver from having been infected with hepatitis-B sexually. So, I have cirrhosis of the liver and a large number of liver complications. In the end, that may do me in rather than the HIV. I also have low platelets which is why I take the AZT. The cirrhosis of the liver also appears to be getting worse, which means shortly or not at all, depending on how life goes on, I may require a liver transplant, which is not a happy thing to look forward to either. I take an enormous number of medicines for one thing or another and I hope for the best. But I seem to have a lot of good energy.

BB: So, how do you spend most of your days?

LK: This interviewing and speaking can really take over your life sometimes. I try to do a lot of my own writing every day. I'm not so certain why the requests for interviews go in spurts. Suddenly you're "the gay" everyone wants to talk to. It's a mixed bag. It's hard because, especially in the straight world, it's important that there be a gay representative interviewed. There's a book coming out soon on people who have accomplished things. Everyone in the book is ostensibly straight and I'm the token gay. Initially I had said no to the request from the author, Barbara Lee Diamondstein. In a way I resent this. My work isn't finished and I'm not dead. But then I think that it's better to be "the gay" in the book. Then the gays can say "we got someone in the book" and, of course, it would make me very angry if there wasn't a gay person in the book.

BB: When is the film of *The Normal Heart* coming out?

LK: I don't know. It seems to be going full steam ahead. Streisand is trying to cast it. Speedy Gonzales, she's not. But she seems passionate and committed. The script still seems to have a lot of the things in it that I feel strongly about. So it hasn't been watered down. She's more interested in the love story than in the political story, and that's fine.

BB: Are you going to be actively involved in the making of this film?

LK: I don't know. I was very actively involved and she has brought in some other people, but she's got to make it her way and her story and I understand that. It's got to be a pain in the ass to have the person who the story is about still alive and breathing down your neck. I may or may not like what she does, but that, unfortunately, is the price of admission.

BB: You and Streisand seem to be cut out of the same mold.

LK: Everybody says that. We get along well. I love being with her and she has been very loving and supportive to me. We both have very high standards and I think people who do respect that in each other. She doesn't like yes men and I don't like yes women. So there has been a good interchange. I've told her what I thought and she's done the same, and we've both licked our wounds and we're still friendly.

BB: I noticed in *Reports from the Holocaust* that one of your essays was critical of Streisand. She sat on the board of AMFAR and you questioned why she wasn't using her money and clout to really make a meaningful contribution. So, how has your past criticism of her affected your relationship now?

LK: Well, you'd be surprised what you can say to people. I told it to her face. When she gave a million dollars to AMFAR and a million dollars to APLA, I told her she threw the money down the toilet. She didn't like hearing it, but I told her. I have called the man who is the head of the office of AIDS research, Dr. William Paul, a wimp who should resign. I found myself at a dinner last week and he rushed to find a chair to sit next to me. We spent the whole dinner talking and he spent the time defending himself and I said to him that if he ran his office with half as much fervor as he displayed at this dinner, I would be pleased. Gay people are always saying that we're supposed to love each other and not fight and be divisive, but I don't think there's a community anywhere in the world that doesn't have the same fights. We've got to learn how to deal with them because they're not going to go away. How can Bob Dole go out to dinner with Ted Kennedy after they've fought and said terrible things to each other all day on the Senate floor? But that's what the politics of life is all about. Barbra Streisand is a big girl. William Paul is a big boy and so is Larry Kramer. I've been called names, too. But you don't close the doors in each others' faces. It's all part of the game. We have to become stronger out of that. It is a hard lesson to learn. It's usually learned when you have the opportunity to get out there and *tummel*, what the Jews call "*tummel*."

BB: What are your latest thoughts about the religious Right? What should the strategy be to combat their words and actions?

LK: I actually think we're doing sort of an interesting job as a visible population. That's part of the reason why there's such an uproar. It's because we're so visible. More and more people come out of the closet and get married and have children—or write books. That's the best way to show people that they don't have anything to be afraid of. I think that the polls show a bigger tolerance of us, which also scares the religious Right.

I wish we had stronger organizations fighting for our rights. I wish we had more money from our wealthy members, which include women, by the way. There is an enormous amount of lesbian money especially in the South, in Texas, and in California. Maybe not David Geffen kind of money, but close to it in some instances. That has to come into the fight at some point.

Will we be destroyed? I don't think so. I can't help but believe that we can't be pushed back. Once you're out, you're out. I lecture a lot and teach a lot at colleges around the country, which I love. You see some colleges, like Yale, where there will be an enormous gay dance once a month and straight kids will also go to it. You'll see gay young men and lesbians necking with each other. Then you go to the University of Tulsa where there'll be forty people sneaking into the room to hear you speak. You feel that you're back in the Dark Ages. There does seem to be more of the former rather than the latter. Kids seem more accepting of gay friends in some places than in other places. Also, there are a lot of books out there. We have our own bookstores. The last couple of years were probably the first time in history that you could make a living as a gay writer, writing about gay issues—that Dorothy Allison could make a living being an out lesbian writer. Sales of my stuff keep going up year after year. That's why it's important to support our bookstores. They sell a lot and it forces the national chains to stock our writing. The fact that the Greg Louganis book is a number one best seller is fabulous. It's unheard of that we've been able to achieve that. Even though I'm critical of so much that we do and how we are organized, there seems to be something going on quite apart from that. Whether the two can marry each other, I don't know. I keep waiting for something else. Why isn't there another movement? What happened to all the activists? I know a lot of them died. All the energy couldn't have evaporated. Is this younger generation so completely apolitical that they don't care?

BB: Do you think this could be the case?

LK: I don't know. From 1987 to 1992, there was such fervent passion in the younger kids. Where did it go? You tell me.

BB: Well, I was one of those "younger kids" during that time. But so many people died. I think that many of us just got burned to a crisp by the constant dying and loss of our friends and lovers.

LK: But doesn't it get replaced and replenished? Don't other kids come along? Is it a pendulum swing?

BB: I know when I stopped. No one took my lead with the same kind of fervor and picked up on the activities I created. I think this generation is apolitical, but I also think we haven't created any kind of clear leadership.

LK: So, why doesn't somebody come along and lead? Why do we wait for the leader? Why don't you start an organization of women who feel as you do?

BB: Well, as you said it takes money. Who will plant that seed money for me or for some other take-charge lesbian?

LK: Well, you can get away without the money in the beginning. You need the money later. In the beginning, you need a vision and a like purpose with others. Then the money comes.

BB: Well, are there any up-and-coming leaders that you are impressed with— young leaders, or even middle-aged leaders?

LK: I don't see anyone who wants to do it. I see a lot of young people who have interesting voices, but they all tend to be into what they're doing. Everyone knows it's a pretty thankless job. Enough of them have had darts thrown at them for what they've said at some time or another. I always look upon it that if you haven't offended someone, you haven't done it right.

BB: Okay, Larry: your final opportunity to talk about anything we may not have touched on during this discussion.

LK: Okay, let's talk about the Harvard AIDS Institute, since this interview is going to appear in *The Harvard Gay & Lesbian Review*. It's been sad to watch something that was so vital, promising, and interesting become so pale over the years. It was a great place for a few years. They put out a dynamite publication which has now been reduced to a mimeographed tear sheet. I was very angry when I discovered that the president of the board of directors was Maurice Templesman and has been for a number of years, and I called Max Essex at the Institute and said, "He has been the president of your board for all those years Jackie Kennedy was alive and you never once asked him for anything, or you never asked Jackie to front something, or to show up?" Max was dumbfounded that I even asked those questions. Doctors are such lousy politicians. Here he's had two of the most potentially important voices in the country who could have spoken out for AIDS and he didn't ask them to do anything. I wanted to say, "Max, how stupid can you be?" Those people don't necessarily volunteer, you have to ask. She was probably asked for everything in the world. Jesus, to have Jackie as a possibility! She might have said no, but no one even asked her. Even now, Templesman is still a valid source of power and he's not been asked. He's never given any money. So what's the use of having him as president of the board? He's useless. That's what makes me mad: when we have these chances and don't make the most of them.

Out Comes American Literature

THE HISTORY OF GAY and lesbian fiction is a very short one or a relatively long one, depending upon how one wishes to interpret the writers of the past. Was Walt Whitman or Willa Cather "queer" in a way that gives contemporary gay people the right to claim them as literary ancestors? Does the literature of the closet count at all?

If the answer to the final question is "no," then gay and lesbian literature as such could not have existed much before 1969, the year of the Stonewall revolt. Felice Picano maintains that the group of writers constituting the Violet Quill Club (Edmund White, Andrew Holleran, et al.) were the first serious novelists to write expressly from the perspective of out gay men. Others would push the date further back to include works from the 1940s and 1950s, such as Gore Vidal's *The City and the Pillar,* Radclyffe Hall's *The Well of Loneliness,* Christopher Isherwood's *A Single Man,* Fritz Peters' *Finistère,* among others. Much before that and what we find is essentially a literature of the closet, in which homosexual themes had to be just ambiguous enough to "pass" for straight, if they were present at all. Writers of the past often have to be "outed" through a re-examination of their lives or a deconstruction of their texts. To "queer" a genre or literary period (as in the titles *Queering the Renaissance* and *Queering the Pitch*) is to show evidence for hitherto submerged homosexual themes in the works of, say, Dickinson or Melville or Willa Cather.

To "out" or "queer" a literary figure or period is to make allowances for the social and literary conventions that precluded a more direct discussion of homosexual themes. Whitman was astonishingly bold for his time, but stands alone in this regard, in a society that frowned upon *any* reference to sex, much less its homosexual variant. Next to him we have Emily Dickinson's richly coded references to same-sex love and desire, Melville's bizarre configurations of men inside bunk rooms or whales' carcasses. Decades later, we find ourselves still engaged in deep deconstruction when it comes to writers like Henry James or Willa Cather, both evidently queer in their private lives, but both taking pains to reveal just enough to let on (we think) without leaving any smoking guns.

Now that we've put Dickinson, Whitman, Melville, Cather, and Henry James on the table, we need to acknowledge that these are also arguably the five most important American writers of the seventy-five-year period they define. Add to this roster names like E. M. Forster, Proust, Mann, Virginia Woolf, Gertrude Stein, and so on, all of whom have been "outed" pretty thoroughly at this point, and one begins to wonder if we're engaging in wishful thinking or if being gay or lesbian is some sort of prerequisite for greatness as a writer. (Okay, so Joyce and Faulkner are no-shows, but D. H. Lawrence and even Hemingway are still up for grabs.)

These writers, along with countless others, offer a wide range of possibilities for revealing or concealing their sexual orientation in both their lives and work. Thus Whitman's relative openness about his homosexual attractions is balanced by Melville's preference for subterfuge and Henry James' obsession with sexless friendships. Among women writers, the trajectory from Dickinson through Cather and Stein shows an increasing openness about sex in general and lesbian sex in particular. The closetedness of James and Forster, who suppressed *Maurice* during his lifetime, can perhaps be attributed to the pall cast by Oscar Wilde's trial in the 1890s; in any case, it wasn't until after World War II that the closet doors started to be pushed open for men, notably with the publication of Gore Vidal's *The City and the Pillar* (1946) and Isherwood's *A Single Man* (1964).

The seven essays in this section offer glimpses at a few critical moments in this slow historical progression toward greater openness, culminating in the fully "out" gay and lesbian literature of the post-Stonewall period. Three of the women in the progression noted above, Emily Dickinson, Willa Cather, and Gertrude Stein, show this trend quite clearly. Martha Nell Smith writes of how Dickinson tried within the extremely puritanical standards of her time to disclose her passion for another woman. By the turn of the century, as Marilee Lindemann documents here, things had loosened up enough for Willa Cather to depict thinly veiled lesbian relationships in her work, as well as gender-bending women, of which Cather herself was one. By the time of Gertrude Stein—whose work is analyzed by Renate Stendhal—it was possible for the poet to live openly with a lesbian lover, albeit in Paris, and to write sexually explicit poetry about their relationship.

The outing of gay literature picks up with some of the male authors that emerged after the war, beginning with W. H. Auden, whose 1995 biography is reviewed by Richard Howard. Reed Woodhouse provides a thorough and now famous historical analysis of the outing of gay fiction in an essay called "Five Houses of Gay Fiction," first published in the premiere issue of the *HGLR*. Woodhouse identifies the completion of this process with the emergence of a self-consciously gay "ghetto fiction," written by and for gay people. And indeed, as the gay and lesbian publishing boom would attest, such a fiction has established itself as a seemingly permanent fixture of gay culture. On the other hand, as gay culture gains wider acceptance in American society, we ought to be able to expect more mainstream acceptance of our works. Two contemporary writers are spotlighted whose works have indeed "crossed over" into mainstream society: Tony Kushner, whose *Angels in America* brought in thousands of straight theater-goers; and Sapphire, whose most recent novel, *Push* (reviewed by Cheryl Clarke), targeted a general audience while making no secret of its lesbian themes.

MARTHA NELL SMITH

The Belle of the Belle of Amherst

APPROACHING THE CORCORAN, they were greeted with a roar from the crowd, blocks-long applause as spectators elbowed one another, pointed, giggled, and smiled at their sign: "Emily Dickinson Scholars for Gay Rights: We dwell in Possibility." One placard among hundreds of thousands of joyous linguistic embodiments featured in the April 1993 March for Lesbian, Gay, Bisexual Rights, the purple and lavender lettering even sporting a curviform "dash" dancing up at the end, an exuberant mark suggesting a fond lick or kiss for the crowd. 1995's National AIDS Awareness Catalog displays this elevating epigraph:

> I'll tell you how the Sun rose
> —A Ribbon at a time—
> > —Emily Dickinson

For nearly a century, from soon after the 1890s publications of the first printed volumes of Dickinson's poetry to the present, lesbians and gays—including poets such as Amy Lowell, H. D., Hart Crane, Adrienne Rich, and Judy Grahn, as well as numerous critics and biographers—have claimed Emily Dickinson as a sister traveler. Claude Summers includes her in *The Gay and Lesbian Literary Heritage* (1995) and, whatever her quibbles with what and who counts as lesbian, Lillian Faderman features her in *Chloe Plus Olivia: An Anthology of Lesbian Literature from the Seventeenth Century to the Present.* Just this fall, a conservative columnist rails in *The Atlanta Constitution* against English professors who plumb Dickinson's images and symbols for signs of the erotic, especially—egads!—the lesbian erotic. Yet as many who have taught Dickinson's poetry well know, readers do not need the prompting of Rebecca Patterson, Paula Bennett, or any other critic to suggest that there just might be something clitoral to all those nuts and berries, something oral and sexual to "Lips" that "sip thy Jessamines."

From the Winter 1996 issue

Scholars bicker and argue passionately over whether or not "lesbian" is a proper term to identify Emily Dickinson's decades-long devotion to her sister-in-law Susan Huntington Gilbert Dickinson or her passionate, early-1860s friendship with Kate Anthon. Theoretical debates fret in the face of Foucault's timeline for the history of sexuality, yet finally tend to leave us in a critical cul-de-sac, wondering what to call this great love of one of America's most renowned poets. In all these can-we-call-this-lesbian? consternations, we are talking more about ourselves and our taxonomies than about the life and passions of Emily Dickinson.

Some parts of the biography are familiar: born on December 10, 1830, in Amherst, Massachusetts, to prominent (and very stern) lawyer Edward Dickinson and his wife Emily Elizabeth, the middle child, a year younger than her only brother Austin, three years older than her only sister Lavinia; never married; nursed her mother in the 1870s; wrote nearly two thousand poems, printed only a few of them, ten at present count, in her own lifetime; bound hundreds of these poems into manuscript books that were found in her room after her death; sent out at least a third of her poems in a thousand letters to friends, both intimate and casual; is rumored also to have nursed an unrequited love for—depending upon whom you believe—a minister, an editor friend of the family, a judge several years her senior, or her sister-in-law Susan; died at home May 15, 1886, at the age of fifty-five.

Other aspects of the biography are less familiar but are becoming increasingly well-known, and these speak to our present concerns: Susan and Emily lived side-by-side for thirty years in the houses Evergreens and Homestead on Main Street in Amherst, Massachusetts (1856–1886); Emily sent more poems, letters, and letter-poems to her beloved Susan than to any other correspondent, more than twice as many as to the correspondent next most frequently addressed (a professional man of letters). That she was writing so much to someone who lived just next door suggests that the writing was central to their relationship, something both took very seriously—seriously enough to have high ambitions for.

Emily actually changed a poem, rewrote "Safe in their Alabaster Chambers," at the behest of Susan, who was a trusted literary advisor as well as a personal confidante.

It was Susan, not her sister Lavinia, who dressed Emily's body to be laid to rest; and it was Susan, not her brother Austin, who wrote Emily's obituary for the *Springfield Republican*. In the posthumous sorting and winnowing of Dickinson's papers, someone excised loving remarks about Susan from Emily's writings to her brother Austin, erasing as many as seven lines from letters and actually inking over the loving poetic tribute, "One Sister have I in the House." As curious and suggestive as these mutilations are (as Marianne Moore reminds us, "Omissions are not accidents"), they point to writings even more telling, the hundreds upon hundreds of poems, letters, and letter-poems to Susan, which even in their exhilarated metaphors tell us about the daily routines and abiding love of Emily Dickinson.

By the time Susan married Austin in July 1856, Emily had been writing her since at least December 1850, proclaiming "we are the only poets, and everyone else is prose" (L 56), lamenting "How vain it seems to write . . . how much more near and dear to sit beside you, talk with you, hear the tones of your voice" (L 73), exulting that "when you come home, darling, I shant have your letters, shall I, but I shall have yourself" (L 85), and that "I shall have you, shall hold you in my arms" (L 93), where "we need not talk at all, our eyes would whisper for us, and your hand fast in mine, we would not ask for language" (L 94). For this last, Dickinson's final punctuation mark is a kiss, rendered "shyly, lest there is somebody there!" and in the next she asks, "Susie, will you be my own again, and kiss me as you used to?" (L 96). Littering these early letters with signs of her devoted blood, sweat, and tears, Dickinson weeps a "tear here, Susie, on purpose for you," when she misses her beloved, simultaneously presenting both evidence of her love and a part of herself in the tearstain on the page. Enshrining fantasies of touching Susan in a kind of emotional/erotic scripture that permeates not only these letters of a woman in her twenties, but the letters and poems written throughout their nearly forty-year libidinously-charged relationship, Dickinson suffuses her dreams of physical intimacy with reveries of linguistic coition—"I'm thinking when awake, how sweet if you were with me, and to talk with you as I fall asleep, would be sweeter still" (L 178).

"Well you know, don't you, that women in the nineteenth century talked to each other in that loverlike fashion and they certainly didn't mean what we mean when we say 'lesbian.'" So goes the usual explanation for Dickinson's hundreds of passionate proclamations written over several decades to Susan. Yet such shushings predicate their conclusions on the notion that nineteenth-century women who kissed, held each other, caressed, and slept with one another did so unself-consciously. "If they were being sexual, they would be self-conscious about their activities, and they are not" says the asexualizing ideology of romantic friendship. Yet about her loving expressions to Susan, Emily Dickinson was self-conscious: after declaring the vanity of writing when she could be touching and kissing Susan, Dickinson anxiously inscribes, "Oh what will become of me? Susie, forgive me, forget all what I say, get some sweet scholar to read a gentle hymn, about Bethlehem and Mary, and you will sleep on sweetly and have as peaceful dreams, as if I had never written you all these ugly things" (L 73).

Whether self-consciously or not, Dickinson continued for the rest of her life to write seductively to Susan, using comic depiction, verbal wit, and unabashed praise to make herself more appealing, repeatedly approaching Susan with a suitor's designs. Dickinson attends to Susan's appearance, noticing her dress and the way in which her hair is fixed and apologizing for her own "gross" appearances as late as the 1870s and 1880s (L 383, L 554). Though Amherst gossips claimed the two women were estranged late in Dickinson's life, her own letters document one direct encounter after another, expressing profound pleasure at the mere sound of Susan's voice and apologizing for not making an appearance when she didn't know Susan was there, and otherwise noting regular, casual, face-to-face contact. An 1883 letter demonstrates Dickinson's lover-like, playful beseeching of her apparently angry friend, "how could I woo / in a rendezvous where there / is no Face?" (L 856); in this, the writing does not "face" the reader but, around the left and right edges of the page, demands that the document be turned all around to be deciphered, demands that Susan's reading be active, physical.

Early in their relationship, Emily and Susan took long walks, baked cookies, sewed, talked about books and their dreams, and as they grew older continued to share many cultural delights, exchanging food, recipes, tips for reading, mutual passions for gardening and, most importantly for us, for writing. Austin and Susan's guests were sometimes treated to Emily improvising at the piano and were by all reports delighted by her inventive, unusual melodies. An evening in the Evergreens, Susan and Austin's home, might even involve literary luminaries such as Harriet Beecher Stowe recounting the plays she had enjoyed in Paris, or Ralph Waldo Emerson recommending Julia Ward Howe's "Passion Flowers." In solitude, like Emily, Susan read voraciously, and Shakespeare, Milton, Tennyson, Elizabeth Barrett Browning, the Brontës, Lydia Maria Child, George Eliot, William Dean Howells, Henry James, and Rebecca Harding Davis were all subjects of their epistolary conversations. Thus Susan and Emily shared a cultured, sophisticated world of literature, music, and fine dining—menus with shrimp vermicelli, asparagus, salad from the garden, sherry, and tables decked with arbutus and wild violets. Not surprisingly, in Dickinson's letters to Susan, readers witness an ever-deepening fusion of the erotic and the intellectual.

Susan applauds the publication of "Safe in their Alabaster Chambers" in *The Republican* and characterizes it as the launching of "our Fleet." In fact, if we compare the ten printings of poems during Dickinson's lifetime with the versions her mentor Susan had in her possession after the poet's death—and remember that Susan played host to each of the editors who printed Dickinson's verse—it is reasonable to conclude that Susan acted as agent and was responsible for their publication. But Susan is also the beloved, Emily's muse, her poetic wellspring. Dickinson equates the writing of their love with that penned by great poets: "We remind her we love her—/ Unimportant fact, though Dante didn't think so / nor Swift, nor Mirabeau" (L 393). In a moment giddy with being deeply in love, Emily gleefully rhymes:

> To own a Susan of my own
> Is of itself a Bliss—
> Whatever Realm I forfeit, Lord,
> Continue me in this! —(L 531)

Susan is a "Siren" for whom "Emily would forfeit Righteousness" (L 554); "To be Susan is Imagination" (L 855); her syllables are "impregnable," like "Gibraltar" (L 722), her words "Silver genealogy" (L 913); and "With the Exception of Shakespeare," Susan "told" Emily "of more knowledge than any one living" (L 757).

Emily Dickinson's passionate, exuberant love for "Sweet Sue" demonstrates that in those houses on Main in Amherst, "Poetry" and "Love" indeed "coeval come" (P 1247):

> Take back that
> "Bee" and "Buttercup"—
> I have no Field
> for them, though
> for the Woman
> whom I prefer,
> Here is Festival—
> Where my Hands
> are cut, Her fingers will be
> found inside   —(L 288)

Quickly overturning the obvious sadomasochisms of this letter-poem, Emily, on the creative field of her Eden with Susan, appropriates the site of crucifying wounds to rewrite the biblical myth of human creation and tell a story about relations between two women who, like Adam and Eve, are flesh of each other's flesh, limbs of each other's limbs. Describing the emotional and intellectual engrossment in terms that transform what promises to be but a gory scene of bloodletting into that of female figures who cannot be crucified, whose vibrance is revealed beneath the site of pain, Dickinson underscores just how monumental is their orgasmic suffusion of selves. Embedded within this gash, ecstasy is excruciating and festive, a more than appropriate sign for women who love one another but know there is a "Will of God" (L 312) and there are laws of society. For lesbian love struggling without a "Chart" or "Compass" (P 249) in an Amherst culture compulsively structured around heterosexual coupling is both a crucifixion—a "Calvary of Love" (P 1072)— and resurrection—"Rowing in Eden" (P 249). And living side-by-side their whole adult lives, they had made their choice: the one never married and wrote her passionate adoration over and over, while the other loved "dear Emily" but took a husband, Emily's brother.

I could catalog many more examples of Emily Dickinson's startlingly passionate expressions to Susan Dickinson. Rumor, unseemly innuendo, and the frictions inevitable in any passionate lifelong affair have all been used to dispute the erotic importance of Susan to America's sweetheart poet. But I ask that we depend neither on theory nor its histories to evaluate this coupledom. Instead, let's use a little common sense. If all these wildly effusive remarks had been written to a man whom Dickinson called an "Avalanche of Sun" (L 755), no one would be asking if they actually "did it," had genital contact, a question frequently invoked to discredit use of the term "lesbian" to characterize this emotional entanglement. Questions of bisexuality inevitably arise as well, with everyone pointing to a century of tattle about a minister and Dickinson's supposed late-life affair with Judge Otis P. Lord. Yet these assumptions are based on gossipy hearsay and on a "correspondence," no item of which anyone can prove was ever mailed. Nor can anyone prove that the "Lord" letters were indeed written with the Judge in mind. What we do know about those letters is that they were trotted out by Millicent Todd Bingham in 1955, as if to counter Rebecca Patterson's assertions about Dickinson's lesbian attachments in *The Riddle of Emily Dickinson* (1951). A great lover, Emily Dickinson probably knew heterosexual as well as lesbian desire. But one desire does not invalidate the other, and nothing can change the fact that the love of Dickinson's life was lesbian, and for Susan, Emily's "Eden" (L 584).

Dickinson returns again and again to the imaginative place Eden, continually revising the site of humanity's mother's seduction. At age fifteen, she muses, "I have lately come to the conclusion that I am Eve.... You know there is no account of her death in the Bible, and why am not I Eve?" (L 9). By tasting the forbidden fruit, Eve tested God's dictum and introduced critical inquiry, or the quest for knowledge, into the world. In analogous ways, Dickinson's extraordinary poetic project continues to test received wisdom about literary production and reception. And her extraordinary lesbian love, a consuming dedication of four decades, tests understandings and theories of sexuality, sexual history, sexual practices, and lesbian existence.

MARILEE LINDEMANN

Willa's Case

WILLA CATHER must have cut quite a figure on the streets of Red Cloud, Nebraska, the prairie town her family moved to in 1883 when she was nine years old. At fourteen, the future Pulitzer Prize winner embarked on a four-year masquerade as William Cather (also known as Willie, William Cather, Jr., and William Cather, MD), an elaborate and public episode of male impersonation documented in studio photographs that show her sporting crewcuts and dressed in masculine attire. According to Sharon O'Brien (1987), one unnerved neighbor recalled Cather for "her boyish makeup and the serious stare with which she met you," but the young gender-bender bravely continued to cross-dress, even in her first two years at the University of Nebraska in Lincoln.

There, she met and fell in love with Louise Pound, who would go on to achieve prominence as a folklorist and the first woman president of the Modern Language Association. In a passionate letter of 1892—the historical moment when sexologists were radically redescribing love between women as pathological rather than innocently romantic—Cather repeatedly notes how queer she had felt at a party earlier in the evening, as she anticipated leaving Lincoln, and thus Pound, for the summer. Struggling first to express her admiration for the dress Pound had worn and then to minimize her obviously intense feelings, Cather rails in the course of the letter against the fact that feminine friendships should be regarded as unnatural. She winds up blaming the weather for her frame of mind, but signs the letter, "Yours, William."

From such maverick beginnings one might expect a lifetime of sexual defiance to spring, but that was not exactly the case for Willa Cather, though all of the intimate, long-term relationships of her life were with women, including a partnership of nearly forty years with Edith Lewis. Born in Back Creek, Virginia, on December 7, 1873, Cather left Nebraska shortly after graduating from college and settled permanently in the East. Already a writer but compelled to earn a living, she worked, mostly in magazine journalism, for more than fifteen years before she was able to devote herself full time to writing fic-

From the Winter 1996 issue

Willa Cather

tion. These years included stints as editor of a women's magazine in Pittsburgh and managing editor of New York's great muckraking magazine, *McClure's*. During this period, she became acquainted with Sarah Orne Jewett, the New England writer whose *The Country of the Pointed Firs* (1896) is a masterwork of American regionalism and of the proto-lesbian fiction produced out of the pre-Freudian world of female romantic friendship. Jewett's literary success and her "Boston marriage" with Annie Fields, dazzling hostess and widow of publisher James T. Fields, supplied Cather with important models of personal and professional achievement, and Jewett's advice and interest in the younger writer's work helped ease Cather out of journalism.

Long before this crucial transition occurred, Cather had repudiated the sexual radicalism of her youth, trading in William's "boyish makeup" for the less threatening no-nonsense look of the early twentieth-century career woman. As early as 1896, she wrote a letter chiding an old Lincoln friend, who had known "William" well, accusing her of being Bohemian. She goes on to say that she could most effectually surprise her friends and pain her enemies by living a most conventional existence, and that she intended to do precisely that. Several months later, she wrote to the same friend of building a new life for herself in Pittsburgh in broad daylight with neither short hair nor any other of the old things queer to her. Even as she pursued relationships her culture deemed as "unnatural"—whether or not they were genitally sexual, which isn't clear from existing records—first with Pittsburgh socialite Isabelle McClung and then with Lewis, Cather battled publicly to repress the old "queer" things and maintain the façade of a conventional existence.

The suspicion that enemies were out to get her grew more acute as the years passed, despite the fact that her success as a novelist brought fame, awards, and wealth. By the end of her life, in 1947, Cather's desire to control her privacy and her reputation was so obsessive that she destroyed all the personal letters in her possession, asked friends to destroy any they had, and even stipulated in her will that quotation from or re-publication of any surviving letters be forbidden. Which is why, in the preceding paragraphs, though I have used some of Cather's exact words—most importantly the word "queer"—I have not used quotation marks to indicate where I have done so. Her longing for mainstream respectability has forced all scholars of her life into similarly unsatisfying compromises and resulted in inestimable losses to Cather scholarship and to gay and lesbian history.

Nonetheless, Cather's twelve novels and several collections of short stories are a substantial and luminously written part of that history. Her popular success and her (modest) place in the canon of American literature were secured by works such as *O Pioneers!* (1913) and *My Ántonia* (1918; revised, 1926), which could be read as celebrations of women whose energies and intelligence were devoted to the expansion and settlement of the nation. Recently, though, attention to gender and sexuality issues has brought to the surface of Cather's texts some of the old "queer" things she sought desperately and systematically to repress in her life. Given that she herself associated "queerness" with the sense of deviance she experienced in cross-dressing and loving women in the 1890s, the (re)"queering" of Cather and her fiction in the 1990s seems justifiable and necessary, so it is not surprising that such prominent theorists of sexuality as Eve Sedgwick and Judith Butler have recently written on Cather. Indeed, the texts readily avail themselves of such a process, supplying ample evidence to support a range of queer interpretive possibilities. In what follows, I briefly sketch out just a few of those possibilities. I do so not to reduce Cather's fiction to a covert sexual autobiography or to fulfill my own wishes as a lesbian reader, but to demonstrate how much is obscured when critics, like authors, repress queerness in favor of "conventional" readings.

The "queerness" of Cather's texts—if I might resituate her term into a broader contemporary context that includes not only a range of sexual deviations (from whatever "norm" might be said to operate these days) but also a multifaceted sense of the subversive, the disruptive, the dissenting—is manifest in at least three primary ways: first, in their massive resistance to compulsory heterosexuality as a social institution; second, in their deployment of a model of character that destabilizes the connection between biological sex and sociological gender; and third, in their persistent, if quiet, celebration of same-sex relationships as an alternative to the emptiness or the destructiveness of socially sanctioned opposite-sex relationships. These three points are overlapping and complexly connected, but for the sake of clarity I will discuss them separately.

From her first novel (*Alexander's Bridge*, 1912) to her last (*Sapphira and the Slave Girl*, 1940), marriage—the most visible sign of compulsory heterosexuality as a social institution—is depicted in Cather's fiction as coercive and corrosive, a structure erected primarily to regulate desire by ensuring that it flows through "proper" channels. Marriage generally succeeds, however, not in regulating desire but in crushing it, twisting it—or forcing it into "improper" channels outside of marriage. In *Alexander's Bridge*, *O Pioneers!*, and *A Lost Lady* (1923), infidelity is the result of disappointment in marriage, and in the first two cases adultery leads directly to death. In *My Ántonia*, *One of Ours* (1922), and *The Professor's House* (1925), such disappointment leads only to estrangement, but it is also tied to the profound anguish that marks the three male protagonists of these tales. Godfrey St. Peter, of *The Professor's House*, seems to speak for the whole miserable gang when he remarks, shortly before nearly dying of asphyxiation, that his whole adult life, "his career, his wife, his family, were not his life at all, but a chain of events which had happened to him. All these things had nothing to do with the person he was in the beginning."

Critics have frequently noted the dissatisfactions of Cather's middle-aged characters and their tendency to reject their adult selves as inauthentic in comparison to their (remembered) childhood selves. Rather than reading these characters as repressed homosexuals (which in my view flattens them into psychological case studies), I prefer to see them as vehicles for Cather's relentless critique of the regime of heterosexuality, a regime maintained, as St. Peter notes, through strict enforcement of the "penalties and responsibilities" one incurred in becoming "a lover"—St. Peter's term for the "secondary, social man" he became by participating in the rituals of courtship, marriage, and family-making. St. Peter's longing to reconnect with the "Kansas boy" he describes as "the original, unmodified Godfrey St. Peter" also ties him to my second point about the "queerness" of Cather's texts, for his longing is for a fluidity and freedom from constraint typically associated with gender instability in her fiction.

For most characters, such instability is possible only in childhood. Ántonia, for example, boasts that she can "work like mans" when she is young but embraces the gender-appropriate roles of wife and mother—and, indeed, becomes a mother so prolific that Jim compares her to "the founders of early races"—in adulthood. Jim himself feels "erased, blotted out" in the prairie landscape of his childhood, but in that state of dissolution he is free to travel between genders, as it were—to be equally (and erotically) fascinated by Jake and Otto, the hired men who work on his grandfather's farm, and by the immigrant girls of the neighborhood. Otto's mustache, the ends of which were "twisted up stiffly, like little horns," is as compelling to Jim as the spectacle of Lena Lingard's "plump, fair-skinned" body.

For a few characters, the capacity to bend or blend genders persists beyond childhood. In *O Pioneers!* Alexandra Bergson is able to combine a patience with and insight into the land that the text marks as feminine with a shrewd sense of business and a strength of will that it marks as masculine. In *The Song of the Lark* (1915), Thea Kronborg revels ecstatically in her female physicality—taking baths that have a "ceremonial gravity" and being cheered by the sight of her own body—but manages her singing career with a single-mindedness that novels generally deny female characters or punish them for having.

The critique of marriage and the subversion of gender identity are combined in the figure of the same-sex couple, which Cather deploys with some frequency. The most prominent of these pairs are male, though the comely Lena Lingard remains unmarried and closely connected to Tiny Soderball—living around the corner from her in San Francisco—to the end of *My Ántonia*. The male couples seem less a sign of Cather's masculine identification or a misogynistic rejection of femininity (as some readers have recently averred) than a further destabilization of the connection between sex and gender and a complex process of mingling, switching, and redistributing of attributes and energies that seems possible only within the unit of the couple. Such pairs include the soldier boys Claude Wheeler and David Gerhardt in *One of Ours*, the cowboy archaeologists Tom Outland and Roddy Blake in *The Professor's House*, and to some extent Tom Outland and St. Peter in *The Professor's House*, but the same-sex couple that absorbs most narrative attention is that of the two French priests, Jean Marie Latour and Joseph Vaillant, in *Death Comes for the Archbishop* (1927). In this case, the story of the couple—their long personal and professional partnership, the rhythms of their life together, the strains created when duty forces them to live apart—really is the story the novel aims to tell. Cather's stunning descriptions of the Southwestern landscape and the story of the Catholic Church's role in the "Americanization" of New Mexico are merely tributaries to the narrative's main stream, which is the richest and most satisfying love story the author ever wrote.

That said, it must also be acknowledged that Cather's same-sex couples are not figured without some ambivalence—without, indeed, clear signs of homophobia or a more general erotophobia. Latour and Vaillant are, after all, priests. They take seriously their vows of celibacy, and Latour works hard to rid his diocese of those who do not—to clean up the "Augean stable" of the church in the Southwest, as the missionary bishop who chooses him for the job puts it. Latour and Vaillant's relationship can be safely idealized because it is predicated upon an explicit renunciation of sex. In *The Professor's House*, when Tom recalls being nursed through a bout of pneumonia by his friend Roddy Blake, he remarks, "He ought to have had boys of his own to look after. Nature's full of such substitutions, but they always seem to me sad, even in botany." Tom's skittishness about Roddy's caretaking and his ultimate betrayal of their friendship (in the argument over Roddy's sale of the artifacts) suggest that Cather fought to repress signs of "queerness" in her characters as vigorously as she fought to repress them in herself—even as she fought, on other levels, to express them or merely to live them. Tom later says of his treatment of Roddy, "Anyone who requites faith and friendship as I did, will have to pay for it. I'm not very sanguine about good fortune for myself. I'll be called to account when I least expect it."

In the battle between the queer and the conventional, Willa Cather made similar sacrifices, particularly in repudiating her own daring alter ego, William Cather. I wonder sometimes if she, too, thought she would be called to account.

NOTE: My discussion alludes to and paraphrases the following letters: Willa Cather to Louise Pound, 15 June 1892, Louise Pound Papers, Manuscript Department, Duke University Library, Durham, North Carolina; Willa Cather to Mariel Gere, 4 August 1896 and 25 April 1897, Willa Cather Historical Center, Red Cloud, Nebraska.

RENATE STENDHAL

Stein's Style: A Passion for Sentences

THE REVOLUTIONARY SPARK STRUCK by Picasso in painting was kindled by Gertrude Stein in writing. She wrote the way the Cubists painted, moving beyond the spatial limitations of their three-dimensional perspective. Her early "word portraits," for example, were verbal still lifes capturing the salon guests from different angles simultaneously, in a single "cubist" plane. Her writing and theories about writing liberated language from the nineteenth century, from all romantic, naturalistic, and symbolic overtones. With her most famous words—"A rose is a rose is a rose is a rose"—the nonrepresentational rose of the twentieth century was created.

Yet, in her own time, recognition of Gertrude Stein's language revolution was slow to come. From a traditional perspective, there was "no there there": the words of a woman could not possibly be at the beginning of modernism. The American Gertrude Stein gave her contemporaries a lot to swallow. She was not only a woman, she was an independent woman. She came from a well-to-do German-Jewish family and had her own income (a family allowance). At age fourteen, she had lost her not particularly beloved mother; at eighteen, her much detested father. She had studied psychology and medicine before coming to Paris. She would not tolerate the domination of a man and replaced her brotherly companion with a woman. With all this, the female language pioneer was a step ahead of her time.

Readers of the monumental work of Gertrude Stein (about 600 titles) are sentenced to a challenge. The author had a "lifelong passion for sentences." Endless sentences. Stenographically short sentences. Constantly repeated, minutely changed sentences. Sentences that refuse to move anything on, that do not move toward any end of a story, any aim or future. Sentences insisting on the continuous present, i.e., "continuous presence." Sentences consisting of word play, double entendres, and seemingly nonsensical linguistic hide-and-seek games.

From the Spring 1995 issue. This reading is excerpted from the Introduction to *Gertrude Stein in Words and Pictures*, edited by Renate Stendhal (Algonquin Books of Chapel Hill, 1994).

Gertrude Stein

The works of the male avant-garde—Joyce, the Futurists, Dadaists, Expressionists, Surrealists—were auscultated word for word. Not so the works of the female avant-garde. Gertrude Stein had to wait for her first success until she was fifty-nine years old. Until then, she hardly managed to publish anything unless she paid for it herself. Her freeing of language from its grammatical and emotional traditions was considered absurd, not to be taken seriously. Together with Picasso, she liked to speculate: "Braque and Joyce, they are the incomprehensibles whom anybody can understand. *Les incompréhensibles que tout le monde peut comprendre.*"

As death approached, Stein asked Alice B. Toklas the now legendary question, "What is the answer?" And, when there was no reply, said, "In that case, what is the question?"

The legend still holds. Everybody knows of Gertrude Stein, even if only a few have read her. "A rose is a rose is a rose is a rose" is an evergreen, self-sufficient and satisfying to the point where inquiring further into her writing might seem unnecessary. Here, the idea and practice of modernism are captured in a single line, a magical "Open, Sesame" that promises access to the avant-garde literature of the twentieth century. Here, at the literary threshold, one can linger and weigh with a pleasant shudder how far the experiment of language has moved out into impassable terrain. In Stein's phrase, the rose is still recognizable as what it had been for centuries in the Western lyrical tradition. Yet, it has gained a concreteness of irreducible presence and, at the same time, awakens an intimation of strangeness, the estrangement of a new era. The line is a literary "invitation to the dance": we, the readers, are invited to create the well-worn rose anew.

Familiar and strange. The photographic image of Stein's beautiful, massive head with the Caesar haircut belongs to the culture of our century as solidly as Picasso's 1906 portrait of her. A modern equivalent to archetypal Western images of women—the Mona Lisa, for example—Stein's head raises the timeless question of identity. "I want to be historical," "In my generation I am the only one," "I am a genius"—the pronouncements of a woman who stepped onto the world stage at a time when other women were just beginning to demand egalitarian treatment.

Gertrude Stein, born in Allegheny, Pennsylvania, to parents of German-Jewish descent, learned English at the age of five. Her first language was German. She spent her early years in Vienna and Paris before her family moved back to America. From that time on, and for the rest of her life, she knew how to remain the five-year-old child who discovers the English language for the first time, tries it out without prejudice, endlessly repeating, wantonly changing, destroying, and re-creating it. She played with every possible literary genre, from nursery rhymes to opera libretti. No matter how difficult her texts appear, she always insisted they were perfectly simple. And many are disarmingly simple and playful:

> If you hear her snore
> It is not before you love her
> You love her so that to be her beau is very lovely
> She is sweetly there and her curly hair is very lovely.
> She is sweetly here and I am very near and that is very lovely.

> She is my tender sweet and her little feet are stretched out well
> which is a treat and very lovely.
> Her little tender nose is between her little eyes which close and are
> very lovely.
> She is very lovely and mine which is very lovely.
>
> —*Portraits and Prayers*

Having come into the world as the spoiled youngest of five siblings, Gertrude Stein described her childlike quality as freedom from "sentimental feeling" and as "aggressive liveliness" ("that is the way I was and that is the way I still am, and any one who is like that necessarily liked it. I did and I do"). The "child within man," as the German language has it, in this case survived within a woman.

FOR ME, composing Gertrude Stein's life story in pictures and quotations was giving in to the temptation of a riddle. There was not only the question, Who was Gertrude Stein? There was the unavoidable challenge of the question, How to read Gertrude Stein?

The riddle fascinated me from the moment when, as a schoolgirl, I heard how a comma is "holding your coat for you" ("Poetry and Grammar"). The fascination lasted even when it turned into avoidance: whenever I advanced from her more accessible theoretical and autobiographical texts into the hermetic fields of her "Cubist" writing, my courage would desert me. Her continuous present tense seemed to have left the past, the literary tradition of the fathers, so far behind that the literary connection between them was cut. I would find myself face-to-face with a sphinx holding a mirror to my incapacity. Is she making fun of language? I would ask myself. Is she intentionally fooling us?

I sensed that there was something else at play. If one could only find the rules of the game, one would be able to play along with her and share the fun. With an excluded reader's agony, I would look for the "useful knowledge" my author had promised (in a book of that title, in 1928). I would go back and forth between my possible sources of understanding, puzzling over her cryptic words, her personality, her psychology, her life story, then trying to read her face, the foxy but good-natured, serious fun it radiates. I sensed that if this sphinx had hidden the answers to her questions, well, she must have also left sufficient clues about how to find them. "If there is no answer, what is the question?" My hunch proved right. My lack of courage would be countered to the extent that pieces of the verbal puzzle kept falling into my hands.

I remember the night when I first tried my teeth on Stein's famous portrait-poem "Susie Asado," written in 1913. The portrait begins:

> Sweet sweet sweet sweet sweet tea.
>   Susie Asado.
> Sweet sweet sweet sweet sweet tea.
>   Susie Asado.
> Susie Asado which is a told tray sure.
> A lean on the shoe this means slips slips hers. . . .

Reportedly the portrait had been inspired by the flamenco dancer La Argentina, whom Stein and Toklas had admired when they were in Spain in 1913. How then could the first evocation of the dancer be dominated by the highly un-Spanish association of tea on a tray? I did not find poetic peace that night. I continued hearing the staccato rhythm of flamenco shoes in these lines, but I fell out of rhythm every time I came to the "Sweet tea." The turnoff or cutoff at the end of these lines seemed so jarring that I sensed a purpose behind it. Did the abrupt shift from Spanish "sweet" to English "tea" capture a dislocation Stein herself had experienced? I literally had no clue. I felt duped and slighted. I decidedly did not like Susie Asado, that fake Spanish dancer with a half-English name.

The next morning, however, when sweet Susie had become an annoying "earworm" (a German notion), I suddenly heard it. "Sweet tea": sweetie. It was a revelation that changed the entire portrait for me. Stein's sound play suddenly pulled the rapid dance of "Sweet sweet sweet sweet sweet . . ." over the end of the line—and over the edge of proper British manners—into a rapturous calling of "sweetie Susie Asado." Now the whole beginning sounded like the beginning of a lover's plea, with "tray sure" melting into "treasure," another tenderness. "Told" seemed to speak of "bold," of something risqué having been communicated between the adorer and the adored. On the sound stage that had suddenly opened before me, I could take the liberty of playing with associations. The passionate context of flamenco music, song, and dance held another, private, and perhaps secret, passion—a passion involving an author who spoke English (and who had just been in England before coming to Spain) and whose communication of her admiration may not have been as easy as she had desired. Movements of desire may have run into obstacles (broken-off lines) because of different languages—English and Spanish, perhaps even French ("tray sure" can be read as "*très sûre,*" the French feminine version of "very sure"). Desire may also have run into invisible lines of manners, drawn by Alice's presence as a guardian of tea on a tray, the virtues of the home. The dancer's mysterious English name, Susie, may point to the French word for worry, "*souci.*" Any too-passionate leanings ("lean on the shoe") might have caused slippings, a loss of balance, especially if the dancer's movements ("slips slips hers") had conveyed too bold a message (with her slippers, her lips, or revealing her slip) as the sounds seem to suggest.

I felt bold myself in this speculative reading, but encouraged by the fact that my playing with Stein's text never seemed to leave the text. I rather felt that I was finally playing inside her own playfulness, dancing along with her own verbal dance. I was fortunate to know some of the bilingual "steps" of that dance. To read "Susie Asado," knowing French as well as English seemed a precondition. In other cases, I soon noticed, a knowledge of German and Yiddish also helped in keeping up with Stein. (My first language, as for Stein, was German; I learned English at age ten, French at sixteen, and Yiddish at twenty, shortly before leaving Germany to live in Paris as my chosen place of "exile.")

"Susie Asado" made me aware that biographical knowledge can be useful indeed for reading Gertrude Stein. I am not sure I would have found access to her text had I not known about the multilingual context of her writing and taken a few hints from what I knew about the erotic side of her life. Then, by reading and repeating the words (in the way Stein liked to call "caressing"), the "abstract" portrait had revealed itself as equally evocative, risqué, and rich in color as the portraits Picasso had painted at the same time.

In the past two decades, feminist scholars have confirmed my own tentative reading. Linda Simon, Gloria Orenstein, and others have clearly established the eroticism that crosses through Stein's work, partly in disguise, partly with surprising explicitness. The discovery led scholars to a new hypothesis: perhaps more than erotic deviance was hidden in Stein's texts. Perhaps even her most experimental work was not altogether abstract, but strategically coded. The coding, in Orenstein's view, was a device to disguise anything that would have hindered Stein's literary success. In order to hold her own against her male rivals, the female author had to veil the disturbing elements of her identity: being female, Jewish, and lesbian. According to this thesis, Stein over(p)layed these disturbing elements with the less provocative identity of an American in Paris. Hidden in the text, she played out her true identity in word games, sound associations, false abstractions, maskings, and masquerades.

Stein's "Susie Asado" can be read as a perfect example of such a masked homoerotic subtext. Another example is "Caesar," an image that appears repeatedly in her work. "I say lifting belly and then I say lifting belly and Caesars. I say lifting belly gently and Caesars gently. I say lifting belly again and Caesars again. I say lifting belly and I say Caesars and I say lifting belly and Caesars and cow come out" ("Lifting Belly"). "What are Caesars. Caesars are round a little longer than wide but not oval. They are picturesque and useful" ("Today We Have a Vacation"). Or, "A fig an apple and some grapes make a cow. How. The Caesars know how. Now" ("A Sonatina Followed by Another"). The name Caesar contains a sound play on "sees her" and "seize her," as well as an allusion to Stein herself, the author with a claim to literary authority and with the haircut of an emperor famous for his homosexual leanings. Again the ear decodes what is partly hidden to the eyes.

It has been argued, however, that Stein's way of loading a word/sound/name/image with complex associations does not necessarily indicate coding. "Opaqueness" is characteristic of the entire modernist avant-garde. Instead of being a special case, Stein can be read simply as a prototype of modernism. Indeed, if she wrote in code, we would have to explain an obvious contradiction: she, whose language insistently abstracts itself from the personal and representational, presents her physical self with such shocking liberality.

No Oedipus will once and for all unriddle this sphinx. The most enticing riddle is precisely the one that promises and, at the same time, withholds its solution. Continuously tempting, it stays continuously present.

The guessing game of reading Stein demands patience and sufficient motivation to listen to and around her words, to feel them out, let them roll over one's tongue, and read them aloud (or listen to Stein's recorded voice). Aloud and, I would add, administered in the right dose, in a rhythm similar to that in which she wrote: every day a bit. In my experience, this practice best brings out the unity of sound, rhythm, sense, and ambiguity in her writing. Even the most seemingly absurd statements do, after all, make sense.

Take a line from one of her hermetic texts, *Tender Buttons* (1912–14): "A little called anything shows shudders." What are we to make of it? Does anything show shudders when called "little," or when called only a little bit? The sentence is evocative without evoking anything clearly recognizable. It stays abstract, pure "Steinese."

The mystery, in this case, happens to have been solved by Gertrude Stein herself. She revealed in an interview, in 1946, that the sentence referred to her car, to "the movement of one of those old-fashioned automobiles, an old Ford . . . [a]

movement that is not always successful." The "absurd" sentence instantly fills with life. There is tenderness, worry, a hint at nicknames for a beloved car. Every word vibrates with associations, with the "peaceful and exciting" certitude of meaning. Readers who are not satisfied with Stein's practical explanation, however, may seek further inspiration from the intriguing title of the book, *Tender Buttons*. "Button" is a slang word for clitoris. Read with this in mind, "a little" and its "shudders" radically change meaning. One and the same sentence can be abstract on one level, realistic on another, and a double entendre on a third. With her own interpretation the author has pointed toward a possible *explication de texte*, in the sense of a personal, creative relation to language in which meaning and interpretation are necessarily private and consistently in flux. Commenting about her sentences, Stein once evoked "the intense feeling that they made sense, then the doubt and then each time over again the intense feeling that they did make sense."

Stein's strategy is obviously different from the "female voice" (*écriture de différence*) celebrated by recent feminist authors. The "Mother of Modernism" was not particularly interested in being a woman. On the contrary, she used every possibility of the English language to neither reveal nor conceal her gender. She chose to leave the question open. She, the outsider, wrote about herself as "he," "one," "someone," "nobody," and "everybody." She called the second part of her autobiography *Everybody's Autobiography*. As she considered her writing self-explanatory, she never commented on what she intended with this tactical move. We are left to speculate. Did she intend to proclaim the universality of her—female—person?

RICHARD HOWARD

Auden Agonistes

A Review of *Auden*

by Richard Davenport-Hines
(Pantheon Books, 1995)

THERE APPEARS to be a contradiction in genre between the poet who asked
that anyone owning his letters burn them (a ludicrous and entirely emblematic request: I myself possess three communications from Wystan Auden, two
of great interest for their discussions of prosody, and I wouldn't dream of destroying any of them; Auden's own relish in writing about the letters of all
kinds of writers and artists suggests the perversity of his crematory impulse)
and that there be no biography (I have read two, Osborne and Carpenter,
while waiting for the second volume of the entirely superior Mendelson).
There are also two book-length memoirs, one ridiculous (Farnham) and one
rewarding (Clark), as well as three volumes of Oxford *Auden Studies,* the
Newsletter of the Auden Society, and any number of memorial tributes that
bid fair (and even unfair) to continue while the Princeton edition of *The
Complete Works,* which has so far produced only two volumes, the *Libretti*
and the *Plays,* drags its slow length along—there is a contradiction, then, between the poet of such biographical reticence (if that is what it is) and the
poet who asked that (a recording of) *Siegfried's Funeral March* be played at
his obsequies.

For Auden apparently did think of himself as a hero, and however disputed
the heroism of his life may have been, he wanted that much attestation to it,
that much acknowledgment of it (pretty broad, I should say; not even Robert
Lowell, had he known the possibilities afforded, would have gone in for *The
Twilight of the Gods!*). Mr. Davenport-Hines—the author of a book called *Sex,
Death and Punishment* and the editor of *Vice,* a literary anthology—has been
entirely loyal to Auden's realization of himself as an heroic, certainly as an ag-
onistic figure, and his biography is a delicately limned portrait ("Auden's last

From the Summer 1996 issue

W. H. Auden

three teeth were extracted in January 1956, and after this depressing start he seems to have been deeply unhappy for much of the year"). Better than any of the other biographers so far (I except Mendelson, whose returns are not yet altogether in), Davenport-Hines has managed to stir Auden's homosexuality into the pudding without indigestible lumps, and without too much poking and prodding of the poems themselves he has provided a pervasive sense of a specific poetical character from youth to age, the public mask laid upon the private face, i.e., Auden plain.

The man's social *Stimmung*, sensational though it frequently was, is not insisted on—Davenport-Hines gestures to the poetry as the source of our in-

214

terest in most instances—but it is implicit in the dark brush strokes of the descriptions ("touchy, demanding, tyrannical, disruptive"), in the grimmer medical details ("the anger is that of a prematurely ageing man accused by pain"), and though there is necessarily a difference in emphasis about the New York years as perceived by those of us who shared them with the poet and as Davenport-Hines reports them from England, this is a true biography—not backwritten from the work to the life (like Painter's *Proust*), nor "interpretive" from the life to the work (in Sainte-Beuve's manner), but a close account of the writer and talker Spender called "sometimes agreeable, sometimes illuminating, sometimes brilliant, sometimes funny, sometimes irritating."

Quotations like this last one are liberally spattered through the book—Davenport-Hines has not passed up anything anyone said which might amuse or enlighten an outsider, and if I miss something it is the absence of the biographer's own resonance, though I guess such "impersonality" is intended. Only rarely do I hear what must be the author's "view," as here: "[Auden's] efforts were not a connivance to become a permanent character in the dramatis personae of the twentieth century, though that was certainly a result." For the most part, Davenport-Hines has been eager to let the famous and the clever do his characterizing for him; his own and intensive effort has been to articulate the ongoing travail of the life as lived, the feeling for the man's quality as he speaks in the work, prose, and verse, throughout, from the early Hardy imitations to the elaborate late poems (which seem to dissatisfy so many readers who pastured so readily on the poems of the forties, when they were in their forties) with their nonce words, their Jamesian syntax, their high information-quotient.

The special problem of any Auden biography—which Carpenter muffed altogether, which Osborne too much gloated over, and which Mendelson doesn't, so far, seem to consider a problem at all—is of course Chester Kallman. Thekla Clark's memoir, which has been published subsequent to this book, is a great help in seeing why it was possible—and even poetically useful—for Auden to be trapped with this "partner" in an erotic, financial, and characterological labyrinth that appears to have been spared Stein in her life with Toklas, and Britten in his with Pears. Certainly Davenport-Hines is perceptive and fair in this regard, and his subsidiary portrait of the man who was both the "onlie begetter" and "Chester my chum" is vivid enough (God knows). The mystery abides, however, and perhaps we are yet having to learn, in our biographical speculations, that love is love, still, which alteration finds (think of the Carlyles, of Forster and his policeman!). But that is the only bare place in this handsomely carpeted narrative, and there are characteristic virtues not to be found elsewhere—the discovery, for instance, that Auden's commonplace book *A Certain World* is a disguised autobiography; and the careful, lively, and *charitable* figuration of Auden's parents (Mr. Davenport-Hines is much kinder to Constance Rosalie Auden than I can find it in my heart to be—yet another instance of his general superiority of character). Altogether, a valuable study, the one to read after you have read the criticism and the plays and the libretti and the table-talk, should you still be curious about the Englishman who, after Hardy, wrote the grandest body of poetry in the twentieth century.

REED WOODHOUSE

Five Houses of Gay Fiction

VIRGIL THOMSON ONCE SAID that when he was working on a new piece he kept at it until (as he put it) the piece "improvised itself the same way" three days in a row. Several years ago, my friend Michael Schwartz and I began teaching a course at the Cambridge Center for Adult Education called "Gay Male Fiction"—literature (as we put it) "by, for, and about gay men." Our course has confirmed Thomson's experience, for it has now improvised itself in basically the same way three times. Each time, we have come back to the same core of texts, around which we then situate certain others. This core I am calling "ghetto literature"; its periphery I am dividing into various categories: closet, proto-ghetto, assimilative, and "queer."

When we first conceived this course, we were faced in the most practical sense with the question of a "canon." Which books had to go on the syllabus? Which would be fun to teach if we had time? Which were irrelevant or bad? Further questions occurred to us: What is the essence of a "gay" fiction? Are the gayest books necessarily the best books? Or does the book's "gay-density," so to speak, have nothing at all to do with its literary value? What follows is my own attempt to justify the "canon" we have repeatedly improvised, and in so doing to make a rough and ready taxonomy of modern gay-male fiction.

It is not, I hope, a restrictive, let alone a prescriptive taxonomy, for I am aware of having left out a great deal. I am, for instance, deliberately confining myself to American gay male fiction of the post–World War II period. I have done this mainly because I think it is almost impossible to speak of openly gay fiction—books "by, for, and about gay men"—before this period. There are exceptions, of course: Parker Tyler's *The Young and Evil*, for instance. But most books claimed for gay literature from earlier periods (e.g., Van Vechten's *The Blind Bow-Boy*) are so severely coded as to require sophisticated literary cryptography: they are not the focus of this essay. For the same reason, I do not attempt to bring out the homosexual meanings of Melville, James, or Proust: a task which literary historians like David Bergman, Eve Sedgwick, and Robert

From the Winter 1994 issue

Martin have undertaken. The tradition I am invoking is far more recent and far less grand. Whether its works will be judged by future readers as "great" remains to be seen. They are, nonetheless, our books in a way that *Billy Budd* and *A la recherche du temps perdu* are not; and as such they attempt a synthesis of homosexuality into literature that earlier writers, no matter how great, simply could not have imagined.

I believe that there is a distinguishable body of first-rate work "by, for, and about gay men," a literature I am calling "ghetto" or "proto-ghetto" fiction. I further believe that this fiction ought to be considered the trunk, not a mere branch, of our particular literary tree. By "ghetto" fiction, I do not mean only the books whose authors lived in the gay ghettos of San Francisco, Los Angeles, or New York; nor those whose characters did. In a sense, it would be more accurate to say they are books whose *readers* did indeed live there, but that even that residence need not have been a literal one. The more important reason this is "ghetto" fiction is that it occupies a place in literature analogous to the place occupied in the city by the gay ghetto; a place where homosexuality is both taken for granted (and thus invisible) and at the same time easily identifiable (and thus highly visible): a sort of parallel city, in fact. "Ghetto literature," then, is in one sense literature "by, for, and about gay men." In another, wider sense, it is literature that resembles the ghetto by embodying the virtues of separateness and pride, by insisting on a gay identity, and by existing for itself alone, not for the straight world.

These are not books, in other words, whose characters "just happen to be gay"; any more than the ghetto can be defined as a place whose residents "just happen to be gay." Its characters (whether truly or mistakenly, comically or disastrously) see their sexuality as a key to their lives. These books, like the gay ghetto itself, represent a gay world at its furthest point of self-definition, and are an expression of homosexuality at its most concentrated: that is, as nearly as possible without normative reference to the straight world. The proto-ghetto books differ from ghetto books mainly by lacking a gay community, and sometimes even the *name* "gay" for who and what the characters are. They nevertheless belong with ghetto literature, rather than with either closetted or assimilative fiction, sharing with ghetto fiction an astonishing, sometimes arrogant disregard for the surrounding straight world. Some of the works I would put in the ghetto or proto-ghetto category are: Tennessee Williams' early and amazingly unabashed short stories ("Hard Candy," "Desire and the Black Masseur," "Two on a Party" and others); Christopher Isherwood's masterpiece *A Single Man*; James Purdy's novels of rapturous violence *Eustace Chisholm and the Works* and *Narrow Rooms*; Andrew Holleran's *Dancer from the Dance*; Ethan Mordden's three volumes of short stories on gay life in Manhattan in the late 1970s and 80s; and, most recent and one of the best, the English author Neil Bartlett's beautiful *Ready to Catch Him Should He Fall*.

Ghetto literature was preceded by, and in some ways formed against, something we might call "closet" literature: fiction which saw homosexuality as something defining indeed, but horrifyingly so. One wants to say that this is literature so remote from an ordinary modern gay man's experience that it is now irrelevant. But such a judgment would not be quite true, for in a sense the closet can never die. So long as homosexuality continues to be defined (as, in an obvious way, it must) as a sexual identity, books about it will be quintessentially sexual and thus quintessentially threatening. That is the source of closet-literature's truth and power. ("Queer" theorists and artists insert their skewer precisely here: the closet *can* die, in their view, if sexual identity—being "gay" or "straight"—is no longer considered defining or constitutive. Hence their eager embrace of bisexuality as theory and practice; and their extension of "queerness" to forms of identity that are non-sexual.) James Baldwin's *Giovanni's Room*, the closet novel *par excellence,* is a reminder of where we have come from, and where most of us, at some point in our gay lives, have been: alone, fearful, disgraced. It is also true, in some horrible way, to an ongoing sexual need and sexual shame that are never entirely erased. Gloomy and unfair as much of it is, closet fiction is at least not Pollyannish. It has the great virtue of taking sex seriously. It does not whimsify it, nor denature it of moral meaning.

Both ghetto and closet literature have been replaced, in recent years, by different kinds of gay fiction, most of it very polished, much of it popular, and some of it well-reviewed in the mainstream press. The two main branches of this new literature I call "assimilative" or "homosexual," and "transgressive" or "queer."

Assimilative gay literature embraces many of the best-known gay writers in America, including the late Robert Ferro, David Leavitt, Stephen Mc-Cauley, Christopher Bram, Michael Cunningham, and others. This literature breaks away from the ghetto tradition by placing its gay characters either outside the literal gay ghetto or in a hostile relation to it. But the characters are also outside of the symbolic, literary ghetto: Nothing but their inclusion of a gay character would make us think these were gay books. Assimilative stories are deliberately integrative and frequently concern a gay character's coming to terms with his family, living with straight friends (often women), or finding a lover and settling down in a monogamous relationship. An astounding number of them are about raising children.

Assimilative literature is fiction about gay men for straight readers. It shows gay life within the implicit or explicit context of mainstream life, and tacitly appeals to mainstream values—especially those of the family, or of monogamous love—to bless its gay characters. It is not the same thing as closet literature, for it claims the right of gay people to exist—provided they resemble straight ones. These books, while well-written, are rarely brilliant or witty. (Stylistic brilliance of the Wildean sort is perhaps too identifiably "gay.") Their strength lies in an appeal to a common humanity: "We're all looking for love" or, "We're all trying to figure out our parents." These novels are about people who "just happen to be gay." Some homosexual titles: Gore Vidal's brave early novel *The City and the Pillar*; David Leavitt's *Equal Affections* and *The Lost Language of Cranes*; Stephen McCauley's *Object of My Affection*; and Michael Cunningham's beautiful *Home at the End of the World*. Perhaps the most popular of all gay books (among both gay and straight readers) would fall into this category: Armistead Maupin's *Tales of the City* series.

The transgressive, or "queer" writers are quite different, at least on the surface, from the assimilators. And they too number some respected, if less known gay writers, many if not all from the West Coast: Dennis Cooper, Robert Glück, Kevin Killian, Paul Russell, the late Sam D'Allesandro. Their stories are frequently ones of horror, dissociation, or emotional numbness. They are often shocking in their presentation of extreme psychological states and extreme sexual acts, such as mutilation and murder. They are like the assimilators in disdaining the ghetto, though for a different reason: what they loathe is its bourgeois complacency, indeed its rather vulgar success. And indeed, they seem to be assimilative themselves—only to a different larger group.

The queer writer is queer first; homosexual second. "Queer" in this context does not primarily mean "homosexual," but "estranged," "marginal." He is in reaction against not only the straight world, but the gay one as well, especially the middle-class ghetto. He is a professional distruster of authority. Queer writing is peculiarly contradictory about sex. On the one hand, because it sees homosexuality as "transgressive," it can present gay characters as heroes of the sexual margin. On the other,"transgression" takes so many forms—including cross-dressing, bisexuality, radical or reactionary politics, or mere anomie—that it's hard to keep the homosexuality as such separated from the general transgressiveness that is praised. If the characters are gay, their gayness is not as central as their alientation.

The queer writer par excellence these days is Dennis Cooper, whose novels *Closer* and *Frisk* exemplify the frightening coolness and unemotionality of radical narrative. In *Frisk*, for example, one of the characters asks another to shit in the toilet and not flush. He adds: "I'm not being abject. . . . It's not, 'Ooh, shit, piss, how wicked,' or anything. It's, like I said, information." Queer writing is often pornographic or a parody of pornography; and it brilliantly captures the dissociation of sexual obsession. Its great insight is that, just as "love" can be put in ironic quotation marks, so can something seemingly real and objective like "sex." Nearly all the sex scenes in Cooper are fascinating—the right, obsessed word—because they are mechanical. In no case do they call forth irrelevant words like "beautiful" or "ugly," "good" or "bad." "Queer" titles might include Killian's *Shy*, Glück's *Elements of a Coffee Service* and *Jack the Modernist*, Paul Russell's *The Salt Point*, Sam D'Allesandro's collection of stories *The Zombie Pit Stories*.

Neither the assimilationists nor the queers are attempting quite what the earlier gay authors attempted: namely, to create a literature of gay awareness, heroism, and separateness. Neither group seems to proceed from a sense of *joy* (even privilege) in being gay. None of them finds the "world well lost" for it. The assimilative books, while completely un-abject and "pro-gay," continue a narrative of acceptance by the straight world that was present in earlier, more lachrymose works like the saccharine *The Lord Won't Mind*. The transgressive titles repudiate the straight world (construed as something much larger than the mere mass of heterosexuals), but in that repudiation continue its power, and assign homosexuality a position only on the margins of society—powerless, undignified, desperate. In both assimilative and transgressive texts, homosexuality loses all particularity of social reference; the gay characters don't act or talk "gay." Whether insiders or outsiders, they are virtually indistinguishable from straight ones.

Is this a step forward? Many would say yes; I would disagree. It seems to me that there is a tremendous, and unacknowledged pressure on gay writers to "tone down" the sexuality of their characters and their story, to make them more "universal." I am an Aristotelian in this matter, and believe that universality, if it is to be found, must come in the form of particulars. I do not think that a literature, or a life, that blurs the outlines of our gay identity represents us fully to ourselves or to the straight world. While assimilative or queer texts may be excellent books, therefore, they are only partially "gay" books. However interesting or beautiful they may be in other respects, they are not the books I would recommend to someone, gay or straight, who wanted to know what a *gay* life was like.

The ghetto writers, by contrast, do insist on a gay particularity and are thus as necessary (I would argue) as the actual ghettoes many of us inhabit. Both fictional and urban ghettoes "stand for" an identifiably gay life, and thus are living refutations of the belief that gay people don't really exist, or are not really different. Both institutions, ghetto and ghetto literature, make a radical and complex claim: that gay life is different from straight life in some important ways; and that that difference won't go away. Ghetto writers have posed, if not solved, the peculiar difficulties and triumphs of gay life by insisting on three things. The first and most important is that sexuality must be central; to make it peripheral or adventitious risks erasing the characters' homosexuality altogether. Second, and related to the first, is the insistence on the characters' slight, but important, separateness from the straight world. Third, they insist on joy, even arrogance, in that separateness, rather than shame or guilt. The sexual and social particularities of their characters may be social disabilities, but are personal advantages.

What I am calling "ghetto literature" is then gay, not incidentally but essentially. It is not enough that it simply take place in the ghetto; it must, as it were, be written *for* the ghetto. It is not intended primarily for a non-gay audience: like life in the actual ghetto, it will take homosexuality for granted, and will not explain it. It is not enough for there to be one or two gay characters swimming in a welter of straight ones, even if the gay characters are "good" and the straight ones "bad." The purpose of ghetto literature is not to award points for sensitivity. The gay protagonist will see himself in only incidental relationship to the straight world: George in Isherwood's *A Single Man,* for instance, teaches with straight people at his state university. But they are not the important people in his life. Even his best friend Charlotte, who thinks she is more important to George than she is, is kept at a distance. These books describe a homosexuality which sees itself as separate, confident, unself-pitying. By the same token, they see heterosexuality and the life of the straight family as interesting, perhaps, but essentially irrelevant. The separateness the gay character feels, in other words, liberates him more than it enchains him. It is the condition of his particularity, and he would not give it up, even if he could.

It has been noticeably easy for critics to praise a fugitive and cloistered voice: that is, to give their blessing to a homosexual fiction which represents few gay characters, few gay tropes (irony or camp), and few gay sexual acts. David Leavitt's *Equal Affections,* for example, seems to have won acclaim for its representation not of the gay son, but the dying mother. (A reviewer for the *San Francisco Chronicle,* carried away by exaltation, compares him to Tolstoy.)

Stephen McCauley's *Object of My Affection* tells the *Times Book Review* "what it is like to be young in these crazy times." ("Young," not "gay.") And at the opposite pole, the cold horror of Dennis Cooper has proven almost equally tolerable, at least to the avant-garde. ("A minor classic," says the *Washington Post* of *Closer.*) In much recent writing, homosexual love is purged of lust (as in Leavitt), or nihilistically reduced to it (as in Cooper). In the older books, by contrast, specifically gay desire is important, romantic, and—most dangerous of all—*attractive.*

TO GIVE AN IDEA of the different branches of gay-male fiction from the last fifty years, I have taken descriptions of five homes from different branches of gay literature: the closetted, the proto-ghetto, the assimilative, the transgressive, and the full ghetto fictions. Each shows the gay protagonist in a particular relationship with himself, with the outside, non-gay world, and with the outside gay world. The kind of place it is, the way it's described, the sort of person who's living there (and the sort who is not) are all indications of the author's vision of homosexuality. They will help us focus on some larger generalizations I'll make about these branches of gay fiction and what I see to be their main trunk.

The Closet

The closet is not quite invisible: that is its glory and its terror. It is not quite *enough* of a hiding place. It is consequently a place of shame, and the closet-novel focuses on that shame as its main topic and emotional effect. If it damns homosexuality, at least it does not trivialize it. The story of the closet is also surprisingly long-lived: we see late and unworthy versions of it in *The Boys in the Band* and the strangely gloomy life of John Rechy's "sexual outlaw," so promisingly bold in claims of liberation, so unecstatically guilty in fact. (Ecstatic guilt, as in James Purdy on the other hand, is quite alien to Rechy's depressed sex-hunt.) The closet-narrative will always hold some interest for us, as will its more upbeat relative, the coming-out story, because we can all remember a time when we dreaded to see, acknowledge, or express our homosexuality. Further, the strength of the closet-novel, which is intensity of feeling, will always be more popular than mere happiness, or the complex perspectives of irony.

The great novel of the closet is, of course, James Baldwin's *Giovanni's Room,* published in 1956. We say "coming out of the closet," but *Giovanni's Room* is about entering it. We should perhaps remember that in the bad old days, a closet was at least in part a good place: the place where you were private. Even so, Giovanni's room is plainly a symbol not so much of privacy as of imprisonment. It is described as a pool of standing water: "Life in that room seemed to be occurring underwater." Everything there is blurred and softened and distorted: light doesn't quite penetrate it, action is impossible in it. Its waters are the amniotic fluids of a perverse unnatural womb, one that kills rather than brings to life. It is a place not of ordering but disordering: things spill onto the floor—violin music, wine, empty bottles. The horror David feels at the sight of this room is the horror at a sinister life-in-death, at something that cannot or will not die. The past is artificially preserved here, symbolized in stacks of old newspapers. What was lively and intoxicating once—a bottle of wine, its contents spilled on the floor— is now deadening, though paradoxically not dead itself. Its "sweet and heavy" aroma hangs over the room. An old potato—that gift of the New World to the Old, like David himself—is so neglected that even its sprouted eyes have rotted.

The thing that is most symbolically rotten is sex. The half-torn wallpaper, for instance, depicts a "lady in a hoop skirt and a man in knee breeches perpetually walking together, hemmed in by roses." Only in a closet could we be asked to think of a rose garden as a prison. Even the light-fixture is repellent: it "hung like a diseased and undefinable sex." The disease we might have expected; the characteristic Baldwinian twist is that the narrator cannot tell what *kind* of diseased sex-organ it is, male or female. Deformity, unnaturalness, indecisiveness, and sexual confusion thus hang over the bed on which David and Giovanni make love.

Inside, then, is intense shame. But outside is danger. The courtyard "malevolently pressed" against the windows, "encroaching day by day, as though it had confused itself with a jungle." Passing shadows make Giovanni "stiffen like a hunting dog . . . until whatever seemed to threaten our safety had moved away." You can't see or be seen through the translucent, whited-out windows, but you can nevertheless hear the voices of singing children, a mocking code for the "natural," and thus a continual reproach to Giovanni, who bitterly wants to be straight. These voices are like a parodic inversion of that voice St. Augustine heard at the moment of his final conversion: the voice of a child ("whether of a boy or a girl, I don't know") chanting in sing-song fashion: "*Tolle lege, tolle lege*": "Pick it up, read it." Augustine at that point opens the Bible to Romans, where he reads: "Let us walk honestly, as in the day; not in rioting and drunkenness, not in chambering and wantonness." But there is no honesty for Giovanni; he is condemned to "chamber" in his room, to live outside of the day. The children's voices damn, and do not save him.

The world of normality, of family, heterosexuality, nature, is thus shown to be the homosexual's enemy. But the space Giovanni has built to protect himself, a kind of male womb, is no protection. Not only is it precarious, it is itself diseased. Nature itself is not wholesome; for outside his window even the man-made courtyard (another anti-womb) threatens to "encroach." Inside there is a rose-garden gone to seed. The jungle of Nature is not banishable; it has invaded his room like a virus. All he can do to ward it off is maintain himself in a perpetual timelessness. He is a sinister Sleeping Beauty around whom a monstrous forest has grown up, and who hopes in vain to be rescued by the inadequate Prince Charming, David.

The Fortress

To turn from *Giovanni's Room* to Christopher Isherwood's great proto-ghetto novel *A Single Man* is to travel more than the eight years that separate the two works' publication: it is like coming out again into the light. It tells the story of a middle-aged Englishman, George, now living in Los Angeles, where he teaches at a third-rate state university. A year earlier, his lover Jim has died in a car accident. George is now alone, the "single man" of the title. The novel, based loosely on Joyce's *Ulysses*, follows George around through the day, from his waking up to his falling asleep—or perhaps dying.

As a "proto-ghetto" novel, *A Single Man's* main difference from the full-blown variety is its protagonist's isolation from other gay men. The only ones that might count are the hustlers George spots "scowling" on the street corner, with whose youth and sexual energy he claims a distant kinship. For all his isolation, however, George is quite free of self-pity or self-doubt—at least about his homosexuality. He is in many ways part of the outside world. His archetypally straight neighbors the Strunks know he's gay, for instance. "Mr. Strunk, George supposes, tries to nail him down with a word. Queer, he doubtless growls. But, since this is after all the year 1962, even he may be expected to add, I don't give a damn what he does just as long as he stays away from me." Mrs. Strunk "is trained in the new tolerance, the technique of annihilation by blandness . . .(Shame on those possessive mothers, those sex-segregated British schools!)." They leave him alone, and treat him with respectful hostility.

George's house is a symbol of his kind of homosexuality. It is, first of all, *separate*: "they loved it because you could only get to it by the bridge across the creek." It is cut off, too, by trees; but not the "jungle" that "encroached" on Giovanni: *this* house is safely "in a forest clearing." To live there would be like "being on our own island." (Indeed islands, like Fire Island or Manhattan, are typical and frequent presences in ghetto and proto-ghetto literature. They are signs of gay autonomy and identity.) The forest is not menacing here, but rather protective. Devouring Nature is comically represented by the ivy, "half-alive, half-dead," which overgrows only the old inadequate garage they don't care about and which will be consequently "useful for keeping some of the animals in." Furthermore, by placing Jim's animals there, Isherwood effectively reclaims nature for this unnatural couple. He rightly sees that the only unnatural thing in their house and garage is their cars, so he has George and Jim keep them on the sagging bridge.

This house is one you can see out of, but not into. It is literally elevated above the other houses in the neighborhood, permitting George to gaze contemptuously down on the Strunks' house below (as he sits on the toilet reading Ruskin). He can see the Strunk-world more completely than they can see his: the gay viewer forms the truer opinion. (Giovanni, by contrast, could neither see nor be seen.) The very smallness of the house has a different meaning in this novel from that in *Giovanni's Room*. Giovanni's room was "not large enough for two." George's is "cozy," "tightly planned. . . . He often feels protected by its smallness; there is hardly room enough here to feel lonely." Finally, even George's love for Jim is characterized by a sort of separateness. There is a marvellous description of them lying at opposite ends of their couch reading, "the two of them absorbed in their books yet so completely aware of each other's presence." They are mutually aware, but not indistinguishable. Love, then, like his house, is built upon a self-respect that preserves boundaries.

The Bridge

One of the most popular gay novels of recent years was Stephen McCauley's *The Object of My Affection* (1987). It is what I would call an assimilative or "homosexual" book. It literally and symbolically places the gay protagonist almost entirely in the straight world, in this case making him the roommate of a heterosexual woman with whom he dreams of raising the child she is carrying when the novel begins (not his child, of course). Indeed the fact that the hero is gay disappears from sight over large stretches of the novel, especially the first half. As most of its reviewers noticed, *The Object of My Affection* is determinedly pacific and bridge-building, its message seeming to be: "All of us, straight and gay, are lonely and looking for love."

The story concerns another George, George Mullen, a twenty-seven-year-old Bostonian who moves to New York to do graduate work in history at Columbia. Quickly realizing he has no passion for the subject (or indeed for anything else), he drops out; but not before he's begun an antiseptic affair with Robert Joley, a professor of Victorian history. Joley is an unpalatable sort of fellow, emotionally closed and unable to sleep with George, or without the whirr of a white-noise machine. If they have sex, it's not mentioned. They quickly break up. Glad to be rid of him, George remembers a woman he'd met at a party who said she had a room for rent in Brooklyn. He crosses the bridge from Manhattan to Brooklyn Heights, and leaves the gay world behind.

What do we notice about this move? The first thing is the narrator's social viewpoint. He is glad to be moving out of Manhattan (unfairly symbolized by Joley's apartment, which was as prissily clean as Nina's is warmly disordered). He is making a trip across a bridge *out* of gay space and into the straight world: an exact reversal of what Isherwood's George had done. At first George Mullen is wary of Nina's street because it's "far more ostentatious than I'd expected." Luckily for him, it gets grittier: "the brownstones were less elaborately decorated here, narrower and flatter and without the polished look of restoration." We note in passing that words like "elaborately," "polished," and "restoration"—queenly terms—have negative meanings in the Mullen glossary, and "narrow" and "flat" positive ones. He likes the fact that the only "ornamentation" is the "trash barrels chained to the fence in front." George's relationship with outward beauty is always problematic, as though he were warding off a suspiciously gay aestheticism.

We notice, too, some morally telltale children—always a sign in this book of virtue and naturalness. Significantly, there are no children around the "ostentatious," "ornamented" brownstones near the park. Children appear, as if on cue, only in the poorer neighborhood, as an earnest of its greater fidelity to "life." Would it be rude to ask who lives in those "ostentatious" Brooklyn Heights brownstones? Could it be gay men, the selfish beasts? If so, it would not be the first, and will not be the last, slur George makes against his fellow homosexuals.

The inside of Nina's house is cozily lived-in; and the reflection that "more than one generation of children has run amok in this place" reassures George, as it is intended to reassure the reader. As George priggishly says, "It was unlike any apartment I'd been inside in Manhattan." We might notice, too, the honorable place assigned to dirt and grease. Like a sort of inversion of Giovanni's room, Nina's apartment is desirable precisely because "the air was heavy and intoxicating." It is perhaps no accident that the building is owned, and presided over, by a warm-hearted stage Italian, Mrs. Sarni, the smell of whose motherly cooking has been absorbed by its greasy walls. Her presence "naturalizes" George's perversity in more ways than this, for she herself has a gay son who lives in the Village that George has spurned. She is, in other words a sort of fag-hag. If Baldwin's poor Giovanni had only had *her* for a mother, none of his suffering need have happened!

Nina's bedroom itself George pronounces to be "feminine," which apparently means "messy." But Nina's messiness, unlike Giovanni's, is found eccentrically charming. And not only messy, but isolated: McCauley even bestows on her the same blocked-out windows Baldwin's David was so horrified by! The cards crowding the mirror tell us that she doesn't actually use it and is thus innocent of "narcissism" (that gay neurosis). The detritus of her bedroom is the sign of whimsicality, not (like Giovanni's) of despair: "feather necklaces, yellowed lace, wind chimes, and a little girl's straw bonnet with a sky-blue ribbon." They are props that testify to Nina's childlike soul. Not Giovanni's violin music (too arty?), but clothes spill from her bureau. In place of the undead potato are "three vases of dead flowers" and "four coffee cups with spoons sticking out."

George tells Nina after surveying this scene of squalor, "You know what, Nina? I could easily live here." He could, and does; for this place is George himself writ large. Notice that by fitting himself into this "feminine" space, he effectively neuters himself. And indeed his sex-drive vanishes as soon as he moves in. (Not that there was much to vanish: the first event in the book is George's decision not to go on an arranged blind date.) Indeed there is very little sex or sexual identity in the book. His best friend Timothy, for example, lives not in Brooklyn but off Sheridan Square, and could be a representative gay urbanite. But he is unfortunately neither butch enough to be a clone, nor witty enough to be a queen. He's merely (like Joley) a self-absorbed neatnik. But George's attitude toward other homosexuals is really worse than indifference. On a trip to Vermont, for instance, he does find the "object of his affection," a solemn former hippie named Paul; but until then George doesn't mind trashing every other gay person in Vermont: "I recognized our host standing at the far end of the bar. . . . I crossed the narrow room, choking briefly on the smoke, and shook his sweaty hand. The top of his head was covered with a greasy, pitch-black toupee that drained the color from his face and gave his complexion a jaundiced shine. 'I want you to meet Tommy,' he said in a drunken slur. 'He owns this dump with me.'" Grease, so honorable in Nina's apartment, is apparently disgusting when associated with a gay man.

It is no accident, finally, that Nina is pregnant, that Paul has adopted a child, and that George works as a teacher for a snotty East Side elementary school. Children are invoked as a kind of sanction for his sexuality, removing its perverse sting. They make his homosexuality acceptable. When he finally settles down with Paul, he is not so much embracing homosexuality as allying himself with a superior version of Nina: sexier, but just as much a shield from the gay world he fears and despises. In an odd way, George's supposedly extinct Catholicism resurfaces in his assumption that sex for the sake of children is permissible, but not for pleasure. While George doesn't literally procreate, his story is about becoming a father: an act whose moral beauty apparently redeems the perversity of his homosexuality. While it would be untrue to call *The Object of My Affection* a "closet" novel exactly, it is astonishing how much its fundamental premise resembles that of, say, *Giovanni's Room*. That premise is, of course, that homosexuality *needs* to be redeemed. The main difference between Baldwin's and McCauley's books is simply the possibility or impossibility of such a "redemption." And one may feel that George Mullen's happy ending is bought at the too-heavy price of squeamishness about the actual gay world, and other gay men.

Noplace

As an example of "queer" story-telling, I'm going to take a beautiful, if little-known story by a writer who died at the horribly early age of thirty-one of AIDS, Sam D'Allesandro. Its appropriateness will be obvious from its title, "Giovanni's Apartment." The story, to the extent that there is one, is about an unnamed narrator who is followed home one night by Giovanni, a handsome man whom he'd seen in a movie. Giovanni takes him to his apartment, where the narrator stays for the next eighty days, leaving only to walk in zombie-like straight lines through the unidentified city. For the first thirty-two of these days, he never leaves, content to stay among Giovanni's erotic but semantically blank possessions. On the thirty-third day he goes outside and "zombies" into a dime-store, where he strikes up a conversation with the clerk, a dwarf named Mary. He immediately invites her to dinner. From that point on, Mary, Giovanni, and he become friends and spend all their time together. The narrator has dropped all his previous friends, as well as his job. At the end of the story, there is a suggestion that he'll go back to work, not because he's bored—he's literally incapable of boredom—but in order to buy Giovanni a VCR: "Then we can all watch *The Flintstones* and *Our Miss Brooks* reruns at night. Except Tuesdays, cheap beer night, Gio's pool night." And there the story ends.

Giovanni's apartment has "black walls," and is illuminated only by the erotic red light of a lava lamp on the floor. It is "a warm and luscious hell." Its only furniture besides the lamp is a "fat mattress on the floor," the scene of Giovanni's nightly "killings and revivings." There is no day or night in this place; time is suspended. But who needs day? "If I tired of sunbathing on the floor, I could go to the window and look out. Flowers, trees, dirt, garbage, a child's swingset but no child, two women having coffee on an iron table. I couldn't be bored." It is a womb, a place of rebirth into "emptiness." As the narrator says, "I felt clean for the first time since I was born."

As the title suggests, we are invited to consider this place in the light of Baldwin's classic room. There are obvious similarities, including the allusion to being underwater, the womb-like timelessness. But how different is his reaction to that timelessness! Far from being horrified by it, as David is, he is enchanted by it; it frees him (to be happy? or is the word irrelevant?); it purifies him. The very tone of the passage is unemotional and unemphatic.

And if he's clean, he's plainly different, too, from McCauley's George Mullen. Giovanni's apartment has none of the warm eccentric squalor of Nina's house in Brooklyn or the upright orderliness of Paul's house in Vermont. Though he might recognize himself in the narrator's passivity, George would not be happy here. For one thing there's too much sex, and it seems too violent and too ecstatic: "killing and reviving" would hardly have appealed to Mullen. For this gay man, unlike Mullen, is both physically and emotionally *penetrable*. Indeed, he is *nothing but penetrability*: he has no boundaries of any kind. He is totally invadable by the world. Unlike Mullen, he has no dishevelled charm with which to joke away passion. The room itself offers no distraction from the "fat mattress" on the floor. While George Mullen can lose himself in the sheer random proliferation of things in Nina's apartment, the minimalism of Giovanni's apartment keeps the narrator focussed on sex. This place is sparely furnished, and becomes more so as the story continues: Giovanni gradually and without explanation gets rid of most of the existing furniture, though leaving the mattress and the lava lamp. The lava lamp, which would have been only a social marker in McCauley—something George and Nina could feel superior to, something that would further clutter and conceal their lives—is completely functional here. It is not meant to be whimsical. Indeed there is no wit in this story at all, as there is no judgment. Judgment of all kinds is suspended, as being part of the dirt the narrator sloughs off. The dirt in Nina's apartment, we may now realize, was ironically what prevented George from seeing how dirty he thought his own sexuality.

This is a "queer" place for several reasons. One is, simply, that it is not a ghetto place: there are no other gay men in the story; the only other person who joins them is the presumably heterosexual Mary. At the same time, it is not a closet, for no one feels shame, guilt, or indeed any other strong emotion. Nor finally is it an "assimilated" world. The presence of Mary, for example, far from heterosexualizing, and thus naturalizing, the narrator's relationship with Giovanni, makes it seem even weirder than it already is. These characters all share an isolation from the world which is the antithesis of the integrative assimilating vision.

Another way Giovanni's apartment is queer is its utter and essential lack of boundaries, names, and definitions. We never know where it takes place, what the narrator's job used to be, or even what his name is. Such details, essential to the bourgeois realist tradition, are irrelevant here. What would it mean for such a narrator to call himself "gay" and someone else "straight?" His dissociation from the world goes far beyond that of mere sexual identity. Finally, the point of the story really is not the narrator's homosexuality, but his aloneness and Zen-like indifference. Sex is crucial to it, but not gay sex. Do we even know for sure that the narrator is male?

The Ghetto

By their drugs ye shall know them. If "Giovanni's Apartment" is like being "drowned in heavy waves of barbituate-like nothingness," Andrew Holleran's *Dancer from the Dance* seems written on speed, its co-protagonist Sutherland's drug of choice. It is brilliant, funny, melancholy, and exact. It is not content to be dissolved in a postmodern "emptiness," like Giovanni and his lover. Neither is it a closetted fiction, for the character lives an openly, obviously gay life. Finally, it completes, and complicates, the proto-ghetto journey by moving its main character, Malone, into the heart of gay New York. And this is the symbol of a far more profound narrative move: the experiment of imagining a gay character who is, for once, almost totally *free*, unconstrained by small-town mores, cowardice, social disability, or a novelist's need either to "doom" or "redeem" him. Malone, in other words, can theoretically choose happiness. That he doesn't, or that the happiness he thinks he has chosen turns out to be delusive, is the source of the book's ineradicable melancholy and wit.

The world Malone comes to inhabit is both straight and gay, both public and private: that of post-Stonewall New York. (Indeed, in the Bantam paperback edition he arrives on Sheridan Square promptly in 1969, three months after the Stonewall Riots.) His journey there is a coming-out story and, like all coming-out stories, also a homecoming—to a place he has never been before. It is initially a catalogue of *wrong* places, of anti-homes. They include the seemingly paradisal tropical island where Malone spent his dutiful childhood; the Vermont prep-school where he "studied diligently and postponed happiness to some future time"; the suburban home of the "widow of an ambassador who had been a friend of his grandmother's when they were girls" where he lives on a "vast floor of empty rooms in whose hallway outside his own the odor of cold cream, the sound of a television program being watched downstairs, hovered." New York City, which will become his true home, "he saw . . . with the eyes of most of his classmates: an asphalt slag heap baking under a brown shroud of pollution."

The half-comic, half-poignant moment when Malone finds his home in the new gay ghetto comes when he is visiting New York, working late on a "promissory note for the Republic of Zaire." When a messenger comes into his office, he looks up: "How could he know that his desire, his loneliness, were written on his face as clear as characters on a printed page?" The messenger, less inhibited than Malone, bends over to kiss him, and Holleran writes, with amused exaggeration: "It was the kiss of life." The messenger leaves him "with an expression on his face such as the Blessed Virgin wears in paintings of the Annunciation." It is because of this kiss that Malone finally decides he must become gay, that he must throw in his lot with the gay men he had previously seen, desired, and feared. With a touching, ridiculous hope he moves to Sheridan Square, the heart of the nascent gay ghetto, where on a late-summer evening he "watched the Puerto Rican boys unloading soda pop for the Gem Spa on his new corner. . . . And so the last Sunday evening of August 1969 found him sitting on his stoop like a monk who comes finally to the shrine of Santiago de Compostela—devoted not to Christ, in whom he no longer believed, but love."

The comic, rueful religious vocabulary is telling. For what is it to make a pilgrimage to a shrine? It is to make yourself public, to declare yourself. It is to remind yourself of your true home, and of your long exile in a false one. (It is no accident that Malone, on the night of his "engagement" and death, is brooding over St. Augustine in Point O' Woods.) "The false years of dutiful behavior" can now "fall away." The great cry of triumph that is present even in Holleran's most muted, wistful phrases is an almost religious one, then: the realization that those early, respectable years were simply "false."

Coming out since Stonewall brings you to your own stoop, your own new corner—that is, a place which is simultaneously public and private. One consequence of his move to the ghetto is that Malone becomes real for the first time to himself. Before, he had been what he calls a "ghost"; now he has a body, and can therefore be seen. Seen, furthermore, *as gay*. If we could imagine the men who are unloading soda pop turning their heads in his direction, they would see not just "Malone," but a gay man, emblem of an unmistakable homosexuality. In fact, the whole city of New York, in page after brilliant page of Holleran's novel, becomes a gay neighborhood—as indeed it is, to the eye of erotic faith.

HERE, then, are examples of five important kinds of gay-male literature. Let me conclude with a few generalizations about each, and a brief defense of the centrality of ghetto literature.

I would be disingenuous if I didn't admit that I find most of the non-ghetto works limited in their ability to tell the truth about gay life. The closet novel finds doom too easily, and indeed unnecessarily: the terrible self-laceration of David in *Giovanni's Room* was already in 1956 (after the stories of Tennessee Williams, after Vidal's *The City and the Pillar*) a mere stage-prop. Closet texts are like baroque arias: exciting in a way, but monotonous in their single-mindedness. There is absolutely no other voice in Baldwin's novel but the tragic one, and its story is uncontaminated by contradiction or by life.

The queer alternative is as unironic as the closet novel, if for completely different reasons and with far different effects. The lack of irony here stems from the narrator's, author's, or character's radical unself-consciousness. There is in fact no self to be conscious of in "Giovanni's Apartment" or in Dennis Cooper's *Frisk*—except by the most minimal, detached definition of "self." The characters can watch their thoughts as intently as a Zen Master; but they scrupulously, phobically avoid the dimension of the self one might call "deep": the moral, the aesthetic, suffering dimension. There is certainly nothing so old-fashioned as a Faustian double-soul dwelling, alas! in a single, tormented breast. Interesting, indeed brilliant as this inner minimalism can be, its effects seem to me strictly limited. In this style one can "speak" only a few passions: numbness, boredom, suppressed hysteria. Far from being primitive or elemental, queer fiction is an example of what George Santayana called in 1922 "Penitent Art," an art which "childish as it may seem at times, is a refinement, perhaps an over-refinement . . . not so much crude or incompetent, as ascetic or morbid."

This leaves the "homosexual" or assimilative novel: Leavitt's or McCauley's, for example. Assimilative writers are the Human Rights Campaign Fund of gay literature: decent, politically and socially middle-of-the-road, interested in the "naturalization" of homosexuality and the satisfaction of rational desires. Their work is neither ascetic nor morbid, but bouncingly healthy, liberal, generous, common-sensical. Its characters are generally as well-observed as they are well-behaved. Many "homosexual" writers seem determined to prove gay life just as dull as straight: a useful corrective to gay arrogance and inflation, I suppose, but pallid fictionally and untrue historically. For many of us, after all, living in a gay world has been anything but dull: promiscuity made it thrilling in the 1970s, deadly in the 1980s; political battles have made it restless, heroic, or absurd; friendships make it precious. Assimilative fiction tends to mock or otherwise "punish" the passionate. In *The Object of My Affection*, for example, Nina's boyfriend Howard, who actually loves his job, is made to seem ridiculous for it. Similarly, in Leavitt's short story "AYOR," the narrator's friend Craig gets into predictable trouble by cruising in dangerous areas: his sexual adventurousness is primly called "tragic" by the writer-narrator. Sometimes these authors, in their automatic preference for the prudent emotional compromise, seem prematurely middle-aged. They are able to tell a certain valuable truth, but throw away something yet more valuable in the process: namely, that separateness, that sense of an identity which both liberates us for political and personal action, and from complacency. From doubtlessly good motives they take the gay label from us, finding it divisive rather than liberating. Like Rilke in his famous response to Freud, however, I find myself wondering if getting rid of one's devils (anti-gay stereotypes, for instance) means also getting rid of our angels (our sense of election and joy).

It is a choice we ought to be hesitant to make. However rightly we desire acceptance and rights, we need to insist on preserving in literature, and also in life, the "slight angle to the world" that Forster saw in the (proto-ghetto) poet

Cavafy. Indeed I would claim that a certain apartness is essential to a full homosexuality, as well as to the literature that celebrates it. The actual gay ghettoes of American cities remain not merely places where a gay man can be among others like himself, and thus find a workable happiness. They are also places that *straight* citizens can identify *as being gay*. They thus serve a double purpose, both private and public. The private life being lived in the ghettoes, and made possible by them, is also a public symbol of homosexual existence. The great impediment to our success in the past has been our invisibility, or our reluctant visibility. The ghetto makes the presence of gay people in the big cities a simple and undeniable fact of urban life.

Ghetto literature is performing an analogous feat. It is not only a place for gay readers to find images of themselves that are neither simplistic nor demeaning. It is also an identifiable literary site. In the most concrete sense, it means sections in mainstream bookstores called "Gay and Lesbian." In a deeper sense, it means there is now fiction that refuses to make homosexuality invisible—not simply by presenting sexual talk, sexual acts; but by insisting that its characters are gay, first and foremost. They are not generically "queer," they are not "just people," and they are certainly not "closet cases." Ghetto and proto-ghetto fiction is the only place in literature where this is true, with the sole, and limiting exception of pornography.

Is ghetto literature then necessarily better than non-ghetto literature? Yes and No. There are undoubted successes in all the genres I have listed, and there are many failures or partial-successes among the ghetto texts. The claim I would make is that when the ghetto texts succeed, they are more complex, more audacious and more lifelike than the non-ghetto texts when they succeed. For if, like Holleran's Malone, many of us have come to the ghetto as to a shrine, we come with a complex and contradictory burden: that of a past we do not wish to jettison and a present which that past would not understand. Ghetto fiction does not simply lament this burden, nor simply celebrate it. It tries to hold it in a creative tension. Ghetto literature is, so far, the fullest expression of that tension. Thus, though ghetto texts are often deeply contradictory, indeed precisely because they are, they do more complete justice to gay life *qua* gay, than assimilative, closet, or queer fictions.

Dancer from the Dance is, to my mind, the best of all modern gay novels, not because it is formally the most perfect, but because it is simply larger in its scope: large enough to risk contradictions. Its "failures" have to be measured against its far greater ambition. Its most radical attempt is to bring together Malone's past and present, his straightness and his gayness, without disparaging or eliding either; to give him, as it were, more experience than he can possibly contain. That both he and the book fall apart is therefore hardly surprising. To me it means only that Holleran has tried to do something impossible, and therefore interesting. While other perfectly good books have presented a more coherent view of homosexuality, they have usually, to my mind, simplified it out of recognition. They have either seen homosexuality as a terrible doom, thus leaving out irony and happiness altogether (like *Giovanni's Room*); or they have so blurred it that its "happy endings" seem virtually heterosexual (like *The Object of My Affection*); or they have made it a mere special case of marginality (like *Frisk* or "Giovanni's Apartment"). In none of these other categories does gay life seem desirable in and of itself, but either a damnation, a *pis-aller*, or a sardonically desired disintegration. Even Isherwood's great novel *A Single Man*, while technically far more accomplished than *Dancer from the Dance*, attempts less than Holleran's. George is finally content to be "single," to take what he can get, "eating his poached eggs humbly and dully, a prisoner for life." Malone, ridiculously, pathetically, and heroically demands more.

The Victorian novelist George Macdonald once wrote: "Home is the only place where you can go out and in. There are places you can go into, and places you can go out of, but the one place, if you do but find it, where you may go out and in both, is home." Neither wholly public nor wholly private, neither entirely solid nor evanescent, the ghetto is the closest we have yet come to a "home." It has both an inside and an outside, and we enter and leave it freely. And what I have called "ghetto fiction" is like the actual ghetto because it is neither hermetically sealed, nor overly porous, but flexibly distinct. When it works, ghetto fiction thus seems to me the largest and most livable of the existing "houses" of gay fiction.

TONY KUSHNER

Three Screeds from Key West

For Larry Kramer

THESE ARE prefatory remarks written for the three panels upon which I sat at the recent Key West Seminar on "Literature in the Age of AIDS." I wrote each one about an hour before the panel; Larry Kramer called them "screeds" and that sounded right so I've used his title. The titles of each section are simply the titles somebody else assigned to the panels. I think everything I write sounds like a dramatic monologue, which isn't surprising; these monologues were written by and for the almost-entirely fictional character Tony Kushner, a playwright, who, as he said in the last of the three panels, spent the weekend feeling like the bastard child of Neville Chamberlain and Attila the Hun. There's a reference in the second screed to a struggle Sarah Schulman and I had over several instances of thoughtless exercising of privilege and exclusion. Better, I said, borrowing a lesson I've learned from my collaborator friend Kimberly Flynn, to be awkward in admitting a mistake than to be a totally irresponsible fuck-up: and this I think is in a sense the point of all that follows.

I. The Theater and AIDS

I can't imagine I'm the only one here—I certainly hope I'm not—who feels odd that she or he has benefited, even profited from the epidemic. This is an ugly statement and I hesitate to write it or utter it, but I've been haunted all weekend, and was anticipatorily haunted before coming here, and even considered not coming up till the last moment, because of strong feelings of unworthiness, inadequacy, and fraudulence. I've acquired a habit now of confessing to these feelings before crowds of people, and I probably should have stayed at home and sought out the appropriate 12-Step program, Playwrights' Anonymous, instead of mortifying myself before artists and activists I admire

From the Spring 1997 issue

Tony Kushner

so much—whose presence, I suspect, made the promise of suffering a really intense abjection entirely too tempting to pass up.

I didn't set out to write a play about AIDS, I set out to write a play about what it was like to be a gay, Jewish, Leftist man in New York City in mid-eighties Reagan America. I really think I set out to write about Reagan. I'd seen a few plays and TV films "about" AIDS, and with one single exception they were all terrible, in my opinion, disease-of-the-week weepies addressing something manifestly monumentally of another order—an order, I felt, like the Holocaust, the scale of which was incommensurable with representation on the tacky-tawdry-showbizzy stage. The one (and without attacking other play-wrights and screenwriters, I'd like to stress this one) towering exception was *The Normal Heart,* of course, which galvanized its audiences like no play any of us—any of my generation of theater artists, certainly—had ever seen; and which—and I'm certain this was the least of its author's intentions, if indeed it figured at all—awoke in theater people a long-dormant ambition to make popular theater that enters full-bloodedly into civic life, into immediacy, cri-sis, and public debate.

The Normal Heart, scene for scene, is a great American play. People have an annoying tendency to call it a polemic, but "1,112 And Counting" is a polemic—a historically significant polemic, that rare thing, a sermon that works; *The Normal Heart* is a great play. It has depth, complexity, symbolic and political and psychological and musical strata, strains which proceed, unerr-ingly orchestrated with the gripping, terrifying narrative until all the pennies drop at just the right moment to move a large, impatient, distracted house full of people to terror, pity, empathy, reflection, and outrage.

But the play set an impossibly high standard and we suspected, and we were not wrong in this, that its urgency and phosphorous brilliance were not exclusively the effects of its author's talents and technical skills, but also of his activist engagement with AIDS. As we have demonstrated with AIDS and every other human and political calamity, and with our passive acquiescence to the destruction of the National Endowment for the Arts, among theater folk the activist impulse is forever devoured, or rather eviscerated, by our fatal attraction to its inherent drama. We love the flash and thunderclap and are too impatient to do the work of constructing the bomb. We could not, and I think we have not, followed Larry's lead.

(In a way, this is just a nineties version of what grand old theater queens used to say to excuse appalling, inexcusable sloth or misbehavior, quoting Duke Theseus, usually in a tremulous voice when accepting your award at the Sarah Siddons Society dinner: The best in these are but shadows, the worst no worse, blah blah blah.)

We all know that there's been a lot of theater about AIDS, a lot of dra-matic literature, and some of it is very good, even if it is only "dramatic liter-ature" and hence a thing of indifference outside of annoyed envy at the size of dramatic royalty checks to many novelists and poets and scholars and book reviewers and (dare I say it? and I say it with the greatest respect) Keynote Speakers.

We all know that the form, the public forum, the instant community of actor and audience, collective attendance, catharsis, can in the right hands suit any subject of a vast shared grief and rage. We know that theater originates in the sacred, but we should also remember that the Church banished actors, once full-throttle mimesis, representation, and narrative had insinuated themselves into the Mass; not because of a good actor's power to inspire idolatry but rather because the whole business started to smell of something dangerously cheap, risible, carnal: the ecclesiastical rapidly became the dialectical opposite of its Sacred subject. The proximity of the Divine and the Preposterous, the Infinitely Grave and the Infinitely Embarrassing, made the theatrical bits more exciting than the sacramental ritual and hence the theatrical became ripe for, and deserving of, anathema.

We come to the theater—and to literary conferences, which are also affairs of voices and bodies and flashes of excitement and lingering doubts and disappointments, mean and bruising and cruisy and fun—to be mortified, and to delight in the mortification of others, to suffer with those we see (and cause to) suffer and pay money to see suffer. Theater is always self-evidently political because it is always dialectical and always dialectical because this paradox, Inspiration Flashing and Modesty Blushing, simultaneously, is at its heart, it's what makes the engine go. All theater is a waste of time, which reminds us that our best and dearest dream for ourselves and for our fellow humans ought to be oceans of time to waste in a cozy seat in which you have (and here we see the difference between the theatrical and the literary) very little work to do to receive the best kind of pleasure: free of consequence.

I think what I'm trying to say is that it is theater's inappropriateness that makes it a likely place for the staging of scenes from a pandemic. To borrow an image used by Herbert Blau, Shakespeare, and Beckett, where else but the theater can we go to mourn, and mourn deeply, over a corpse, noting all the while that the corpse over which we grieve, oh beautiful, impossible sight! is breathing.

I did not set out opportunistically to write about AIDS because it's such great material; but it is, isn't it? And so am I not opportunistic? Am I not, as I have been accused of being, an AIDS profiteer?

Perhaps I haven't heard this said because I haven't been at the panels where it's been said, or perhaps it's too despicable or vulgar or in some sense unnecessary to say, or perhaps survivor guilt is a sufficient rubric, but something has compelled me to make this declaration to the conference. I know my play has helped people and helped the cause. It has also made me comfortable. And there's something unbearable about that. Which, maybe, I ought to keep to myself, but, playwright, theater worker that I am, I am too much in love with the drama of declaration and mortification.

We've talked about a fear of using AIDS metaphorically, about comparing AIDS to the Holocaust, and this dilemma I think speaks to my theme: *Using AIDS*. Using AIDS to make art, to make a political point, to achieve a desirable goal. Of course we're squeamish. But I have always thought that the only point in remembering and then organizing memory into an event and then naming that event "the Holocaust" or "the AIDS epidemic" is to provide ourselves and the future with a standard by which comparison can be made. Otherwise, *forget*, for God's sake; do us all a favor.

But in this standard-construction business is implicit the notion that the Holocaust and the epidemic are *for* something, are utilitarian, can be turned into phenomena by which we might profit—morally, spiritually, and yes, materially. We must approach this dialectically, I suppose is my point: to use human suffering, whether it originates in viral infection or from malignant human agency or from a blending of the two—is necessary and appalling, neither more one than the other, always unbearable, always unavoidable, a terrible mandate, always both.

II. "Seeking the truth, a matter of life and death," Part One

I struggle a lot with what I've come increasingly to describe to myself as a divide between Wisdom with a capital W, which I am reasonably certain I do not possess, and the something that I do possess—opinions? In my opinion, my opinions are the correct opinions to have, but having the correct opinions is not the same as knowing the truth, having Wisdom; some people have that, but I don't know where they got it any more than I know, really, why I'm gay. But I'm reasonably sure I'm gay and I'm reasonably sure my opinions are at least sixty-five percent right seventy percent of the time, which makes me cleverer than all of the Republican Party and ninety percent of the Democratic Party and a whole lot of others besides, and that really is all I know of truth and how to get it.

My favorite writer Melville loved those pearl divers, he wrote in a letter to his boyfriend, Hawthorne, who go deep down seeking the truth, rising to the surface again with bloodshot eyes, their pressurized, lachrymal stigmata indicating how hard a struggle it is to seek Wisdom. Some dark nights I can guess at what Melville meant, but I'm too afraid of the bends to try it myself; and why should I, really, when Wisdom doesn't work as well in the theater as having the correct opinions, and I can always get Wisdom seated in my armchair, reading novels?

Truth is a matter of life and death and nothing proves that more than this plague; lies, as often as silences, equal death. Wisdom will save you, reliably, that's how you know it's Wisdom, or at least if it can't save you it will help you make sense of your demise. And it lasts: truth is the daughter of time. But I have been bewildered since 1981. Opinions work in the moment, if you're voluble enough, but they can betray you. Here are some of my false truths, opinions that betrayed me: In 1981 I thought AIDS was a distraction from the real struggle, which was for a lesbian and gay rights bill in New York City. In 1983 and 1984 I refused to be tested and encouraged others not to, certain that it was a mistake, a hysterical over-reaction, cooperation with an oppressive medical/political homophobic establishment—and maybe back then it was, who knows? I have held the opinion that AIDS was legionnaire's disease, swine flu, a monkey virus, and practically become a maintenance illness (on several occasions, which is why protease inhibitors make me feel glad but very cautious).

The illnesses, sufferings, nightmares, struggles, heroism, and deaths of friends and idols, such involvement in the movement as I can claim, reading, writing *Angels*—my opinions get corrected, but there's still so much I don't know and am afraid to know, and some of it may be life-and-death. Is it okay to suck cock without a condom? Should I or shouldn't I say that I do, sometimes? My bemusement is a luxury, which Amiri Baraka has defined as living in ignorance, comfortably. But it's also genuine un-knowing in the face of mysteries, and so I seek out my multicultural fallible rabbinate, for exegesis, for rescue. My chiefest wisdom, I think, is knowing myself to be unwise. I don't mean this to sound as bromidic as it does, it's not universally true, thank God. And it goes without saying you can probably hear it, that my greatest danger is my complacency. For agnostics, both of the secular and of the sacred order, complacency is the most venal sin. That, and having the wrong opinions. Lots of people have the wrong opinions and know them to be wrong and still act in accordance with their error, and every morning I thank God I'm not one of those.

I have a few truths, which I believe to be truths and not opinion, because I don't understand them fully or even partially after thinking about them for a long time, and in that quality of unfathomableness these truths resemble

God as I intuit God to be; if God is anything at all, one thing S/He is, is unknowable. I know three truths: Democracy, because I can't imagine justice without it, nor can I imagine anything better; Socialism, because capitalism sucks; and Internationalism, or Solidarity if you will, because we'll never have the first nor the second without this third. It is almost always for a lack of solidarity that democracy and socialism (or whatever you choose to call a more sane and just way of organizing human economic affairs in the global community) fail.

It is very easy to say this and it makes me feel good to say it, but solidarity is immensely difficult, especially for the privileged—my friend Kimberly Flynn gave me a quote once from Gayatri Spivak about "the slow unlearning of privilege" being the necessary work of the privileged interested in participating in justice. Slow because painful. Sarah Schulman taught me a painful lesson in that unlearning today; learning hurts; I'm going to try to learn. I don't want my opinions to fossilize in the honey-colored amber of my ignorance, or cowardice, I don't want to start defending ignorance, which is always indefensible.

I think the cure for AIDS is Democratic Socialist Internationalism, or Internationalist Democratic Socialism, or Socialist Internationalist Democracy—help me out here. This may be opinion rather than Wisdom; but if it's Wisdom to despair, I'd rather be opinionated; if, as Larry Kramer seems to write in the program, it's a choice between opinion and artistry, I'd rather be opinionated. Activism and art about AIDS have run up against the wall of Economics; so has race, gender, homosexual rights, disability rights, immigrant rights—the whole rainbow of progressive causes has hit the Milton Friedman Memorial Firewall barricade, and balkanized. All await a decent answer to the pitiless capital-logic of the Balanced Budget; we must make this barricade budge. This is why I so thoroughly despise gay conservatism. They don't believe in regulation, they want to cut the capital gains tax, and cutting the capital gains tax is homophobic, preserving the capital gains tax a lesbian and gay rights issue. Cutting taxes is racist, sexist, homophobic: if it is any one of these it is all three. That's my opinion.

We people have two hedgehog questions, it seems to me: How much trouble are we in? And can we do anything about it? If the answer to the first question is "a lot!" and if the answer to the second question is "no," then it would be a kindness to die, the only decent thing, really. And if that's Wisdom, who wants it? If the answer to the second question is "yes," then a third question inevitably follows, my favorite: "What is to be done?"

III. "Seeking the truth, a matter of life and death," Part Two

Theodore Adorno wrote a really great essay called "On Commitment," which I think reaches the wrong conclusions but lays out pretty much the same dialectic we struggled with last night, and I think we've struggled with it through much of this conference, at least the parts I've attended. Adorno, as I recall, writes of art which moves in its urgency right up to its audience, or at least towards it; and art which almost seems to retreat from its audience—"reticent" art, to borrow an apt word Robert Dawidoff used on Friday—but for all its reticence, still committed, still purposeful, art which persists in indulgence in a grand and necessary luxury, the hope and faith in human beings that whatever it was that compelled them to pick up a book, a poem, go see a play—that this same impulse will get them moving when they cease to be consumers and spectators of culture and return to the social world and its demands for action, for agency.

Of these two aesthetic stratagems, one which addresses you aggressively and one which demands of you exertion by virtue of its flight from you (we might choose to call one political and the other literary, or accessible and difficult), Adorno prefers the reticent, the literary and the difficult, while recognizing that each contains elements of the other, and both seek different means to engage in public, political struggle. But this doesn't mean his essay is a kind of "I'm OK you're OK, I say potato you say rutabaga" affair. He writes: One is better than the other. He reaches a conclusion about committed art many of us have reached: that the faith in one's audience or reader to perform empathic leaps (empathy perhaps being art's most sublime gift and function) must be matched by the artist's embracing a rigorous discipline of non-partisan (to the extent that it is possible) observation, self-investigation, eschewing of pretentiousness, and metaphysical, rhetorical posturing—to become the constantly-retreating horizon point upon which the wayfarer, the reader, expects to find redemption, wisdom, peace, succor, epiphany—the future.

Adorno, because he thinks dialectically, and does not feel the need we Americans seem to feel to pretend that we don't struggle, or to pretend that the struggling, the wriggling, isn't Life, and isn't Infinite as long as there is a species and unceasing unto our deaths and, who knows? perhaps beyond. Adorno, unarguably an elegant writer, a great stylist, is comfortable with difficulty; indeed he revels in it, even in the scars difficulty can leave. He doesn't do something I think a lot of us do. He doesn't announce his mastery by clobbering the dialectic, he doesn't get sere, or vatic; he doesn't say, "I personally

know how to do this impossibly difficult thing, and so I no longer struggle."
He says, "I know what is best," but he leaves open the possibility, dangerous
to him, that in 1997 a gay forty-year-old Jew facing four more years of Speaker
Gingrich and Bill "Bipartisan Compromise" Clinton, young friends and family with AIDS and breast cancer because the world is poisoned and the whole
endless catalogue of it, who is *frightened* by the whole endless catalogue of it,
the greed and the bigotry and the terrible death, because last year one of his
secular rabbis from whom he has come to expect hope and marching orders
told him, in a confidence he now compulsively betrays by sharing it, that in
one hundred years he is certain that there will be *no life left on earth*—
Adorno's fidelity to dialectics forces him to forsake the burnished glow of "the
solution" and offer up the very tools with which this frightened queer American Jew in 1997 might conclude that Adorno is a very great thinker who finally—Brecht was right about him—finally was in some regards a compromised paid state intellectual talking out of his hat.

I guess what I'm saying is that truth is dialectical. Which does not mean
that it politely nods to the opposition, which nods and winks back signaling
brandy and cigars in the back room after the rubes have been fooled by wit-
nessing a sham fight. A live model for this sort of false opposition might be the
House Republicans and Democrats, and now the Ethics Committee's Primate
Parody of justice in calling the tax thief Gingrich to an utterly zipless account.

Dialectics should be the opposite of polite, or reassuringly relativist.
Neville Chamberlain was not a dialectician. Dialectics is messy. A dialectically
shaped truth is a heated argument, and it should be three things: first, outra-
geously funny, because puzzles are fun and because, faced with the improba-
bility and impossibility life's contradictions present us with, what else is there
to do but laugh; secondly, absolutely agonizing, because faced with the above,
what else is there to do but feel terrible pain, fear, pity? because a proper dialectics will make us face something most of us can't, namely the probable
truth that suffering, as E. H. Carr writes, is indigenous to history, and that's
horrible; and, thirdly, a dialectic should move us forward. Don't, in other
words, lose sight of the fact that you are probably almost as wrong as you are
right but knowing, if it is given to you to know, requires the courage to combine your contemplation with your action and act—Praxis, in other words,
movement; because we are, after all, bodies on this earth and it is as much a
chalkboard and a laboratory as it is a temple, and always remember what
Robert Duncan once said in an interview: Symmetry is what life resists arriv-
ing at; symmetry is stasis; symmetry equals death.

CHERYL CLARKE

An Identity of One's Own

A Review of *Push*

by Sapphire

(Alfred A. Knopf, 1996)

SAPPHIRE, the author of *Push*, goes back further than the "rap tradition," though in the late 1980s I once heard her deliver, in a lesbian space in Manhattan, a poem about fist-fucking in that jolting, close-rhymed cadence we have come to associate with rap. Since the days of Gap Tooth Girlfriends, an early 1980s workshop for black women writers (where Sapphire spent some time), conducted by poet, playwright, essayist, and teacher Alexis De Veaux in Brooklyn, Sapphire has honed and tempered herself as a writer in the black and white lesbian-feminist literary movement of the 1980s. In fact, the texture of *Push* shows an indebtedness to De Veaux's early experimental novel, *Spirits in the Street* (1973). That's why I say that Sapphire goes back further than rap, contrary to what Alice Quinn, *New Yorker* poetry editor, is quoted as saying in *The New York Times Magazine* prior to the publication of *Push*: "Sapphire comes out of a rap tradition. . . . I think rap can breed poets. These things are written things" (February 19, 1995). Well, Sapphire was bred before she started using rap techniques and before her performances at the famous Nuyorican Poets Café on the Lower East Side.

As one who got her chops as a writer and editor in the lesbian-feminist movement also, I have crossed paths with Sapphire numerous times at readings, political events, conferences, and movement fund-raisers from Manhattan to San Francisco. Sapphire did a long apprenticeship as an identified black lesbian writer. During the nine years (1981–90) that I was a member of the editorial collective of *Conditions*, a literary journal for women with an emphasis on writing by lesbians, Sapphire's poetry and prose appeared several times, as they did in other small and alternative press publications of the time. She's been out there for quite a while.

From the Fall 1996 issue

246

Sapphire

Sapphire's first book was *Meditations on the Rainbow* (1987), a long poetic reflection on multicultural conflicts and white racism, published in 1987 under her own imprint. *American Dreams* (1994), her second book, which several reviewers have erroneously listed as her first, was published by High Risk Books and reprinted by Vintage, each a beautifully packaged "mixed genre" volume of unevenly achieved writing. The horror and beauty of Sapphire's work on the page and in performances are electrifying, incantatory, sometimes evangelical. Sapphire reaches back further than to the 1960s black nationalist, counterculture politics by which she was influenced before she came to New York in 1977. In *Push*, her first novel, she pays homage to the rich antecedent texts that gave her her voice.

> Dear God
>
> I am fourteen years old. . . . First he put his thing up gainst my hip and sort of wiggle it around. Then he grab hold my titties. Then he push his thing inside my pussy. When that hurt, I cry. He start to choke me, saying You better shut up and git used to it.
>
> —Alice Walker, 1982

Claireece Precious Jones, the first-person narrator of *Push*, begins her interior monologue in much the same way as Walker's letter-writing protagonist, Celie, quoted above from the stunning first page of *The Color Purple*. Like Celie, who is trapped in one and then another abusive family system, like Pecola in Toni Morrison's *The Bluest Eye*, who's driven insane by the impoverished emotional system of her family and community, Precious is trapped on the terrain of contemporary Harlem in a system of abuse and emotional deprivation: "I was left back when I was twelve because I had a baby for my fahver." Sexually assaulted repeatedly by her father and bearing two children as a result, physically and sexually abused by her mother, to whom she is depicted as virtually enslaved, Precious, in the tradition of famous nineteenth-century black narrators of slavery and religious conversion, such as Frederick Douglass, Harriet Jacobs, William Wells Brown, Jarena Lee, and Zilpha Elaw, makes her break for freedom. Says the acerbic *Publisher's Weekly* reviewer, "Precious comes under the experimental pedagogy of a lesbian miracle worker" (April 22, 1996), namely Blue Rain, the Shug Avery of adult basic education, who endows Precious, at the age of sixteen, with literacy: "'Everyday,' Miz Rain say, 'we gonna read and write in our notebooks.'" Precious is then able to escape her mother's tyranny, her low self-esteem, and most of her dependency upon others' definition of her.

In this exceedingly explicit and sometimes didactic narrative, we witness Precious and her classmates, Rita, Rhonda, and Jermaine ("a butch"), who together resemble nothing so much as a 1970s feminist consciousness-raising group or a twelve-step self-help assembly, achieve a politics of sentience under the tutelage of Ms. Rain, a "butch" too: "Periodically we'll be getting into a circle to talk and work." Ms. Rain is a persona for the author, who taught "remedial reading" in Harlem and the Bronx and who admits that her characters are composites of her students. (Judging from the tenor of some of the reviews, the identities of Precious and Sapphire are elided in the minds of the reviewers. Of course, people always think poets are revealing autobiographical truths in their writings.) However, Precious discovers, like her literary forbears, that the rewards of literacy are dubious. Just as Precious seems to have triumphed over her environment, she is smacked with the news that her scum of a father has died of AIDS. Upon being tested, she discovers she is HIV-positive.

> I look my friends in the circle and tell them, test say I'm HIV positive. . . . Ms. Rain say, You not writing writing Precious. I say I drownin' in river. . . . Writing could be the boat carry you to the other side. . . .

I still don't move. She say, 'Write.' I tell her, 'I am tired. Fuck you!' I scream, 'You don't know nuffin' what I been through.'

And yet, Precious is undaunted and irrepressible, tripping off to an incest survivor group in the West Village, joining the "HIV community" at the urging of her friend Rita, and fighting to maintain her maternal autonomy as workfare and welfare reform loom. In fact, Precious' overdetermined maternal identity is finally hackneyed. "He my shiny little boy. In his beauty I see my own," is Precious' penultimate realization. Do I resent the smokescreen of motherhood? I much prefer Precious' newly acquired poet's identity, which is revealed to us in chapter IV and "Life Stories: Our Class Book," at the end of the novel. Very much like the subjects of *The Children Coming Home* (1991), a volume of poems by Gwendolyn Brooks about the dangers faced by children in contemporary urban settings, each woman in Precious' class, including Precious herself, publishes her own horrific story. We learn, as we learned in Morrison's *Beloved*, that the atrocities are as infinite as the stories that recount them. But telling the stories is never enough.

Certainly *Push* deserves the high praise it has received. It is a substantial first novel, and Sapphire has worked toward its completion for more than sixteen years. She has had many teachers—not just Susan Fromberg Schaeffer and Allen Ginsberg at the City University of New York, from which she recently received a MFA. Sapphire did not just get "discovered" in 1989 when Jesse Helms vilified her poem, "The Wild Thing" and "accidentally made [her] famous" (*Harper's Bazaar,* July 1996) during the Senate shake-down of the NEA for its support of venues that featured sexually explicit and transgressive work. Sapphire has been a poet a long time, and a lesbian a long time. She has a context and a history. I, for one, am looking forward to much more from this always challenging and important writer. Push on, Girlfriend!

On Liberation Strategy:
An Exchange

LESBIANS AND GAY MEN constitute one of the most heavily Democratic voting groups in the U.S., with upward of eighty percent reporting support for that party in *Advocate* surveys and election-day exit polls. And while a left-of-center position has been largely taken for granted at Pride rallies or HRC dinners, a small but dedicated minority has emerged that supports Republican candidates and advances a number of traditionally conservative positions. The emergence of the latter voice, whose semi-official national organization is the Log Cabin Republicans, has given rise to a lively debate that touches on matters both philosophical and strategic.

It is the question of political strategy that animates the exchange featured here, which took place over four issues of the *HGLR*, all in 1996. In the second of a two-part article on party politics and strategy, Rep. Barney Frank takes conservative gays to task for supporting Republican candidates who are clearly less friendly to gay and lesbian rights than their Democratic opponents, eliciting a response from Rich Tafel, national head of the Log Cabin group. While conceding that on balance the Republican Party has not been as supportive of gay rights as the Democratic, Tafel argues that categorical support for Democrats risks a "one party strategy" in which the gay vote is merely taken for granted rather than in play. Moreover, support for selected Republican candidates is the only way to gain any leverage over their future voting behavior if elected. Frank's response is that political support must be retrospective and not based on hope: reward candidates for their past support and work to defeat our detractors. This rule applies to Republicans, too, but in Frank's assessment they almost never field the better candidate; if they did, and only if they did, would a "two party strategy" make sense.

While neither Frank nor Tafel turns the debate into an explicit test of one's loyalty to the gay rights movement itself, there is an unstated assertion on Tafel's part that there just might be other issues that matter as much to gay people as gay rights—a point he has made elsewhere. He freely concedes in this article that Democrats *are* better on balance than Republicans on gay rights issues, but wants to balance this against other considerations. Frank's position takes for granted that advancing gay and lesbian rights is foremost on our agenda, overwhelming other issues. Now Frank happens to be an honest liberal on other matters as well, and clearly sees a connection between gay rights and other traditionally liberal positions; but what about those who see no contradiction between being gay and, say, opposing abortion or wanting to reduce capital gains taxes? The Log Cabin Republicans may seem an odd group to raise this question, since they are a specifically gay organization ostensibly lobbying for gay rights, but the question is a reasonable one: to what extent should a commitment to gay rights dominate our political lives, trumping other ideological commitments? The converse of this question is, to what extent can the support of gay and lesbian voters be counted on, both by our own leaders and by party politicians? The answer could be critical to the electoral role that gays will play in the future, and in turn their ability to influence the legislative process in the struggle for equality.

BARNEY FRANK

Why Party Politics Matters

AT EVERY LEVEL of government, and in every region of the country, the Democrats are significantly better than the Republicans on the issue of defeating homophobia and protecting us against unfair discrimination. Why, then, the ambivalence on the part of gay men and lesbians about following the advice of Samuel Gompers, who in the early days of the labor movement in America announced the political principle that he said should govern those seeking to use the political process to advance important goals—"reward your friends and punish your enemies"? For gays and lesbians in the current American political climate, this means strongly supporting Democrats nearly all the time.

Parties do mean something in American politics, more than ever in the last year, what with Newt Gingrich having made great strides (along with Rush Limbaugh, Pat Robertson, and Ralph Reed) in hammering the Republican party into a disciplined right-wing organization. We have seen this in the Republican presidential contest, in which there has been a stampede to the right, and in which the only arguably moderately conservative candidates, such as Pete Wilson and Arlen Specter, have been trampled. Which party controls the Congress makes an enormous difference, even beyond the fact that when we can receive seventy-five percent of the Democrats and ten percent of the Republicans, we can win only if Democrats outnumber Republicans overall. When the Democrats were in control, the party leaders, the people who scheduled floor action, the committee chairs, the people who structured amendments, tended to be people who believe that homophobia is a bad thing.

With the Republicans in power, the levers are in the hands of people who want to strengthen discrimination, whether because they believe in it personally or because they think it will win them votes. Even for the Republicans who are not personally homophobic—I would put Gingrich in this category because I do not think he is a man of very strong conviction on this or any other issue—their need to activate their political base drives them to take homo-

From the Spring 1996 issue

Barney Frank

phobic positions. Had the Republicans controlled Congress during the eighties, public policy regarding AIDS would be a nastier and meaner one by far.
Should the Republicans win the presidency, we would see an end to the
appointment of openly gay and lesbian officials, and very possibly an end to
the right to appeal discriminatory actions in the federal government, and a re-
imposition of the ban on security clearances for gay men and lesbians. We
would have a president who denounced gay rights legislation as "special
rights." Presidential influence would go to helping pass anti-gay and lesbian
referenda in the states rather than to opposing it.

Judicial appointments would be especially significant. Judicial decisions
are critical in our efforts to win our rights. The Colorado case is pending. The

Supreme Court decided by five to four that it was constitutional to make sodomy a crime, and at some point the nine justices will be deciding on the constitutionality of the prohibition on our being allowed to serve openly in the military. The current Supreme Court is fairly closely balanced, with the side that would vindicate our right to full constitutional protection probably now in a five-to-four minority. The president elected in 1996 will almost certainly appoint two new justices and possibly three. If Bill Clinton appoints the next two or three Supreme Court justices, based on the sort of judicial appointments he has already made, a majority on the Supreme Court is likely to hold that discrimination solely on the basis of sexual orientation by government is inappropriate. Should Dole or any other possible Republican win, we will get another Scalia or Thomas or Rehnquist. And a similar effect will occur in the lower courts. When the Circuit Court of Appeals in Washington, D.C., dealt with gays and lesbians in the military, we were generally supported by those appointed by Democratic presidents and opposed by those appointed by Republican presidents. The pattern is similar elsewhere.

The basic political facts, then, are clear. Where there are differences between Democratic and Republican candidates on questions of discrimination, the Democrat is better in the great preponderance of cases. Outside white-dominated districts in the deep South and a few central city areas, there is increasingly likely to be such a difference between the parties' candidates. Even where the individual Republican has a record as good as his or her Democratic opponent, the Democrat is likely to have an advantage in fighting homophobia, since, where Republicans control executive and legislative branches, they are pulled by party ties to enemies of our rights. Democrats are pulled in the opposite direction—to people who believe that gay people are entitled to the protection of their Constitution. Voting for a Republican candidate for the House who is simply about the same as his or her Democratic opponent on our issues makes sense only if you think it is really helpful for Newt Gingrich and Dick Armey to lead the House instead of Democratic leaders, all of whom have consistently voted to end bigotry based of sexual orientation. For example, two of the Republican House members with the best record in their party on our behalf, when asked by the Human Rights Campaign to be the lead sponsors of the bill to outlaw discrimination in employment based on sexual orientation, specifically refused. When I urged them to reconsider, they explained that they could not do so because they didn't want to anger Newt Gingrich. They did agree to be among the 150 cosponsors.

Gay and lesbian appointees and staffers of Republican officials and candidates are under sustained pressure to stay in the closet. More and more these days their Democratic counterparts feel free to be honest about their sexuality. There are dozens of openly gay and lesbian people serving responsibly and well in policy-making positions in the Clinton administration; I can think of none in the Bush and Reagan years. All but two or three of the members of the Congressional Gay and Lesbian Staff Caucus work for Democratic members of Congress; all but two of the elected officials who are honest about their homosexuality are Democrats. Even Bob Dole's inexplicable gay defenders—there appear to be no lesbians in this group—acknowledge that all of his gay employees are deeply closeted.

Voting with Your Head

This is not an argument for merging the movement for gay rights with the Democratic Party. It certainly doesn't mean that we should support in any way homophobic Democrats. Before Sam Nunn decided to quit the Senate, I was urging supporters to do whatever they could to defeat him next year, even if that meant supporting a Republican, since any replacement would be less influential. Straining a commitment to gay and lesbian rights through a pre-existing partisan screen is a betrayal of our cause. But so is straining that commitment through a predetermined, anti-partisan screen.

The argument against supporting Democrats as a general rule goes something like this: that while the Democrats are better than the Republicans in resisting homophobia, they are not nearly "better enough"; we should not reward the Democrats with any permanent commitment so long as the party falls short of full support for our rights. The short answer to this is that gay men, lesbians, and bisexuals should support the Democratic Party most of the time not as a favor to the Democratic Party, but as a favor to ourselves. The problem may be partly semantic. This point might be easier to make if Samuel Gompers had used a different word than "reward" when urging groups like ours—not that he had us particularly in mind—to throw our support to our friends in the electoral process and then try to defeat our enemies. Given the state of American politics today—and for the foreseeable future—our support for the Democratic Party is not a *reward*; it's a *strategy*. The more Democrats who serve in the House and Senate, the better able we'll be to fight homophobia and win our rights.

A similar pattern is true in most of the states, and there are no states in which the reverse holds. More Democrats in office also means more gay, lesbian, and bisexual appointees free to be honest about their sexuality, and to work for equal rights with the passion and dedication that comes from having experienced bigotry firsthand. Choosing Clinton over Dole means preferring a president who has banned discrimination based on sexual orientation in the granting of security clearances, required all federal agencies to reject sex discrimination in federal employment, provided remedies for federal employees who have been discriminated against, appointed openly gay men and lesbians to a wide range of positions, including judgeships, extended protection to persecuted gay men and lesbians overseas, and spoken out strongly against anti–gay and lesbian referenda—versus a man who has been on the opposite— i.e., the bigoted—side of virtually every gay and lesbian rights issue that has come before Congress in the past twenty years. And given the current field of Republican candidates, Dole is the best we can expect.

Part of the problem is that many Americans, with the distaste for "partisanship" that they grew up with, misunderstand what it means to identify as a Democrat, and to be generally supportive of the Democratic Party. When I was a Democratic state legislator in Massachusetts in the seventies, I won office entirely on my own and received no great favors from the Democratic legislative leadership. I therefore felt free to support Republicans when they came close to my views—that was at a time when there was still a healthy moderate faction within the Republican Party. In 1978 I publicly supported a Republican candidate for governor of Massachusetts and the U.S. Senate. When I sought election to the U.S. House, covering a much larger district, I entered into a somewhat different relationship in which I incurred a set of obligations to my fellow Democrats both in the party structure in my congressional district and in the House leadership. I believe that incurring these obligations has in fact enhanced my ability to fight for the values I most care about, but I recognize that they constrain me somewhat. Consequently, I no longer feel free publicly to support Republican candidates, but neither am I obligated to support Democrats of whom I disapprove. In William Weld's race against John Silber in 1990 for governor of Massachusetts, given among other things Silber's anti-gay record as president of Boston University, I confined my activities on behalf of the Democratic ticket that year to posing for one picture with Silber and my congressional colleagues in Washington, and issued no statements urging anyone to vote for him. When asked at one gathering, I said that on gay and lesbian issues Weld was a better candidate. The model here is that of the conservative Democratic leader in New York when confronted with the candidacy of the radical—by his standards—William Jennings Bryan as the Democratic nominee for president in 1900, who was heard to comment, "I am a Democrat still. Very still."

Those of us who have some positions where we have incurred obligations to the party ought not explicitly to support Republicans. But no such constraint applies to the great majority of Democrats. It is entirely reasonable for advocates of gay and lesbian rights to support the Democratic Party most of the time, and to support Republicans where that better advances the cause. Indeed, I wish Democratic supporters of gay and lesbian rights were more frequently confronted with a situation in which the Republican was the better candidate on our issues. Sadly, given the right-wing grip on today's Republican Party, that is very rarely the case anywhere in the country.

The Double Standard

Paradoxically, while this argument against identifying with the Democrats is based on the Democrats not being good enough and not deserving our support, there is a variant of it which builds on the fact that the Democrats have in fact been much better than the Republicans. This is the argument that we should hold the Democrats to a higher standard because we have a right to expect more of our friends. The problem here is that it states only half of a sensible political approach. It becomes whole only if you couple it with a recognition that because your friends are in fact your friends, you have an interest not just to criticize them but also to help them win.

The argument that we should not give the Democrats full support because they aren't good enough is an emotional one—and it's an emotion I fully share, having experienced it myself much of the time over the past twenty-five years in which I have been working my legislative colleagues and Executive Branch officials to persuade them to oppose homophobia. It's bad enough having to plead, trade, and argue for rights that we should be able to take for granted. And as with any cause that is important, it's especially aggravating to have to argue with someone who you think should know better. The statement "we expect more from our friends" is not so much a statistical prediction as it is a value judgment. Harry Truman said that being president meant spending an enormous amount of time persuading people to do what they should have been smart enough to do on their own in the first place. That is true of all politics. I understand how frustrating it is to have to persuade someone who should know it already that ending officially sanctioned homophobia is very important. I wish that it weren't necessary. But I also wish that I could eat more without gaining weight, and that I could work as long and hard today as I could twenty-five years ago without getting tired. But I restrict my food intake and say no to invitations and proposals that I would like to accept. And I spend time pushing my friends to do better when I wish I could simply insist that they behave appropriately and have them instantly respond.

If this were simply a matter of some Democrats having their feelings hurt because they weren't given enough positive reinforcement, it would not be worth mentioning. But taken with the intellectual error that it reinforces, it diverts us from the best use of our political energies. Intellectually, the argument that we should expect more from our friends translates all too often into a strategy of ignoring the need to help our friends get into office or to stay there. Indeed, those supporters of gay and lesbian rights who are articulating this viewpoint that the Democrats should be held to a higher standard seem to be operating with an implicit model that assumes a world divided into friendly elected officials who are Democrats and unfriendly elected officials who are Republicans. In this model, the role of activists is to criticize our friends when they are less than perfect, and cheer for our enemies when they are less than terrible.

The problem is that this ignores the most important political goal, which is to increase the number of your friends in office. As we relearned in the 1994 elections, there is nothing pre-ordained about Democratic majorities in the Congress. One reason that the number of hostile congresspeople increased in 1994 was that we were more focused on criticizing our friends' failings than on helping them stay in office. Not just gay activists but other groups as well—civil libertarians, feminists, environmentalists, supporters of racial fairness—acted as if they assumed that a given number of Democrats would be in office, and that their job was to make the officeholders' lives somewhat miserable until they improved their position. Instead, they undermined their friends and wound up with people in power much less sympathetic to their causes.

Another problem with this model is that it betrays a very unsophisticated notion of how to get people to move closer to your position. Several times this year I have heard angry complaints from Democrats who were confronted by gay and lesbian activists criticizing them for the shortcomings of Democrats. In one case, a Democratic leader was criticized because only seventy-six percent of all Democrats supported D.C.'s domestic partners ordinance. Given that eighy-five percent of all Republicans had voted the wrong way, he was understandably distressed to be treated as a laggard in need of correction. In another case, some supporters of sensible AIDS education spent a good deal of time denouncing Democrats for not being unanimous in opposing a Republican effort to undermine AIDS education. Again, the vote on the critical issue was lopsidedly in our favor on the Democratic side and overwhelmingly opposed on the Republican side. But because the Republicans had produced nearly twenty percent of their membership, close to an all-time high, the response was to leave them alone and denounce the Democrats for not being unanimous. The final example comes from the *Washington Blade*. On March 1 they reported on the anti-gay marriage bill in Colorado. The vote was, among Republicans, thirty-one in favor of the bill and nine opposed. The Democrats opposed the bill by a margin of twenty-two to two. How did the *Blade* report this? The subhead read "Two Democrats Blamed for Narrow Passage." That is, on a bill where more than seventy percent of the Republicans voted against us, while more than ninety percent of the Democrats supported us, the conclusion of the *Blade* was that this was the Democrats' fault. It is factually true that, if the Democrats had been unanimous, apparently the bill would have lost. It is also true that this demonstrates the central point: the more Democrats we have in virtually all legislative bodies, the less likely we are to be victimized by anti-gay and lesbian legislation. To give the Republicans credit, as the *Blade* article does, because only about seventy percent of them voted against us, and to blame the Democrats because only ninety percent of them voted for us, is indicative of the kind of confusion that hurts our efforts.

There is a version of game theory which says that you should, if you're trying to get people to do something, never appear to be satisfied with their efforts until they are one hundred percent on your side. In this view, one should always be pressing for more and never express too much satisfaction lest people "take you for granted." This is very poor human relations and very bad politics. Groups that adopt this attitude tend to take themselves out of the political marketplace. Elected officials who find themselves criticized because they are only eighty percent on your side are much more likely to figure that they might as well stop trying to please you as to make an extra effort to accomplish the remaining twenty percent.

Holding your friends to a higher standard is half an argument. The other half is recognizing that they are your friends, that you and they have common interests, and in particular in the political context that you have an interest in helping them win. This is why the Human Rights Campaign finds itself overwhelmingly supporting Democrats, not from any partisan predisposition, but as an inevitable consequence of their commitment to advance fairness for lesbians and gay men. Where individual Republicans are supportive, the Human Rights Campaign responds—indeed it looks hard for Republicans it can support. This is reasonable, but even with this accommodation, their fealty to the cause results in the HRC supporting Democrats more than ninety percent of the time. The unfair criticism the HRC received from some Republicans because of this probably contributed to the rare error they made recently when they contributed to the Republican Campaign Committee. Contributions to individual Republicans who have been strongly supportive of our fight make sense, but the attempted outreach to the broader Republican Party was futile, given its relentless march to the right.

While the Human Rights Campaign has on the whole struggled sensibly and effectively with this dilemma, the record of the Log Cabin Republicans is a much less defensible one. Given the vast disparity between the two parties in their support for gay and lesbian rights, these Republicans have a dilemma of their own. How do you urge gay men and lesbians to vote Republican when that will almost always mean a strengthening of those dedicated to enacting homophobia into law? This dilemma was made worse by the 1994 elections. Gay Republicans can point to our defeats on issues such a domestic partners and gays in the military when the Democrats controlled Congress, despite the fact that, on the roll call on these issues, we received the support of a significant majority of Democrats, only to lose because of the extremely heavy percentage of Republicans voting against us. But once the Republicans took control of Congress, the Log Cabin Club and their allies understood not only that there was no chance that the Republicans would be supportive of us, but that we were also likely to suffer significant setbacks in some of the areas where we had previously been successful. That has in fact been the case: we have seen significant cutbacks in housing for people with AIDS; the Ryan White Bill has still not been re-enacted into law as of March 1996 and, whereas the House in 1993 under the Democrats rejected the effort by Congressman Robert Dornan to expel military people who are HIV-positive, in the current Republican Congress we lacked the votes to prevent this vicious, bigoted piece of legislation from being enacted. And, of course, only President Clinton's veto has prevented the Republicans from abolishing the federal Medicaid program, which has been the single greatest source providing care for people with AIDS.

The Log Cabin's response has been twofold: using a double standard to judge the parties; and blaming the victim—ourselves—when even that double standard cannot justify a pro-Republican stance for gay and lesbian rights advocates. The Log Cabin Club asserts that the Democrats should be more supportive in gratitude for the votes they have received from our community. In their version of history, liberal advocates led gay and lesbian voters into the Democratic Party years ago, but we have not been adequately compensated. But that gets history exactly backwards. Up until 1970 there was no organized gay or lesbian activity in either political party of any significance, and neither party was at all responsive to our claims. Gay and lesbian support for Democrats has resulted in large part from the greater responsiveness of the Democratic Party to our quest for fairness. Gay men and lesbians have been more active in the Democratic Party not out of some predetermined partisan commitment, but because Democrats, with a greater orientation towards human rights and using the government to protect minorities against discrimination in general, have been far more hospitable to our efforts than have the Republicans. Thirty years ago there were virtually no openly gay or lesbian political figures in either party. Today, there are a large number of us who feel free to be honest about who we are, and well over ninety-five percent of us are Democrats.

Based on inaccurate history, the Log Cabin Club consistently criticizes Democrats more harshly than Republicans on the record. A recent statement from the Log Cabin Club noted the defeats we suffered in Congress in 1993–94, with no mention of the fact that this came because eighty to ninety percent of the Republicans generally joined thirty percent of the Democrats to inflict these defeats. When Bill Clinton takes firm executive action to ban discrimination in federal employment based on sexual orientation, appoints openly gay and lesbian officials to office, and writes a strong letter opposing anti-gay referenda in the states, the Log Cabin Republicans criticize this as inadequate. When Newt Gingrich compares gay men and lesbians to alcoholics in a grudging assertion that we should be tolerated, or when Bob Dole says in a fourth reversal that he is now sorry he returned the Log Cabin Club's campaign contribution, the Log Cabin response is to congratulate them for their open-mindedness.

The Proof Is in the Voting Record

This one-sidedness in judgment hit a peak recently when the Log Cabin Club issued its analysis of Republicans in Congress. Recognizing that you cannot make an intellectually honest case for voting Republican if your primary concern is advancing gay rights, the Log Cabin Club did an analysis of only the Republican Members of Congress. Their purpose was to show that the Republicans are not nearly as bad on gay and lesbian rights as we think. Having worked with very little success over the past fifteen years to try to get any significant amount of Republican support on the floor of the House to fight homophobia, watching the last few Republican conventions and national presidential campaigns, and looking at the data the Log Cabin Club itself puts forward, when I read their conclusion that the Republicans are really not so bad, I am reminded of the question Chico Marx asks in a movie: "Who you gonna believe, me or your own eyes?"

If you apply the extraordinarily generous criteria that the Log Cabin Club uses to rate Republicans—people who make homophobic remarks and almost always vote against us are rated as "tolerant"—the Democrats come out as the Legion of Superheroes. While they understand how fatal it would be to their arguments if they actually compared the parties, the Log Cabin analysis attempts to discredit the pro-Democratic result by pointing to regional and urban/rural differences. Specifically, they argue that their "report also demonstrates that rating scores have more to do with regional demographics and culture than with political affiliation." In other words, it's not fair to compare Democrats and Republicans because Democrats tend to come from areas that are more supportive of gay and lesbian fairness issues than Republicans. Unfortunately for them, there is one set of statistics that completely demolishes this argument. It is one that they scrupulously avoid.

We have a very large number of political constituencies in the last two Congresses that have had both Democratic and Republican representatives in exactly the same district. Thus, we have a basis for comparison in which only partisanship is at issue. And the results, not surprisingly, show an overwhelming Democratic superiority. We have fifty-six House seats where Democrats who served 1993–94 were replaced by Republicans in 1995. It is true that these districts are on the whole less supportive of gay and lesbian rights than those districts which are solidly Democratic, because demographics are a factor. But this gives us a chance to see what difference it makes in those districts that do not swing between the parties.

Fifty-seven percent of the Democrats who held these seats in the 103rd Congress voted to allow the District of Columbia to continue its domestic partnership law. In 1995, when the Republicans proposed an even harsher anti-domestic partnership motion concerning the District of Columbia than they had in 1993, only six percent of the Republicans who replaced these Democrats voted with us. A second important issue in the previous Congress was the Republican effort to penalize school systems that treat gay and lesbian students with compassion. Some seventy-eight percent of the Democrats who were replaced by Republicans in the current Congress voted against bigotry in that instance. While there was not a comparable vote in 1995 because no bill came up that could have been a vehicle for such an amendment, we did have a vote on a Republican motion to restrict severely the administration's AIDS education program, in which similar anti-gay and lesbian sentiments came into play. On this vote, only nine percent of those Republicans who had replaced Democrats upheld the sensible AIDS education program.

In the Senate, there is a similar measure. In 1993–94, there were twenty states where one senator was a Democrat and one was a Republican. In 1995, there were eighteen such states. In 1993–94, in nineteen of the twenty states where there was divided representation, the Democratic senator had a better voting record than the Republican on gay and lesbian issues. In one state they were tied. Last year the Republicans did better. There was one state where the Republican was marginally better than the Democrat—Strom Thurmond got a twenty-five percent record in 1995 while Ernest Hollings got a zero percent in South Carolina. And in five states the Republican and Democratic votes were the same. But in twelve states, the Democrat was better than the Republican. So, in both years, there are large, statistically significant differences between senators from the same state and different party when it comes to supporting our rights. In thirty-one instances over the two Congresses, the Democrat was better than the Republican. In one instance the Republican was better than the Democrat, and six came out even.

The final argument that the Log Cabin Club advances is that a Republican who's supportive of gay rights will do more good than a Democrat because he or she will be able to influence fellow Republicans. That argument has some appeal in theory but has produced no success in practice. After fifteen years of serving in the House, I can think of no Republican other than Steve Gunderson who has consistently and actively worked with any success to bring other Republican votes to our cause. The anti-gay and lesbian feelings among Republicans are so deeply rooted that even when a powerful and strongly supportive person like Governor Weld tries to be helpful, the results are nil. Thus Weld failed when he tried to get his fellow moderate Republican John McKernan not to veto a gay and lesbian rights bill. And Governor Weld, Congresswoman Connie Morella, Congressman Chris Shays, and others of the small handful of Republicans who are consistently supportive of our rights find themselves pressured by the partisan necessity overwhelmingly in support of strong anti-gay and lesbian Republicans for other offices. Personally they are with us. Politically, their influence when they are not themselves on our ballot is almost always used to hurt our friends and help those opposed to our rights.

Of course, it is important for us to have lesbians and gay men who are in agreement with the Republicans on a range of issues but who are also willing to fight against the tide within that party for gay and lesbian rights. It is essential for our ultimate success that Republicans know that if and when they are prepared to move to a less homophobic position, they will receive support for it. My problem is not with the Log Cabin Club trying to move Republicans into a more sympathetic position, but the fact that they pretend to a far greater degree of success than they have accomplished. In fact, during the period the Log Cabin Republicans have been the most active, the Republican Party has if anything gotten worst on the issues of concern to us. It is not the Log Cabin Republicans' fault that they have had no influence. It is their fault that they pretend to a greater influence than they have, because this misleads other gay and lesbian voters.

The problem is that few political organizations can succeed forever if they are unable to claim any success. Having had no success in moving the Republican Party to a less bigoted position, the Log Cabin Club instead claims credit when the Republicans do not dismantle the Ryan White Bill. And while Ryan White is a very important piece of legislation, it is defended in Congress by a wide range of interests, including the major metropolitan areas where most of the funds are spent. At the same time, the Log Cabin Club is absolutely silent on the Republicans' dismantling of Medicaid, which is a far more important source of funds for treating people with AIDS than is Ryan White.

It would be very useful to us if we had an organization that succeeded in preaching gay rights to Republicans. Sadly, over the last few years the Log Cabin Club has been much more notable for preaching Republicanism to gay and lesbian activists.

RICH TAFEL

Why a One-Party Strategy Fails

IN HIS TWO-PART essay in *The Harvard Gay & Lesbian Review*, Representative Barney Frank argued in favor of a one-party political strategy for all that gays and lesbians seek to accomplish. To make his case, he used a method of creating a straw man opponent and then ripping it apart. However, there are some hard realities that confront Rep. Frank's passionate argument for a one-party gay movement, ultimately showing it to be a failure.

It is revealing that Rep. Frank began his piece by suggesting that the gay community take a lesson from Samuel Gompers, an early leader of the labor movement. Of all the examples of a movement which has so weakened its political effectiveness by employing a one-party strategy, labor is the best example. Indeed, a recent poll of union members showed that the labor movement's $35 million campaign to toss every Republican out of Congress this year is overwhelmingly opposed by the very people that labor claims to represent. Their strategy is so flawed and so ideologically narrow that it has forced them to break with their own, albeit dwindling, constituency.

However diminished it is today, labor will always have bigger numbers and more money than gay men and lesbians have. But labor's downward political spiral still offers us a clear view of what happens when a movement adopts what Rep. Frank so passionately advocates. Labor, for all of its members and money, is taken for granted by the Democratic Party and written off by the Republicans. That is political reality, no matter which party is in power. The NAFTA and GATT debates are but two recent examples of where the Democratic leadership easily rebuffed a frenzied opposition campaign by labor, only to receive the movement's loyal and generous support in the 1996 elections.

The reality of American politics is that it's a two-party affair, and anyone who studies American political movements will see that they are successful only when they are bipartisan. That's a reality that even Rep. Frank recognizes. When he cites his own record from time to time, he openly boasts about working with and having access to Republicans.

From the Summer 1996 issue

Despite Rep. Frank's repeated claims, Log Cabin Republicans has never said that the Republican Party is better than the Democratic Party on gay issues. We have made the point that, for the past thirty years, the gay community has pursued a one-party strategy with the Democrats and vilified the Republicans so relentlessly as to drive any possible GOP allies away. What's more, when the Democratic leadership has really been put to the test ("Don't ask, don't tell," same-sex marriage), they have repeatedly tossed us over the side. While Rep. Frank will scramble to defend his party by saying "the Republicans started it," this is an undignified defense of a failed and politically cruel strategy. Log Cabin merely calls for opening a new flank in the gay struggle to increase our political leverage within the two-party system.

Rep. Frank still has not quelled the explosion of criticism against his defense of President Clinton over "Don't ask, don't tell." He still must confront the reality that in 1993, with Democrats in control of all three branches of government, the gay community witnessed its worst public beating in American history over the military issue. Clinton never took to the airwaves to explain his positions in defense of the gay community, or act as heroically as he has in defense of social programs targeted for cuts by the Republican Congress.

The problem was not with the anti-gay Democrats and Republicans in Congress who fought him on the issue. The problem was with the one-party strategy of Rep. Frank, which gave Clinton a free hand to back down without paying a price in the gay community. Witness the early endorsement of President Clinton by the Human Rights Campaign this year, and the hard right turn Clinton subsequently took on same-sex marriage. It seems that when we should be at the zenith of our power in Rep. Frank's paradigm, we are in reality embarrassingly powerless.

Indeed, the one-party strategy is a brilliant way to let Democrats abandon our cause altogether, because they can't lose if they do. If Democrats don't deliver, blame the Republicans. And if anyone tries to change the Republicans, do everything in your power to stop them. This guarantees that the Democrats will always look good, Republicans will always look bad, and no one will ever have to advance a single issue of concern to gays and lesbians. The emotional roller coaster ride that has been the Clinton era should be evidence enough that we need real accountability and real choices in politics or we will not have real and tangible progress. The slow work of building a foundation for gay support in the Republican Party requires vision and leadership, something utterly lacking in Rep. Frank's blueprint.

The 1990 gubernatorial election in Massachusetts, which Rep. Frank refers to in his piece, is a case study in the failure of a one-party strategy. In that race, pro-gay Republican William Weld was running against staunchly anti-gay Democrat John Silber. While Rep. Frank concedes that Silber was a clear homophobe, he took no steps to defeat him. He admits posing for an endorsement photograph with Silber and other Democratic leaders, but he didn't campaign for Weld, one assumes, because his party would punish him. Did Rep. Frank gain any leverage with the Democratic Party by tacitly endorsing Silber? Did it move our community ahead? The answer is no. The election of Bill Weld, however, has been an enormous benefit to gays and lesbians in Massachusetts. I'm glad, for their sake, that the one-party strategy was rejected in that election.

Indeed, Weld's predecessor, Michael Dukakis, aggressively went after gay foster parents, going as far as to remove a child from a gay couple's home and to place it in an abusive heterosexual environment. Rep. Frank supported Dukakis for president, and I'm sure he would say that there was no better choice. What a depressingly powerless refrain. The question for gay voters is how to get beyond the choice between lesser evils to the day when we have a choice between two relatively friendly candidates.

If we break out of the two-party strategy, we'll not only have real progress but we'll be liberated from single-issue voting. The current U.S. Senate race between Weld and Democratic Senator John Kerry is a perfect example of the world that Log Cabin envisions. I recently sat on a discussion panel with a liberal lesbian activist from Massachusetts. She praised Weld's record on gay issues in great detail, but when asked whom she would support in the election, she responded, "John Kerry, of course. Bill Weld and the Republicans are out to hurt the poor."

I can't imagine a more empowering situation, where a lesbian can comfortably vote her conscience on the wide range of issues facing everyone in the state, and still be assured that her rights and her concerns as a lesbian will be promoted. That's the world that Log Cabin wants to help create. Why doesn't Rep. Frank share this vision for our community? Instead, Rep. Frank regularly makes the false claim that Log Cabin endorses anti-gay Republicans, and that we spend our time trying to make the gay community vote Republican instead of trying to change the Republican Party. This is another example of how little he knows about what we do. We spend *all* of our time educating Republicans on gay issues and promoting legislation that will help gay and lesbian people.

The results are already starting to show. I had the opportunity to work for

Governor Weld, who is the best governor, Republican or Democrat, in the country when it comes to delivering for our community. Mayor Rudolph Giuliani of New York, Mayor Richard Riordan of Los Angeles, and Mayor Susan Golding of San Diego publicly embraced the gay community in their election campaigns. Governor Christie Whitman of New Jersey, Governor Arne Carlson of Minnesota, and Governor Lincoln Almond of Rhode Island have taken swift steps to promote the interests of the gay and lesbian community.

Just last month, Dan Burdish, a long-time Log Cabin activist, was appointed as the executive director of the Nevada State Republican Party, the GOP's first openly gay, high-level party official. This year, Log Cabin activists organized a concerted grass roots attack on the extreme right within the GOP, ousting notorious anti-gay leaders such as Morton Blackwell from party positions and defeating anti-gay resolutions in Christian Coalition bastions like Texas and Virginia. All of this has happened just since Log Cabin came on the scene, and it's a track record we will continue building on every day. This Republican Convention will witness the first ever openly gay delegates, which is an important step.

I am convinced that if we succeed in changing the Republican Party on gay issues, even by a modest measure, the whole picture of gay life in America can radically improve. There will be real accountability among politicians. There will be greater political leverage in the gay community. With more choices, there will be broader discussion about how to solve our unique problems as a community. Ultimately, we will be better served and better protected by our government if we widen the spectrum of our political involvement. If we take the path of least resistance, as Rep. Frank suggests in the heat of an election year, then we will stifle our potential as a movement. In the end, we should reject a strategy that has already proven to be a failure.

BARNEY FRANK

Republicans Must *Earn* Our Vote

RICH TAFEL'S RESPONSE to my article is important both for what he says and for what he doesn't say. What he doesn't even try to do is to refute my article, which documented that on every issue important to the rights of lesbians, gay men, and bisexuals, the Democratic Party is overwhelmingly better than the Republican Party, and that the Democrats have gotten better as the GOP has gotten worse.

His only reference to the comparative record of the two parties is his defensive statement that his organization "has never said that the Republican Party is better than the Democratic Party on gay issues." Can readers think of any other political organization that tries to get them to believe that it is irrelevant that one party has a far better record on the issues than the other party? And I must note that, while for polemical purposes Mr. Tafel ducks the central question as to which party has the better record, he often tries to give the impression that the Republicans are better for us, indefensible as he knows such a statement to be. For example, after the 1994 elections, Mr. Tafel and other Log Cabin Republicans asserted that the Gingrich-Dole-Helms-Armey takeover of Congress was a good thing for gay men and lesbians, and that we would be better off as a result.

What he does say is seriously flawed because it completely misrepresents my position. Mr. Tafel falsely claims that my position is that gay men and lesbians should support the Democrats no matter what. In fact, I said exactly the opposite. Because Mr. Tafel so egregiously misstates what I say, I quote here what I said in my previous article:

> Of course it is important for us to have lesbians and gay men who are in agreement with the Republicans on a range of issues but who are also willing to fight against the tide within that party to support gay and lesbian rights. It is essential for our ultimate success that Republicans know that if and when they are prepared to move to a less

From the Fall 1996 issue

homophobic position, they will receive support for it. My problem is not with the Log Cabin Club trying to move Republicans into a more sympathetic position, but the fact that they pretend to a far greater degree of success than they have accomplished. In fact, during the period the Log Cabin Republicans have been the most active, the Republican Party has if anything gotten worse on the issues of concern to us. It is not the Log Cabin Republicans' fault that they have had no influence. It is their fault that they pretend to a greater influence than they have, because this misleads other gay and lesbian voters. . . .

It would be very useful to us if we had an organization that succeeded in preaching gay rights to Republicans. Sadly, over the last few years the Log Cabin Club has been much more notable for preaching Republicanism to gay and lesbian activists.

I would be delighted if Republicans understood that they can get votes from gay and lesbian voters if they are supportive of our positions. My problem with the Log Cabin Club is that their strategy consists essentially of rewarding the Republicans before they move in our direction, which means that they have absolutely no incentive to move that way. And in pursuit of their pro-Republican policies, the Log Cabin Club exacerbates our political problems because their influence is overwhelmingly on the side of Republican candidates who are almost always worse on gay and lesbian issues than Democrats.

Mr. Tafel says that I falsely accuse them of supporting anti-gay candidates. What in the world does he call endorsing Robert Dole, who has been one of the leading homophobes in America through his position as Republican Leader? Yes, we lost on gays in the military—and the beginning of that loss came early in 1993, when Republican Leader Bob Dole got most of the Republicans to back a proposal to add an anti-gays-in-the-military rider to the bill that established family and medical leave. Because Dole, with the aid of the homophobic Sam Nunn and a minority of Democrats, had the votes to prevail at that point, gay and lesbian groups acquiesced when the president deferred on the Executive Order lest we see the family and medical leave bill go down. It is true that a Congress controlled by Democrats later voted for a bad policy, which I fought hard against. It is also true, as I pointed out in my article, that we got a significant majority of Democrats to vote against that policy, but lost because approximately ninety percent of the Republicans voted for it in both Houses.

This is the central problem with Mr. Tafel's pro-Republican strategy—not that it is badly conceived, but that it is abominably executed. Yes, it makes sense to say to the Democrats that if they don't support gay and lesbian rights, and if there are Republicans who are better on the issue, gays and lesbians will vote Republican. But that is not what we confront. The fact is that at the national level, as Mr. Tafel implicitly agrees, the Republicans are overwhelmingly worse than the Democrats by any measure one wishes to use. Thus, while his strategy sounds reasonable in his formulation of it, in practice it consists of penalizing Democrats by supporting Republicans who are worse on our issues. But it makes no sense to penalize Democrats for inadequate support by urging people to vote for Republicans who are even worse on our issues.

When the Log Cabin Club welcomed the Republican control of Congress that took place in 1994, they hailed an event that happened in large part because a number of Republicans who have one hundred percent anti–gay and lesbian voting records defeated Democrats with voting records up to eighty, ninety, and one hunred percent supportive. I know of many congressional races in 1994 in which Democrats were attacked by Republicans because the Democrats had supported fairness for gay men and lesbians. I know of absolutely no races in which the reverse was the case. When the Log Cabin Club welcomes the triumph of homophobes over people who have supported us, I find it hard to understand why they think I criticize them unfairly.

Mr. Tafel counters by pointing to their support for Mayors Rudolph Giuliani and Richard Riordan in New York and Los Angeles. It is true that in those cities, given the demographics, there is a great deal of support for gay and lesbian rights. But it also should be noted that the election of Giuliani and Riordan as Republican mayors has not altered one very important fact: the Republicans in Congress from both of those cities continue to have virtually one hundred percent anti–gay and lesbian voting records. And both of these men are much less loyal Republicans than the Log Cabin Club, because they are less inclined to put partisan politics first. Giuliani backed pro-gay Mario Cuomo, while Log Cabin New Yorkers backed his anti-gay opponent George Pataki; Giuliani boycotted the Republican convention, and, unlike Mr. Tafel's organization, he has not endorsed Robert Dole for president.

That is the other point that Mr. Tafel ignores. Even where we have occasional, exceptional Republicans such as these two mayors, along with Governors Weld and Whitman, who are free to be supportive of our rights to fair treatment in their own local and state spheres, they are either useless or harmful to our efforts at the national level. Weld tried very hard the last time we were redistricted to change Gerry Studds' district so that Gerry would be defeated. Fortunately, Gerry's strength with the voters allowed him to frustrate this effort. Governor Whitman is strongly supporting a Republican candidate for the Senate, Richard Zimmer, who has an overwhelmingly anti-gay and lesbian voting record, against Robert Torricelli, who has been very supportive of our rights.

If Weld goes to the U.S. Senate, he will help perpetuate a right-wing Republican regime that is wholly negative on the issues we care about. During Bill Clinton's first two years, several openly gay and lesbian officials were appointed to presidential positions and confirmed by the Senate—although in Roberta Achtenberg's case it was over the negative vote of Bob Dole, the intended recipient of the Log Cabin Club's thousand-dollar contribution of recent memory. Since the Republicans took control, no gay or lesbian officials have been confirmed, because the first time the president considered nominating one, it became clear that the nomination would be blocked by Jesse Helms.

To summarize, I think it is a very good idea for there to be an incentive for Republicans to be more supportive of gay and lesbian rights, and for Democrats to understand that, if they fail to help us gain victory in our fight against discrimination, there will still be people for whom gay and lesbian voters can vote. The problem with the Log Cabin strategy is that it does virtually nothing to accomplish these goals. Instead, they give aid and comfort to people who are on the whole our enemies, apologizing for, underplaying, and ignoring their leaders' homophobia, while denigrating the efforts of Democratic officials to vindicate our rights. National Republican leaders are of course delighted at this, since they understand that they are unlikely to get votes from those who think gay and lesbian rights are important, and for them the next best thing is to have gay and lesbian voters not vote at all.

IN MORE RECENT MONTHS, we have seen Newt Gingrich—whose accession to the Speakership was hailed by the Log Cabin Club—take the final steps to drive Steve Gunderson out of politics, because Gingrich understands, as Mr. Tafel does not, that the Republican Party simply will not tolerate any openly gay people in high office. Gunderson has been a leading Republican and a very close ally of Gingrich. When Dick Armey referred to me as "Barney Fag," Gunderson, as he notes in his book, came to Armey's defense. But when Gunderson reconsidered his decision to leave Congress, given the fact that he would be chairman of the Agriculture Committee next year if the Republicans retain control of the House, Gingrich stepped in to insist that he stick with his original decision to quit.

According to Gunderson, Gingrich met with him and told him "as a friend" that he, Gingrich, thought Gunderson should not run. According to both men's version of the conversation, Gingrich told Gunderson that, while he personally would support Gunderson, there would be a brutal campaign against him, with Republican activists engaging in vicious personal attacks on Steve and his lover. (The right-wing activist who was supposed to be leading this charge, Paul Weyrich, denied that he had any such plans.) Moreover, Gunderson could not count on becoming chairman of the Agriculture Committee if he were re-elected, due to strong opposition within the Republican Party to having an openly gay leader. Gunderson got this message and reaffirmed his decision to quit, bitterly denouncing the anti-gay feeling in the Republican Party. This *coup de grâce* was administered by Mr. Gingrich himself, whom the Log Cabin Club will be working hard to retain as Speaker. Note that the right-wing activist whom Gingrich claimed would be leading an assault against Gunderson, Paul Weyrich, denied that he had any such plans and asserted that Gingrich had simply made up this story. All in all, Gingrich's role in forcing Gunderson to quit elected politics resembles nothing so much as the scene in *Oklahoma!* when Curly tries to persuade Judd to commit suicide, explaining to Judd that he'd be a far more popular figure in that part of Oklahoma dead than alive.

A similar eagerness to blind themselves to homophobia describes the Log Cabin Club's enthusiastic response to Jack Kemp's nomination as vice president on the Republican ticket. Kemp has an unbroken record of homophobic activity. As a member of the House in the eighties, when we were fighting desperately to defeat Dannemeyer's right-wing amendments that would have crippled the fight against AIDS, Kemp could usually be counted on to support Dannemeyer. As Secretary of HUD, Kemp rejected a contract negotiated by lower-level HUD officials and the union that gave some recognition to gay and lesbian domestic partnerships. The Clinton administration has since reversed Kemp's homophobic position. And, of course, the platform on which Dole and Kemp are running is actively and vigorously anti–gay and lesbian, denouncing efforts to protect us against discrimination and, most egregiously, denouncing the current military policy—as far too soft on gays and lesbians.

Finally, we have their votes on the Defense of Marriage Act. It is unfortunately true that President Clinton said he would sign the bill, and that a majority of Democrats in the House voted for it. As of this writing, Senator Edward Kennedy plans to offer an anti-discrimination bill as an amendment to the Defense of Marriage Act, and President Clinton is actively supporting that amendment. I cannot be sure of the outcome, but one thing is very clear: a large majority of Democrats will vote for adding the bill, which would protect gays and lesbians from discrimination in the workplace, and an overwhelming majority of Republicans will vote against it.

The Defense of Marriage Act has two provisions. One says that no state need follow any other state that adopts same-sex marriage. My own view is that the Supreme Court would probably find this to be the case anyway, certainly given its current composition. (And of course if the Log Cabin Club is successful in electing Bob Dole, more justices will be appointed to that body who will take an anti–gay and lesbian position, in contrast to the two justices appointed by President Clinton who voted to strike down the Colorado anti-gay ordinance.)

The second provision has the clearest negative effect on same-sex marriage. In direct contrast to the supposed states' rights philosophy that the right wing claims it supports, this bill says that if any state were to allow same-sex marriage, the federal government would refuse to recognize it. This means that same-sex couples married in Hawaii or anywhere else would find themselves without any federal tax benefits, immigration benefits, social security benefits, and so on. This is a direct attack not only on same-sex marriage but on the right of states to make such a policy decision. I offered an amendment to strike this part from the bill, which would have thus allowed states to legalize same-sex marriage and have these marriages be fully recognized. My amendment lost heavily, but I received a majority of Democratic votes. It was not nearly as large a majority as I would have liked: 99 Democrats voted for and 87 voted against it. The Republicans opposed my amendment by a vote of 223 to 3.

I should add that those Democrats who voted for my amendment—and especially the sixty-five who voted against the entire bill (versus the one Republican who voted against it: Steve Gunderson)—have already come under attack from their Republican opponents. This is an illustration of my central point. Yes, we have a lot of work to do to get the Democrats to be better on gay and lesbian rights. But one of the major obstacles we face in trying to do this is the fact that Democrats from districts where gay and lesbian rights are controversial can expect to be demagogued by their Republican opponents, who will in general be supported by the Log Cabin Club. This does not mean that the Log Cabin Club will endorse individually homophobic Republicans. It means that their enthusiastic welcoming of the Republican majority in 1994, their support for a continued Republican majority, and their contributions to Republican Party efforts—when the party deigns to accept them—all reinforce the Republicans' anti–gay and lesbian efforts.

The central point remains. Thirty years ago both parties were terrible on gay and lesbian rights. Over the past twenty years, the Democrats have gotten better and better, while the Republicans have, if anything, gotten worse. Mr. Tafel's prescription for dealing with this is to support Republicans anyhow, apparently on the theory that this will somehow inspire the Democrats to be even better than they have been. I can think of no other example in American politics where supposedly rational people tell us that when you are unhappy with one group for not being good enough on your issues, the way to respond is to give support to those who are worse. His approach to the Republican Party reminds me of the joke about the parent who comes to school and tells the first grade teacher that while his son *will* misbehave from time to time, he is a very sensitive child, and the teacher should show what could happen by slapping the child next to his son. Encouraging the Democrats to be better by supporting Republicans who are incomparably worse makes about that much sense.

To Assimilate or
Not to Assimilate?

I T IS A SIGN of the matriculation of gay culture that lesbians and gay men have had to come to terms with a question that other minorities have confronted in the past, namely, whether to strive for a separate cultural identity or to assimilate as much as possible into mainstream American life. The most dramatic example of a confrontation between these two visions of minority status occurred when the Civil Rights movement of the 1950s met the Black Power movement of the 1960s, presenting one model that sought full integration of the races and another that completely rejected the culture of white society. The question of assimilation versus a separate ethnic identity has been on the minds of American Jews for many decades and remains a topic of debate and concern to this day.

It is only recently that a similar question has arisen in the gay and lesbian world—perhaps because it's only recently that we could even dream of thinking of ourselves as a "people" at all. The most obvious sign of this change is that sexual orientation has come to be widely viewed as a minority status potentially on a par with race or sex, subject to discrimination and thus legal protection. In addition, a national gay and lesbian culture has emerged in the past decade that for the first time makes it possible for a person to define his or her existence almost completely around being gay. One can live in the gay neighborhood of any big city, surf the Net for sex or chat exclusively with other gay people, vacation at a gay resort, spend one's free time entirely in gay environments, whether gyms, bars, or coffee houses, and so on.

Okay, so it's possible to live that way, but *ought* we to? What are the implications of building one's identity almost entirely around a sexual orientation? These are ethical as well as strategic questions that lesbian and gay writers have started to wrestle with in recent years. Perhaps the most direct challenge to the "ghetto" culture was that of Bruce Bawer in 1993's *A Place at the Table*, which argued that cultural separatism was detrimental to the cause of gay rights, since it provided an excuse for the dominant society to deny gays full access to its benefits and privileges. This book gave rise to an "Open Letter" from David Bergman that was published in the second issue of the *HGLR*. In it, Bergman charges that Bawer's call for assimilation amounts to a wholesale surrender of a distinctive gay identity—even the very concept of "outness"—in the interest of being accepted by straight society. Bawer responds that the gay subculture Bergman is defending offers but a single model of gay life, and a very deviant one at that, which presents itself as a compulsory lifestyle rather than one of many options.

The debate over assimilation is underscored by a pair of books with confusingly similar titles that came out in the fall of 1995: Urvashi Vaid's *Virtual Equality* and Andrew Sullivan's *Virtually Normal*, both reviewed by Michael Schwartz. Sullivan's position is that our goal should be to achieve simple equality as citizens and not minority status, much less cultural autonomy in gay ghettos. Vaid argues that engaging in gay sex automatically places a person in radical opposition to mainstream society, suggesting that a subculture of opposition can be expected to endure for some time to come. Finally, in a brief interview, playwright Edward Albee questions whether it makes sense for a sexual orientation to serve as the basis for a ghetto literature of the kind that has emerged over the past two decades.

DAVID BERGMAN

An Open Letter to Bruce Bawer

I'VE READ YOUR BOOK, A *Place at The Table: The Gay Individual in American Society*, and some of the reviews of it. A few of the reviews I've read have been positive, but none of them, I think, have been just to you. They have failed to note the really heroic sincerity of your book, your painful effort to be evenhanded to those you oppose on both the left and the right. They've ignored the passion of the book and your deep love for your companion, Chris Davenport. In some way A *Place at the Table* is a long valentine to him, and I find that very moving.

The reviews have ignored the deep moral examination of your own conduct. But most of all they have ignored your concern for young gay men and women growing up in this society. I am sorry that these virtues haven't been acknowledged by the critics, because without recognizing these qualities they will not be able to account for the profound influence your book will have. I don't want to hide the fact that I think your book is very wrongheaded, but I am glad you have written it because it articulates what many people feel in ways that can lead to much better mutual understanding.

Like me, you show a great concern for young people; in fact, you see the worried, frightened, isolated teenager as your ideal reader. You open your book with an account of a young man, whom you assume from his "neat dress and good posture" and from the "wholesomeness and sensitivity" he radiates to be "the much-loved son of a decent family." You watch him at a magazine rack slowly gravitate to a copy of the *Native*, and you are "irked" because the journal contained "the narrow, sex-obsessed image of gay life" which "bore little resemblance to my life or to the lives of my gay friends—or, for that matter, to the lives of the vast majority of gay Americans." (I will spend a lot of time quoting you, because I don't want to put words in your mouth in the way that you put words in other people's mouths.) However, at the end of the anecdote, you do nothing to help the young man, and it's not clear from anything in the book that, with the exception of writing A *Place at the Table*, you have done anything for young people despite your expressed concerns for their welfare.

From the Spring 1994 issue

I'm sorry your contact with young gay people has been so limited. They need the help. Moreover, you might learn from them not to be so anxious about the harmful effects of the *Native* or other gay publications; and, finally, if you spent some time with young people you might be less censorious of others—the teachers at the Harvey Milk School, professors in gay studies programs—who have dedicated themselves to working with the young.

I know it's been a great privilege for me to serve for the last few years as the faculty advisor to the gay, lesbian and bisexual student organization at Towson State University, a rather large state institution in Maryland. I've also taught such courses as "Images of Masculinity," a look at both gay and straight male autobiography, and "The Literature of AIDS"—courses you may sneer at as being "subcultural-oriented courses." So I've done my share of working with just the types of young people you're concerned about.

What I learned is that teenage and college-age people don't have to read the *Native* to be "sex-obsessed"; their hormones will do that quite nicely. Even your well-scrubbed, much-loved boy is no stranger to sexual obsession. Second, the students are quite good at deciding which fantasies are theirs and which are someone else's. Your young man had enough self-knowledge that he didn't want to look at *Penthouse*, and I feel confident that he won't start wearing nipple clamps just because he saw them advertised. Finally, if you want to help young people develop as individuals, you can't impose on them your standard of how they should express themselves as gay men or lesbians.

That well-scrubbed boy may, in fact, want to wear leather or taffeta. One of the nicest, sweetest men in my student group—who has adoring parents and who works part-time in a bookstore—took an extra job as a go-go dancer at a local bar. It's not something I or his school friends encouraged him to do; they are as puzzled by this decision as I am. When I asked him why he took the job, he told me he liked dancing and the job brought in good money. I don't think those are the only reasons, but I'm not going to presume to know his motives. I would not be helping the young man if I said, "How awful! How disgusting! That's not what decent, middle-class males do." Nor would you be helping the young man at the magazine rack if you told him, "Believe me, most gay people don't do those disgusting things." He might feel even more alone than he already feels.

What is of the utmost importance in working with young people is not to impose what you like, what you feel comfortable with, on them, or to presume that you know their hearts better than they do. As you point out, the range of human emotion, the rate of growth and maturity, the levels of comfort differ in every individual. Again, as you point out, one needs to be more than tolerant; one needs to be accepting. It seems to me that you should take your own words to heart if you really mean to help people develop as happy individuals.

Helping that young man is not at all as simple as you seem to think. Twenty years teaching have not always shown me what to do. I don't suppose you've gotten calls in the middle of the night from a gay student ready to commit suicide because his parents threatened to kick him out onto the street, or from a bisexual mother whose two-year-old daughter has been diagnosed with leukemia, or from frightened teenagers of both sexes who have learned that their best friend has AIDS. Their lives are more complicated than ours ever were, and the picture of a drag queen or a man in leather doesn't faze them.

If you had worked with young people, maybe you wouldn't be so critical of the teacher at the Harvey Milk School who excused the lateness of students by saying they were on "Gay People Time." You thought the teacher was reinforcing a stereotype, and "stereotypes are prisons." I understood his joke as an attempt to bring the students' attention to their tardiness and their stereotypical behavior without turning the matter into a big deal. As you point out, the students at the school are "emotionally bruised young people," and coming down hard on them at this time in their lives may not be the best strategy for their overall development. I suppose the point I'm making is that for all your talk about wanting to foster individuality, you don't give people much room to find their own way to live their lives. You make your pronouncements about what's good and bad for people from a safe distance. I'm not so ready to second-guess the teacher at Harvey Milk as you are.

But it's not only the teacher at the Harvey Milk School you patronize; it is everyone involved with education. You tar with a very wide brush anyone involved in gay and lesbian studies. First you claim that we're interested in "therapy" more than in "education." But since Socrates the basis of Western education has been the injunction that "the unexamined life is not worth living" and that educational institutions are meant to help young people to be fully productive members of society. I don't see how helping students understand themselves and function better (which is what I suspect you mean by "therapy") can ever be divided from the accumulation of facts and the development of cognitive skills (your limited idea of "education"). The two must go hand-in-hand.

You mock any attempt to teach students—gay, straight, and in-between—about homosexuality. Here's what you say based on reading merely the titles of workshops and course descriptions (a typical strategy of the reactionary right):

> Gay Studies might have a valid purpose if it could help students bet-
> ter understand certain heretofore neglected aspects of Marlowe's
> plays, say, or Raphael's paintings, or Benjamin Britten's music. In real-
> ity, however, far from probing and questioning and attempting to un-
> derstand, Gay Studies imposes reductive, politically correct ideas
> upon its subjects, mindlessly celebrating gay solidarity and the unty-
> ing of lesbian tongues, for example, instead of seeking to understand
> major historical figures as individuals in whose lives and work sexual-
> ity functioned in very different ways.

Now I am highly critical of much of the work in gay studies, and have published my criticism in some detail, but your statement takes no notice of the
very wide debates going on within gay and lesbian studies about methodology
and subject matter. In your words, no one is studying major figures; all gay
studies celebrate "solidarity"; no distinctions are made among different artists.
How many of these classes have you attended? How many conferences have
you gone to? I don't know what works in gay studies you've been reading, but
a more careful examination will indicate that it is you who are reductive. May
I suggest Claude Summer's *Gay Fiction*, Mark Lilly's *Gay Men's Literature in
the Twentieth Century*, James Saslow's *Ganymede in the Renaissance*, Michael
Moon's *Disseminating Whitman*, Jonathan Goldberg's *Sodometries*, or my own
Gaiety Transfigured? These books take very different approaches, come to very
different conclusions, have very different goals. Some of these books I thoroughly disagree with; in others I find larger areas of agreement; but nobody
who has read these books carefully and without prejudice could come away believing they are cut from the same cloth. Did you think you were doing young
people a service by tearing at everyone who tries to address gay and lesbian
studies?

Indeed, one of the largest contradictions in your book is between your
rather moving attacks on the inadequacy of labels, the dangers of pigeon-hol-
ing people, the intellectual dishonesty of large groupings, on the one hand,
and the way you like to pin labels on people, on the other, just as you've done
in the passage above, where you lump all people in and classes on gay studies
together. Here, for example, is what you say about labels:

> Labels, political and otherwise, have often seemed to me to create di-
> visions where there need be none, to magnify minor divisions into
> greater ones, and to bind people to extreme positions that they might

> in other circumstances find anathema. . . . A friend of mine once com-
> plained that my views on various issues didn't add up neatly into any
> ideologically orthodox position. . . . She wanted to be able to label me,
> to put me on a shelf. This is what most people want, because focusing
> on labels makes life easier. Label yourself and you'll always know what
> to think, even without thinking; label others and you'll always know
> who are your enemies and who are your friends.

Bravo! These are fine words. And yet your analysis over and over divides gay
people into two camps. "There is a broad cultural divide," you tell your reader.
"We might call them, at the risk of drastic oversimplification, 'subculture-oriented gays' and 'mainstream gays.'" This oversimplification could admittedly
be useful if you then went on to show that the groups are far more complicated
than that. But, to the contrary, even though you know the dangers of labels
and that your own labels are a "drastic oversimplification," you stick to them.
Is it because with these labels you can pretend to know who are your friends
and who are your enemies?

I must admit that I never really understood this distinction between "subculture-oriented" and "mainstream" gays. Whenever I thought I was getting
a clear notion, you'd say something that thoroughly confused me. Here, for example, is how you describe the "subculture-oriented gay" living "near one extreme" of the gay lifestyles: he is a person "born into a more or less ordinary
family in Wisconsin or Missouri or Georgia" who comes to live in a gay ghetto,
work at a "marginal [or] at least vaguely artistic" job, patronize gay businesses
and cultural events, belong to "at least one AIDS-related organization," and
whose "'life-style' would probably be considered aggressively nonconformist
by most Americans." What first struck me about this description is that it
doesn't seem to me extreme at all. I know a lot of people a lot more "deviant"
than this man. In fact your aggressive nonconformist in many ways appears to
be a model citizen. After all, here's a guy who works for a living, pays his taxes,
obeys the law, contributes to the local economy, remains politically informed
and civically conscious, helping out people less fortunate than himself. If most
people regard him as "aggressively nonconformist," where's the terrible sin?
Isn't this a land of liberty and freedom where people are supposed to be allowed
to live as they choose as long as they don't hurt anyone? What's the difference
between being a "nonconformist" and "individualistic"?

In your disdain for the "aggressively nonconformist," I am reminded of
John Stuart Mill, who wrote in *On Liberty:*

In this age, the mere example of nonconformity, the mere refusal to bend the knee to custom, is itself a service. Precisely because the tyranny of opinion is such as to make eccentricity a reproach, it is desirable, in order to break through that tyranny, that people should be eccentric; . . . the amount of eccentricity in a society has generally been proportional to the amount of genius, mental vigor, and the moral courage which it contained. That so few now dare to be eccentric, marks the chief danger of the time.

You might find that those nipple clamps and bike pants are not an enemy of democracy, but two of the foot soldiers in the war against "the tyranny of opinion."

Anyway, after reading the above description, I believed I did know what you meant by the "subculture-oriented gay," but then I came to your encomium to the characters in *Longtime Companion*. Unlike the hypothetical man described above, the couples in *Longtime Companion* were drawn from "everyday life of middle-class gay male couples . . . like me and my lover; they walked the same streets we did, shared the same body of cultural references, . . . held up a mirror to a version of 'gay life' that was familiar to me." In short they represented the "mainstream gay male." But how do the characters in *Longtime Companion* differ from the extreme "subculture-oriented gay"? In *Longtime Companion*, much of the action takes place on the Pines at Fire Island, which is as much of a gay ghetto as one is likely to find. Their friends seem to be exclusively gay, except for the one young woman, who is clearly (to use the vulgar expression) a "fag hag." When one pair goes out to celebrate, they patronize a gay restaurant. One is an actor on a daytime drama, another a writer for a daytime drama, a third a gym instructor—these seem to be the marginal or "vaguely artistic" jobs you criticize the poor extremist for holding. And, like the extremist, the characters in *Longtime Companion* don't seem to be from New York—two are clearly Southern. By the end of the movie, four work for "AIDS-related organizations." So why are the people in *Longtime Companion* "mainstream gays," whereas your early figure was "subculture-oriented"?

The only answer seems to be that "subculture-oriented gays" are poor whereas these men are not, as you claim, "middle-class," but fairly wealthy. David, for example, is described as "filthy rich" and his lover is a writer for a network show—clearly they have big bucks. Fuzzy is a theatrical lawyer, and seems to be doing quite well for himself, while our soap opera actor makes well over a hundred thousand dollars a year. And they are all so pretty. When I showed *Longtime Companion* in my AIDS literature class, the students—most of whom were straight women—disliked it. They said it had the blandness of "an afternoon special," although they were disturbed by seeing men kiss in bed together. These suburban teenagers wanted to know where the black people were. (The only black person is a practical nurse.) It didn't strike them as "real life" in the least.

I found my students' reaction especially interesting, because one of your greatest claims about "mainstream" gays is that they face reality. For example, one of the components that divide "subculture-oriented gays"—and as a usually graceful writer you should have recognized that there was something wrong in your analysis by the clumsiness of these classification titles—from "mainstream" gays is that subcultural gays like to live in ghettos, whereas

> most adult homosexuals simply don't want such a life. They were raised in conventional middle-class neighborhoods, and they want to spend their lives in similar homes and neighborhoods, and they don't see why being gay should prevent them from doing so. Nor do they like the idea of inhabiting an exclusively, or even mostly, gay world: such a world feels artificial to them, feels like an escape from reality. They want to live in the real world.

Like you, I grew up in Queens, and I know those Queens neighborhoods. They are almost always racially divided; they are usually ethnically and religiously divided. They tend to be economically homogeneous. Richmond Hill, for example, is the neighborhood of Archie Bunker. I grew up in Laurelton, an all Jewish, all middle-class ghetto. I'm not sure what is the real world, but I do know that Laurelton is no more "real" than Chelsea or the West Village. In fact, I can't think of anyone but you who would call the Lower East Side, where many gays and lesbians live, an escape. I now live in Baltimore, which has lively neighborhoods, almost all of them fairly divided along racial, ethnic, and economic lines. The area I live in around Hopkins University is a place where many gays and lesbians live, but it is also one of the most ethnically, racially and socially varied parts of the city. Do you really want us to believe that the suburbs are the real world, and the urban centers are an escape? Really, Bruce, that is too, too easy.

But I will agree with you that gays and lesbians should be able to live wherever they want, which is why those subcultural types—that supposed cadre of alien escapists—worked so hard to try to pass housing and employment antidiscrimination laws, and why in Baltimore, when a gay couple was being harassed by their neighbors because they didn't want gays living in their neighborhood, subcultural types rallied to the couple's support and made sure they got the police protection they needed. If there is an element of escapism, it is in the person who wants to shut himself off in the neighborhood he has always known, unwilling to explore what it would be like to live elsewhere among less familiar surroundings. If you want to live in Queens, all the more power to you. But don't defend your choice, by claiming that others want to escape reality.

Another oversimplified distinction you make is that "to be a subculture-oriented gay, then, is to center one's identity on one's homosexuality." Toward the end of the book you write: "homosexuality is not (or should not be) a fixed, defining identity; for each gay person it should be a part of a *distinctive individual identity*" (italics yours). Yet you also write: "As with Jewishness or blackness, a gay person's homosexuality is almost invariably a key component of his identity" and "for the average gay person, sexual orientation is at least as important an element of individual identity as race, ethnicity or gender." Later you write, "Sexual orientation is an essential element of a person's identity." And you write that "homosexuality is so essential and deeply rooted a part of . . . identity as to be unchangeable."

Now as I quoted above, you've written that labels can be used to exaggerate difference that are really only small semantic distinctions. I suppose there is a shift between the subculture-oriented gays who would center their identity on the sexuality, and your claim that it is an essential and key component. But, honestly, are these positions so far apart? Don't you both believe that sexuality touches all areas of a person's life? In fact, it seems to me that both you and queer theorists hold similar notions of identity and are hostile to identity politics for similar reasons. You both regard identities as rigid formulae that inhibit behavior and require highly regimented behavior. Identities, you claim, give people a false sense of themselves and stop the processes of development and growth.

Of course, identity can and does force people to conform to certain standards. But it does other things that both you and the postmodern theorists you dislike conveniently forget. If one regards identity not as a normative formula but as a name for relationships held together as Wittgenstein argues by "a family relationship," then much of what you resent and resist will be less threatening. Take, for example, your identity as a son. It has not remained something unitary, but has changed—I hope—as both you and your parents have changed. Moreover, it has altered in relation to other sorts of identities—as a lover, as a writer, as a Christian. Rather than something rigid and well defined, identities tend to be very vague, baggy, and interlocked with other identities. It seems to me that being gay is just as much an evolving identity as being a son, and it means something very different when you first identify yourself as gay than when you have lived as a gay man for many years. The mistake that so many people make is assume that everyone who shares an identity has to be identical. But one of the reasons people join groups is so they do not have to duplicate behaviors; groups allow people to focus on what they prefer to do, while leaving others to perform their own preferred tasks. Look at a family: the shared familial identity allows each member of the family to cultivate his or her own individuality. If they lived as strangers, there would be much more duplication.

Both you and your much-despised subcultural gays ignore the benefits of identities. First, identities allow people to feel less alone, and for young gay people this is a particularly important benefit. Few things can be as frightening and alienating as believing you're the only homosexual in the world. This need to belong is probably the reason that young people when first coming out seem to drift to the most easily identifiable, most stylized and stereotypical behaviors. But I have noticed that people, once they have achieved a sense of security, begin to see that under the rubric lies a wide area of behavior, and they begin to define themselves in less stereotypical terms.

More important, identities can provide a sense of purpose. Because identities arise in part out of relationships to others or to certain causes, they can give people a sense of acting for something larger than themselves. As a son, as a Bawer, you act with other people in mind, and it's not surprising that the postmodern attack on identity comes from a generation that arose in the "age of narcissism." The AIDS programs that developed rapidly across the country could not have existed had there not been a shared identity that gave some people a sense that they should act beyond their own immediate self-interest.

Your narrow sense that all people who share an identity must be nearly identical affects not only how you regard gay people but your sense of being an American. Thus you attack multiculturalism, because "instead of recognizing the many things that unite people with one another across lines of race, ethnicity, class, gender and sexual orientation . . . these scholars are preoccupied with the differences that divide group from group." I think you've got it all wrong. By emphasizing the diversity of class, gender, race, and sexual orientation, multiculturalism is celebrating the way all groups are tied together in society, united together, sometimes by tensions and conflicts, but also by the interlocking mesh of identities. But as scholars describe the push and pull between groups, the complex interactions among and within identities, you feel threatened rather than confirmed. You want all the rough edges filed away, the mirror made smooth so that it can reflect your own glowering stare. It is you who can't take any joy in the polyphony of voices within American culture or within gay people; it is you who want to impose a monody—that most primitive of musical forms. You don't like the raucous, sometimes vulgar, often cacophonous sounds of the Gay Pride March or the March on Washington.

And with this emotional and imaginative failure to appreciate the invigorating complexity of society, you also seem unable to recognize the inconsistencies in your own argument. For example when discussing the speeches at the March on Washington—admittedly not my favorite part of the event— you describe such "eloquent speakers" as Ian McKellan alternating with "vulgar comediennes," Eartha Kitt leading a "rousing" rendition of "God Bless America" followed by someone who argued that "America was irredeemably corrupt," "fire-breathing radicals" versus "a brave, intelligent speech by the first openly gay member of the Canadian parliament." As you described it, the March on Washington last year seemed a livelier event than I remembered it. But despite this variety, you draw the conclusion that the speeches "confirm[ed] every last stereotype about homosexuals." How could an event so diverse confirm stereotypes? What stereotype could you make out of RuPaul, Jesse Jackson, Martina Navratilova, Kate Clinton, and Ian McKellan? True, a bigot could find in this highly diverse crowd any stereotype it wanted to see, but the bigot can find what it wants to see wherever it looks, even if the only speakers had been you and Marvin Liebman. The open mind, I hope, would come away realizing that all gay people are not alike, that there is no single gay lifestyle, that some gay people are silly and vulgar while others are wise and polished. In short, they would get a better idea of the range of lesbian and gay experience than they would have gotten from one eloquent speech in the manner of Martin Luther King.

The problem is not merely intellectual—it's deeper, on the gut level. You don't seem to connect with people who are clearly different. Uptight, prim, stiff, you can't enjoy the great spectacle of human difference and variety even as you proclaim the utmost respect for individuality. And this limitation goes along with your seeming lack of humor. Frankly, Bruce, your book lacks any sign that you can laugh at yourself or the world. You exude an earnestness, which, although at first somewhat charming like the deadly seriousness of my best students, soon grows tedious with its air of self-importance. I agree that you're not a self-hating homosexual—that is far too facile a diagnosis. If anything you are far too pleased with yourself. Even at the end when you discuss the snobbery of others, you seem complaisantly delighted with your own modesty.

Because you are so pleased with yourself, you can't believe that others might hate you for being gay. You want to blame those others, those subcultural types—those really weird gay people—who are messing things up for people like you. The heart of your political position is wonderfully simple and utterly naive: "prejudice . . . can be most dramatically challenged by personal exposure to the object of prejudice." "Our aim," you write, "should be not to use 'power' to change laws but to use our humanity to change hearts and minds. If the heterosexual majority ever comes to accept homosexuality, it will do so because it has seen homosexuals in suits and ties, not nipple clamps and bike pants; it will do so because it has seen homosexuals showing respect for civilization, not attempting to subvert it." If only a three-piece suit would win us love, then, Bruce, we would all gladly don them! But as your own experience reported in your book over and over again shows, the hearts and minds of heterosexuals don't want to change even when they're shown the most respectable, civilized behavior.

Let us go back in history. My father was one of the first American soldiers at Bergen-Belsen. He rarely speaks of it, but he knows that German Jews were the most assimilated minority in Weimar Germany. They wore suits and ties. They showed respect for civilization and did not want to subvert it. They believed that this alone would protect them, and they were exterminated. As a Jew I was brought up never to forget, and as a gay man I am constantly reminded that assimilation is no guarantor of acceptance. The tactic you are advocating is exactly the tactic used by the Mattachine Society. In their demonstrations, lesbians and gays had to act like little ladies and gentleman. The effect: zero.

But if that is not enough, look at your own experience at the *American Spectator*, which published vitriolic attacks on homosexuality, knowing perfectly well that they were untrue. You even admit: "The truth is that conservative publications and foundations that oppose gay equal rights nonetheless publish and employ numerous individual homosexuals, many of whom they know perfectly well to be gay." Did you fail to wear the right clothes to work? Were you insufficiently civilized? Why hasn't your friendship changed their minds? And how could you, Bruce, be a part of this hate-mongering journal for six years?

You discuss the letter of a Robert B. Reilly in *Newsweek,* who believes that homosexual practices are being shoved in his face. Your conclusion is that people like Mr. Reilly don't "even want to be reminded that homosexuality exists." If people don't even want to hear that homosexuality exists, then how can you make them understand it, win their hearts and minds—unless you're willing to make them uncomfortable?

Yet the saddest story—the most revealing tale—comes at the end of your book. Two straight friends whom you and your lover had introduced, who asked you to be the best man at their wedding and Chris to be in the wedding party, these people who knew your lives and saw how deeply committed you were to one another, how civilized and respectful you were of mainstream values and Christian beliefs, and had even seen you in suits with matching ties— these very people wrote into their wedding vows that the "marriage between a man and a woman . . . was 'the only valid foundation for an enduring home.'" How did you explain this "traumatic" experience, which you rightly felt was "patronizing"? Your explanation is "that some straight people consider a close friendship with a gay person to be a part of their wild and colorful youth. . . . Then they reach a certain age and decide to settle down; they find responsible jobs, get married—and kick the gay friend in the teeth."

What does this incident do to your theory that "prejudice . . . can be most dramatically challenged by a personal exposure to the object of prejudice"? That all we have to do is make America understand us as suit-wearing, civilized human beings, and it will gladly extend to us the equal rights which are our proper share? You are "disheartened" because "many 'enlightened' opponents of gay rights . . . don't rethink their opposition" even "if an argument they have advanced fails to stand up to scrutiny." But do you rethink your position, when your own painful experience shows it to be, if not wrong, then inadequate? For I do believe that education and understanding and, yes, personal exposure are necessary steps in winning equal rights, even if they are not sufficient engines of change. Come on, Bruce, if people were so generous, so rational, so empathetic, would there be the kind of hate we now face?

Let's be clear about it: I'm not saying that all Americans are yahoos and bigots, but I'm also rejecting your fantasy that they are just bewitched, bothered, and bewildered. There are a great number of people out there who don't want to think about homosexuality. There is an even greater number who don't have the intellectual or emotional flexibility to understand that difference is not a threat. They believe that only one way can be right, and they have come to live the way they do, not because they have selected it from among different options, but because they have been told it is the only right way to conduct themselves. Gay rights threatens their fundamental belief systems. And there is a final group who can feel good about themselves only if they can feel superior to others. For these groups—and I don't know how many of them there are, but from votes in Cincinnati, Colorado, and Oregon we can assume they form a large number—just being nice won't do the trick. Organizing, exerting political pressure, raising money, using the media—all the tricks of political power you rather balk at as being rough and uncivilized—are necessary to win our fair share of equal rights. And it's not going to be clean, polite, or civil. There's no hostess from Mrs. Porter's serving at the table, but a lot of hungry, demanding lodgers who believe that we are another mouth to feed—which means less grub for them. I wish it wasn't so because, like you, I'd rather have pleasant dinner conversation than the pandemonium that usually happens when the family of man sits down together; but there it is.

Nor does it have to be as particularly grim as I've painted it. In fact, the kind of carnivalesque atmosphere of many gay events—a raucousness you so sniffily turn away from—is exactly the antidote to the serious work that needs to be performed. I know you didn't find much sense for the March on Washington to be both "serious and festive": "At a party there was room for frivolousness and self-indulgence; a serious protest required restraint and self-discipline." But many occasions are both serious and festive—weddings, Christmas, political conventions. The March on Washington was an event more important for showing numbers and re-energizing activists than for changing the minds of the Joint Chiefs or Jane Doe. Do you really think those "enlightened" conservatives would have changed their minds if the march had been grimly sober?

What I want to say, Bruce, is that there is a place at my table for you—with starched linen napkins, and my grandfather's silverware, and pleasant dinner conversation, all the things you like. The guests may be a little wild, and the cuisine a little rich and spicy, but it's good home cooking. Yet I don't think you will set a place for me at your home, because you keep telling me that I'm not your sort. I'm a bit too different; I might speak too loudly and embarrass you, and I do have the habit of spilling the wine, as well as my beads. Nevertheless, you're welcomed at our place anytime you want—you and Chris—just pull up a chair and dig in. We don't stand on ceremony.

BRUCE BAWER

What *A Place at the Table* Really Says

DEAR DAVID,

The editors of *The Harvard Gay* and *Lesbian Review* have kindly sent me a copy of your open letter about *A Place at the Table*. Since you call me Bruce and sign the letter "Best wishes, David," I'm addressing you as David.

David, you begin by saying that the reviews you've seen of *A Place at the Table* have been positive but haven't been fair because they've failed to acknowledge several of the book's strengths. The implication is that your remarks will be fair. Indeed, your first two paragraphs consist of praise. Once that's out of the way, however, you dig in your heels and spend the next several pages on what is by far the most systematically dishonest and unfair account of the book that I've seen, excepting perhaps the six-page attack by a reactionary Catholic priest in *National Review*.

You say that "I will spend a lot of time quoting you, because I don't want to put words in your mouth in the way that you put words in other people's mouths." I don't know whose mouths you think I've put words into; when I comment in the book on other people's views, I'm careful to quote them, to comment directly on those quotations, and not to take their words out of context. My intent is not to set up straw men to knock down, but to examine honestly the things that people are really saying about homosexuality. By contrast, despite your ample quotation from the book, your open letter gives a highly distorted picture of who I am and what I've written.

Your criticism of the book begins with the opening anecdote about my observation of a teenage boy in a bookstore whom I recognized as gay and who worked up the courage to pick up a copy of *New York Native*, which contained ads for escort services, S and M equipment, and so forth, all accompanied by graphic photographs. By way of disputing my impression that such pictures weren't what that young man was looking for, you say that he may well have wanted to wear leather or taffeta. I hope so, because in that

From the Summer 1994 issue

case those pictures were more up his alley than I suspected they were. But I doubt it. The fact is that most gay men don't have such longings, and chances are that this particular boy didn't either. Such young people, and such needs, do exist. To say so is not to condemn anybody's interest in leather or taffeta.

You note in an accusatory tone that I did "nothing to help that young man." David, that's my point: I felt powerless. My position in that bookstore was emblematic of the way many gay adults feel in relation to gay youth. What could I do to help that kid and kids like him? Eventually I wrote a book. You say "it's not clear from anything else in the book" that I've done anything for young gay people besides write the book. You're right, it's not clear. My book is not about congratulating myself on my personal accomplishments. It is, in part, about examining my own past failings and trying to learn from them—thereby providing people like you, of course, with ammunition to use against me.

You say that "teenage and college-age people don't have to read the *Native* to be 'sex-obsessed.'" I agree. But you're wrong to deny that some of the images of gay life in the pages of publications like the *Native* can confuse the hell out of a kid coming to terms with his homosexuality. You also suggest that I haven't known many young gay people and don't know how complicated their lives are. Well, I do know a lot of them, and I've met a lot more as a result of my book, either at talks I've given or through correspondence. Most of them seem to feel that I understand their lives quite well. Since you make such a point of putting people into categories, I'll add that these young people have been black and white, male and female, from a range of economic, social, and religious backgrounds. Their politics are all over the map. And they identify with that boy in the bookstore. Since you think I'm "very wrongheaded," you probably think by extension that these kids are wrongheaded, too, along with the hundreds of adult readers who have told me, in letters and in person, that I've spoken the truth about their lives, who saw their younger selves in that boy in the bookstore, who have said that I'm right about their reaction as teenagers to publications like the *Native*, and who have said they wished they'd had a book like *A Place at the Table* at that age, because it would have helped them come to terms with their sexuality.

I might also mention the several readers who have said that my book opened their eyes to new possibilities in life and made them realize that they didn't have to live in the subculture cages they'd constructed for themselves.

I don't understand your strident unwillingness to recognize this as a real issue, and to see the difference between lifestyle choices freely made (which I don't object to at all) and lifestyles that people get into simply because they think they have to.

You accuse me of mocking any attempt to teach young people about homosexuality. That's absurd. My book is such an attempt.

Another important point: you base much of your open letter on the unwarranted assumption that in describing two hypothetical individuals at different ends of the gay spectrum—the closeted suburban Republican and the urban-ghetto left-winger—I approve wholeheartedly of the former and see the latter as my "enemy," as someone that I "despise" and whom I consider to be guilty of some "terrible sin." Absolutely not! Like most gays, I'm more or less mainstream-oriented, but I'm not closeted or suburban or Republican; I think coming out is extremely important; nor do I claim to be immune to subculture tastes or influences. When it all evens out, I'd say I'm somewhere in the middle of the gay spectrum. Your mistake is assuming that I'm criticizing where I'm merely describing. This assumption on your part explains your inability to view my strong identification with the characters in *Longtime Companion,* who are hardly closeted suburban Republicans, as anything but a self-contradiction. Likewise, when I say that the person toward the subculture end of the gay spectrum "would probably be considered aggressively nonconformist by most Americans," you assume—wrongly—that I'd agree on this point with most Americans, which gives you the opportunity to see my supposed "disdain for the 'aggressively nonconformist'" as contradicting my enthusiasm for individuality and to counter that supposed disdain by quoting a stirring passage about nonconformism from John Stuart Mill.

I say that those hypothetical closeted Republican gays "want to live in the real world." Your comment: "Do you really want us to believe that the suburbs are the real world, and the urban centers are an escape?" No, I mean that the real world is mostly straight; in any case, my remark about living in "the real world" is part of an attempt to characterize the way such gays view themselves and their lives. Speaking for myself, (a) I live in Manhattan (not Queens, as you seem to think); (b) I've never lived in a suburb (the part of Queens where I grew up was urban, not suburban like the part you grew up in); and (c) I don't want to live in a suburb. My point in the book about suburbs is that (a) a lot of gay people do live in suburbs, (b) it's good for straight people to know this, and (c) we should be striving to create a country where living in the suburbs, or in small towns, for that matter, is as realistic and safe an option for gays as it is for straights.

You speak of my "narrow sense that all people who share an identity must be nearly identical." No; I say in the book that it's vitally important for gay people to accept their gay identity, but that it's also important not to cling so tightly to any group identity that one loses a sense of individuality. A *propos* of my criticism of multiculturalism, you say that I "want all the rough edges filed away, the mirror made smooth so that it can reflect [my] own glowering stare." On the contrary, I think that multiculturalism's easy division of identity into compartments of race, sex, class, and sexual orientation is altogether too smooth and simple; real life has rougher edges than that.

You make a series of ad hominem accusations that have no basis in what I've actually written and that focus on my supposed narrowness of mind and spirit. You say, for example, that I "can't take any joy in the polyphony of voices within American culture or within gay people." I don't know where you get this from. If I didn't take joy in the rich variety of American culture, I don't think I'd have spent the last ten years writing about fiction and poetry by a wide range of authors who fall into the categories of race, sex, and so forth that appear to be what you're talking about when you speak of "polyphony."

In the same vein, David, you say I "don't seem to connect with people who are clearly different." I don't make such a big deal of those differences of race, sex, etc., that seem to you so important; if I connect with a lot of people who don't fall into the same categories I do, it's not because I'm making a conscious effort to connect with people who are "different" from me but because those supposed differences don't seem anywhere near as important to me as the things that I share with them. In any case, A *Place at the Table* is an attempt to build bridges between people who are different, between gays and the heterosexuals who don't really understand homosexuality and who consequently fear and hate us, and between different kinds of gay people who often have contempt for one another.

Likewise, you say that I'm "uptight, prim, stiff," incapable of enjoying "the great spectacle of human difference and variety," and that I lack humor. "Frankly, Bruce, your book lacks any sign that you can laugh at yourself or the world." Well, gee, frankly, David, there are a lot of things I laugh at; the persistence of homophobia isn't one of them, and it was my deep frustration at that enduring homophobia—and my belief that I had a few things to say about how we might overcome it—that impelled me to turn my life upside down and write the book. I don't remember Elie Wiesel's books about the Holocaust being particularly humorous, either.

You accuse me of being "far too pleased with" myself. I don't know what you're talking about. My book contains a handful of personal anecdotes, in none of which I figure as a hero; on the contrary, I routinely use myself as an example of human failings that I wish to criticize. By contrast, your open letter consists largely of tributes to your own open-mindedness, integrity, dedication to gay youth, etc., which form a neat contrast to what you represent as my intolerance, selfishness, dour disposition, and so forth. I wish I were half as comfortable as you are with blowing my own horn.

Even after months of being misrepresented in the gay press, I was open-mouthed in astonishment at some of your charges. "You can't believe," you write, "that others might hate you for being gay." What on earth can you mean by that? The whole book is a response to that hatred. I've gone on dozens of talk-radio shows around the country and had conversations with callers who are brimming with that hatred. All I can make of your remark is that you take offense at my attention to the ignorance and fear that underlie that hatred. I gather that you consider antigay hatred essentially ineradicable, and that you think the best we can do is to protect ourselves from it by such essentially political acts as lobbying legislators and pressing for pro-gay court decisions; I, for my part, think we can do an enormous amount to foster acceptance by talking honestly to straight people about who we are. On the radio, in small groups, and one-on-one, I've spoken to countless parents about what it means to be a gay kid. Even to supposedly sophisticated urban professionals, the truth about gay kids' loneliness and pain and alienation comes as an utter shock. It makes those parents think, and it changes their attitudes profoundly. To you, such efforts presumably sound naïve, assimilationist, apologetic, quixotic; perhaps you feel that in doing such things I'm committing treason against the Queer Nation. Perhaps it also makes you feel uncomfortable to think of putting oneself in such a vulnerable position.

You mock my expectations of change by pointing out that my editors at *The American Spectator* didn't learn to accept me. You're right, they didn't. It doesn't work with everybody, and certainly not with cynical, careerist folks at right-wing institutions where homophobia is part of the job description. You also try to use my wedding anecdote to challenge the possibility of acceptance. But the point of that anecdote is that a disposition toward unequal treatment is very deep-seated, and that, in the context of a wedding—the ultimate public heterosexual ritual—such a disposition can surface even in people who seem thoroughly accepting and who don't even realize they're treating gay friends hurtfully and inequitably. The anecdote demonstrates that we're not dealing so much with conscious malice, which would seem to be your view, as with unconscious attachment to certain conventional ways of thinking about human relations, and that in order to make life easier for the gay people who come after us we need to bring those conventional ways of thinking to the surface and talk about them.

You accuse me of blaming antigay prejudice on subculture-oriented gays who are "messing things up for people like me." No, I blame antigay prejudice largely on a widespread ignorance about and fear of homosexuality. My experiences have confirmed my sense that such attitudes can be changed enormously through frank personal contact. Why haven't gay people done more of this? Because it's not easy. Because some of us are closeted, and some of us marginalize ourselves, avoiding contact with the people whose opinions of us most need to be changed. My book is an attempt at once to do some of that educational work among straight readers and to explain to gay readers why neither the closet nor marginalization is in our best interests and certainly not in the best interests of the generations of gay people to come. To characterize my book as you do—as something I wrote because I was angry at certain types of gay people who were messing things up for me—is unconscionable. If I were worried only about my own well-being, I wouldn't have written A *Place at the Table* in the first place, for I knew very well that in writing it I'd be putting myself at the center of a firestorm. By writing the book and going around the country talking about it, I've exposed myself to more harsh invective in the last six months, both from homophobes and from gays who think I'm their enemy, than I would otherwise have had to endure if I'd lived to be a thousand. My life is changed forever, my privacy shattered. I brought all this on myself knowingly, and I did it not because I enjoy being hated, mocked, and misrepresented, but because I wanted to do something for other gay people—all of them, not just ones who are "like me" (whatever that means).

I certainly didn't do it for myself. Of all the gays in the world, I'm one of those who are in least urgent need of social change. I'm one of the very lucky ones: I live with someone I love; my family accepts me; I live in a part of the world where I've always had landlords who didn't care that I'm gay; I write for publications and belong to a church where I feel welcome as a gay man. It will make relatively little difference to my life if a husband and wife in Idaho, say, read my book and stop hating gay people. It can make a great difference, however, for their kid, if that kid happens to be gay; for a gay man who might happen to work for one of them; or for a lesbian couple who might happen to live next door. That's another big reason why I wrote this book. Gay readers in such circumstances have realized this and been grateful. I don't know which is harder to believe: that you, David, an educator supposedly devoted to the best interests of young gay people, could genuinely fail to recognize this motive on my part, or that you would consciously misrepresent my intentions.

But then you're hardly the first to do so. It's ironic: while reviewers for the mainstream press—e.g., *The New York Times, The Wall Street Journal, The Los Angeles Times, The Detroit Free Press*—have almost universally praised *A Place at the Table* for its fairness and conscientiousness and for helping them to understand homosexuality, many writers in the gay press have responded to the book as you have, by mocking its "earnestness" and by drawing a grotesque, dishonest, and baseless caricature of me as some kind of stuffy, sex-negative Tory who wants all gays to live in suburbs, dress in suits, and sip wine out of a certain type of glassware, and who doesn't like people who aren't "like him." None of that nonsense has anything to do with what my book is about, but it's easier for a lot of gay-press critics and Gay Studies professors to weave such fantasies than to deal with the fact that the book has hit home with lots of gay readers across the political spectrum. It seems to me, David, that the responsible way for someone in your position to respond to the success of *A Place at the Table* is to acknowledge that things are changing very rapidly, that gays are coming out of the closet in record numbers, that this is shifting the political, cultural, and social center of the visible gay population closer to the center of the straight population, and that this is a very good thing for both gay and straight America, even if it's not really a very good thing for the careers of P.C. professors who want to be seen as speaking for gay America.

The other night I gave a poetry reading in Westchester County. Afterwards a woman came up and told me that her lesbian daughter had given her a copy of *A Place at the Table* and that the book had turned around their relationship and made the family closer. I've heard this sort of testimony dozens of times since the book came out. To me it reflects less on the merits of the book, which I don't think is any great masterpiece, than on the remarkable fact that no one else had written such a book sooner. Instead of being so condescending and contemptuous toward me, David, you might more usefully address the curious fact that there are hundreds, if not thousands, of Gay Studies professors in this country, and yet virtually all the books that are really helping to advance understanding and acceptance of homosexuality and gay rights in America are being written by non-academics like Eric Marcus, Robb Forman Dew, and the late Randy Shilts. Let's face it: Gay Studies is a huge growth industry, but so far it's done far more to advance the careers of a few hundred fast-track academics than it's done to educate the people who most need to be educated about homosexuality and gay rights. It's outrageous to me that instead of putting your own house in order and doing something constructive, you've put so much effort into writing a mendacious, malicious piece about a book that has actually helped to promote acceptance and understanding of homosexuality in America.

Like you, David, several reviewers in the gay press have responded to the metaphor of my title by suggesting derisively that people who are "different" from me (the reviewer usually offers himself as an example) wouldn't be welcome at my table; two or three critics, including you, have added a little sardonic flourish to the effect that I, of course, would be welcome at their tables. You write: "There's a place at my table for you—with starched linen napkins, and my grandfather's silverware, and pleasant dinner conversation, all the things you like. . . . Yet I don't think you will set a place for me at your home, because you keep telling me that I'm not your sort. I'm a bit too different; I might speak too loudly and embarrass you, and I do have the habit of spilling the wine, as well as my beads." Linen napkins? Silverware? Little did I—a graduate of SUNY at Stony Brook who is writing this letter while eating a pastrami sandwich off a plate bought at Woolworth's—ever think I'd be characterized as some kind of upper-crust oenophilic snob in the pages of a publication out of Harvard University. [*The Harvard Gay & Lesbian Review* is not a publication of Harvard University.—Ed.]

Of course the truth about all this, David, is really quite the opposite of what you would have people believe. As I state very clearly in my book, I want all gay people to have a place at the table; you, like a lot of other Gay Studies folks, feel threatened by moderate gay voices, because you've begun to realize that our views are closer to those of the majority of gay Americans than yours are, and you're willing to misrepresent us in order to deprive us, to the extent that you can, of a place at the table of gay American social and political discourse.

Despite all this, however, David—despite your gratuitous insults and your mischievous misrepresentations—you are welcome at our table. Why? Because I really do think that personal contact can make a difference; I think that almost all people have good sides and that the way to effect positive change is to put aside their insults and misrepresentations and to speak truthfully and patiently to those good sides. Be warned, however, that unlike you, Chris and I don't have linen napkins or inherited silverware; I'm afraid you'll have to put up with paper napkins, ordinary flatware, and a rather rickety table from Conran's. In spite of these shortcomings, however, I think we can promise an interesting conversation—not a "fine" one, perhaps, but one that's substantive and meaningful. One thing that Chris and I both believe is that honest, face-to-face conversation between erstwhile antagonists can help close the distance caused by resentment, misunderstanding, and mercenary distortions, and can recall the participants to the highest motives of their best selves.

DAVID BERGMAN

No Back-Pedaling, Please

DEAR BRUCE,

I hoped that my letter would open up a dialogue that would be a useful attempt to bridge the differences between our positions, and I am pleased that you have replied. But let me say out front although I said you were wrongheaded and humorless, I never doubted your sincerity, honesty, and goodwill— just the things you accuse me of. If I had wanted to be "mendacious" the essay would have been quite different in tone. I didn't spend the time carefully examining your book because I thought it was unimportant and negligible. I know that you have had an enormous impact on young people, and if it has been to the good I am delighted. Indeed, I thought it was important enough that it deserved close scrutiny. Perhaps I misunderstood you, but perhaps you said things in your book that you're not happy to see examined so carefully, for my method was to compare different parts of your book, to show their contradictions. Your letter indicates that you are backing away from some of your more extreme positions.

What is striking about your letter is how much at variance it is with your book. You say that it is I who "make such a point of putting people into categories," when in fact I only used the categories you developed. One of my criticisms of your book is that your labels don't make much sense, and that you tar people with a very wide brush. I notice that your reply involves the same sort of broad attack. Gay studies, you say, has "done far more to advance the careers of a few hundred fast-track academics that it's done to educate the people." A few hundred! Here I am teaching at lowly Towson State University, which can't even supply a ribbon for my typewriter. I must be on the wrong side of that fast-track. What you fail to understand even yet is that your categories don't make much sense either as descriptors or proscriptors. One of your central categories is what you call the "subculture-oriented" gay. You wrote in your letter, "Your mistake is assuming that I'm

From the Fall 1994 issue

criticizing where I'm merely describing." But you're far more than descriptive. Here, for example, is how you characterize the 1992 Gay Pride Day March: "If at its best the event hints at the diversity of the gay population in America, altogether too much of it is silly, sleazy, and sex-centered, a reflection of the narrow, contorted definition of homosexuality that marks some sectors of the gay subculture." You're not criticizing that type? "Silly," "sleazy," "narrow," "contorted," these aren't pejorative terms? Come on, Bruce, let's be honest, you don't like these people. And you're angry that their behavior is used by the extreme right to stir up homophobia. You call them a "public relations nightmare"; if that's not at least putting some of the blame on them, I don't know what is. Please, don't rewrite your book in your letter.

Indeed, from your reply, I wonder how recently you've read your own book. For example, you describe the point of your episode about being insulted by a bride and groom as showing "that a disposition toward unequal treatment is very deep-seated, and that, in the context of the wedding—the ultimate public heterosexual ritual—such a disposition can surface even in people who seem thoroughly accepting and who don't even realize they're treating gay friends hurtfully and inequitably. The anecdote demonstrates that we're not dealing so much with conscious malice, which would seem your view, as with unconscious attachment to certain conventional ways of thinking about human relation." How reasonable and equitable that sounds. When I read your letter I wondered how I could have misunderstood you so badly. So I went back to look at the episode as it appears in A *Place at the Table*. Here's what you wrote there:

> This episode reminded me of something Chris had said to me once—namely, that some straight people consider a close friendship with a gay person to be a part of their wild and colorful youth, along with taking drugs and sleeping around and being financially irresponsible. Then they reach a certain age and decide to settle down; they find responsible jobs, get married—and kick the gay friend in the teeth. Suddenly, to the friend's surprise, he's out in the cold, like Falstaff when he's rejected by his old chum Prince Hal at the end of *Henry the Fourth, Part Two*. I'd never experienced such a renunciation before—and I hope never to experience it again.

I hope you can see why I might have thought this was a story about conscious maliciousness. In your book you don't sound as calmly philosophical as your letter indicates. In the book there's no hint that the insult was merely a gaffe that occurred in the excitement of a wedding, like sitting Aunt Bess next to the Cousin Vinnie, whom she cannot abide. Rather, in the book you make the insult sound very premeditated—one more part of shedding the unseemly past. It's hard to kick a friend in the teeth unconsciously. (That was your head down there? I thought it was an old joint. Sorry for kicking you.) Indeed, your allusion to Prince Hal is especially misleading since Hal does consciously forsake Falstaff. You don't say the couple "ignored you" or "was blind to you," or even "denied you," phrases that might have indicated that their actions were unconscious. The term you used was "renunciation," and renunciation is not an unconscious activity. I'm sorry that I misunderstood your intent, but I hope you can see how one could honestly draw what you now claim to be the wrong conclusion from the book. In fact, I think it would be hard to draw the conclusion you say you intended given the words you use.

On your part, you simply ignore things that I made perfectly clear. You write to me "you think the best we can do is to protect ourselves from [anti-gay hatred] by such essentially political acts as lobbying legislators and pressing for pro-gay court decisions." What I wrote was "I do believe that education and understanding, and yes, personal exposure are necessary steps in winning equal rights, even if they are not sufficient engines of change." My point is that we need to use all the methods available to us to win justice including "organizing, exerting political pressure, raising money [and] using the media." My experience as a Jew is "assimilation is no guarantor of acceptance." But to be honest, you're correct in assuming that I cannot foresee a time when antihomosexual prejudice will be completely eradicated. Eternal vigilance will be the price we'll have to pay for liberty. Still, I'd like to be proven wrong.

But there is a great deal we do agree on. I think you're right—at least I hope you're right, that "things are changing very rapidly, that gays are coming out of the closet in record numbers." If A *Place at the Table* helps in the effort, I will be happy. But that process was happening long before you penned your book. Anyway, I don't fear this change—I've been working for it for a long time. I welcome the greater acceptance of gays, lesbians, and bisexuals, I also agree that much more needs to be done to help gay, lesbian, bisexual, and transgendered youth. If your book has helped young people, I'm delighted. But it would be nice if you acknowledged that others have been working hard even before you saw that boy in the bookstore. I don't want the acceptance of people who are close to the center to be won at the expense of people who are not. That is my worry. I don't want the door opened wide enough so that only people who can pass as mainstream can get in. I want it opened all the way. And you say you do, too. So give a call now that we've gotten to know each other so publicly and we'll talk. I like pastrami, too.

MICHAEL SCHWARTZ

A Civil Libertarian States His Case

A Review of *Virtually Normal: An Argument about Homosexuality*

by Andrew Sullivan

(Alfred A. Knopf, 1995)

THE SUBTITLE OF Andrew Sullivan's *Virtually Normal* tells us that the book is "An Argument about Homosexuality." By "argument," Sullivan, who is the editor of *The New Republic*, announces his intention to offer a rational presentation of the weaknesses of his opponents' positions and the strength of his own, with the goal of persuasion through superior reasoning. The subject of the argument is what Sullivan calls "the homosexual question": "how a society should deal with the presence of homosexuals in its midst."

Sullivan's prologue asks "What Is a Homosexual?" and seeks an answer in his own early life, which he cites as proof that homosexuality is not a choice. He then takes a long look at the four basic approaches to homosexuality, and explains why they're all wrong. The first is "The Prohibitionists," represented by the Catholic Church, which wants to banish homosexuality from society. The second group, "The Liberationists," takes its political theory from Foucault. The third and fourth groups are "The Conservatives" and "The Liberals." After showing the logical contradictions within each philosophy, Sullivan proposes his own "Politics of Homosexuality": the only goal of the gay movement should be to end all "proactive discrimination" by the government against homosexuals, especially its bans on gays in the military and on gay marriage. Finally, in an epilogue, Sullivan asks, "What Are Homosexuals For?" and points out the contributions that homosexuals make to society.

So, does the argument work? I had my initial problems with the core of the book, Sullivan's analysis of the four philosophies. His method of debating his opponents is to assume that he's triumphed when he has turned up a logical inconsistency in their position. This may work in a debating society, but in the

From the Fall 1995 issue

304

Andrew Sullivan

real world people are able to hold inconsistencies and still function quite adequately. A related problem is that some of the inconsistencies arise only because of the way in which Sullivan presents them: he builds in the inconsistencies that he later "reveals" with great fanfare.

For the prohibitionist or Catholic position, Sullivan describes a philosophy that's based on faith and doctrine, but that is amenable to the rational counter-argument he offers. Specifically, he asserts that Paul's and Aquinas's condemnation of homosexuality falls apart if homosexuality is not a choice. He hopes this logical inconsistency will lead the Church to reconsider its stand on homosexuality, although the evidence he offers suggests only a hardening of the condemnation. The "rational Catholic" Sullivan presents may show up at Dignity meetings, but he is probably not representative of those with the power to prohibit homosexuality.

Sullivan's description of the liberationist position is particularly misleading. He cites Foucault's theory of social constructionism as the basis of liberationism, but his summary of Foucault is simplistic to the point of misrepresentation. On the other hand, anyone who counters Foucault by invoking "the core of the homosexual—the human—experience" probably wasn't very sympathetic to social constructionism in the first place. It gets worse when Sullivan describes liberationist politics. He uses outing as an example, even though he admits "there is no direct link between this tactic and the philosophical structure" offered by Foucault. He then fabricates a liberationist position on gays in the military, spinning out an image of what "queer" soldiers would be like. It's a delirious nightmare of what the Left is up to, and bears little resemblance to reality.

Sullivan's depiction of conservatives also centers on a fantasy figure: conservatives who "combine a private tolerance of homosexuals with a public disapproval of homosexuality." Maybe there are a few such figures, but Sullivan doesn't include any actual examples, and they aren't a significant force on the political scene anyway. It seems misguided to base an analysis of conservatism on them. But this combination does let Sullivan express the hope that conservatism will move "toward an alliance with conservative trends among homosexuals and a cooptation of responsible gay citizenship."

In analyzing liberalism, Sullivan focuses on its support for anti-discrimination laws. This, he claims, leads to a logical inconsistency because it requires liberals to impinge on the liberty of private contracts between individuals in the areas of employment and housing. But liberalism can also hold that employment is not a private contract: a corporation or business is not an individual and therefore does not have the rights of an individual. An individual can discriminate; an employer or landlord cannot. There is no contradiction here. But Sullivan goes off in another direction as well, faulting liberalism because it doesn't cure "the pain of the closet, the trauma of being forced to renounce or disown the object of one's love and attraction." This seems like blaming aspirin because it doesn't heal a broken heart. It wasn't supposed to.

As I look at Sullivan's analysis, I get the feeling that, although he finds something wrong with all four positions, he doesn't find them equally wrong. His subtext, it seems to me, is to open up space for gays within Catholicism and conservatism by showing how these philosophies could accommodate a certain brand of respectable, coupled homosexuality. At the same time, he wants to show how liberalism, traditionally the basis for lesbian and gay politics, is in fact a dead end. He wants to limit severely the goals of gay activism so they can be consistent with an enlightened conservatism. Accordingly, as an alternative to the four discredited philosophies, Sullivan proposes his own political goal: an end to government discrimination, specifically the ban on gays in the military and gay marriage—and no more (that is, no laws against "private" discrimination).

It's probably clear that my own sympathies are with Sullivan's liberals, although I prefer the term "progressive." Does this bias disqualify me as a reviewer? I don't think so. I'm a test case, to see whether Sullivan's argument is persuasive. And it isn't. His analysis of the "contradictions" of liberalism didn't convince me of the error of my ways. Nor do I think I'm the only one who will remain unpersuaded. Sullivan may suggest a re-interpretation of Paul's condemnation of homosexuality, but I somehow don't see the Pope reading it, slapping his forehead, and exclaiming, "Of course! How could I have missed this?" This kind of argument doesn't persuade the opposition. Its purpose is to find readers whose feelings already tend in this direction, and to articulate those feelings as a political position. Who are these readers? I suspect the book will find its audience among readers who believe that the government shouldn't do much of anything, except maybe lower their taxes. These people are basically happy with their lives—they know they won't be fired from their jobs or thrown out of their homes. In fact, the only thing they may be lacking is a lover.

Sullivan addresses this issue, too. The biggest problem facing homosexuals, it seems, isn't discrimination; it's the failure to find love. In his autobiographical prologue, Sullivan describes his first crush, which brought him "the first strains of the homosexual hurt that is the accompaniment of most homosexual life." Given society's opposition, he finds it "no wonder . . . that male homosexual culture has developed an ethic more of anonymous or promiscuous sex than of committed relationships." Invoking Orwell's Room 101, Sullivan decries the prejudice of society that can get a man "to betray the integrity of his love," and asserts that this is the fate of homosexuals, who are thus kept from "the possibility of the highest form of human happiness." This theme runs throughout the book and proves central to Sullivan's politics, culminating in his demand for gay marriage, "the only reform that truly matters." In Sullivan's view, legalizing gay marriage is good for homosexuals and for society. It gives young homosexuals a role model and an "eventual chance at some kind of constructive happiness." It also, like heterosexual marriage, contributes to the stability of society.

So what is there to argue with here? First, I think the book oversells both the "homosexual hurt" and the glories of love. Yes, there are obstacles, but many of us have managed committed relationships even without the benefit of marriage. The propensity of lesbians to mate is legendary, and suggests that male promiscuity may have causes other than societal oppression. And, yes, love is nice, but the prose poems in its honor seem extravagant. This rhapsodizing, however, plays its rhetorical role in Sullivan's argument. By praising love so extravagantly, he makes all other considerations seem trivial, and even unworthy of our attention when compared to "the basic bonds of human affection and commitment that make life worth living." Well, love may be a many-splendored thing, but so are housing and a job that you can't be thrown out of just for being gay. Sullivan's emphasis on the private and de-emphasis of the public define his politics: love, yes; government "interference," no.

Moreover, Sullivan's praise of love and marriage leaves some questions unasked. For example, he takes marriage as an unexamined, unproblematic good, a heterosexual model that homosexuals should uncritically emulate. It's as if feminism had never happened. Granted, the dynamics of a same-sex marriage will be different from a heterosexual marriage, but the similarities and differences must be examined and evaluated. In fact, the basic meaning of marriage needs to be examined. My own interest in gay marriage has nothing to do with a deeper commitment or more role models; it has to do with legal protection and economic benefits, topics that Sullivan barely mentions.

I have no interest in gay marriage as a means for making society more stable, or for fitting homosexuals into society as it currently exists. This is my basic problem with the book. Sullivan assumes not only that marriage is good, but that society is good, and that homosexuals want to be assimilated into society. This homosexual, however, doesn't—not until society has undergone a lot of structural changes. There are people who are demanding these changes, but they don't show up in this book. In setting up his four-point political compass, Sullivan creates the illusion of covering all possible political positions. But, of course, he hasn't. What if he had added chapters on "The Feminists," say, or "The Socialists"? These philosophies support gay rights, but not (as Sullivan would have it) for the purpose of fitting gays and lesbians into society. Instead, getting gay rights will be one part of the total restructuring of society. For example, gay marriage isn't the goal; instead, it's rethinking all relationships in a more equitable and inclusive way. Why not think big? And if it means adhering to norms that are themselves problematic, why settle for being "normal," virtually or otherwise?

MICHAEL SCHWARTZ

The Persistence of Liberalism

A Review of *Virtual Equality*

by Urvashi Vaid

(Anchor Books, 1995)

THE COMPARISON is inevitable. In a coincidence that bookstore clerks must be cursing, *Virtual Equality* by Urvashi Vaid has appeared shortly after Andrew Sullivan's *Virtually Normal*. The books themselves define sharply contrasting positions on the gay political spectrum: they even disagree about what we should consider "gay politics." Sullivan, representing a recently emerging conservative gay voice, argues for a strict narrowing of the gay political focus: overturn the bans on military service and same-sex marriage, and no more. Vaid, a veteran progressive, also sees a problem with the movement's current focus, but she wants to broaden it to encompass issues not traditionally identified as gay ones, such as racism and sexism.

But the contrast goes beyond the substance of their positions to what might be called their packaging. Sullivan's book is sleek, short, compact. It's more like a long essay stretched to book length by a small page size and vast margins. Vaid's, on the other hand, is undeniably a book: over four hundred large pages where the text squeezes the margins to the vanishing point. And packaging isn't irrelevant. Unfortunately, conservatives tend to be better at packaging than progressives. When the right wants to get an idea across, it reduces it to a sound byte or slogan; the left produces a position paper. Sullivan's packaging is efficient: a reader can breeze through his book—the pages practically turn themselves—and come away assured that there are philosophical arguments to back up his conservative beliefs. Reading Vaid's book, I was reminded of the many times I have been standing at a rally for some progressive cause, listening as too many speakers (chosen to represent a diversity that was seldom reflected in the make-up of the audience) give long, earnest, but artless speeches, usually through a faulty sound system. Anyone who's not already

From the Winter 1996 issue

Urvashi Vaid

a true believer will walk away long before it's over. Fewer speeches, or a shorter book, could have conveyed the same ideas more effectively.

As for the content of the book, Vaid says in the preface that it is in part "a document of self-criticism," in that it looks at the history, achievement, and ultimate failure of the gay and lesbian liberation movement, specifically the National Gay and Lesbian Task Force (NGLTF), where she served as executive director. Vaid begins with the assertion that our recent political gains in fact constitute a "virtual equality"—"a state of conditional equality based more on the appearance of acceptance by straight America than on genuine civic parity." She attributes this compromised achievement to the fact that the lesbian and gay movement is "rights-based" rather than "freedom-based." She then traces this contrast through this century's history, showing how the movement's conservative wish for legitimation alternated with the more radical goal of liberation. After examining the effect of AIDS on the movement, she describes what she sees as the "prevailing strategy" of the movement today, and then demonstrates the failure of that strategy by giving a minutely detailed account of the attempt to lift the ban on gays in military: this debacle, she insists, demonstrates in microcosm the limitations of the prevailing strategy, with its emphasis on political mainstreaming at the national level.

Having established this historical context, Vaid next analyzes the problems of the current movement and suggests some solutions. She first argues that the movement must look beyond a "civil rights paradigm" to a goal of complete "cultural transformation." The current movement, she points out, aims at gaining access to the current system, and access is not the same as equality. She analyzes the meaning of political power, the compromises caused by the need for fund-raising, and the debate over the issues of sexism, racism, and classism in the movement. She examines the threat posed by the "supremacist Right," looks at the lesbian and gay leadership crisis, and ends with specific recommendations for the things that are still to be done.

As a progressive myself, I found much to agree with in this book. Even my disagreements with specific points of Vaid's interpretation were stimulating. I certainly endorse her overall contention that the best future for the movement lies in a broad-based progressive coalition focused on local politics. But I have to wonder whether the book has an audience beyond readers like me who already care about the movement, and who are probably already progressive. Will it be as effective for a reader who isn't political, or whose politics are conservative? For example, Vaid alludes frequently to "the intersection of race, sexuality, gender, and class," and insists that the movement must come out of its "gay policy ghetto" to address these other issues as well. Yet she never explains how exactly they intersect; this remains an article of progressive faith. Nor does she refute the counter-arguments of conservatives; she merely restates the progressive positions as the correct ones. To those who say that an issue like welfare has no place in the gay agenda, she points out that there are lesbians and gays on welfare. "Why is the voice of the middle-class Republican man eager to reduce his tax bill more credible than the voice of the gay man on welfare?" Or vice versa, I imagine the gay Republican replying. If there is to be a gay position on economics, why should it necessarily be a progressive one?

The book also assigns the national movement more importance than it may in fact have. Vaid blames the military ban disaster on "Clinton administration abdication and the self-interested and short-sighted way in which the movement acted." This seems myopic. Even if the national movement had been as co-ordinated as the Rockettes, the ban would have been upheld. Too many people hated us too vehemently to let us into the military. The lesson I draw from the debacle is that any action we attempt at the national level is going to run up against Southern senators, and we're going to lose. Action can proceed at the local or even state level; but for now, at least, the national level is not fertile ground.

I also have problems with Vaid's explanation of why more gays and lesbians aren't involved in the movement. She seems to assume that the masses out there are eager to become political but are turned off by the elitism of the national movement, what with its boards of millionaire directors and $500-a-plate fund-raisers. To arouse these masses, she includes a list of "suggestions for the anti-political." The list comes, however, on page 395. The truly antipolitical won't get that far. Unlike Vaid, most people don't see their lives in a political context, and they don't see how politics could make their lives better.

In fact, they may not think their lives need to get better. Vaid asserts that most lesbians and gays live lives "dominated by fear, permeated by discrimination, violence, and shame." But in fact actual firings, evictions, beatings, or murders are rare. It's my sense that most gays and lesbians are basically comfortable; at the very least, their lives are better than they once dared dream they could be. Granted, many are semi-closeted or worse, and we are denied a lot of benefits. But if we're free to look for love and sex and friendship, it doesn't occur to us to ask for more. (Even those of us who are political may not be involved in the gay movement. The ACLU card in my wallet is always current, but I don't know if I'm a member of NGLTF. The national movement simply doesn't seem relevant to me.)

What we all need is something to shock us out of our comfort, to make us see how compromised our lives are. In spite of the power of her ideas, Vaid can't provide this spark, because her writing is diffuse and abstract. It never gets down to the concrete examples that make ideas come alive. The whole concept of "virtual equality" could shake our complacency, but it too remains "virtual," unreal. I need to see what the limits on my seeming equality are. I need to see in detail how much more equal my life could be.

Vaid's recommendations suffer from the same abstraction: I can't see them. She says we should turn our focus from national politics to "grass-roots organizing." I like the sound of this, but I'm not sure what grass-roots organizing consists of. There's voter registration—but, after that, what? Elsewhere, Vaid makes the excellent point that the civil rights paradigm is inherently limited because it fails to address the fear of sexuality that underlies so much homophobia: "we have to figure out how to talk in mixed company—heterosexual as well as across gender lines—about what sex means to us." This gets to the heart of the matter, and then drops it immediately. What would such talk sound like?

For me, the most disappointing moment comes when Vaid calls for a completely different approach to the movement: "Rather than asking how gay and lesbian people can integrate themselves into the dominant culture, what if, instead, we affirm that our mission is explicitly to assimilate the dominant culture to us." This is revolutionary, and it sounds like fun, too. Vaid gives a concrete example, using the movement against anti-gay violence. "What if we allied in our neighborhoods with all others who fear violence to understand the construction of violent people, and to expose the conditions like alcoholism, drug addiction, insecurity, and economic anxiety that contribute to violence." My hopes deflated on reading this. To "understand" and "expose"—this sounds like discussion groups, followed by an article in a publication of severely limited circulation. It's not the revolution any more.

It may be unfair to fault Vaid for not being the visionary our movement is waiting for. Visionaries are rare beings. What Vaid has done is to write a book on a subject that matters deeply to her, a book that has much to offer anyone who does care about lesbian and gay politics. It also works as the record of a life lived politically. Seen in this more autobiographical light, the problems I've been citing become virtues of a sort, because they seem inseparable from the personality of the author. Where Andrew Sullivan's acknowledgments took only a paragraph, Vaid needs three pages for her lists of friends, supporters, and colleagues (all in alphabetical, non-hierarchical, order). Like much of the book, they go on too long, but they testify to a feeling for inclusiveness, to a connection to an extended community of activists. That's the strength of Vaid's life and of her politics, and it's a strength that comes through in her book as well.

AN INTERVIEW WITH EDWARD ALBEE

by LESTER STRONG

"Aggressing against the Status Quo"

EVER SINCE HIS THEATRICAL DEBUT in the late 1950s, Edward Albee has been recognized as one of the foremost American dramatists of the twentieth century. He and his works have also been controversial, not the least because he is a playwright who happens to be gay. When I interviewed Albee in the winter of 1994, his Pulitzer-Prize-winning play *Three Tall Women* was just embarking on its national tour. *Three Tall Women* takes place in two acts. In Act I, a twenty-six-year-old woman and a fifty-two-year-old women visit the sick room of a dying ninety-one-year-old woman. In Act II, all three become different ages of the same dying woman as they debate the shape they have given to their collective life.

LESTER STRONG: Critics and commentators have used the following terms to describe your plays: avant-garde, nihilistic, experimentalist, absurdist, existentialist, postmodern, surrealist, and realistic. Where do you yourself place your work among all those labels?

EDWARD ALBEE: I don't categorize myself. They are talking about one play after another, because I work in very different styles depending upon the reality demands of the play. If the play wants to be naturalistic, it'll be naturalistic. If it needs to be highly symbolic, it'll be that. If it needs to be avant-garde and fairly obscure, it'll be that. Form and content codetermine each other.

LS: Where would you place *Three Tall Women* among these different styles?

EA: Well, you see, I think all of my plays are absolutely realistic—every single one of them, no matter what degree of stylization they have. *Three Tall Women* is an absolutely naturalistic play about three ages, three women who happen to be three ages of the same woman in an impossible but realistic conversation with each other.

LS: Why does the theater appeal to you as a writer? Why not write fiction, for example?

From the Winter 1997 issue

Edward Albee

EA: I started writing poetry when I was a kid, and it wasn't very good. I wrote
two novels, and they weren't very good either. And I didn't do very well
with the short story or the essay, so there wasn't very much left. But to give
you the simple answer, I write plays because I'm a playwright. I think like
a playwright, I walk like a playwright, I smell like a playwright, and I write
like a playwright. You know, playwrights have slightly different minds than
novelists and poets do. That's why most novelists and poets don't write
very good plays, most playwrights don't write very good novels, and so on.
There are a few exceptions—Chekhov, Beckett. But not too many.

LS: It has occurred to me that your plays have received such different recep-

315

tions from different people because of certain ambiguities they can present when performed.

EA: Well, mind you, the plays get such different responses because they're being reviewed by different people. And no two people see the same play, whether they're critics or not. No two people bring the same intelligence, the same sophistication, the same perception, the same willingness to participate. No two people bring those same things to the viewing of a play. So you'd expect different reactions from different people.

LS: You've been writing what I would call confrontational dramas and even comedies about powerful, in-your-face characters for a long time now. Have your theatrical themes and interests changed over time?

EA: I think some of my concerns have remained fairly constant—people not communicating with each other, preferring to skid through life rather than participate in it; some intentional cruelties, some avoidances. All that stuff, yes. That's a pretty large field to concern yourself with.

LS: You say in the Plume edition of *Three Tall Women* that you can pinpoint the genesis of the play in terms of your personal history—

EA: Well, this particular play, sure, since it was a takeoff or theme-and-variations on a real character.

LS: Can you pinpoint its theme?

EA: That's difficult to do. I hate doing that with any play because if you can describe in a couple of sentences what a play should be, that's probably as long as it should be. But—what is the theme of *Three Tall Women*? I think we have to be terribly careful as we go through our lives to stay right on top of ourselves so that we don't end up as the lady does in *Three Tall Women*, filled with anger and rage and regret. She gets trapped into getting by, making do. Everybody has to make choices. Some of them turn out to be terrible compromises, of course.

LS: Turning to another subject: You've been accused of being a "closet gay" who surreptitiously imports gay themes into your works, into heterosexual situations—

EA: That's bullshit, of course. There's a distinction to be made between a playwright who's gay and a professionally gay playwright. There are some playwrights who concentrate on writing gay themes in their plays. I know the difference between men and women. Back in the old days, there was a suggestion that *Who's Afraid of Virginia Woolf?* was written about two gay couples. Nonsense! A hysterical pregnancy in a gay relationship?

LS: I also want to ask how your homosexuality does relate to your writing. It doesn't seem to be quite at the center of your writing self in the same way it is, say, for Tony Kushner or Harvey Fierstein.

EA: Well, I made a statement at a gay OutWrite conference in San Francisco about four or five years ago. My speech was about anti-ghettoization in gay literature—that I think gay writing by itself has no virtue, and that there are a lot of publishers out there who are taking advantage of gays because gay people will read anything with a gay theme. I started off by saying I belong to a great number of minorities. I'm male, to begin with, which is a minority; I'm white, which is a minority; I live in the United States, which is a minority; I'm educated, which is a minority; I'm a writer and creative person, which is certainly a minority; I'm agnostic, which is probably a minority; and I also happen to be gay. These are all minorities, and I don't know why I'm supposed to be responsible to just one of them. That I should limit myself to writing about only one of the minorities, to begin with, is absolutely ridiculous. I don't think being gay is itself a theme. Nobody thinks of being straight as a theme for a play; no one has ever written a play about being straight. It's so weird. Some of the characters in my plays are gay. But in terms of being gay, it's not my overriding preoccupation.

LS: Getting back to your plays in general, you're usually considered part of the avant-garde, and many critics have stated that at least in your younger years you were very much influenced by Beckett, among others.

EA: Well, you know, there are four or five playwrights in the twentieth century that anyone's a damn fool not to be influenced by. They include Chekhov, Pirandello, Beckett, and Brecht. I think they're the four giants of twentieth-century drama. Among American playwrights, I've been influenced by both Eugene O'Neill and Tennessee Williams. You're supposed to be influenced by people who come before you who have done interesting work. You're meant to be influenced. The only thing with influence is that you turn it as much as you possibly can into yourself so that the influence becomes integrated into your work and nobody is aware of it. You don't want to go around copying people. You know, early on in his career people used to say that Harold Pinter was influenced too much by Beckett, that Harold's rhythms were very similar to Beckett's rhythms, which is interesting and curious because Sam's ear came from Ireland and Harold's from the East End of London, which are slightly different things. But I guess the trick is to be influenced by the right people and not the wrong people.

LS: How do you distinguish your own writing from these influences?

EA: I hope I have a voice that is individually me.

LS: And what do you think that voice is?

EA: Damned if I know. People keep telling me, "Oh, go see this new young playwright. He's very influenced by you." I'll go, and I can't see it for the most part. I don't know what it is. But people do tell me that the way I write is very specific and clear. I try not to think about that, you see, because then if I started to write a play I would start thinking, "Is this sounding like me?" What a dumb question to ask yourself! No, I wouldn't do that, because you're thinking about yourself in the third person that way. I don't like to do that.

LS: You've talked about the audience as an active participant in the dramatic experience. Could you comment on that?

EA: To a certain extent a good play is an act of aggression against the status quo—the psychological, philosophical, moral, or political status quo. A play is there to shake us up a little bit, to make us consider the possibility of thinking differently about things. Now this involves the audience. Another way of involving the audience, of course, is to write the type of play in which the actors—or the characters, rather—talk directly to the audience, engaging the audience in conversation. This involves the audience in a different way because the audience can't be a passive spectator. It can't be sitting at the keyhole.

LS: I remember one time in the late sixties or early seventies walking into a theater where the performers came out and started bringing people right onto the stage. It was a scary experience.

EA: Of course. Because audiences, you know, want to be invisible.

LS: Is there anything you're working on currently that you'd care to comment about?

EA: I'm working on a play called *The Play about the Baby*, so that when anybody asks someone, "Have you seen *The Play about the Baby?*" they'll reply, "No. What's it about?" or "What's it called?" And the person can answer, "The play about the baby!"

LS: In preparing for this interview I put on the tape of the movie version of *Who's Afraid of Virginia Woolf?* and found it's still as powerful as I remembered it. I know the movie was changed around from the play in terms of the setting and maybe some of the dialogue—

EA: And the ages of the characters. You know they promised me Bette Davis—James Mason and Bette Davis, who were both the right age for it. It would have been a different experience.

LS: Well, I have to say that Elizabeth Taylor and Richard Burton will always be Martha and George for me, and I expect they will be for anybody who saw that movie.

EA: I imagine so. Sure.

LS: That covers all the questions I have. Is there anything else we've talked about that's brought anything to mind you feel is unanswered?

EA: The unanswered question. The unanswerable question is really what you're talking about.

Postmodernism and Its Discontents

N 1987, at Brown University, a small conference offered the first airing of a debate that would become the dominant theme at such conferences for years to come. It was there that the forces of "social constructionism" and "essentialism" squared off directly and staked out their rival theories as to the nature and origins of homosexuality. The constructionist position, which was new to most people but had been filtering down from Foucault for the previous decade or more, was represented by David Halperin and the late Jack Winkler. The position that most people had previously taken for granted, now dubbed as "essentialism," was represented by the late John Boswell, whose 1980 book, *Christianity, Social Tolerance, and Homosexuality,* had already become a classic. Now Boswell was being taken to task for having assumed throughout his opus that it was legitimate to apply words like "gay" or "homosexual" to people from the distant past, based on references (often oblique ones) in ancient and medieval texts; Halperin and Winkler were saying that what we mean by "gay"—the very type of person to whom this word refers—is an invention of modern Western society.

Much of the argument that evening, as in subsequent debates, focused on the case of the ancient Greeks, a society whose well-known tolerance of male homosexuality has served as a beacon for contemporary gays. But are we justified in connecting ourselves to an ancient institution that differed so markedly from contemporary same-sex relations? Halperin and Winkler would point out that Greek homosexuality was strictly defined by the pederastic relationship between a male citizen and a boy or slave, and had more to do with rank and class than with sexual object choice. Boswell conceded that this was indeed the official norm, but pointed out that not everyone was equally enthusiastic about the pederastic option, while some men were very enthusiastic indeed, displaying a dominant homosexual orientation that even earned them a label as sexually deviant.

Underpinning this historical debate are two very different accounts of the nature and origins of homosexuality. Boswell's essentialism represents the common-sense notion that a homosexual orientation is deeply rooted in the person's psychological or even genetic make-up, and that such an orientation is a given fact of the human species; ergo it shows up in societies both ancient and modern. Social constructionism, a.k.a. "postmodernism," "queer theory," or "French theory," following Foucault, asserts that sexual categories like "gay" or "straight" are constructions of our own society and meaningless when applied to ancient Greece. The fact that many people *experience* their sexual orientation as "deeply rooted" or immutable is a matter that requires explanation. An essay by April Martin explores the ways in which language and cultural categories infiltrate our consciousness in a way that makes things seem "natural" or inevitable when in fact they are culturally constructed. The radical relativism present in Martin's account is the hallmark of the general position known as "postmodernism," which comes under attack in an article by Richard Mohr. If we start with the proposition that the category "gay" or "homosexual" is just an arbitrary invention of society, Mohr points out, then what's to stop society from simply dissolving these categories and denying our existence (it's happened before)?

Echoes of the Brown debate can still be heard and have even intensified in recent years, stoked by scientific research that continues to suggest biological or genetic linkages, on the one hand, and by re-evaluations of Foucault that find new levels of subtlety in his thought. David Halperin even went so far as to "canonize" Foucault in a book (*Saint = Foucault*, 1995), reviewed by Andrew Holleran, while John Boswell left a final legacy before his death, a book called *Same-Sex Marriages in Premodern Europe* (1994, reviewed by Denise Kimber Buell) that stimulated a cottage industry of research on this topic.

APRIL MARTIN

Fruits, Nuts, and Chocolate:
The Politics of Sexual Identity

WILLIAM JAMES IS REPUTED to have observed that there are two kinds of people in the world, those who divide the world up into two kinds of people and those who don't. I'd like to argue that there is nothing inherently natural about categorizing sexuality by the gender of the partner involved. There is nothing inherently natural about categorizing people by the gender of their sexual partners. Nature didn't create the dichotomy of homosexual and heterosexual; people did, and in fact it has been done only fairly recently, historically speaking. The sexologists of the late nineteenth century are responsible for shifting the focus away from same-sex acts of sexuality, and onto the idea that the people who engaged in those acts were a different breed. Foucault wrote that up until that time, "The sodomite had been a temporary aberration, the homosexual was now a species."[1]

Since then we have divided human sexuality into two types, which, while perhaps not mutually exclusive, are considered distinct enough that each is seen as having its own intrinsic nature. A great deal of cultural effort, on the part of scientists in many disciplines, religious leaders, political activists on the left and the right, social theorists, and the media, has gone into proving that the distinction between homosexuals and heterosexuals is in fact meaningful, and that it reflects forces of nature which we can study, uncover, and ultimately turn to for confirmation. The danger here is that we may reify the categories we create, sometimes forcing real observations onto a procrustean bed of theory. In the process, we may miss the true importance of human sexual variety and the politics that surround it.

Let me suggest an analogy with eating behavior. In the same way that we are all more and less sexual beings, it is true that we all are involved with eating food to varying degrees. Consider the fact that like sex, the desire to eat has a biological basis. There are some purely biological factors which will affect one's preferences or distastes for particular foods. I personally would rather starve than eat asparagus, and I know that there must be some biolog-

From the Winter 1994 issue

ical basis for this: it simply cannot taste the same to asparagus-lovers as it tastes to me. I have no doubt that it will someday be possible, if it isn't already, to identify substances or structures in one's taste buds or olfactory receptors, and maybe even in one's genes, that show clearly which of us are destined to be lifelong asparagus-haters.

Unlike sexual behavior, however, we have never seen fit to categorize eating behavior based on the choice of food eaten, undoubtedly because society does not feel that the consequences of different eating behaviors are important to it in the same way that it feels the consequences of sex are. There is no category of food, except perhaps in the case of cannibalism, which when eaten or not eaten will cause a person to be deprived of his or her civil rights. We have never divided up the world into those who eat X and those who eat non-X, and we have never presumed that there is anything inherently different in the natures of those who do or don't eat X. And though I am in possession of a tongue-in-cheek article entitled "Oral Sadism and the Vegetarian Personality",[2] to date I have heard no serious suggestion that we study the psychological, biological, and social concomitants of a tendency to eat one or another category of food. Instead, we seem fairly comfortable acknowledging that we are a very diverse species with respect to eating behavior, and leave it at that.

I'm going to leave it to the social theorists to explain why our society is so intent on controlling sexual behavior, and hardly interested in eating behavior. There are economic theories, feminist theories, Marxist analyses, and so on, written by people with a much broader perspective than mine. But imagine if we lived in a society which was intolerant of food diversity. Suppose global forces conspired such that society suddenly felt it had a huge stake in controlling eating behavior, and eating chocolate were declared illegal, as well as immoral, unhealthy, and an indication of a deranged or distorted sensory development. Well, it's safe to guess that there would be far less chocolate eaten under such a regime, just as we are likely to find fewer acts of sex between people of the same gender in societies which enforce harsh penalties for homosexual activity.

Many people would just give up chocolate. Oh, there would undoubtedly be some people who would sneak an occasional piece, but basically think of themselves as mainstream citizens whose lapses occurred only in the absence of other suitable food, perhaps, or under the influence of alcohol. Of course, some people might go on eating chocolate, perhaps hating themselves, and consulting doctors and religious leaders for help in overcoming their affliction.

A number of us might insist (and I probably have to count myself in this group) that we, indeed, have no choice—that while we could forever be deprived of the opportunity to encounter chocolate, nothing will stop us from longing for it, dreaming of it, fantasizing about it, and feeling we are not able to live our lives to the fullest without it.

Well, if you take a socially despised phenomenon and add psychologists, psychoanalysts, physicians, and other researchers to the picture, a likely consequence is that we will soon develop a profile of the perpetrator. Chocolate eating will become not merely something we do, but an essential facet of who we are. That is, compared to the rest of the population, we will be identified as a different breed—chocophiles. And having been thus defined, we will be lumped together as if we had things in common (despite the fact that some chocolate eaters I know only eat white chocolate, the point of which I can't begin to see, while many of them also like asparagus, which leaves us with shockingly little in common). Loving chocolate has now gone from something we do to something we are, and acknowledging that fact about us is presumed to convey something meaningful about our essential natures. The notion of a chocolate-eating identity is thus created.

While biologists go on to search for the physical manifestations of a chocophilic constitution, psychoanalysts would be writing endless papers on the meaning of a given case of chocophilia, suggesting that devotees of milk chocolate were fixated on mother's breasts, for example, while those who loved candy bars were clearly evidencing phallic yearnings. Rigid or unusual preferences for chocolate in its more exotic forms could be seen as resulting from serious narcissistic wounds in early childhood, and so on.

Depending on the intensity of the political struggle between chocolate eaters and a chocolate-negative society, one's identification as chocophilic or choconegative might even become more important than one's class, race, or gender identifications. Consider a personal ad under such a regime: Attractive bi-coastal chocophile desires bittersweet encounters, nonsmoker, any race or gender. Furthermore, explanations would have to be developed for those people who were neither chocolate lovers nor chocolate shunners, but who could take it or leave it at will. Are they really, deep down, chocophiles who will not acknowledge the true intensity of their desires because of internalized chocophobia? or are they truly another breed, an unexplored middle ground requiring an identity of their own? And what about those people who suddenly discover passions for chocolate in midlife—have they just come out of the closet with their true natures, long suppressed out of fear and shame? or have their preferences indeed undergone a change? and if the latter is true, how can we understand such a change in the light of biological and other theories?

The point is that to divide the population into those who do and those who don't engage in a complex and varied group of behaviors, which intertwine biological phenomena with cultural prescriptions and personal psychologies, both presumes the naturalness of such a division, and then starts us down the path of creating theories to reinforce such a presumption.

Our existing theories of homosexuality and heterosexuality do a fair amount of violence to the human variety that they claim to describe. We presume that if we know someone is homosexual or heterosexual, we therefore know something about his or her sexual life. The reality is that knowing someone is gay or straight tells us absolutely nothing about which sexual acts that person enjoys, the importance sex has for him or her, the contexts in which sexual acts occur, the nature of that person's dream and fantasy life, whether behavior, preferences, or fantasies have changed over time or have remained stable, the degree to which that person has a psychological experience of choice or flexibility about his or her desires, the degree of satisfaction the person has with his or her sexual experiences, and so forth. Nor does it begin to tell us anything about that person's affectional ties—with whom they talk, feel safe, fall in love, seek companionship. And yet somehow we think it tells us something to say that someone is homosexual.

In the process of slotting people into one or the other category, we distort our own data. On a research level, we face the knotty problem of having to define what we mean when we say we are studying lesbians, for example. What criteria does a woman have to fulfill to be considered acceptably lesbian for a research study? Some studies require that a woman have nothing to do with men sexually, despite the fact that many self-identified lesbians have sex with men. Others require that a woman not list political motivations for defining herself as a lesbian, despite the profound political implications of any woman calling herself lesbian. Some research projects require that a woman identify herself as lesbian, yet there are many women who engage in exactly the same sexual and affectional activities as those women, but who do not call themselves lesbians. Are we truly learning about women's loves for women in such research? Or are we supporting notions of what we expect to find based on biased and misleading definitions?

On a personal level, encouraging the idea that people are by nature essentially either homosexual or heterosexual causes a fair amount of internal conflict for many women, in particular, for whom there may be no category that conveys the complexity of their experience. I frequently hear women distressed by the question of whether they are "real" lesbians or not. For some it is a question filled with genuine pain, as they feel somehow inadequate to fit the roles designated for them. Here are some of the realities of women's lives:

- Among self-designated lesbians, there are some who have sex occasionally or even exclusively with men, some who have deep, committed love relationships with men, some whose primary buddies and comrades are men. There are also women who designate themselves as heterosexual with exactly the same patterns.
- Among self-designated lesbians, there are some who want little to do with men, who feel most emotionally safe and comfortable with women, who live in the company of women and choose a woman as their most intimate and committed relationship. There are also women who designate themselves as heterosexual who do exactly the same things.
- Among self-designated lesbians, there are women who feel strongly erotically attracted to women and always have. Their interest in women feels primarily like an interest in getting them into bed. There are heterosexual women who report similar feelings.
- Other self-designated lesbians say they have chosen a woman partner simply because they happened to fall in love with a particular person, and that person's gender was an incidental aspect of their choice. Some women who describe their life partnership with another woman in this way also say that they are heterosexual.
- Some women say their primary reason for exclusive involvement with women has to do with the strong feminist feelings they have, and their feeling that relationships with men contain unacceptable power inequities. Yet there are strong and vocal feminists who choose male partners, for a variety of reasons.
- Some women who are attracted to women do not identify themselves as lesbians because they feel that their other identities, for example, memberships in ethnic or racial minorities, take precedence over their sexuality.

Further compounding all this diversity is the fact that, while some women's experience of their sexual identity is fixed and unchanging from childhood on, for many others there are radical shifts at different stages in their lives. The shifts may go in either direction, from heterosexual to homosexual or the other way around, and may represent shifts in self-definition with or without changes in sexual or affectional behavior.

Our culture has constructed a homosexual minority out of what may well be a wide variety of people with potential for same-sex erotic interests. The invention of the homosexual minority, and the dichotomy between homosexuality and heterosexuality has had profound effects, not only on how people label themselves, but also on what they do sexually, and on what they think, feel, dream, and fantasize about—in short, shaping the very nature of desire itself. These effects in turn influence and reinforce our observations that there seem to be two kinds of people in the world.

By and large, the invention of the homosexual constitution derives most of its data from observations of men. (And, in fact, discussions tend to define sexuality with a focus on genital acts, which is not necessarily the way women define sexual relationships.) Just as women have been left out of the history books in general, women's erotic attentions to other women have been relatively ignored, as well. It appears that there is more sexual diversity among women than among men. For example, within the lesbian and gay communities, self-identified lesbians report attractions to men and sexual activity with men with some frequency. Self-identified gay men, by contrast, are much less likely to report desires to sleep with women, or to act on such desires if they have them. Similarly, among self-identified heterosexuals, it is more common to find women who describe fantasies of or interests in a sexual encounter with another woman than to find men who report same-sex erotic interest. The fact that men in American culture today are seemingly more sexually dichotomized than women has undoubtedly helped to reinforce the myth of "the" homosexual identity.

So let's take a look at some of these differences between men and women and see if they offer any clues about the cultural contributions to the notion of homosexuality.

One factor which has contributed to the apparently greater sexual diversity among women has to do with societal repression of homosexual acts, which appears to be more stringently applied to men than to women. (Women may be more seriously punished for wanting to live independent of men, but not necessarily for their sexual acts.) Heterosexual culture has seen fit to appropriate a certain amount of woman-to-woman sexuality as part of its sphere, as evidenced by the lesbian scenes in basically heterosexual pornography. There is no corresponding blurring of boundaries to include erotic activity between men. While a woman may admit to attractions to women without being called a lesbian, a man who admits to sexual feelings for men is much more suspect. He would therefore be less likely to report such feelings unless he were willing to be labeled a sexual outcast.

Since there is so much pressure for men to deny homoerotic interests, is it not therefore likely that only those men who possess both strong erotic interests in men and very weak or absent erotic interests in women will cross the line and risk being thrown on society's garbage heap? And is it possible that once there, they are under more pressure to construct a gay identity to help them survive, one which contains pressure not to experience or act on any heterosexual inclinations, thus adding to the appearance of dichotomy between gay and straight men?

We get some support for this notion if we extend our observations beyond the white, middle-class gay communities of North America. In Latin America, for example, epidemiologists concerned with the rapid spread of AIDS among women have noted widespread bisexual activity among their male partners.[3] Latin American men who sleep with men are not necessarily considered homosexuals unless they are the receptive partners in sex. They can therefore feel freer to enjoy a wider range of sexual options without risking being dismissed as "faggots." In other words, assigning the label and the identity changes the phenomenon itself.

But repression alone is not sufficient to account for the existence of sexual dichotomies. If it were, changing the laws and social mores would be enough to change people's experience of their sexual selves. We have to delve further into the notion of identity, because even though the concept of a sexual identity is a cultural creation, it is experienced by individuals as if it were something basic to their natures.

What one does, wants, thinks, and feels, along with the culturally derived meanings one attributes to those experiences, becomes organized psychologically into what we call identity. What we experience as our conscious identity is the intricate weave of our intrinsic uniqueness with the happenstances that life sends us, all filtered through the culture of our time and place, which we take in with our mother's milk. The identities we develop in this way shape our recollections of our personal history, and our future dreams and behavior.

An important aspect of identity is that once we have established it, we seem quite invested in maintaining it, and in reinforcing a sense of its consistency and continuity over time. In fact, we spend a lifetime refining and elaborating our notions of who we are. Not to do so, I imagine, would make us vulnerable to a level of existential *Angst* that few of us would want to endure. The personal identities we construct for ourselves are vital to our emotional well-being. They help to affirm our sense of existence and give meaning to the lives we live.

Furthermore, our experience of self-esteem is intimately related to our sense of identity. That is, we have to feel we know who we are in order to like ourselves.

I want to illustrate some of the things that culture may contribute to sexual identity. Let's start, for example, with the fact that in our culture we recognize only two genders. We assign people at birth to one or another based on external genitalia, and tremendous importance is attached to one's designation as male or female. As devotees of *Saturday Night Live* have observed, not having the information about someone's gender provokes considerable discomfort in people. Knowing whether someone is male or female allows us to relax into assumptions about who they are, based on the constellations of meaning assigned to maleness and femaleness in our society.

Most of us have accepted the notion that we belong to one of two genders, and we strive to keep our membership in good standing. The recipe for maintaining one's gender identity differs for men and women on many ingredients, including sexuality. For most people, sexual life figures more in sustaining a sense of being male than of being female.

Here's an illustration: It is fairly common when I see men in my psychotherapy practice that in the course of our work they will spontaneously volunteer a great deal of detail about the kinds of sex acts they enjoy, the fantasies that accompany them, their masturbatory frequency, the size and other characteristics of their own and their partner's sexual organs and so on. These are frequently related with the ease of someone discussing his exercise regimen. They also seem to take it for granted that these details are important and relevant to my understanding of their basic selves. By contrast, women don't often mention masturbating unless asked, rarely discuss their genitals, and only go into the mechanics of their sexual behavior if it is deemed essential to tackle a problem. When they do, they are likely to choose the least colorful words to convey the story, saying little more than "We had sex." If sex was less than satisfying, I might hear "We sort of had sex." Trying to get more detail on who did what to whom is likely to elicit embarrassment, vagueness, and a general feeling that that information has no particular relevance.

I believe two things are going on here. One is that women have been culturally enjoined from speaking about their own sexuality for a long time, under pain of being labeled immodest, crude, low, and so on. But along with simple suppression of speech about sexuality is something else. Women don't seem to regard the sexual details of their lives as having the same relevance for their sense of identity as men do. A man with an impotence problem, for example, is more likely to feel personally inadequate than a woman with an equivalent problem, because his genital activity is more directly connected to his sense of self. In fact, a man's sexual frequencies, difficulties, and achievements are very much tied in to his sense of being a man.

By contrast, women's sexual activity (in general), while of no less value or pleasure to them, is not necessarily an organizing principle of their sense of being female. A woman's confirmation of her identity as a woman can be achieved through other means, without necessarily including her sexual behavior, or at least without giving it a prominent place.

What does this mean for sexual orientation identities? One thing it may mean is that men may have a stronger need to construct sexual identities that are stable and unchanging. To do so, they may have to narrow the focus of their sexual expression. For women, a narrowing of their sexual field would contribute little to their sense of being female, making it a less necessary construction, and therefore less likely to occur.

I do not mean to imply here that women are in any way freer to feel and be sexual than men are. On the contrary, the cultural restrictions on women's sexuality are profound, and women are more likely than men to be inhibited in their fantasy life and in their explorations of their sexuality. I only mean to suggest that women are somewhat less likely to divide themselves quite as sharply into total lesbians and total heterosexuals.

It needs to be considered that it is not just the cultures of our childhood or the mainstream media that shape our sexualities, it is also our gay and lesbian cultures. The things lesbians want to do in bed have changed over the decades, since the requisite butch-femme fifties, through the tyrannical politically correct seveties and eighties (nonpatriarchal, nonpenetrating mutually vanilla sex), and into the toys and leather of the nineties. Similarly, since AIDS, gay men now talk about how they no longer want a lot of quick, easy sex as in the old days.

In addition, in both gay and lesbian cultures, there is considerable pressure to define oneself as not being interested in sleeping with the "opposite" sex. Those who cross the line into heterosexual behavior risk being seen as self-hating social conformists, afflicted with internalized homophobia, trying to fit in with society's norms at the expense of their own true desires. While such a description may at times be accurate for some, it may do serious injustice to others.

Furthermore, the language used to describe one's desires can prompt a negative diagnosis. A woman who claims to be in love with another person who "just happens to be a woman" is often accused of having an undeveloped sense of her lesbian identity. Once she has truly arrived, goes the theory, she will recognize that she has always wanted women primarily, if not exclusively, and it was only her homophobia which kept her from that realization. The effect of this is, needless to say, coercive.

So by now I trust I have made the point that our clumsy categories of gay, bisexual, and straight are political divisions, primarily, much more than descriptive categories. Human sexuality not only does not polarize into two varieties, it isn't even adequately represented by a Kinsey continuum. It is more accurately described by one's position in a complex matrix that includes data about actual sexual behavior, preferred behavior, sexual fantasy, the social contexts of such behavior and fantasy, and one's affectional ties, all considered over the life span.

To make matters worse, we have also confused the issue of sexuality and socially prescribed gender role behavior. That is, we have assumed that choosing a female sexual partner constitutes maleness, in both men and women, whereas choosing a male partner indicates femininity in both men and women. From there, biologists have expended great efforts to correlate hormone levels associated with maleness and femaleness with data about the gender of the partner chosen.[4] What about women who like butch women? What are they? Or, for that matter, men who like butch women? And the psychoanalysts have had a field day making presumptions about what is essentially and naturally male and female, postulating such concepts as phallic identifications and innate wishes for babies, and so forth. Psychoanalysis is particularly guilty of taking complex behaviors that may be observed more often in males, for example, and calling them therefore "naturally" masculine. A recent article by a feminist psychoanalyst asserted that a woman had a masculine identification because she went to the gym every day. Given that men tend to be taller than women, might we not regard tallness as biological evidence of masculinity? The idea is ridiculous, and yet other delineations of what constitutes masculine and feminine have been based on far less.

I am not arguing here against the idea of a biological component to sexual interests. Nor am I suggesting that everyone, deep down, is bisexual, or could be if they wanted to be. I am inclined to believe that if we could someday remove the restricting effects of sexual orientation categories and all traces of heterosexist bias, there still would be some people who report that from as early as they can remember they had exclusive attractions to one sex or the other and never for a moment experienced any variation in that. And under those circumstances it might perhaps be interesting to ask some of the research questions we now ask, like what makes those with exclusively homosexual attractions different from those with exclusively heterosexual attractions, in the same way that we might research what makes someone love or loathe asparagus. But we have to be very careful if we think that its more important to do research on questions of sex than of asparagus. We need to ask ourselves why we think so, what it would mean to us, and what conclusions we might want to draw from the data. Because the answers to these last questions have less to do with science and more to do with politics.

So we see that one may reject the idea that being labeled homosexual in any way explains or identifies the range of one's sexual and affectional life; however, one may embrace the idea of a homosexual identity as a mark of one's active struggle with society's repressive forces. In other words, society calls me a lesbian because it has a controlling stake in underlining the fact that my life partner is a woman. But I call myself a lesbian as a very personal expression of my opposition to those societal forces. That is, I have formed a psychological identity as a lesbian as a way of saying "Yeah, do you want to make something of it?" In the absence of repression, there would be no need for such an identity. In the presence of it, however, my identity as a lesbian is a vital part of how I give meaning to my life and acquire the strength to survive and surmount social obstacles. As Jeffrey Weeks put it: "Gay and lesbian identities are fictions, the necessary ways we mobilize our energies in order to change things."[5]

Acknowledging that, we can put the political debate where it belongs. As much as it feels to many gay people that they are being legitimized by the evidence of a biological basis for homosexuality, it also does some damage, and a feeling of legitimacy can be had in much less destructive ways. The question of whether homosexuals should have full legal and civil rights and social acceptance has nothing whatsoever to do with whether we can or can't help or change our inclinations. It has nothing to do with whether we were born this way, or whether we evolved into our own creations. It has to do with the fact that it is morally wrong to oppress people based on characteristics or behaviors which cause no harm to anything except the established social hierarchy.

It is not only morally wrong, it's tragically stupid. Especially in this age of AIDS, society can not afford the consequences of continued sexual intolerance, which is the single biggest obstacle to accurate and detailed education programs, accurate reporting of statistics, and honest communication between sexual partners.

And though I am a practicing psychoanalyst, I believe that on an individual, psychological level, the recognition of one's position in the political struggle for sexual tolerance can be the best antidote to the painful and costly ills that accompany being sorted into society's reject pile. It helps to direct the attention away from "Am I really gay?" and "How did I get this way?" and focus instead on "What can be done to change a system that uses fear and ignorance to pit people against one another, out of an investment in keeping power in the hands of the heterosexually partnered?"

NOTES

1. Michel Foucault, *The History of Sexuality. Volume I: An Introduction* (Vintage Books: 1990).
2. Glenn C. Ellenbogen, *Oral Sadism and the Vegetarian Personality: Readings from the Journal of Polymorphous Perversity* (Brunner/Mazel: 1986).
3. Richard G. Parker, *Bodies, Pleasures, and Passions: Sexual Culture in Contemporary Brazil* (Beacon Press: 1991).
4. Wendell Ricketts, "Biological Research on Homosexuality: Ansell's Cow or Occam's Razor?" in *Gay Personality and Sexual Labeling*, edited by John P. CeCecco (Harrington Park Press: 1985).
5. Jeffrey Weeks, *Against Nature: Essays on History, Sexuality, and Identity* (Rivers Oram Press: 1991), 98.

RICHARD D. MOHR

The Perils of Postmodernism

THIS ARTICLE is a second shoe dropping. In my 1992 book *Gay Ideas*, I pointed out theoretical problems in contemporary academic understandings of gay identities—of what it means to *count* as a homosexual being. In particular, I criticized the view widely dubbed "the social construction of homosexuality," which holds that lesbian and gay identities are to be understood on a par with abstract expressionism or baseball as social forms and forces that have not always existed and that are clearly the products of culture rather than nature. Just as there were no baseball dugouts or color-field paintings in the twelfth century, neither (the social constructionists claim) were there gays, lesbians, or homosexuals back then. I argued that all the standard interpretations and defenses of the social constructionists' thesis contain some flaw of concept, logic, or fact.

In this essay, I criticize contemporary academic understandings of gay identities along another dimension. I point out the moral, practical, and political deficiencies and dangers inherent in these understandings and in the wider received opinions and dominant paradigms at work in contemporary Leftist-dominated academe. Again, my perspective in the main is critical rather than constructive, though along the way I flag some attractions of traditional political liberalism.

If the current intellectual trends that have taken over the social sciences and humanities are absorbed into law and society generally as governing styles of thought, they will have dire consequences for the defense of rights. In particular, should these trends come to govern in the courts and case law, they would have disproportionately disastrous consequences for gay rights. They would cause privacy rights to collapse into equality rights, which, in turn, would collapse into speech rights, which, however, would prove to be untenable.

The trends march under a variety of banners: post-structuralism, social constructionism, deconstructionism, and the new historicism—collectively,

From the Fall 1995 issue

Richard Mohr

postmodernism. Institutionally the trends have clotted together under what is coming to be called cultural studies, an emerging discipline which also includes a fair number of *old* ideas and styles of thought recycled and transmuted from the last century—notably the debris of Marxism. For the uninitiated, here are five minutes of "Postmodernism 101."

Basics of Postmodernism

All the trends that make up postmodernism have as their central saint and hero, archangel and evangelist, the French philosopher Michel Foucault, whose most influential books are *Discipline and Punish* (1975) and *The History of Sexuality* (1976). What these trends have in common ideologically is Foucault's belief in the cultural or social origins and nature of meaning, values, identities, knowledge, and power. But culture itself (the more deconstructive postmoderns hold) is not one uniform thing but a multi-strand, everchanging thing, so that "meaning," "identity," "knowledge," and "power" themselves are always plural, ambiguous, fuzzy, multiform, strained, even contradictory. In definition or understanding, everything is both determined by and inevitably, in turn, dissolves into its social context. Nothing has meaning or value in itself, and the meaning of no "thing"—be it a text, individual, or institution—is stable. Everything is both socially constructed and yet also self-deconstructing.

Because in the postmodern view everything is dependent on its relational placement for its meaning and even for its existence, there are no free-standing individuals, only shimmering variable "types." Within this view that the world is composed of socially constructed yet slippery "types," the postmoderns dilate and alter the Marxist belief that the core contests of power and meaning lie in the structures and struggles between classes. They believe that contests of power and meaning range across any number of differences, but especially differences of race, gender, and sexuality: the postmodern trinity. Since these types are social constructs or products rather than, say, natural properties, they take their meaning from their relations toward and against each other and other types, identities, and concepts.

In consequence of postmodernism's belief that the source of meaning, value, and existence is the interrelatedness of concepts or types, there can be no "real" world outside of, beyond, over and against the web-like lattice of concepts, a world that could either underwrite concepts or provide a pivot for a critical assessment of them. As a result, truth for Foucault and his followers is not to be understood as correspondence—a match-up of a proposition or statement to the world. Concepts do not hit or miss the world; they create it—are constitutive of it. Truth is the coherence of the web of concepts that make up the world.

In ethical consequence, the truth does not make you free and does not—indeed cannot—provide ideals and guidance for a society. Rather, truth for Foucault is a "regime," a thing with effects. It is just whatever concepts influence and sway the mind. Truth is the going regime of ideas in a society—whatever the regime's coherence happens to be at the moment. Truth acts as a social lens through which one views, interprets, and constructs everything. One can never step beyond this social lens, which is embedded in and perhaps even constitutes the mind, and which filters and manipulates all we take in.

For postmoderns the distinction between fiction and fact, myth and reality, collapses. Language and ideas are never essentially descriptive. They are always means of persuasion, never tools for independent critical inquiry and assessment. The postmodern lesbian philosopher Cheshire Calhoun puts it bluntly: "The point of telling gay and lesbian history. It is a political one." Rhetoric is all, reason nothing.

In the postmodern view, politics permeates all our ideas, and the values that inform that politics are always, like everything else, culturally determined. Since the meaning of a thing is derived from its social context, there can be no values lying outside of a society on the basis of which one could evaluate or criticize the society itself. And so, postmodernism is deeply committed to moral relativism between societies.

Because knowledge is a product of social forces rather than derived from nature, science's claims to objectivity and impartiality are always bogus, cooked up to hide whatever political agenda the science as a social project is necessarily pushing. But the reverse is also true in postmodernism: knowledge is power—not in the sense that practical wisdom enables us to do things efficiently, but in the sense that what is in our minds determines who we are, and so, in the end (it is claimed), determines how we will act. Thus postmodernism is deeply committed to cultural determinism.

In the evolving modern age, power has become ever more diffuse in its scope, ramified in its penetrations, and refined in its manipulations. And it works not so much by pushing and shoving as by luring and inducing. In the first instance, its effects are on the mind. It does not cause or coerce a person to do something against his or her interests; rather it seduces one into viewing oneself in a certain way, as having certain interests, even desires, as being a certain type of person, and then into acting in accordance with the type.

With this sketch as background, I want to suggest that the rights most important to gays—privacy rights, equality rights, and speech rights—if brought within the force field of postmodernism, will telescope into each other and implode. First, the dependence of the individual on the social—the social construction of the individual—will eliminate the unique self as a vehicle for privacy by dissolving the individual into a type or types. But then, in turn, the social relativity of values will undercut the core rationales for the equality rights that should protect individuals as types. Finally, because of the social relativity of meaning and the interpenetration of knowledge and power, individuals as types become contested zones of meaning—battlefields in what are now called the cultural wars, where to win means to control meaning and thus to control ideas and speech. The ability to articulate ideas is cultural war booty, rather than part of the agreed-upon ground rules—the "Geneva conventions"—of cultural warfare. And so further, freedom of thought and rights to free speech, too, must finally go by the boards.

Privacy and the Self

In the postmodern view, it is a mistake to think of personal choice and individual decision-making as motor concepts in social theory. There is no individual prior to social processes. The individual (or what we mistakenly call the individual) is a product of culture, a social construction. The individual is at most a bud or excrescence emanating from the social mind or what postmoderns call "social discourses." But as the plural "discourses" suggests, society is not of a single mind. So the constructed thing is not a unity. The "individual" is simply the point where a number of social identities intersect. The constitutive identities themselves, though, according to deconstructive principles, are disparate and contradictory.

But then, there is no thing that is properly called a person if by person we mean a creature with ends of its own choosing and the ability to revise those ends in light of critical self-reflection. First, the individual cannot have a core content or identity of its own making; nor can it have a core set of desires over and against what is socially imposed on it, so the first requirement of personhood cannot be met. Second, socially imposed categories affect, even *effect*, self-perception. Indeed it is chiefly through the social causing the self to perceive itself as a certain type (say, homosexual) that the self becomes the type and comes to have desires in accordance with it (say, homosexual ones). And so, the second prong of personhood, call it autonomy—the ability to critically assess and revise one's ends—is also beyond the horizon of possibility for the socially constructed individual.

Further, there is no, and can be no, privacy in the sense of the personal— a region of activity in which a person, simply as a person, is sovereign in her decisions and in her ability to act on them. More specifically, there are no "central personally affecting values"—the formulation for privacy rights offered, for example, in *Roe v. Wade* (1973), the Supreme Court case that held that abortion is protected by the right to privacy. In postmodernism the individual cannot have core interests or make core decisions that privacy protects against social forces. For social manipulations and interests have invented the individual's interests.

To sloganize: No persons, no rights. Foucault himself saw that once the individual is dissolved as a source of independent desire and autonomy, appeals to rights are pointless against the ever more ramified and sinuously intrusive state. Rather, at the end of *Discipline and Punish*, Foucault feebly supposes that micro-level resistances to the state will somehow automatically spring up from within the very webs of power laid out by the state. This assumption seems to be little more than a pledge taken to the Hegelian dogma that theses always contain within themselves antitheses that spring up automatically from them.

Privacy and Equality

Beyond "the personal," other senses of privacy also wither under the postmodern gaze. In postmodernism, there cannot even be a sense of privacy that emanates from and guarantees a person's control of his or her own body. In the postmodern view, the body is not a constitutive factor in the individual, but is at most a blank slate over which the gas-cloud-like social mind drifts and writes its script, which the individual then reads off to find out what type of person she is. The body as a principle of uniqueness, as a determinate source of desire, as a receptacle of pleasure, and as an essential instrumentality of freedom—all this is denied by postmodernism. The fine filaments of the social, especially operating through the mind of its target, are like a spider's cocoon that gradually encases, obscures, and desiccates the body. Or as Foucault, inverting Plato's Orphic maxim, puts it: "The soul is the prison of the body."

In its most recent abortion ruling, *Planned Parenthood v. Casey* (1992), the Supreme Court surprisingly put a great deal of emphasis on the body as a source of the "general right" of which the case holds abortion to be a part. We hear twice of a right to "bodily integrity," of a right to "the ultimate control over one's destiny and one's body . . . implicit in the meaning of liberty," and of "the right to physical autonomy." But on a postmodern understanding of the body, the Supreme Court would be benighted should it now reverse its 1986 "homosexual sodomy" decision, *Bowers v. Hardwick*, and find a right to gay sexual privacy in *Casey's* right-granting talk of the body. For the body, in this understanding, is at most a valueless, inert, functionless nothing.

In sum, individual uniqueness and distinctiveness have no place in the postmodern view, and with their vanishing so too vanish the conditions and equipment with which to assert privacy rights. But postmoderns generally do not bemoan this disappearance. Under a lingering Marxist, mechanically feminist, or conservative communitarian sway, postmoderns hold the impoverished view that privacy rights are merely either a bourgeois power grab by and for the propertied elite or a means of insulating pornography and domestic violence from the law. Lesbian legal theorist Ruthann Robson in her 1992 book *Lesbian (Out)law* claims, for instance, that "there is nothing inherently private about sex. . . . Privacy is ultimately dependent on the legally sacred concept of private property."

Rather than prizing privacy rights, postmoderns put a premium—or at least appear to—on *equality* rights. For instead of viewing an individual as an individual, postmodernism always views the individual as a type or cluster of types. The individual is constituted as the intersection of diverse social forces, roles, identities, and interventions. And indeed, if the individual is always to be viewed as a type or kind, then the sorts of rights that the postmodern theorist might reasonably attempt to assert are rights to equality—rights, that is, which protect individuals as belonging to some type, kind, identity, or "difference." In current federal law, such protected groups include blacks, women, Latinos, paraplegics, resident aliens, illegal immigrant children, Democrats, Marxists, veterans, people with AIDS, and Mormons. Future law might protect queers, the homeless, drug addicts, punkers, skinheads, students, and ex-cons.

The problem for postmodernism, though, is that the relativisms that rest at the core of its commitments will undo attempts to give any adequate analysis of equality and inequality. And this failing explains why postmodernism rarely gets beyond mantra-like invocations of The List of its favorite "differences"—race, class, gender, sexuality, and other othernesses—to analyze equality, as though what equality rights are and who has them are somehow obvious, the elasticity of The List notwithstanding.

The specific problem confronting postmodernism (it will turn out) is that its ethical relativism eliminates any analysis of equality that turns on an understanding of oppression or oppressed groups. This result is perhaps ironic, for given the usual make-up of The List, this sense of equality—equality as non-oppression—is the one about which postmoderns give every appearance of being centrally concerned.

Now the postmoderns are right about a couple of things here. First, equality in its fundamental sense is not to be understood as *merely formal* equality—the treating of similar cases similarly, making sure that everyone has equal access to whatever *other* rights there are. Foucault and his followers have shown a great sensitivity to rules that are neutral on their face but that in application disadvantage some group. Thus, for example, a law that bars sex both to unmarried heterosexuals and unmarried homosexuals is hardly neutral in its application though it formally treats gays and straights identically.

Second, in expanding The List of contested social categories well beyond familiar Marxist categories of class and wealth, postmodernism implicitly appears not to be concerned primarily with *substantive* equality, either. We can have millionaire gays and millionaire blacks who are nevertheless oppressed. And there are poor folk who are nevertheless oppressors; indeed such people make up the bulk of neo-Nazi movements.

Equality is neither a merely formal nor a substantive principle, but is, I suggest, a structural one. Equality is chiefly a principle of non-degradation. Inequitable treatment is the holding of members of a group in lesser moral regard, as less than full human beings, by virtue of their group membership alone, independent of any behavior that might constitute them as members of this group. It is not inequitable to treat murderers in lesser moral regard, since they are classified by what they have done.

But this sense of equality as non-degradation presupposes a culturally neutral claim that each and every person presumptively is worthy of equal regard and that we have some means of determining this moral fact outside of the moral twists and turns of any given society. Due to its relativistic commitments, postmodernism can never provide this presumption.

If a society thinks, in the manner of the Supreme Court's 1857 *Dred Scott* decision, that slavery is acceptable because blacks *are* lesser beings, *and* if values are all socially and historically specific—all culture-bound and culturally determined as postmoderns claim—then there is no fulcrum and lever with which one could dislodge this belief about blacks by showing it to be false. But then, if blacks are inferior, they are not treated worse than they should be when they are treated as slaves rather than as full persons.

We can tell from within a culture (say, from its jokes and slang) that some group is humiliated, held in contempt; but without culturally neutral values, one cannot tell whether that group does or does not indeed deserve that contempt. Without such values, we cannot know that certain groups aren't simply being put in their proper place. Postmodern theorists like Judith Butler, author of *Gender Trouble*, brand as fascist any appeal to culturally neutral values and the metaphysics such values inevitably entail. But without such values we are unable to tell when ill treatment and ill-will are warranted and when they constitute oppression.

The moral relativism of postmoderns leaves them unable even to refute Nazi views on homosexuals:

> Himmler recounted to his SS generals the ancient Germanic mode of execution for homosexuals—drowning in bogs—and added: "That was no punishment, merely the extinction of an abnormal life. It had to be removed just as we now pull up stinging nettles, toss them on a heap and burn them" (from James Steakley's 1975 *The Homosexual Emancipation Movement in Germany*).

The moral relativism of the postmoderns destroys the very foundations of the sort of equality which they want to espouse.

Talk, Discourse, Free Speech

When, as in postmodernism, there are no culturally neutral criteria with which one could properly show to be false a socially held belief that some group is worthy of derision, all one can do is to try to change the belief itself from within the culture, thus transforming the culture into a different one with its own, new values, which again, thanks to moral relativism, are unassailable. Inevitably, then, under postmodern pressures, equality rights have no separate standing from concerns about how to persuade people to change their values. At best, equality rights against oppression and degradation must be abandoned in favor of rights to free speech, by means of which one side or faction in a society tries to upgrade the status of certain groups within the culture.

But most postmoderns have not embraced free speech rights. Ruthann Robson, for example, guts the First Amendment in one sentence: "The First Amendment is a rule of law with its roots in European liberal individualism and property-based notions. Its value to lesbians must be decided by us, not assumed by us." Free speech rights are good only if they "assist us"—that is, us lesbians. This stance, holding that asserted rights really are rights only when the asserting group says they are, does away with free-speech rights altogether once some other competing and winning group makes the same claim for itself: "we believe in free-speech rights only when they work for us, and we've won, so no speech rights for you." In short, majorities, on this account, get to determine what rights there are—which is to say the "rights" are not rights at all, but majority privileges.

Perhaps the best-known postmodern attack on the First Amendment is Stanley Fish's 1992 article titled "There's No Such Thing as Free Speech and It's a Good Thing, Too." Fish holds that speech "impinges on the world in ways indistinguishable from the effect of physical action." This position is silly when taken literally, as it would imply that I can move mountains with my mind and tongue as easily as with dynamite and a steam shovel. What Fish is really doing is taking the postmodern pledge that people's ideas determine what they do because they determine who they "are." To make people good, we, like Plato's Philosopher-Kings, must control what people hear and must hold them legally responsible for their utterances as though these were thrown knives—only worse.

Speech for postmoderns is nothing but politics by other means. It cannot be subject to rules other than those of political power, which include the acceptability of its suppression through the machinery of majority rule. Fish's hope is that majority rule, free of the burdens of the First Amendment, will choose to suppress such speech as the shouting of "faggot" and so sweep in a millennium of gay liberation. After all, how else could one do that but with words? Liberation on this account will be cheap, quick, and easy, because talk is cheap, quick, and easy.

Fish gives no acknowledgment to the sorts of arguments made by traditional liberals in favor of free-speech rights—arguments like those from John Stuart Mill's *On Liberty* (1859). Fish fails to see that the free exchange of ideas is the chief means by which we critically assess our beliefs to see if they are warranted and is what allows us, to a significant degree, to evaluate courses of action without having previously performed them ourselves. It is this critical capacity of speech, language, and thought that distinguishes words conceptually from actions and that positions them as things that centrally need to be protected if individuals are to be autonomous, and so warrants speech's protections even if these produce incidental harms in the world of action.

Lessons of recent history should teach us that Fish's hope of liberation through the control of speech is a misguided fantasy. When governments suppress speech, it is lesbian and gay speech that they suppress first. In February 1992, the Canadian Supreme Court accepted Catherine MacKinnon's and Andrea Dworkin's analysis that pornography may be legally banned because it is degrading to women. After this ruling, the very first publication in Canada to lead to a bookseller's arrest was the lesbian magazine *Bad Attitude.* The Glad Day bookstore, Toronto's only gay bookstore, continues now to be harassed by customs officials and police just as it was before the MacKinnon-rationalized decision, because the police view gay sex itself, in whatever form, as degrading to the humanity of its participants.

It is not just lesbian feminists who should fear unleashed censorship. *The New York Times* (June 29, 1994) reports that "earlier this month, the America Online network shut down several feminist discussion forums, saying it was concerned that the subject matter might be inappropriate for young girls who would see the word 'girl' in the forum's headline and 'go in there looking for information about their Barbies.'"

THE COST OF postmodernism is high. It eliminates privacy rights, equality rights, and free-speech rights. Ironically, it turns out that postmoderns themselves, when they deign to descend from their ivory towers, also believe the cost of postmodernism is too high. When confronted with the real world and the need to act politically, they resort to what they call "strategic essentialism"—essentialism here is a code word for the assumptions about human nature that are embedded in liberal individualism. Postmoderns recognize that their own sort of relativistic talk will not get them anywhere in the real world, and that they will have to resort at least to the strategies, styles, and cant used by liberal humanists—that is, if gay progress is to be made. But bereft of the substance and principles of liberalism that are its real tools and that postmodernism supposes it has destroyed, liberal strategies will hardly be effective.

Moreover, despite postmodernism's thick jargon and tangled prose, there is no reason to suppose that the courts won't eventually see through the postmodern bluff and, like Toto, pull back the curtain of its liberal guise to reveal machinery which conservative justices can effectively use to further restrict rights.

It is not too difficult to imagine a scenario in which Justice Scalia signs off on an opinion upholding the mass arrest of gay Marchers on Washington by block-quoting Stanley Fish: "In short, the name of the game has always been politics, even when (indeed, especially when) it is played by stigmatizing politics as the area to be avoided by legal restraints."

Indeed the Supreme Court's most recent gay case gives evidence that it is already able to co-opt postmodern discourses as means of oppressing gays. In its June 1995 St. Patrick's Day Parade ruling, the Court voided the gay civil rights protections of Massachusetts' public accommodations law as applied to parades. In order to reach this conclusion, the Court had to find that Boston's

St. Patrick's Day Parade constituted political speech despite the fact that the Court could find no discernible message conveyed by the parade; as far as any message went, the Court analogized the parade to the verse of Lewis Carroll and the music of Arnold Schönberg. What to do? Well, the Court sought out a source that would claim for it and against common opinion that all parades are inherently political. And where better to find such a source than in post-modern beliefs that hold that everything is politics? The Court quoted the requisite claim about the inherently political nature of parades from an ob-scure 1986 academic book *Parades and Power: Street Theatre in Nineteenth-Century Philadelphia*, which, on the very next page after the one quoted by the Court, signals its intellectual allegiances: "The concepts framing this study flow from . . . E. P. Thompson . . . and Raymond Williams." These two men are the Marxist scholars who founded cultural studies in England. The Right-wing Supreme Court here used postmodern Marxist scripture to clobber gays.

Global Postmodernism

It used to be that tyrants—be they shah or ayatollah—would simply deny that human rights violations were occurring in their countries. But in the last few years, tyrants have become more "theoretical" and devious. Their underlings have been reading Foucault. Now, when someone claims that a ruler is violat-ing some human right, say, religious freedom, the ruler simply asserts that while the purported right may well be a right in Northern European thinking, this fact need have no moral weight in his own way of thinking. Indeed, if, as postmoderns claim, values are always historically and culturally specific in their content, then the ruler can claim not only that North European think-ing about rights need have no weight in his own thinking, but moreover that it cannot have any weight in his own thinking, determined as it is by local con-ditions and cultural forces. Recently Muslim fundamentalists have defended their religious cleansing of Coptic Christians out of Egypt by asserting that there is no international human right to religious freedom.

In a similar spirit, Saudi Arabia's ambassador to the United States took out a full-page ad in the Sunday *New York Times* titled "Modernizing in Our Own Way" (July 10, 1994). The ad couched moral relativism in pseudo-liberal ver-biage—appealing to "rights to our own basic values" and "respect for other people's cultures"—in order to justify Saudi Arabia's barbaric departures from "Western human rights."

For a gay example of such judgment-arresting relativity, consider the case of the 19-year-old Jamaican reggae singer, Buju Banton. In 1992 he had a hit song, "Boom Bye Bye," with lyrics that translate approximately to "Faggots have to run or get a bullet in the head." A spokesman in the singer's defense claimed, "Jamaica is for the most part a Third World country with a different ethical and moral code. For better or worse, homosexuality is a deep stigma there, and the recording should be judged in a Jamaican context." If postmodernism is right, such fundamentalists, ambassadors, and spokesmen are irrefutable.

Surprisingly, such moral relativism has even infected Amnesty International—a group that is a conceptual joke if the very idea of international human rights comes a cropper. Through the 1980s, British, Dutch, and American sectors of Amnesty International argued that people arrested for homosexual behavior should be classified as prisoners of conscience— Amnesty International's blanket designation for those whose human rights have been violated. But for a long time, these arguments were drowned out by Third World voices, which claimed that while sexual privacy may be a right in some First World places, it certainly is not where they speak. If postmodernism is right, these Third World voices are irrefutable. Finally, in 1991, "hegemonic" Western voices got the Third World to go along with the reclassification of gay sex acts, but not without a proviso holding that any work that Amnesty International directs at enforcement of rights to sexual privacy should be as deferential as possible to local conditions. No other right recognized by Amnesty International comes with such a morally deflationary fillip. Human rights won this battle, but in a way that holds out the prospect that they will lose the peace.

DENISE KIMBER BUELL

Did They or Didn't They?

A Review of *Same-Sex Unions in Pre-Modern Europe*

by John Boswell
(Villard Books, 1994)

SAME-SEX UNIONS *in Pre-Modern Europe* builds from Boswell's ground-breaking earlier work, *Christianity, Social Tolerance, and Homosexuality* (1980), in which he argued for a tradition of sexual tolerance within Christianity up to the fourteenth century. In *Same-Sex Unions*, Boswell narrows his focus considerably, from same-sex behavior and relations of all types to a specific form of same-sex relations: long-term partnerships.

Boswell's source materials account for this shift: *Same-Sex Unions* is built around a number of related Christian liturgical texts, ranging in date from the eighth through the sixteenth century. Boswell contends that these liturgies provide evidence of a medieval Christian tradition of blessing same-sex relationships, analogous to matrimonial liturgies for heterosexual relationships. He further asserts that this tradition has its liturgical roots in non-Christian same-sex union ceremonies performed in late Antiquity and its social roots in a long history of same-sex couples forming permanent unions.

In making these claims, Boswell identifies two major hurdles he seeks to overcome: (1) an interpretive bias against reading the texts as same-sex unions, which he attributes to contemporary Western heterosexism and homophobia; and (2) difficulties in interpreting the liturgies.

Boswell's thesis depends upon how he resolves the interpretive difficulties inherent in the liturgies. He opens his first chapter by calling attention to the interconnection of interpretation and translation: "only a naïve and ill-informed optimism assumes that any word or expression can be accurately rendered in another." Although he does in fact attempt to offer "accurate" translations, the value of his point remains—translation is an act of interpretation.

From the Fall 1994 issue

The difficulties begin with the liturgies' titles, which all contain a peculiar compound noun. I shall discuss the Greek terms, since the liturgy was first composed in Greek. This compound noun, *adelphopoēsis* (or the variant *adelphopoiia*), consists of the common Greek verb *poieō*, whose meanings overlap with those of the English verbs to "do, make, create," in combination with a gender-neutral prefix formed from the masculine form of the noun *adelphos*, which frequently refers to a male sibling, a brother. But just as one could not explain the full meaning of the English compound noun "ice cream" merely by defining its constitutive parts, "ice" and "cream," so also Boswell argues for the inadequacy of such translations as to "make siblings" or "become brothers" for *adelphopoēsis*. What does it mean for a man to become a brother to another man, or a woman to become a sister to another woman (if, indeed, women had access to this liturgical office)?

Adelphopoēsis has generally been construed as pertaining to bonds of (non-erotic) friendship. Boswell argues that, because of their interpretive biases, virtually all other scholars have failed to consider other possible translations that would convey erotic or marital connotations in English. His translation of this term as "same-sex union" relies upon his assertion that this term, and sibling terms in general, were understood by ancient and medieval Greek speakers to have erotic and marital connotations in certain contexts, including these liturgies. Thus, he argues in favor of an English translation that also conveys this possibility. Certainly, for the modern reader, "same-sex union" is conceptually closer to marriage than a ceremony to "become brothers." The burden of proof rests on Boswell to demonstrate the historical plausibility of this translation.

Boswell begins from the minimalist position that these liturgies are about a union of two men, whether erotic or not. To this extent, he remains in agreement with other interpreters. He parts company with them as to the significance and implications of this union.

The grounds for comparability between these liturgies and ones for marriage that Boswell provides have several serious problems. The two strongest features of his argument for these liturgies to be considered as same-sex counterparts of heterosexual marriage liturgies remain inconclusive. First, the contexts in which the liturgies appear sometimes suggest a link between marriage and *adelphopoēsis*, at least on the part of those compiling liturgical handbooks. Although Boswell notes that the most common placement for this liturgy is following ones for heterosexual marriage, he also mentions the ongoing scholarly debate over how liturgies were composed and according to what principles groups of liturgies were compiled into manuals, thereby indicating that only limited conclusions can be drawn about a given liturgy from its placement in a manual. Secondly, the content of the liturgies share some features with marriage ceremonies. These features, however, notably the joining of hands, the kiss, and the banquet, are not activities reserved only for these two types of liturgies. The most significant problem, however, lies in Boswell's reconstruction of marriage traditions in the Roman period, upon which he relies for his interpretation of these medieval liturgies. He does not attend to the centrality of procreation to ancient concepts of marriage. In addition, in his treatment of kinship he overemphasizes the erotic connotations of sibling language.

To the detriment of his argument, Boswell does not clearly distinguish between cultural norms or ideals and social practices. The latter are invariably more diverse than the former. As a cultural symbol, marriage was essentially heterosexual then, as now, regardless of its variations in practice. This heterosexual character of marriage was both reflected in and reinforced through the close association of marriage with procreation. He does not adequately account for the abundance of sources—legal and philosophical—that virtually equate marriage with procreation. Boswell glosses quickly over his acknowledgment that procreation served as a theoretical justification for marriage within Christianity and de-emphasizes the weight that ancient legal sources placed upon procreation of legitimate children as a defining feature of marriage, a position also adopted by Christians (e.g., Clement of Alexandria).

But ancient marriage was also a matter of status, at least from the perspective of Roman law, which Boswell uses as his benchmark. Not all heterosexual couples had access to marriage, although many formed long-term unions (e.g., slaves and Roman soldiers). Boswell does not examine how or why marriage functioned as an ideal within late Antique society for both same-sex and opposite-sex couples whose relationships did not qualify as legal marriages under Roman law (although they might have according to other legal traditions, such as Greek or Egyptian ones).

While some same-sex couples might have described themselves as "married," as Clement of Alexandria (second-century Christian teacher), Ptolemy of Alexandria (second-century pagan scientist), and Lucian of Samosata (second-century pagan satirist) all claim, these ancient writers condemn or ridicule this appellation. That is, while social practice may have included same-sex couples considering themselves and being perceived as married, diverse Greco-Roman sources portray this practice as counter to the cultural concept of marriage.

Similarly, while Boswell has convincingly shown the possibility that some male couples might have viewed these liturgies as celebrating a bond of intimacy that might be functionally equivalent to marriage in practice, he has not yet shown that marriage is the best interpretive frame of reference for these same-sex liturgies. That is, it is not clear that these liturgies participate in or imitate the cultural norms for marriage among medieval Christians.

As for Boswell's interpretation of kinship, it is striking that he does not comment upon the absence of sibling language in the marriage liturgies. His own examples of male friendships, erotic or non-erotic, suggest that the sibling language was just as likely to signify an unalterable bond, such as blood is commonly assumed to be in Western notions of kinship, as it was to serve as a code for erotic involvement.

Since Boswell mentions collateral adoption as means by which men formed same-sex unions in the Greco-Roman world, it is important to add that women did not have the right to adopt in the Greco-Roman world. Thus, if one accepts Boswell's argument, this would not have been a means available to female same-sex couples. In addition, Boswell rejects out-of-hand the interpretation of the medieval liturgies in light of adoption; this rejection is perplexing, given that he adduces a Roman-period precedent.

Boswell states that a shared feature of sibling languages is a "notion of equality." Equality is also a feature he attributes to male friendship, and less persuasively, to marriage. Boswell does not even raise as a question how this material might or might not apply to women in an historical and cultural context in which there was not a developed tradition or understanding of women as capable of friendship, the equal and mutual affection that Boswell deems central to male same-sex relations. This argument can only hold if gender is considered in isolation from other highly relevant factors in determining one's identity in the ancient world, especially social status. Male same-sex relations could and did occur between men of radically different statuses; a relation between a master and his male slave was not one of equality.

It is ironic that a book that invests so much in the interpretation of liturgical titles should itself bear a misleading one. A reader would not know from the title, *Same-Sex Unions in Pre-Modern Europe*, that the book is specifically about a group of Christian texts. Non-Christian materials receive very little attention; the brief appendix on "Jewish Perspectives" shows little familiarity with the current scholarship on homoeroticism in ancient and medieval forms of Judaism (e.g., that of Rebecca Alpert, Daniel Boyarin, Saul Olyan, and Michael Satlow). In light of the geographical provenance of the liturgies (Eastern Mediterranean and Eastern European), and the considerable attention paid to Roman-period sources, the qualifier "Pre-Modern Europe" is also rather imprecise.

The title also suggests that the material covered in the book concerns unions between women as well as between men. This is not the case. In his discussion of the earliest preserved example of this liturgy (eighth century), Boswell remarks in a cryptic footnote: "In later years a version for two women would be developed. Although *adelpho-* could be understood to apply to women, there is no reason to believe that this particular ceremony was not for two men." Is he asserting that the liturgy was first developed for two men? If so, where are the details of its later development to a version for two women?

The liturgies are constructed as if they were for the blessing of two men (women are only explicitly included in some non-Greek sources), but Boswell does not discuss this matter and its possible significance for interpretation; rather, he excuses it as a mystery. Precisely because of his willingness to explore what has appeared counter-intuitive or impossible within current understandings of Western cultural development, it is especially troubling that Boswell sidesteps questions concerning gender. Citing a paucity of primary references and secondary scholarship as a justification for this lack, Boswell nonetheless claims that "many, many sources indicate that women also formed permanent same-sex unions." Yet he provides virtually no medieval evidence for this claim in his chapter entitled "The History of Same-Sex Unions in Medieval Europe." The examples that he does give do not pertain to the topic of long-term same-sex relationships between women but only to instances of female homoerotic activity. He is silent on the question of the extent to which any of the materials that he adduces about ceremonies between men, both lay and monastic, actually applied to or were practiced by female couples. By structuring his discussion around the dominant sources—i.e., male-centered sources—he leaves the reader guessing about whether to assume that no women engaged in these relationships with the liturgical blessing or, on the other extreme, that everything that he says about men applies equally in every way to women. Clearly neither extreme is likely, and it is disappointing that he appears content not to pursue this matter.

While Boswell includes bibliographic references for most of the key scholarship available on female homoeroticism in antiquity and the medieval world, he does not engage the findings and arguments of these scholars in his analysis (i.e., Bernadette Brooten, Judith Hallett, and E. Ann Matter; he does not cite the work of Mary Rose D'Angelo). His focus is men, his assumption that sources relating to female same-sex relations are analogous to those concerning male same-sex relations; as a result, Boswell replicates the androcentric bias of his sources in his interpretation.

In his epilogue, Boswell anticipates possible responses to this book, specifically on the matter of his discovery of a possible precedent for same-sex marriages, just when some lesbians and gay men are struggling to acquire access to legal marriage or its attendant rights and benefits. He writes, "it is not the province of the historian to direct the actions of future human beings, but only to reflect accurately on those of the past." With this statement, he rejects the notion that the historian has any responsibility or accountability to the future. Further, he holds firm to the possibility and ideal of historical research as the accurate portrayal of the past. His former and current research, however, offers the opposite conclusion: that all historical work is interpretive, that no one accurate version of history is possible—that one's view of history is always forged in light of the interpreter's present. Boswell recognizes that his research affords a precedent for same-sex marriage rights and benefits, one which might receive attention particularly among Christian readers. Nonetheless, he refrains from discussing how his work could shape current debates.

Whether or not the reader finds his arguments persuasive, Boswell's strength lies in his challenge to the current version of historical truth that same-sex unions have never before been liturgically celebrated. Why has this been historically unimaginable? Boswell's answer correctly identifies this as an interpretive problem in the present and recent past. So, too, his presentation of these texts and their meaning in historical context is an interpretive exercise. The meaning and significance of this book lies in and for the present, as we reflect upon the European Christian facet of our cultural heritage. How we understand our past will clearly make a difference for our future; what kind of difference remains a matter for debate.

ANDREW HOLLERAN

Pearls of Jargon

A Review of *Saint = Foucault*

by David Halperin
(Oxford University Press, 1995)

SAINT = FOUCAULT IS A SLIM but sharply entertaining book in which David Halperin, author of *One Hundred Years of Homosexuality*, and professed admirer of the French thinker Michel Foucault, takes issue with biographers and other academics who have, he feels, misinterpreted and reduced Foucault to positions he never took. I picked it up because I was tired of hearing a friend enthusiastically cite Foucault while I knew nothing about him; and I wanted to get a little taste of what the gay academic tong wars are all about.

What they're all about, you might say, is whether or not you put the word truth in quotation marks. Halperin does. "'Truth' is not the opposite of error," he writes, "'truth' is a discursive strategy that . . . blocks inquiry," and requires us to ask:

> Who desires this truth, and why? Who gets to tell it? To whom? For what purpose? With what power-effects? In ways that implicate what other practices or fields of activity? The reason such questions are pressing is that "truth" confers power on those who can claim access to it; it licenses "experts" to describe and objectify people's lives, especially . . . those who, for whatever reason, happen to find themselves fully exposed to the operations of disciplinary power.

The latter, of course, includes us, homosexuals, and is not only, Foucault felt, a great danger, but something Halperin himself experienced when—after a female colleague up for tenure accused him of discriminating against her in favor of a love interest—he saw everything he said in his defense canceled out

From the Winter 1996 issue

by the words a "gay classicist" in accounts of the controversy in *The New York Times*. (There is little in Halperin's book about his own travails: he uses the case only briefly to illustrate what Foucault felt was the danger of the powers-that-be dismissing homosexuals once they were categorized with that noun.)

That noun's advantages and disadvantages are paradoxical—for although Foucault was extremely wary, if not phobic, about being named and system-atized, at the same time, running throughout this glimpse of his ideas is not only the assumption that we do exist, but a call for us to create new cultural forms, new zones of pleasure, new communitarian practices that ultimately heterosexuals might benefit by. It is "the homosexual way of life," Foucault felt, which threatens straight society more than "the sexual act itself." In Halperin's view, Foucault's theories—or rather his non-theories—form the ba-sis for what became ACT-UP. Halperin thinks we are acting out Foucault whether we know it or not:

> No doubt very few of the gay leather men whom Foucault encountered in New York and San Francisco in the late 1970s and early 1980s mod-eled themselves as philosophers. But many of them surely did believe, just as many of us who take part in various forms of lesbian and gay cultural politics still do, that they had embarked on an extraordinary life-experience, an astonishing, unforeseen trajectory that had taken them from isolated, conventional lives, regulated by the routines of heterosexual society and dominated by the tyranny of homophobic at-titudes, and catapulted them into a new, exciting, unpredictable, and dangerous mode of existence, one which had to be made up as they went along and which turned out to be self-transforming beyond any-thing they could possibly have anticipated or imagined.

(Interestingly, Halperin says the ACT-UP demonstrators he asked all said Fou-cault's book was in their jeans pocket; while Andrew Sullivan in *Virtually Nor-mal* doubts the marchers had even heard of him. I believe both.)

Self-transformation—*ascesis*—is a concept that runs throughout many of the quotes excerpted here from Foucault's writings and interviews; as if ho-mosexuality itself were not the important thing, but what we can do with it. What we can do with it is not to be confused, Halperin says, with a kind of California narcissism, or even an Emersonian cult of the self. It's more related to the ancient practice of "working on the self in order to transform the self into a source of self-sufficiency and pleasure." Ascetics, or ethical work, Foucault defined as "an exercise of self upon self by which one tries to . . . transform one's self and to attain a certain mode of being." Both philosophy and homosexuality are "technologies of self-transformation." "To be gay," Foucault said in an interview, "is to be in a state of becoming, . . . the point is not to be homosexual but to keep working persistently at being gay, . . . it is to make a sexual choice into the impetus for a change of existence." Or, as Halperin puts it: "Homosexuality is not a psychological condition that we discover but a way of being that we practice in order to redefine the meaning of who we are and what we do, and in order to make ourselves and our world more gay." Or, as Foucault put it: "It's up to us to advance into a homosexual *ascesis* that would make us work on ourselves and invent (I don't say discover) a manner of being that is still improbable."

Exactly how one does this is not spelled out: in terms of deep-breathing, auto-massage, meditation, or aroma therapy, at least. (This is not *Absolutely Fabulous*.) "Ultimately," Halperin writes,

> the importance of Foucault's work for queer politics does not consist in any improved or more edifying definition of homosexuality but, on the contrary, in the attempt to empty homosexuality of its positive content, of its material and psychic determinations, in order to make it available to us as a site for the continuing construction and renewal of continually changing identities. "Maybe the target nowadays is not to discover what we are," Foucault

Michel Foucault

once wrote, "but to refuse what we are . . . to promote new forms of subjectivity through the refusal of this kind of individuality. . . ." Foucault's treatment of homosexuality as strategic position instead of as a psychological essence opens up the possibility of a gay science without objects, of a queer politics defined not by an ongoing process of self-constitution and self-transformation—a queer politics anchored in the perilous and shifting sands of non-identity, positionality, discursive reversibility, and collective self-invention.

And you thought it was about sucking cock. Or:

> By analyzing modern knowledge practices in terms of the strategies of power immanent in them, and by treating "sexuality" accordingly not as a determinate thing in itself but as a positivity produced by those knowledge practices and situated by their epistemic operations in the place of the real, Foucault politicizes both truth and the body; he reconstitutes knowledge and sexuality as sites of contestation, thereby opening up new opportunities for both scholarly and political intervention.

(With your choice of local or general anesthetic).

I suppose all specialists have their jargon—surfers, steel workers, prostitutes, professors—and of course it is possible that every word of the passage above was chosen because it alone expressed a precisely calibrated nuance of meaning necessary to the argument, but, alas, too often this prose seems merely pretentious—excluding, credential-establishing; a verbal form of Attitude. Which, like all Attitude, is counter-productive—especially if Halperin wishes, as he claims, to mediate between Foucault and the rest of us. Eventually, the sermon has to be delivered in clear prose—or the parish will stop listening, while the priests argue among themselves in language that has lost all connection to reality (which is how much of this controversy sounds to the lay reader).

Because putting "truth" in quotation marks does not make cynics of us all, or convince us that everything is up for contestation—or, God forbid, scholarly intervention, rather, the heady, abstract opacity of such passages—that academic shop talk if you will—raises the question that may invade the reader after several pages of this stuff: Why? Why disaggregate the self? Why empty our homosexuality "of its positive content, . . . its material and psychic determinations in order to make it available to us as a site for the continuing construction . . . of continually changing identities"? Can't we just listen to Haydn? Even political activism is "an experiment we perform on ourselves so as to discover our otherness to ourselves in the experience of our own futurity." Huh?

There is in all this the impression of an ultimately self-conscious man passionately seeking for an escape from the self; even the remark from which Halperin takes the epigraph for his book becomes touching in this respect: "Pleasure," Foucault said, "is something which passes from one individual to another; it is not secreted by identity. Pleasure has no passport, no identification papers." It brings to mind a French intellectual (Renaud Camus, say, in *Tricks*) on vacation in Los Angeles, losing his French intellectual self at the 8709; precisely the reductive image Halperin accuses James Miller, one of Foucault's biographers, of fostering—Foucault as weirdo. It is, of course, ludicrous to reduce Foucault to a man who reportedly said "fist-fucking is our century's only brand-new contribution to the sexual armamentarium," since there's so much more to his thinking than that, as Halperin shows. But eventually this talk of creating new selves, norms, zones of pleasure, will divide readers into two camps: those who find this exciting and new, and those who find it highfalutin language wrapped around ideas that are shockingly banal. I had begun to think of Jane Fonda having sex with David Hemmings in *Barbarella*—fingertips pressed together, in a brisk intergalactic gale—by the time, on page 99, I found instead, as an example of the new cultural forms homosexual *ascesis* may create, the bake sales and fund-raisers leathermen held in the 1970s. Surely these are not new communitarian forms, I thought, but just another version of American loneliness.

Of course, as Halperin points out, Foucault himself would never have wanted to be tied down even to a gay identity. (Like Genet, it seems, another Parisian phobic about the cops, who told the PLO that he would probably abandon them if they gained power. Maybe all this is a French obsession with *l'état*.) Yet much of what excites Halperin about Foucault—his vision of our potential futurities—left this reader skeptical and unconvinced; I suspect homosexuality is a box that words in quotation marks cannot alter, i.e., it's not *just* a socially constructed identity, a prison the powerful put us in.

And so Foucault, even in this book, seems more the professor than the saint. These notes towards a gay hagiography are a fascinating view, through the prism of Foucault, of matters ranging from ACT-UP to the gym culture, from Queer Nation to Bersani, Mohr, and James Miller. They indeed give you an idea of what the commotion in academe is all about. But what it's all about seems so unreal, would-be revolutionary, and idealistic. (There are pearls of jargon in this book one would love to read aloud to a bunch of queens in a bar.) *Saint = Foucault* is interesting where ideas collide with data from real life (where the actual transformations are taking place). But all too often you may find yourself, in purple passages, wishing that Aristophanes, Molière, or especially Charles Ludlam were still around. Were the latter still working, I suspect we'd have seen some of this obsession with the self in the Ridiculous Theatrical Company's next farce. I've a feeling we'd have seen Ludlam empty his homosexuality of its positive content right on stage before our very eyes.

Edward Albee's plays include *Who's Afraid of Virginia Woolf?*, *The Zoo Story*, *A Delicate Balance*, and the 1993 Pulitzer Prize–winning *Three Tall Women*.

Bruce Bawer's most recent book is *Stealing Jesus: How Fundamentalism Betrays Christianity* (1997). He is the author of the widely discussed 1993 book, *A Place at the Table: The Gay Individual in American Society*.

David Bergman is the author *Gaiety Transfigured: Gay Self-Representations in American Literature* and *Cracking the Code*, among other books, and the editor of the biennial series, *Men on Men: Best Recent Gay Fiction*.

Betsy Billard's writings have appeared in *The New York Times*, *MetroSource*, and other publications. Her sports features have been heard on National Public Radio's Morning Edition as well as WBUR-FM in Boston.

Bernadette Brooten, professor of Christian studies at Brandeis University, is the author of *Love between Women: Early Christian Responses to Female Homoeroticism* (1996).

Denise Kimber Buell, an assistant professor of religion at Williams College, recently completed her Ph.D. in early Christianity at Harvard.

Chandler Burr is the author of *A Separate Creation: The Search for the Biological Origins of Sexual Orientation* (1996) and a contributor to *Harper's* magazine.

William Byne, a psychiatrist and director of the Neuroanatomy Laboratory in the Department of Psychiatry at the Mount Sinai Medical Center, has published several scholarly reviews of the biological research on sexual orientation.

Cheryl Clarke is the author of several books of poetry including the 1993 collection, *Experimental Love.*

Robert Dawidoff, professor of history at the Claremont Graduate University, is co-author (with Michael Nava) of *Created Equal: Why Gay Rights Matter to America* and the editor of the Temple University Press's American Subjects Series.

Michael Denneny is a senior editor at St. Martin's Press, where he pioneered the publishing of gay and lesbian books in mainstream houses, and the author of *Lovers: The Story of Two Men* and *Decent Passions: Real Stories About Love.*

Barney Frank is United States representative for the Fourth Congressional District of Massachusetts.

Gabrielle Glancy is a poet and freelance writer whose works have appeared in *The Paris Review, The American Poetry Review,* and *The Kenyon Review.*

Carla Golden teaches psychology at Ithaca College. She has written widely on women's sexuality, gender development, and psychoanalytic theory, and co-edited *Lectures on the Psychology of Women.*

David Hanna, who died in 1993, was a writer and columnist on the *Hollywood Reporter* and other newspapers from the mid-thirties to the early fifties. In the mid-fifties he worked as a movie publicist and was briefly Ava Gardner's manager.

Charles Hefling is the contributing artist for *The Harvard Gay & Lesbian Review* and the illustrator for this volume. He is a freelance artist whose drawings have appeared in several books. He also teaches theology and philosophy at the university level.

Andrew Holleran is the author of the novels *Dancer from the Dance, Nights in Aruba,* and *The Beauty of Men.*

Richard Howard's most recent book of poems, his eleventh, is entitled *Trappings*. He teaches in the School of the Arts at Columbia University.

Holly Hughes, one of the so-called "NEA Four," is the author of *Clit Notes*, a compilation of her recent plays and performance pieces.

Karla Jay has written, edited, and translated nine books, the most recent of which are *Dyke Life* and *Lesbian Erotics*. Her essay in this volume will appear in the forthcoming book, *Tales of the Lavender Menace*.

Larry Kramer, the founder of ACT-UP, is the author of the 1978 novel *Faggots*, the widely produced play *The Normal Heart* and a recent memoir, *The Destiny of Me*, among other writings.

Tony Kushner is the author of *Angels in America, Part One (Millennium Approaches)* and *Part Two (Perestroika)*, *Slavs!*, and other plays, as well as numerous essays and reviews.

Marilee Lindemann teaches English at the University of Maryland. The manuscript of her book, *Willa Cather: Queering "America,"* is currently circulating.

April Martin, a psychologist with a practice in New York, is the author of *The Lesbian and Gay Parenting Handbook*.

Yaroslav Mogutin, an out gay journalist in Russia from 1991 until his expulsion in 1995, has continued publishing essays and articles on cultural topics in Russia. His first book of poetry, *Exercises for the Tongue*, has now been published.

Richard D. Mohr, a professor of philosophy at the University of Illinois at Urbana, is the author of two philosophical inquiries, *Gay Ideas* (1992) and *Toward a More Perfect Union* (1995).

Camille Paglia, who teaches English literature at the University of the Performing Arts in Philadelphia, is the author of *Sexual Personae: Art and Decadence from Nefertiti to Emily Dickinson* (1990), *Sex, Art, and American Culture* (1992), and *Vamps and Tramps* (1994).

Felice Picano is the author of *Ambidextrous, The Lure, Men Who Loved Me: A Memoir in the Form of a Novel*, and *Like People in History*, among other novels.

Richard Pillard, M.D., is professor of psychiatry at Boston University School of Medicine.

Lev Raphael is the prize-winning author of *Dancing on Tisha B'Av, Winter Eyes, Journeys & Arrivals, Let's Get Criminal,* and *The Edith Wharton Murders.*

Vernon Rosario is a resident in psychiatry at the University of California in Los Angeles. He is the editor of *Science and Homosexualities* and the author of *The Erotic Imagination: French Histories of Perversity.*

Michael Schwartz is an associate editor of *The Harvard Gay & Lesbian Review* and a regular contributor to its pages.

Douglass Shand-Tucci is an historian of American art and architecture and New England studies and the author of *Boston Bohemia* (1996).

Martha Nell Smith, an associate professor English at the University of Maryland, is the author of *Rowing in Eden: Rereading Emily Dickinson.*

Edward Stein is the author of *Without Good Reason: The Rationality Debate in Philosophy and Cognitive Science* and of the forthcoming *Sexual Desires: Science, Theory and Ethics.*

Renate Stendhal is the editor of *Gertrude Stein in Words and Pictures* (1994) and the co-author (with Kim Chernin) of *Cecilia Bartoli: The Passion of Song* (1997). She has translated into German the poetry of Susan Griffin, Audre Lorde, and Gertrude Stein.

Lester Strong writes on literature, history, and art for a number of publications. His monthly column, "Gay Arts Beat," is syndicated to a number of gay and lesbian publications nationwide.

Rich Tafel is the executive director of the Log Cabin Republicans in Washington, D.C.

Ira Tattelman is an architect and writer whose articles have appeared in *Creating Place and Forging Identity: Public Sex, Gay Sex, Queer Frontiers,* and *Queers in Space.*

Patricia Nell Warren is the author of several novels including *The Front Runner, Harlan's Race,* and the recently published *Billy's Boy.*

Edmund White is the author of several novels, including *A Boy's Own Story, Nocturnes for the King of Naples, The Beautiful Room is Empty,* and the recently published *Farewell Symphony.*

Reed Woodhouse teaches English literature at MIT. The essay in this volume forms the basis for his forthcoming book on gay literature, to be published by the University of Massachusetts Press.